A Programmed Learning Guide
to Finance

D1613724

A Programmed Learning Guide to Finance

Marianne Hite

The University of Colorado at Denver

IRWIN

Chicago • Bogotá • Boston • Buenos Aires • Caracas
London • Madrid • Mexico City • Sydney • Toronto

Copyright © 1996 Richard D. Irwin, a Times Mirror Higher Education Group
Inc. company.

All rights reserved. No part of this publication may be reproduced, stored in a
retrieval system, or transmitted, in any form or by any means, electronic,
mechanical, photocopying, or otherwise, without the prior written permission of
the publisher.

Publisher: William Schoof
Production Manager: Bob Lange
Marketing Manager: Katie Rose

Design and project management provided by Elm Street Publishing Services, Inc.

Compositor: Elm Street Publishing Services, Inc.
Typeface: 10/12 New Caledonia
Printer: Malloy Lithographing, Inc.

Library of Congress Cataloging-in-Publication Data
Hite, Marianne.
    A programmed learning guide to finance / by Marianne Hite.
      p.   cm.
    ISBN 0-256-17908-5
    1. Finance—Programmed instruction.   I. Title.
  HG173.H55   1996
    332'.07'7—dc20   95-31234

Printed in the United States of America

1 2 3 4 5 6 7 8 9 0 ML 9 8 7 6 5

Richard D. Irwin, Inc.

To Jake and Marshall

PREFACE

This is a programmed learning guide to finance. It is designed to be useful to the individual who is unfamiliar with basic finance concepts, who is having difficulty with basic concepts, or who simply wishes to review these concepts. Each module is designed to stand alone, so regardless of whether the concepts are being covered in a general finance course, an investments course, a corporate finance course, a money and banking course, or an international finance course, a student having difficulty in any of these should find this book helpful. The business person who desires a quick review of a specific financial topic may also find this guide useful. He or she can concentrate energies on one or more modules of this text without having to start at the beginning and progress through the modules. On the other hand, an individual who is entering an MBA program with no previous business courses might work through the entire book to digest some basic background material before being thrust into the rigorous finance courses at a graduate level.

Each module is broken down into numbered "frames." Each frame contains a small body of material ending with a sample application. At the end of the frame, a question is posed for the user to answer. The solution follows immediately, accompanied by a detailed explanation. If the user has answered the question correctly, he or she can confidently progress to the next frame. If not, the detailed explanation must be studied, and perhaps a review of the frame will be necessary until the user understands why the given solution is the correct answer. Some modules contain material that might be too advanced for a student who is studying the topic for the first time. Those frames and their answers are highlighted and can be skipped without any loss of continuity.

At the end of each module, a number of application questions and problems are provided so that the user can test his or her ability to pull all of the information learned in the module together and apply it to practical situations. The solutions to these are provided at the end of the applications section. Should a user be stumped, the frame or frames in which the specific application is addressed is provided at the end of the question so that the user can refer back to that frame for a quick refresher on the concept.

The table of contents is annotated so that the user can easily identify which modules might be relevant to the specific course that he or she is currently taking. A short summary of the topics covered in the module appears at the beginning of each module. Equations that are introduced in a module are also listed at the beginning of the module for convenience.

Appendix A contains the time value of money tables that are referred to in several of the modules. A glossary of all the terms appearing in boldface type is included at the end of the text for easy reference.

Acknowledgments

While there is only one author on this book, and as such I take full responsibility for any errors or omissions, there are a number of people who made significant contributions to it. I wish first to thank Bill Schoof, who believed in my idea and who expanded on it so that the finished product is much better than what I had originally conceived. I am also indebted to the reviewers, Irene Hammerbacher and Anand G. Shetty, both of Iona College, for their very valuable input, and to Laura Fiemann of Alden Capital Markets, Incorporated, for her assistance in factual verification. My students at the University of Colorado at Denver also deserve thanks for their feedback, and I would especially like to thank Patrick Barrett and Cindy Sutfin for their contributions to problem checking. I also deeply appreciate all the efforts of the staff at Elm Street Publishing Services, in particular, Barbara Campbell, Karen Hill, Melissa Morgan, and Betsy Webster. They made a very professional, efficient team.

My deepest gratitude will always be to my family and friends, who have been so very supportive. My final thanks go to my mother, Elizabeth Zeek, who constantly stressed the value of an education; to my sons, Jake and Marshall, who were patient with me when I was involved with my writing to the exclusion of all else; to my many friends, but especially to Nancy, Carol, Jean, Claudia, and Lena, who kept me sane; and last, but not least, to Jack, who breathed fresh life into me as I rounded the final curve of the project. Thank you all so very much.

Marianne Hite
September 1995

Key to Typical Finance Course Coverage

A. Money and banking
B. Investments
C. Corporate finance
D. International finance

Module	Title	Topical Coverage
I	Money, Banking, Interest Rates, and the Federal Reserve	A, C
II	Types of Investments	B, C
III	Options and Futures	B
IV	Security Markets, Regulations, and Market Indicators	B
V	Time Value of Money	A, B, C, D
VI	Stock and Bond Valuation	B, C
VII	Expected Return and Risk	B, C
VIII	Analysis of Financial Statements	C
IX	Financial Forecasting	C
X	Short-Term Asset Management	C
XI	Short-Term Liability Management	C
XII	The Cost of Capital	C
XIII	Capital Budgeting	C
XIV	Leverage and Capital Structure	C
XV	International Finance	A, B, C, D

CONTENTS

I

MONEY, BANKING, INTEREST RATES, AND THE FEDERAL RESERVE

This module will introduce you to the concepts of money and interest rates and the general terminology involving them. It discusses the role of the banking system in the creation and transfer of money among borrowers and lenders. Major regulations regarding the banking system are introduced. You will become familiar with monetary and fiscal policy tools and their effects on the economy. The role played by the Federal Reserve is emphasized.

Equations introduced in this module

$$\text{Maximum change for money supply} = \frac{\text{initial change for excess reserves}}{\text{reserve requirement}}$$

$$\text{Nominal interest rate} = \text{real interest rate} + \text{expected inflation}$$

1.   The study of finance involves money and its transfer among borrowers and lenders. Money can actually be anything that is generally accepted in payment for goods and services. In past times, items such as animal skins, shells, beads, cattle, corn, and metals were used as money. All of these items were accepted as a standard of value and could be used as a medium of exchange, which is the primary role of money. Without the existence of money, a direct transfer of goods and services is necessary; this is known as the **barter system**. The barter system can be inconvenient if you need something from someone who needs nothing from you since you have nothing to trade for that good or service. It can also be inconvenient if you have a future, but not an immediate need, for a good or service. Money proves useful in this situation as well since it serves as a store of value. You can receive money in exchange for goods and services that you produce and save the money for future expenditure requirements. The items that are to be used as the monetary unit for a society must be able to maintain a fairly stable value in order to serve as a store of value. Animal skins, shells, beads, cattle, and corn did not fill this role very well since their supply was often subject to abrupt changes, and some of them, such as shells and beads, were not very durable. Because metals were durable, readily available, and easily divisible into almost any amount, they served both as good stores of value and good media of exchange. To increase their usefulness, the government molded coins out of various metals and fixed their values. As trade expanded, coins became less convenient and paper money, or currency, was developed. With continued expansion of trade, even currency transfers became inconvenient and checking accounts (also known as **demand deposits**) were born.

Technological advances and the needs of modern society have led to the further development of money. Funds can now be transferred by wire, telephone, or computers. Savings accounts, certificates of deposit, and money market accounts are offered as alternative stores of value. These accounts may not serve as convenient media of exchanges, however, although they are becoming more so. For example, historically, the owner of a savings account would have to convert some of the funds into currency or transfer them to a checking account before transferring them to a third party. Today funds held in savings accounts can be transferred electronically, and are sometimes transferred automatically.

The Federal Reserve System, which controls the supply of money in our nation, has developed formal definitions that it uses when measuring the nation's money stock. The traditional measure is **M-1**, which includes coin, currency, and demand deposits (including interest-bearing checking accounts and travelers' checks). **M-2** contains everything in M-1 plus savings accounts and certificates of deposit that have denominations of $100,000 or less. M-2 is a less volatile measure than M-1, and for that reason it is sometimes preferred by analysts who are studying the amount of liquidity in the economy. For example, consider what happens to the levels of M-1 and M-2 if an individual transfers money from her checking account to her savings account. M-1 will fall since savings account balances are not included in the definition of M-1; M-2 will be unchanged, however, since the money is simply being transferred between two M-2 accounts. A third major definition of money supply is **M-3**. M-3 includes everything in M-2 as well as certificates of deposit that have denominations in excess of $100,000 and money market accounts.

? What will happen to the supply of money as defined by M-1 if an individual deposits cash in a checking account?

Answer: Nothing.
Since coin, currency, and demand deposits are all part of M-1, the money is simply being transferred from one M-1 account to another.

2.   The supply of money greatly impacts a nation's economy. Too much money stock can lead to inflation; too little can result in exorbitantly high interest rates. Congress created the **Federal Reserve System (FRS)** in 1913, giving it control over the supply of money and the commercial banking system. The official mission of the FRS is to create conditions conducive to full employment and balanced economic growth with stable prices. It attempts to fulfil this mission by using its **monetary policy tools** (namely, the reserve requirement, the discount rate, and open market operations, all of which will be formally defined and discussed in a later frame) to manipulate the nation's money stock.

The Federal Reserve System serves as the central bank of the United States, but it is not just a single bank. There are 12 Federal Reserve district banks and 25 Federal Reserve district branch banks. Each of the district banks serves a specific region, aided by the branch banks. The district banks are located in New York, Boston, Philadelphia, Richmond, Atlanta, Cleveland, Chicago, St. Louis, Minneapolis, Kansas City, Dallas, and San Francisco. Each district bank and district branch bank has its own board of directors.

The Federal Reserve Banks provide services to the **depository institutions** (commercial banks, savings and loan associations, mutual savings banks, and credit unions) in their district. The Reserve Banks control the flow of currency into and out of circulation, providing more currency upon increased public demand, and accepting surplus currency from the financial institutions in their districts when currency flows in from the public. They supply new paper money as needed and destroy unfit currency. (Unfit coin is returned to a U.S. Mint Facility.) The Reserve Banks operate a nationwide check-clearing mechanism as well. Depository institutions send checks to Federal Reserve Banks for processing. The Reserve Banks in turn route the checks for collection. The Federal Reserve does charge banks for this service, and competing check-clearing organizations exist.

In addition, the Federal Reserve System serves as a banker for the U.S. government. The U.S. Treasury has a checking account with the Federal Reserve and pays its bills with checks drawn on a Federal Reserve Bank. The Federal Reserve Banks also sell and redeem debt issues (Treasury bills, notes, and bonds) for the government when it needs to raise money. For instance, new issues of 3-month Treasury bills are auctioned by the Federal Reserve every Monday. Individuals can buy and redeem U.S. government securities through the Federal Reserve Bank closest to them.

The Reserve Banks are only part of what we refer to as the Federal Reserve System. The System also consists of a seven-member Board of Governors. Each of these seven people is appointed for a 14-year, nonrenewable term by the president of the United States with Senate approval. Each governor must come from a different Federal Reserve District. A chairman is appointed from among the seven governors by the president of the United States. The Board of Governors is responsible for supervising state member banks and all bank holding companies, approving changes in the discount rate that are recommended by the Federal Reserve District Banks, setting reserve requirements, and supervising the activities of the Reserve Banks. The seven governors also make up over half of the 12-member Federal Open Market Committee (FOMC). The remaining five members of the FOMC are presidents of the District Banks. The president of the Federal Reserve Bank in New York City is a permanent member of the FOMC; the remaining four presidents serve 1-year rotating terms. It is this committee that makes decisions regarding open market operations, which is the most important and powerful monetary policy tool that the Federal Reserve has. The FOMC also makes decisions regarding domestic securities markets and foreign exchange markets.

? The Federal Reserve System consists of _____ District Banks, _____ District Branch Banks, and _____ Board of Governors.

Answers: 12, 25, 7.
The Federal Reserve System consists of 12 District Banks, 25 District Branch Banks, and 7 Board of Governors.

3.   A **dual banking system** exists in the United States. Banks can be chartered by either a state government or the federal government. Federally chartered banks are governed by the Comptroller of the Currency, whereas state chartered banks are regulated by individual state agencies. All federally chartered banks must be members of the Federal Reserve System and the **Federal Deposit Insurance Corporation (FDIC)**, which is a government agency that insures bank deposits of its member banks for up to a maximum of $100,000 per account. The FDIC has its own set of requirements that banks must abide by, and it has its own bank examiners to ensure that the banks are doing so. State chartered banks may elect to belong to the Federal Reserve System and the FDIC. Those that do are supervised by the Federal Reserve system and the FDIC in addition to the state agency. All banks that are members of the Federal Reserve System, regardless of whether they are state chartered or federally chartered, are referred to as "member banks." These banks are the *owners* of the Federal Reserve.

In 1978, the Comptroller of the Currency, the Federal Reserve, and the FDIC agreed upon a common framework, known as **CAMEL ratings**, for assessing a bank's soundness in an effort to provide uniformity. Banks are rated on **C**apital adequacy, **A**sset quality, **M**anagement ability, **E**arnings level and quality, and **L**iquidity. Each of the five characteristics is given a rating of 1 to 5, with 5 being an unsatisfactory rating. A composite rating is also assigned. The system has minimized, but not eliminated, conflicts. Disagreements have occurred between the Comptroller of the Currency and the Federal Reserve regarding reserve requirements. In the 1980s, state chartered banks in some states were allowed to engage in activities that were prohibited to federally chartered banks. These activities included securities underwriting, insurance sales, travel agencies, and real estate investments.

? True or False: State chartered banks are regulated by the Comptroller of the Currency.

Answer: False.
Only federally chartered banks are governed by the Comptroller of the Currency.

4. Bank branching has been constrained by both state and federal laws. The **McFadden Act of 1927** allows branching within a state to be regulated by that state. Some states have **unit branching** laws, which means that no branching is allowed. Others have **contiguous county branching**, which means that a bank may branch into a county that is immediately touching a county in which it has existing offices, but it may not skip over a county. **Bank holding companies**, which can control a large number of individual banks, were organized to evade such restrictions. Under this arrangement each individual bank must still have its own board of directors and executive management team, so there is the expense of duplication of effort.

The **Douglas Amendment** to the McFadden Act prohibits holding companies from crossing state lines unless the authorities of the individual states agree to it. The **Edge Act of 1919**, however, does allow bank holding companies to form interstate subsidiary corporations for the specific purpose of accepting deposits and making loans related to international business transactions. The Bank of America has several such subsidiaries. Furthermore, banks and **thrift institutions** (savings and loan associations, mutual savings banks, and credit unions, so called because they were originally established as *savings* institutions) have been allowed to cross state lines in order to acquire financially troubled institutions, with the first such acquisition occurring in 1982.

The **Bank Holding Company Act of 1956**, which was later amended in 1970, established a formal definition for a bank as an institution that accepts deposits that can be withdrawn upon demand and that makes commercial loans. Any institution that engaged in one of these activities, but not the other, was not categorized as a bank and was not subject to Federal Reserve regulations. The **Competitive Banking Equality Act of 1987** closed this loophole by defining a bank as any institution that is insured by the FDIC; however, this new law governs only those institutions established after March 4, 1986.

Historically, commercial banks have not been allowed to engage in investment banking activities. One of the major activities of this industry is **underwriting** securities, or the purchase of stocks and bonds for immediate resale to the public. The **Glass-Steagall Act of 1933** prohibits it. However, in 1987, the Federal Reserve gave banks permission to underwrite municipal bonds and commercial paper, and in 1990 a bank received permission to underwrite corporate stock. These activities are carried out through an investment banking *subsidiary* that is separate from the commercial banking subsidiary although both are owned by the same holding company. Thus, the Glass-Steagall Act is not being violated.

? Interstate banking is prohibited by the
  a. Glass-Steagall Act.
  b. Edge Act.
  c. Competitive Banking Equality Act.
  d. McFadden Act.

Answer: d.
The McFadden Act of 1927 prohibits interstate branching and allows intrastate branching to be regulated by each individual state.

5.   A relatively new piece of legislation, the **Depository Institution Deregulation and Monetary Control (DIDMC) Act of 1980**, had a significant effect on the depository type financial intermediaries (banks, savings and loan associations, mutual savings banks, and credit unions) and their activities. First, it provided for the phase out of **Regulation Q**. Regulation Q was established in 1933 and set ceilings on the interest rate that these institutions could pay their depositors. Because of these ceilings, **disintermediation** would sometimes occur. Disintermediation refers to investors' pulling money out of the financial intermediaries and investing directly in stocks and bonds. Under Regulation Q, when interest rates were high, investors did just that. Although a corporate bond may have more risk, if its expected return was 15%, many investors felt that it was preferable to a savings account that could offer a return of only 5%. Unfortunately, small investors were stuck with the 5% return mandated by the interest rate ceilings since they did not have enough to invest to warrant investing in stocks and bonds. Small borrowers were also hurt in that disintermediation resulted in less loanable funds for the depository type financial intermediaries. Therefore, the price of these loans, i.e., the interest rate that borrowers must pay, increased. Since the phase out of Regulation Q, interest rate ceilings no longer exist.

A second feature of the DIDMC Act provided that all depository institutions could offer checking accounts. Under the Banking Acts of 1933 and 1935, only commercial banks could provide checking accounts. (A 1972 Massachusetts court decision opened the door to **negotiable order of withdrawal (NOW) accounts**, which are the interest-bearing checking accounts, but their legal status was somewhat uncertain until the DIDMC Act.) Since 1980 all depository institutions can offer both regular checking accounts and interest-bearing checking accounts.

A third major provision of the Act was to allow thrift institutions to provide commercial loans, credit lines, and credit cards. Until 1980, these services could be obtained only from a commercial bank. This provision, along with the previous two mentioned, has made all the depository institutions fairly equal in the services that they are able to provide. There is no longer much of a distinction among these institutions.

? Which of the following is *not* a provision of the DIDMC Act?
  a. It allowed for depository institutions to engage in investment banking activities.
  b. It lifted interest rate ceilings that could be paid on deposits.
  c. It allowed thrift institutions to offer checkable deposits.
  d. It allowed thrift institutions to offer commercial loans.

Answer: a.
The DIDMC Act did not permit depository institutions to engage in investment banking activities.

6. The DIDMC Act also gave the Federal Reserve System some regulatory power over the thrift institutions. Since 1980, the Federal Reserve sets the **reserve requirements** for federally and state chartered commercial banks and for the thrifts. The reserve requirements specify the amount of cash that an institution must hold. This amount is based on the institution's deposits. Deposits, which are checking accounts, savings accounts, and other time deposits (e.g., certificates of deposits), are liabilities of the financial institution. They represent money that the institution owes. In 1995, the Federal Reserve requires the depository institutions to hold 3% of all demand deposits over $4 million and less than $51.9 million as cash, and 10% of all demand deposits in excess of $51.9 million. There are currently no reserve requirements on demand deposits less than $4 million or on savings accounts and other time deposits.

? If John Gaelic deposits $2,000 into a bank that has $60 million in demand deposits, how much is the bank required to hold as cash?

Answer: $200.
Since the bank has over $51.9 million in demand deposits, it must hold 10% of these deposits as cash, and $0.10 \times \$2,000 = \$200$.

7. The reserve requirements need not be met daily, but instead must be met on the basis of the daily average deposit balance over the **reserve period**. The current reserve period is 2 weeks. We also have what is referred to as a **lagged reserve requirement**, and the current "lag" is 2 days, which means that 2 days after the reserve period ends the financial institution must have the required cash on hand.

Reserves are not always held in the institution's vault. They may also be on deposit at a Federal Reserve Bank. The Federal Reserve is the banker's bank, and bank deposits are liabilities for the Federal Reserve just as our deposits are liabilities for our bank. Alternatively, a bank's reserves may be on deposit at a **correspondent bank**, which is a large metropolitan bank that serves as a depository for smaller banks in the area. Cash that is held over and above the amount mandated by the Federal Reserve is called **excess reserves**. Excess reserves are the loanable funds that a bank has available since all the bank's other funds are either already invested or are part of the required reserves, in which case they may not be invested in anything. **Total reserves**, the total cash that a bank has, is the sum of the required reserves and the excess reserves of the bank. The term **secondary reserves** refers to high quality, short-term, liquid investments that a bank holds (e.g., Treasury bills). Should a bank fall short of its reserve requirement, it can sell these investments to raise the necessary cash. Secondary reserves are *not* cash, and are therefore *not* part of a bank's total reserves.

? The funds that a bank has available for lending is its _____ reserves.

Answer: excess.
The excess reserves is the cash that the bank has that is over and above the amount of cash that it must hold in a noninterest-bearing account.

8. As was mentioned earlier, the Federal Reserve uses monetary policy tools to control the supply of money in our economy. It does so by using these tools to control the level of reserves in the banking system. If we use the M-1 definition of money supply, the money stock is determined by the level of cash and demand deposits. When an individual deposits cash in a checking account, the money stock is unchanged. However, the deposit *does* increase the total reserves (cash) in the banking system and, therefore, the loanable funds. For example, suppose that Mr. Bigcash deposits $1,000 in his checking account at Bank A. M-1 is unchanged since the $1,000 has simply changed forms, but the bank's total reserves has increased by $1,000. Under current reserve requirements, the bank must hold $100 of that as cash ($0.10 \times \$1,000$), and now has $900 in excess reserves or loanable funds. Next assume that Mr. Hardup gets a loan for $900 from Bank A, and the money is deposited in his checking account. Note that demand deposits have been increased by this transaction. Total demand deposits are now $1,900—Mr. Hardup's $900 account and Mr. Bigcash's $1,000 account. Nor has this been offset by a decrease in cash or some other individual's demand deposit. *A loan creates new money.* Furthermore, the expansion of the money supply does not stop here. Mr. Hardup obviously borrowed the money in order to spend it. Let us assume that he spends $900 on a gold toothbrush from Junk, Incorporated, and Junk, Incorporated deposits the money in its bank, Bank B. Bank B must hold $90 of the $900 as required reserves, but now it has $810 to lend, and that will expand the money supply by another $810. The process can continue until there are no excess reserves left in the system. If this is the case, the banking system is said to be *fully loaned up*. The maximum possible expansion in the money supply can be calculated using the following formula:

$$\text{Maximum change for money supply} = \frac{\text{initial change for excess reserves}}{\text{reserve requirement}}$$

In the example above, the initial change in excess reserves created by Mr. Bigcash's deposit was $900. Dividing this by the 10% reserve requirement, we determine that the money supply can be expanded by $9,000 due to Mr. Bigcash's $1,000 deposit. This is referred to as the **multiplier effect**. If the Federal Reserve wants to expand money supply, it will *lower* the reserve requirement. This will give banks more loanable funds and allow for the creation of money.

? Mr. P. Brothers deposited $500 in his checking account. If the reserve requirement is 12%, how much can his bank now lend, and what is the maximum expansion in money supply that can occur due to this deposit?

Answers: $440, $3,666.67.
The required reserves are $0.12 \times \$500 = \$60$, so the bank has $500 - \$60 = \$440$ to lend as a result of Mr. Brothers' deposit. The maximum possible expansion in the money supply is given by $\$440/0.12 = \$3,666.67$.

9.   A second monetary policy tool that the Federal Reserve has by which it controls the level of reserves and, therefore, the money supply, is the **discount rate**. Depository institutions that fall short of their reserve requirements can borrow money from the Federal Reserve at what is called the "discount window." The interest rate that the Federal Reserve charges on these loans is referred to as the discount rate, and the loans themselves are known as **Federal advances**. (Banks may also borrow reserves from each other in order to satisfy their reserve requirements. These overnight or weekend interbank loans are called **federal funds borrowings** and the interest rate charged is referred to as the **fed funds rate**.) Changes in the discount rate are recommended by the board of directors of the individual Federal Reserve Banks. Final approval or veto to the changes is under the control of the Board of Governors, however.

When the discount rate is increased, it makes it more costly for the depository institutions to borrow money from the Federal Reserve. This serves to make the institutions more cautious. As a result, they may hold more cash, making less money available for loans. They may also choose to sell some of their secondary reserves rather than borrow from the Federal Reserve. This sell-off can cause the prices of short-term securities to fall, and interest rates on short-term securities to increase. An increase in the discount rate might also signal the market that the Federal Reserve is pursuing a contractionary monetary policy. Based on this, lenders may cut back on their current lending activity in anticipation of higher rates, making the tightening effect much more dramatic. On the other hand, it is sometimes the case that a change in the discount rate will follow changes in the interest rates. This occurs when borrowers and lenders are *anticipating* a change in the discount rate due to current market conditions. In this instance, the actual change in the discount rate will have little perceptible effect on current market conditions since the effect preceded the change. The discount rate is changed far more frequently than the reserve requirements. In 1991, it was changed six times.

If the Federal Reserve wishes to expand money supply, it will *lower* the discount rate, encouraging depository institutions to borrow money. If a bank can borrow money at 4% and lend it at 8%, it makes a profit. Furthermore, federal advances are not subject to a reserve requirement, so depository institutions can lend 100% of all its borrowed funds. The discount rate is the *weakest* monetary policy tool, however, in that the Federal Reserve can only *encourage* banks to borrow; it cannot *force* banks to borrow. Federal advances also represent a relatively small percentage of the total reserves in the banking system, which minimizes its effectiveness.

? If a bank that has sufficient reserves to meet reserve requirements borrows $1,000 from the Federal Reserve and the reserve requirement is 10%, what potential effect can this loan have on the money supply?

Answer: Money supply can be expanded by $10,000.
Since there is no reserve requirement on federal advances, the full $1,000 is excess reserves for the bank. Applying the formula, the maximum possible increase in money supply under these conditions is $1,000/0.10 = $10,000.

10.   The most powerful monetary policy tool that the Federal Reserve has is **open market operations**. Open market operations refer to the purchase and sale of Treasury securities by the Federal Reserve to the public. These transactions are decided upon by the 12-member Federal Open Market Committee. If the Federal Reserve wishes to be expansionary, it will conduct an **open market purchase**, i.e., it will buy Treasury securities on the open market. It pays for the securities by increasing the reserve account of the seller's bank. (The seller receives a check drawn on a Federal Reserve bank, and when the seller deposits this check, his bank submits the check for payment. It is at that time that the Federal Reserve makes payment by increasing the reserve account of the bank.) With the increase in reserves, loanable funds are increased, and again the multiplier effect can take place.

On the other hand, if the Federal Reserve wishes to contract the money supply, it will conduct an **open market sale**, wherein it sells Treasury securities *that it owns* to the public. (This is different from the situation in which the Federal Reserve serves as the auctioneer for new Treasury securities in which case it is acting as an agent of the Treasury, and the Treasury receives the proceeds from the sale.) In order to purchase the securities, the public pulls funds out of demand deposits, thereby decreasing the money supply and the loanable funds in the banking system. When the Federal Reserve clears the check drawn on the investor's bank, it will decrease that bank's reserve account.

? Which of the following would be used to *contract* money supply and loanable funds?
  a. decreasing the discount rate
  b. buying Treasury securities on the open market

   c. decreasing reserve requirements

   d. selling Treasury securities on the open market

Answer: d.

When the Federal Reserve sells Treasury securities to the public, the public withdraws funds from their checking accounts to pay for the securities. This immediately decreases the money supply; in addition, total reserves of the banking system decrease, so fewer loans can be made, and loans create new money.

11.   Open market operations may be offensive or defensive. Offensive open market operations are conducted to increase or decrease the total reserves in the system in order to ease or to tighten credit. If credit is eased, interest rates generally go down; if credit is tightened, interest rates will rise since the supply of loanable funds will be less than the demand for loanable funds. An **interest rate** can be defined as the price of credit. Defensively, the Federal Reserve uses open market operations to counteract the effects of some other influences that are affecting reserves, such as **fiscal policy**. Fiscal policy tools are controlled by Congress. The primary tools are taxation, government spending, and deficit management.

If taxes are increased, money is pulled out of the banking system, and this can cause a contraction in the money supply, provided that the government does not spend its tax dollars on domestic goods and services, in which case the money is recycled into the system, perhaps being redistributed. If taxes are lowered, the public has more money on deposit in the banking system, so total reserves and, therefore, loanable funds, are greater. Money supply can be expanded.

If the government increases its spending *domestically*, whether it be on domestic goods and services or an increase in welfare benefits, it puts more dollars in the public's hands. This is expansionary in that total bank reserves are increased. If it cuts spending, bank reserves will be decreased. The tax payments reduce the demand deposits in the system, and the money is not recycled into the system. Note that if tax dollars are spent on foreign aid, this can be contractionary for the U.S. economy since money is flowing out and not coming back in.

When tax revenues exceed government expenses, there is a **government surplus**. If expenses exceed revenues, there is a **government deficit**. Like any other entity, if expenses exceed revenues, the government must borrow the funds from somewhere. The U.S. government borrows money by issuing Treasury bills, notes, and bonds. (This is not unlike an individual who borrows money for a house by issuing a mortgage bond.) The entities that buy these securities are lending the government money. Individual and corporate investors, banks, and the Federal Reserve all invest in Treasury securities. When the lenders are individual and corporate investors, the money supply may not be affected by the deficit management. These investors pull money out of their bank accounts to purchase the Treasury bills, notes, and bonds. However, if the government spends the borrowed funds domestically, the money is recycled back into the economy, and neither demand deposits nor total reserves in the banking system are affected. If, instead, the government spends the borrowed funds outside of the United States, the result is contractionary since demand deposits and, therefore, money supply, is reduced. Furthermore, total reserves in the banking system are decreased, so banks have less capacity to make loans.

When banks purchase the Treasury securities, the result can be somewhat expansionary if the borrowed funds are spent domestically. A bank is *lending* the U.S. government money, and this loan, like any other, creates a new demand deposit and thus an increase in the money supply. When the government spends the money, the funds flow into the hands of individuals and/or corporations, and money supply remains at the new, higher level. However, the excess reserves, which represent the lending capacity of the banking system, are reduced in this transaction since the bank has used part of its loan-able funds to lend money to the government.

The most expansionary method of deficit management occurs when the U.S. Treasury borrows the money by selling its securities to the Federal Reserve. The Federal Reserve gives the U.S. government an account at a Federal Reserve bank in return for the Treasury securities. When the U.S. government purchases goods and services domestically, these funds get transferred into the bank accounts of individuals and corporations, thus increasing money supply. Total reserves in the banking system are also increased, so the available credit in the economy is increased.

? Which of the following is a fiscal policy tool?
   a. the discount rate
   b. taxation
   c. open market sales
   d. both b and c

Answer: b.

Taxation is a fiscal policy tool; the discount rate and open market sales are monetary policy tools.

12.   As previously stated, the Federal Reserve is charged with the responsibility of maintaining conditions conducive to balanced economic growth and stable prices. This is much easier said than done. If money supply is too tight, interest rates can increase and growth can be stymied. On the other hand, too much expansion can lead to inflation. **Inflation** is defined as a general increase in price levels. Changes in price levels are measured by the percentage changes in the **Consumer's Price Index (CPI)**, which is simply the cost of a market basket of goods that the federal government believes is indicative of the consumption of the average consumer. One of the primary causes of inflation is an expansion in money supply that exceeds the growth in the national output. This results in "too much money chasing too few goods," as potential purchasers bid the price of the existing goods up. Inflationary expectations can also lead to higher interest rates as the Fisher effect (named after Irving Fisher, the researcher who first suggested the relationship) depicts.

A simplified version of the Fisher effect states that the **nominal**, or observed, **interest rate** on a riskless asset is equal to the **real interest rate**, or the true price of credit, plus expected inflation.

$$\text{Nominal interest rate} = \text{real interest rate} + \text{expected inflation}$$

The nominal interest rate is the rate that you will find quoted in the newspaper. The real interest rate cannot be observed, but is calculated ex post facto. It can be thought of as the return that lenders get for forgoing current consumption and instead allowing others to use their money. Alternatively, it can be viewed as the price that borrowers must pay for consuming today rather than waiting until they have saved the money. However, if inflation exists, the dollars that are repaid will be worth less than the dollars that were borrowed in terms of purchasing power, so the nominal interest rate also compensates the lender for loss of purchasing power based on *expectations* of inflation.

While the Fisher effect describes the interest rate that we expect to observe on a risk-free asset (such as a Treasury bill), all interest rates will be based on this relationship. A risk premium will simply be added, reflecting the perceived relative risk of a risky loan, such as a corporate bond, a car loan, or a home mortgage.

? If the real interest rate has been averaging 2% over the past 2 decades, and inflation is expected to be 5% over the next year, what would you expect a 12-month Treasury bill to be yielding?

Answer: 7%.

Applying the Fisher effect, the nominal risk-free rate is equal to the real rate of 2% plus expected inflation of 5%.

13. The **term structure of interest rates** refers to the relationship between time to maturity and the yields. The default risk is held constant. The term structure is illustrated by a **yield curve**, which plots the yields on similar risk securities that mature at different points in time. Typically, yield curves are constructed using Treasury securities, which are all considered to be risk-free. A set of Treasury yield curves as they appeared on March 16, 1995 is shown below in Exhibit 1:

Exhibit 1

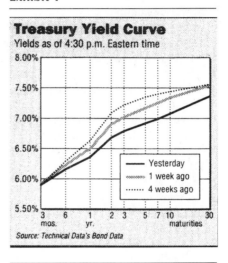

Source: *The Wall Street Journal*, Volume CXXXII No. 52, March 16, 1995, p. C17.

The yield curves shown here are upward sloping, which is the most typical situation. Upward sloping yield curves mean that, given the same risk, longer-term securities pay higher yields than shorter-term securities. A downward sloping yield curve would mean that yields on longer-term instruments are smaller than yields on shorter-term instruments of the same risk. While not a frequent occurrence, downward sloping yield curves *do* exist from time to time, as do *flat* yield curves (in which case long-term and short-term rates do not differ by much) and *humped* yield curves (intermediate term debt instruments may offer the highest yields).

A number of explanations have been proposed for the existence of different term structures. One of the most widely accepted explanations is the **expectations hypothesis**, which states that future interest rates are based on investor expectations about future inflation rates. When the annual rate of inflation is expected to increase, the yield curve will be upward sloping, and when the annual rate of inflation is expected to decrease, the yield curve will be downward sloping.

❓ The term structure of interest rates depicts the relationship between
   a. time to maturity and yields.
   b. yields and default risk.
   c. default risk and time to maturity.
   d. inflation and yields.

Answer: a.

This is the definition of the term structure of interest rates.

14.   The opposite of inflation is **deflation**. Deflation refers to a general decrease in price levels. Deflation can sometimes result in a **recession**, which is defined as an extended period (usually six months or more) of increased unemployment and a reduction in the national output. Obviously, manufacturers cannot allow prices to drop below cost for any amount of time, so when prices decrease, these firms may downsize, laying off employees and decreasing production. High levels of unemployment and a sluggish economy have also coexisted with inflationary conditions from time to time. This is termed **stagflation**, and often occurs when production costs continue to rise even though unemployment is on the increase. This causes unemployment to increase further and prices to continue their upward trend. Another term that is sometimes confused with deflation is **disinflation**. Disinflation refers to a *decrease* in the *rate of inflation*. Unlike deflation, prices are still increasing, albeit at a decreasing rate.

Monetary and fiscal policy tools can be used to fight undesirable economic conditions. For example, if inflationary conditions threaten the economy, the Federal Reserve can use its monetary policy tools to tighten the money supply. The federal government can also use fiscal policy tools to the same end. If a recession appears to be on the horizon, expansionary monetary and fiscal policies may be followed. This is, of course, not as simple as it may sound since too much tightening or expansion can have the opposite effect of what is desired. There is also often a lag between the action taken and the result on the economy. Nevertheless, the astute observer can make an educated guess regarding the direction of the economy and interest rates by observing the current monetary and fiscal policy that is being pursued.

? A decrease in the rate of inflation is called
   a. deflation.
   b. stagflation.
   c. recession.
   d. disinflation.

Answer: d.
This is the definition of disinflation.

Apply It

1. A direct transfer of goods and services is called the _____ system. (Frame 1)

2. What does the M-2 definition of money supply include? (Frame 1)

3. Which element of the Federal Reserve System has the most control over the monetary policy tools? (Frame 2)

4. What is meant by a "dual banking system"? (Frame 3)

5. Who owns the Federal Reserve? (Frame 3)

6. What is the CAMEL system? (Frame 3)

7. What activity does the Glass-Steagall Act of 1933 prohibit? (Frame 4)

8. How are small borrowers hurt when disintermediation occurs? (Frame 5)

9. If the reserve requirement on demand deposits is 10%, and Pat Bain deposits $3,000 in his checking account, how much will his bank have available for loans as a result of his deposit? (Frames 6 and 7)

10. If the reserve requirement on demand deposits is 10%, and Pat Bain deposits $2,000 in his checking account, what is the maximum possible expansion of money supply in the banking system that can occur as a result of his deposit? (Frame 8)

11. If the Federal Reserve wants to fight inflation, will it raise or lower the discount rate? (Frames 9 and 12)

12. If the Federal Reserve wants to ward off a recession, will it conduct an open market purchase or an open market sale? (Frames 10 and 12)

13. What are the three fiscal policy tools? (Frame 11)

14. If inflation is a concern, what is the *worst* source from which the federal government can borrow money? (Frames 11 and 12)

15. What is the difference between deflation and disinflation? (Frame 14)

16. If you observe a 12-month Treasury bill to be yielding 5.8% and you know that the real interest rate has averaged 2% in recent years, what can you conclude about the market's expectations of inflation? (Frame 12)

17. If you observe a downward sloping yield curve, what does this indicate about the relative rates on short-term and long-term securities of similar risk? (Frame 13)

18. Your cousin is considering whether to lock in an interest rate on a mortgage loan that he will be getting in the next 45 days when he reads that the Federal Reserve has lowered reserve requirements and asks you what effect this might have on the economy and what he should do. What might you advise him? (Frame 8)

Apply It Answers

1. A direct transfer of goods and services is called the *barter* system.

2. M-2 includes coin, currency, demand deposits, savings accounts, and certificates of deposit that have less than $100,000 face value.

3. The seven Board of Governors have the most control over the monetary policy tools. They alone determine the reserve requirements; they have final approval or veto power over changes in the discount rate; and they comprise over half the membership of the Federal Open Market Committee.

4. A dual banking system refers to the fact that U.S. banks may be chartered by either the federal government or a state government.

5. Banks that are members of the Federal Reserve are the owners of the Federal Reserve.

6. The CAMEL system is a framework established by the Comptroller of the Currency, the Federal Reserve, and the FDIC to assess a bank's soundness. Banks are rated on Capital adequacy, Asset quality, Management ability, Earnings level and quality, and Liquidity.

7. The Glass-Steagall Act prohibits banks from engaging in investment banking activities.

8. When disintermediation occurs, the deposit type financial intermediaries have fewer funds to lend. This causes small borrowers to pay a higher interest rate on loans.

9. The required reserves on $3,000 are $300, so the bank will have excess reserves, or loanable funds, of $2,700.

10. The required reserves on $2,000 are $200, so the excess reserves created are $1,800. The maximum possible expansion in money supply is $1,800/0.10 = $18,000.

11. The Federal Reserve will raise the discount rate to fight inflation. In doing so, it discourages banks from borrowing at the discount window and encourages them to hold more excess reserves. This means that banks will make fewer loans, thereby hampering the further creation of money, and inflation is caused by too much money supply.

12. The Federal Reserve will want to be expansionary to ward off a recession, so it will conduct an open market purchase. The purchase of Treasury securities from the public will increase bank reserves and allow for the further expansion of money supply through the creation of loans.

13. The three fiscal policy tools are taxation, government spending, and deficit management.

14. The worst source from which the federal government could borrow money during an inflationary period is the Federal Reserve. A loan from the Federal Reserve will result in an immediate increase in money supply, and it will also increase total reserves in the banking system, giving banks the ability to expand the money supply even further through loan creation.

15. Deflation is a general decrease in *price levels* while disinflation refers to a decrease in the *rate of inflation*.

16. The Fisher effect states that the risk-free rate is equal to the sum of the real interest rate and expected inflation, so expected inflation will be equal to the risk-free rate minus the real interest rate. 5.8% − 2% = 3.8%.

17. A downward sloping yield curve indicates that yields on short-term securities are higher than those on long-term securities of similar risk.

18. A decrease in the reserve requirements indicates that the Federal Reserve is pursuing an expansionary monetary policy, which should cause interest rates to fall. You might, therefore, advise your cousin to adopt a "wait and see" stance instead of immediately locking in the rate.

TYPES OF INVESTMENTS

This module is designed to familiarize you with the basic terminology concerning investments in common stocks, preferred stocks, and both short-term and long-term debt instruments. The rights of common shareholders are presented, and the technicalities involving voting procedures, dividend payments, stock dividends, and stock splits are addressed. The various features of preferred stock are discussed, including convertible and callable preferred. Debt instruments are divided into long-term and short-term obligations. Debt securities of the U.S. government, state and local governments, and corporations are discussed separately. Both secured debt and unsecured debt issues are discussed, and common features found in bond covenants, such as call options, convertibility, put options, warrants, and sinking fund requirements, are addressed. Investment in stocks and bonds through investment in an investment company is also presented, and the types of investment companies—closed-end companies and mutual funds—are discussed in detail. You will also learn to interpret *The Wall Street Journal* quotations for each of these securities.

Equations introduced in this module

$$\text{Shares needed per seat} = \frac{(\text{number of seats desired})(\text{number of shares outstanding})}{\text{number of seats being filled} + 1} + 1$$

$$R = \frac{\text{market price of stock rights-on} - \text{subscription price}}{\text{number of rights needed per share} + 1}$$

$$\text{Dividend per share} = \frac{\text{total dividends paid on common stock}}{\text{number of common shares outstanding}}$$

$$\text{Dividend payout ratio} = \frac{\text{common stock dividends}}{\text{net income} - \text{preferred dividends}}$$

$$\text{Conversion value} = \text{market price of common stock} \times \text{conversion ratio}$$

$$\text{Percentage load} = \frac{\text{offering price} - \text{net asset value}}{\text{offering price}}$$

$$\text{Offering price} = \frac{\text{net asset value}}{1 - \text{percentage load}}$$

---

1. Firms such as IBM, Texaco, and Abbott Laboratories are corporations. **A corporation** is a legal entity that is empowered by the state in which it is incorporated to own assets in its own name. A corporation can also be sued and taxed and can enter into contractual agreements. A business that wishes to incorporate must file **articles of incorporation** with the secretary of state in the state in which it wishes to be incorporated. The articles of incorporation contain information concerning the proposed name of the firm, its location, the nature of its business, and the corporate **bylaws**, which are rules established by the founders that govern the internal affairs of the firm. The articles of incorporation also indicate the number of shares of the firm's common stock that can be sold to investors. The **stock** of the firm represents the owners' investment in the firm. Each **share** of stock represents one unit of ownership. The maximum number of shares that can be sold as indicated in the articles of incorporation is called the number of **authorized shares**. The number of shares that have been sold are referred to as **issued shares**. Sometimes a firm will buy back some of its shares. These repurchased shares are referred to as **treasury stock**. The number of shares that remain in the hands of investors is referred to as the **outstanding shares**. The number of issued shares will equal the number of outstanding shares if the firm has not repurchased any of its shares. The number of issued shares can never exceed the number of authorized shares. If a firm has sold the total number of shares that was authorized by its articles of incorporation and wishes to sell more shares, it must obtain permission from its shareholders, who are the owners of the corporation. When the state approves the articles of incorporation it grants the firm a **corporate charter**, which binds the corporation to abide by the articles of incorporation and the laws of the state in which it is incorporated.

? Which of the following relationships could never be true?
a. shares outstanding ≤ shares issued
b. shares authorized ≤ shares outstanding
c. shares issued ≤ shares authorized
d. shares outstanding ≤ shares authorized

Answer: b.
The shares authorized cannot be less than the shares outstanding since the firm cannot sell any more shares than the number authorized by the articles of incorporation.

2. The common shareholders (or stockholders) of a corporation elect a board of directors who are responsible for seeing that the firm is operated in the best interests of its shareholders. Shareholders also have the right to vote on merger agreements and on amendments to the articles of incorporation. The number of votes that a shareholder gets for each share he holds is set forth in the articles of incorporation. Typically, each share gets one vote, but there are cases in which a corporation has different classes of stock, with some classes getting more votes. Shares that have more powerful voting privileges are sometimes referred to as **killer Bs,** since it is often Class B stock that gives its holders more votes for each share.

Some firms use **cumulative voting** in the board of directors elections. Under this system, each shareholder receives a number of votes equal to the number of seats being elected times the number of shares owned. The shareholder can cast all his votes for a single candidate if he chooses. Cumulative voting is designed to allow shareholders who have a minority of the shares to gain representation on the board. If there are 120,000 shares outstanding, five board seats to be voted on, and an investor owns 500 shares, the normal voting procedure would give the investor 500 votes that he could cast for each of the five positions. With cumulative voting, the investor receives $5 \times 500 = 2,500$ votes. He can cast all of these votes for his favorite candidate or he can split the votes up and cast them in any way he wants. If normal voting is used, the investor would have to control 60,001 (50% of the shares plus one) in order to ensure his choice won a seat. A formula that can be used to calculate the number of shares necessary in order to ensure that one or more of the preferred candidates gets elected is shown below:

$$\text{Shares needed} = \frac{(\text{number of seats desired})(\text{number of shares outstanding})}{(\text{number of seats being filled}) + 1} + 1.$$

If cumulative voting is used, the investor would need only the following number of shares to ensure the election of his favorite candidate:

$$\text{Shares needed} = \frac{1 \times 120,000}{5 + 1} + 1 = 20,001.$$

Corporations that have stock which is publicly traded are required by law to send a **proxy statement** to each of its shareholders. The proxy statement explains all the issues on which the shareholder will vote. In addition, this statement reveals other information, such as information regarding the amount of the firm's stock that each of the firm's executives holds, executive compensation programs, and severance agreements. The shareholder can elect to attend the annual shareholder meeting to cast his vote, or he can sign the **proxy card**, a card that is included with the proxy statement on which the shareholder indicates his vote. When one or more groups is trying to gain control of the firm, a **proxy fight** may ensue. The groups will solicit the stockholders for the right to vote their shares for them.

? The Rese Corporation has 200,000 shares outstanding and a 10-member board of directors. Seven of the seats are up for election. You own 1,000 shares and are dissatisfied with the way things are being done in the firm. You would like to ensure that one of the seven vacated seats will be filled by a candidate that you trust. How many shares will you need to control one seat if normal voting is used? How many shares will you need to control one seat if cumulative voting is used?

Answers: 100,001; 25,001.

If normal voting is used, you will need to obtain one more than 50% of the vote. Since there are 200,000 shares outstanding, you will need to control 100,001 shares. If cumulative voting is used, you will need

$$\frac{1 \times 200,000}{7 + 1} + 1 = 25,001 \text{ shares.}$$

3. Shareholders of a corporation have other rights in addition to voting rights. They have the right to obtain the names and addresses of the other shareholders of the firm; the right to inspect the firm's financial statements; the right to call a shareholders' meeting; the right to propose an amendment to the corporate charter; the right to receive any dividends declared, based on their proportionate ownership in the company; and the right to the value of any liquidated assets after prior claims are satisfied, based on their proportionate ownership in the company.

? Which of the following is not a right of shareholders?
a. the right to a list of the firm's shareholders, along with their names and addresses
b. the right to vote on the purchase or sale of a major piece of equipment
c. the right to vote on a merger proposal
d. the right to call a special shareholders' meeting

Answer: b.

Shareholders have the right to vote on merger proposals, to call a shareholders' meeting, and to obtain a list of the other shareholders, but they do not have the right to vote on operating decisions made by the firm, such as the decision to purchase or sell a piece of equipment.

4.   Some corporate charters also give the firm's shareholders **preemptive rights**. A preemptive right gives a shareholder the right to buy any new shares offered for sale in order to maintain his or her percentage ownership in the firm. Assume you currently own 1,000 shares in a firm that has 100,000 shares outstanding, and the firm is going to be issuing 20,000 new shares. At present you own 1% of the company (1,000/100,000 = 1%). The preemptive right would give you the opportunity to purchase 200 of the new shares being sold (0.01 × 20,000 = 200).

If preemptive rights are not authorized by the corporate charter, the firm can still give its current shareholders the opportunity to buy the new shares issued before it offers the shares to the general public by doing a **rights offering**. A rights offering is a formal procedure through which the firm issues rights to the shareholders, which specifies the number of shares that can be purchased, the price at which the shares can be purchased, and the number of rights needed to purchase one share. An expiration date is also specified. The purchase price specified on the right, called the **subscription price**, is less than the current market price of the stock, which encourages existing shareholders to exercise (i.e., redeem) their rights. Therefore, the right has value. Suppose, for example, that a share of Company X is currently selling for $45, and the subscription price on the rights offering is $36. If it takes 10 rights to buy one new share, the value of one right can be calculated as follows:

$$R = \frac{\text{market price of stock rights-on} - \text{subscription price}}{\text{number of rights needed per share} + 1}$$

$$R = \frac{\$45 - \$36}{10 + 1} \approx \$0.82.$$

(The term "rights-on" in the above equation means that an investor who buys the stock will also receive the rights. At some point the stock will trade "ex-rights," which means that the rights will remain with the previous stockholder; in this case, the investor is buying only the stock.)

A shareholder may elect to exercise his rights, sell his rights, or simply let his rights expire. Since a right has value, to let the rights expire is equivalent to throwing away money. If the shareholder chooses to exercise his rights, he must pay the firm the subscription price for each share. In the event that the shareholder does not care to maintain his proportionate ownership in the firm, he can sell the rights to another investor.

? The rights-on market price of a stock is $61. The subscription price associated with the right is $54. If six rights are required to purchase one new share, what is the value of a right?

Answer: $1

Applying the equation introduced in the above frame:

$$R = \frac{\$61 - \$54}{6 + 1} = \$1.00.$$

5.   One of the shareholder rights listed in Frame 3 is the right to receive dividends, *if declared.* Common shareholders cannot mandate that a firm pay dividends. However, if the board of directors declares that common dividends will be paid, then each shareholder has the right to receive dividends based on his proportionate ownership in the firm. (An exception may occur when a firm has more than one class of common stock, in which case it may be stipulated that holders of a particular class of stock will not receive dividend payments.)

The day that the board of directors announce that dividends will be paid is called the **declaration date**. At this time the board also specifies that the dividends will be paid to "shareholders of record" as of a certain date. This date is known as the **record date**. Theoretically, if an investor purchases the stock on or before the record date, he should receive the dividend check when it is mailed on the **payment date**. In reality, the investor must have purchased the stock *five business days before the record date* in order to receive the dividend. Four business days before the record date is the **ex-dividend date**. An investor who purchases the stock on or after the ex-dividend date will not receive the forthcoming dividend payment; the previous stockholder will receive it. This is because there is a lag between the time that an investor calls his broker and purchases the stock and the time that the shares are transferred to his name. (Effective June 1, 1995, the settlement date will be three business days after the transaction date.) The four days between the ex-dividend date and the date of record allows time for the paperwork to be completed.

? On October 4, 1994, the board of directors of X-Rite, Incorporated, announced that the firm would pay a dividend of four cents a share to shareholders of record as of Friday, October 14, 1994. The dividends would be paid on Friday, November 11, 1994. What is the latest date on which you could purchase shares of X-Rite and be entitled to receive this dividend payment?

Answer: October 7, 1994.

Since the record date is on a Friday, the stock will trade ex-dividend on that Monday, which would be October 10, 1994. The shares must be purchased before the ex-dividend date, so they would have to be purchased by Friday, October 7, 1994, in order for you to receive the next dividend payment. (The exchanges are closed on weekends.)

6.   When the board of directors announces that the firm will pay dividends, it generally makes the announcement in terms of **dividend per share**. The dividend per share is simply the total amount of money that the firm is distributing in dividends divided by the number of shares outstanding. (Treasury stock is not awarded dividends.)

$$\text{Dividend per share} = \frac{\text{total dividends paid on common stock}}{\text{number of common shares outstanding}}$$

Investors consider the long-run **dividend payout ratio** of the firm when choosing among investments. The dividend payout ratio is the percentage of a firm's earnings that is distributed as dividends to the shareholders. It is calculated by dividing the dividends by the earnings that are available for distribution to common shareholders. If there is preferred stock (discussed in more detail later in this module), preferred dividends must be subtracted from the net income of the firm to arrive at the distributable earnings.

$$\text{Dividend payout ratio} = \frac{\text{common stock dividends}}{\text{net income} - \text{preferred dividends}}$$

Those who want to augment their current income will tend to invest more in firms that have a high dividend payout ratio. On the other hand, investors who have no need for current income will choose a firm with a low (or no) dividend payout ratio in order to avoid paying taxes on dividends that they reinvest anyway and to avoid the transactions' costs associated with reinvesting the dividends.

? In 1993, Texaco had 258,923,000 shares outstanding. The oil company had net income of $1,068,000,000 and paid preferred stock dividends of $101,000,000. Common stock dividends were $828,000,000. Calculate the dividend per common share and the dividend payout ratio for Texaco.

Answer: $3.20, 0.86.
The dividend per share is found by dividing the aggregate dividends paid to common shareholders by the number of common shares outstanding. $828,000,000/258,923,000 = $3.20. In order to calculate the dividend payout ratio, we must first calculate the earnings that are available to common shareholders. Texaco had net income of $1,068,000,000, but the firm owed its preferred shareholders dividends of $101,000,000, so only $967,000,000 is available to pay common dividends ($1,068,000,000 − $101,000,000 = $967,000,000). The dividend payout ratio can now be calculated by dividing the total dividends paid to common shareholders by the distributable earnings. $828,000,000/$967,000,000 = 0.86, or 86%.

7.   Sometimes a firm will declare a **stock dividend**. In this case, the firm pays its shareholders in stock. For example, if a firm declared a 10% stock dividend and you owned 100 shares of the stock, your holdings would increase by 10%, and you would now own 100(1.10) = 110 shares. Stock dividends do not increase the wealth of the shareholders; they are merely an accounting change. The assets and income of the firm are unchanged, and each shareholder maintains the same proportionate ownership in the firm.

   Stock splits are similar to stock dividends in that stock splits increase the number of shares outstanding while the value of the firm and the shareholders' ownership interests remain unchanged. The major difference between a stock split and a stock dividend is the accounting methodology. If a firm splits its shares two for one (2:1) and you owned 100 shares before the split, you will now own 200 shares, but they will be worth half as much. That is, if the stock was selling for $40 per share before the split, it will now sell for $20 a share. The value of your holdings has not changed. Before the split, you owned 100 shares of a $40 stock, or $4,000 worth of the company. After the split, you own 200 shares of a $20 stock, which is still $4,000 worth of the company.

   One reason that firms sometimes give for offering a stock dividend or a stock split is to communicate good news about the company. Management feels that the market accepts a stock dividend or a stock split as a signal that the company is expecting its future prospects to be good. A second reason given is that a stock split or a stock dividend reduces the price per share of the stock to a more attractive trading range for small investors. Stock splits and stock dividends are not "free," however. There are transactions costs associated with these accounting manipulations, both in terms of management time and money. Some academicians question whether the perceived benefits outweigh the costs.

? A firm currently has 1,200,000 shares outstanding and is selling for $81 a share. If the firm does a 3:1 stock split, what will the price of the stock be after the split, assuming no other events affect the price of the stock? How many shares will be outstanding after the split?

Answers: $27; 3,600,000.

A three-for-one stock split will cause the price of the stock to be divided by three, so the new price will be $81/3 = $27. The shares outstanding will triple, however; 1,200,000 × 3 = 3,600,000.

8.   If a firm wants to *increase* the price per share of its stock, it can do a reverse split. Firms that are selling at very low prices may want to increase their stock prices to a more respectable figure. **Penny stocks**, which are stocks that trade for under $1 a share, often have a negative connotation to investors. A **reverse split** *decreases* the number of shares outstanding and, therefore, increases the price per share since the value of the firm is split into fewer pieces. If you owned 100 shares of a $40 stock before a one-for-two (1:2) reverse split, you will own 50 shares of an $80 stock after the split. As was the case for a regular split, the total value of your holdings does not change.

Reverse splits are also done in order to take the firm private. When a reverse split is executed, any partial shares are redeemed by the firm for cash. If the firm were to declare a 1:2,000 reverse split, any shareholder owning less than 2,000 shares would be paid in cash, so the number of shareholders will be reduced. If the number of shareholders is less than 500, the firm can become a privately held firm under current SEC rules. Its shares *may not* be traded in the financial markets if it wishes to be classified as a private corporation, but the firm no longer has to meet disclosure requirements imposed by the SEC.

? If you own 100 shares of a firm whose shares are selling for $1 per share, and the firm declares a 1:20 reverse split, how many shares will you own after the reverse split, and what will the price of each share be?

Answer: 5 shares, $20.

A reverse split decreases the number of shares outstanding. A 1:20 reverse split means that the firm gives its investors one share for every 20 shares owned. Since 100 shares represents five groups of 20 shares, you will now own five shares. The price per share will be 20 times as great. 20 × $1 = $20.

9.   Some firms also issue **preferred stock** to finance their operations. Preferred stock, like common stock, is an equity account on a firm's balance sheet, but preferred shareholders have *priority* over common shareholders. Preferred shareholders must be paid their dividends before any common dividends are paid, and in the event of bankruptcy, preferred shareholders' claims must be settled before the common shareholders receive anything. Preferred shareholders typically have no voting rights, however. An exception to this may occur if preferred dividend payments are missed too many years in a row; most preferred stock agreements award the preferred stockholders limited voting privileges if this happens.

Most preferred stock issues pay a fixed dividend. The dividend may be expressed as a fixed dollar amount, such as $5 preferred, or as a percentage of the par value of the preferred stock if the preferred stock has a par value. (The par value of the stock is an arbitrary number that is not to be confused with the market value of the stock.) If the par value is $100, and the dividend is 6%, then the dollar dividend is 0.06 × $100 = $6. In the early 1980s, due to a very volatile interest rate environment, **adjustable rate preferred stock (ARPS)** made its debut. The dividends paid on ARPS change periodically according to some benchmark rate, such as the yield on long-term Treasury bonds. This feature is attractive to investors who are wary of investing in any security with a fixed rate, which is often the case when investors expect interest rates to increase. Some ARPS specify a maximum and a minimum dividend; the dividend paid cannot be less than the minimum and it will never exceed the maximum. The maximum and minimum rates are known as a **collar**.

Preferred dividends are *not* legal obligations of the firm; if they are not paid, the preferred shareholders cannot force the firm into bankruptcy as creditors can. As was stated above, though, common shareholders cannot receive any payments until the preferred shareholder dividends are paid. Preferred stock may be **cumulative** or **noncumulative**. (Noncumulative preferred stock is also referred to as **straight** preferred by some in the industry.) Most of the preferred stock issued in the United States today is cumulative, which means that any missed dividends must be paid in full before common shareholders can receive any dividend payments. If the preferred dividend is $5 per share and preferred dividends are not declared in 1995, then no preferred dividends are paid regardless of whether the issue is cumulative or noncumulative. If, in 1996, preferred dividends are declared, the preferred shareholders will be entitled to receive $10 per share in dividends before common shareholders receive anything if the preferred stock is cumulative. They receive $5 for the missed payment in 1995 and $5 for the 1996 dividend payment. If, however, the issue is noncumulative, the preferred shareholders would receive only $5 in 1996. The skipped 1995 payment is lost forever.

Preferred stock may also be **participating** or **nonparticipating**. If the preferred stock is participating, preferred shareholders are entitled to receive a percentage of the firm's earnings in addition to the stated dividend. Most preferred stock issued in the United States is nonparticipating.

[?] Preferred stock for which skipped dividends are carried over to future periods and must be paid before shareholders can receive dividends is called
   a. adjustable rate preferred stock.
   b. participating preferred stock.
   c. cumulative preferred stock.
   d. noncumulative preferred stock.

Answer: c.
This is the definition of cumulative preferred stock.

10. Different issues of preferred stock may have different features. Some issues of preferred stock are **convertible**. This means that the stock can be exchanged for shares of common stock. A **conversion ratio** is specified in the preferred stock agreement. This ratio indicates how many shares of common stock will be received for each share of preferred stock. The conversion ratio may be fixed, or it can change according to some pre-specified factors. In recent years, some firms have issued **mandatory convertible preferred stock**. This feature requires the investor to convert the preferred shares into common shares within a specified amount of time.

Preferred stock may also be **callable.** Callable preferred stock allows the issuing firm to buy the stock back from the investors at a price that is prespecified in the preferred stock agreement. Like the conversion ratio, the call price may be fixed or may change over time. Some firms will issue preferred stock that is both convertible and callable. This allows the firm to "force" the preferred stockholders to convert their shares (or lose value). Suppose an issue of preferred stock is convertible into five shares of common stock and is also callable at $104. The common stock is currently selling for $25 a share. An investor who owns the preferred stock can convert each share into common stock worth a total of $125 (5 × $25 = $125). If the firm issues a call on the preferred stock, the investor will receive only $104, the call price, for each share that he holds. Thus, the investor will be better off if he converts the preferred stock to common stock rather than allowing the firm to buy the preferred stock back from him.

[?] Brian Morgan owns some shares of a preferred stock that is convertible into four shares of the firm's common stock. The preferred stock also has a call feature with a call price of $90. The common stock is currently selling for $18 a share. If the issuer decides to exercise his call option at this time, should Brian accept the call (i.e., sell the preferred stock back to the issuer) or convert his shares?

Answer: Brian should accept the call.
If Brian converts his shares, he will receive 4 × \$18 = \$72 worth of common stock for each preferred share he owns. The issuer will buy the shares back from Brian for \$90 a share. Brian receives more value if he accepts the call.

11. Shares of both the common and the preferred stock of publicly-held corporations are traded on exchange floors or in the over-the-counter market. Daily price information for firms whose stocks trade regularly can be found in *The Wall Street Journal*. Exhibit 1 is a clipping from the May 5, 1995 issue.

Exhibit 1

NEW YORK COMPOSITE

Quotations as of 5 p.m. Eastern Time
Thursday, May 4, 1995

	52 Weeks Hi	Lo	Stock	Sym	Div	Yld %	PE	Vol 100s	Hi	Lo	Close	Net Chg
			-A-A-A-									
	15⅞	11⅞	AAR	AIR	.48	3.5	24	213	18⅞	13¾	13⅞	+ ⅛
	24⅜	18⅝	ABM Indus	ABM	.60	2.6	14	395	23½	22¾	23⅛	+ ⅜
	11⅜	8	ACM Gvt Fd	ACG	.90a	10.1	...	1282	9	8¾	8⅞	...
	8¾	6⅜	ACM OppFd	AOF	.66	9.8	...	437	6¾	6⅝	6¾	+ ⅛
	10⅜	7¼	ACM SecFd	GSF	.90	11.6	...	1944	7⅞	7⅝	7¾	+ ⅛
	9	5¾	ACM SpctmFd	SI	.75	11.8	...	655	6½	6⅜	6⅜	− ⅛
	12⅝	7⅝	ACM MgmdInc	ADF	1.26	13.4	...	682	9½	9¼	9⅜	+ ⅛
	10	7⅜	ACM MgdIncFd	AMF	1.08a	12.9	...	1102	8½	8⅛	8⅜	+ ⅛
	12¼	9⅛	ACM MuniSec	AMU	.90a	7.8	...	76	11½	11½	11½	...
	12¼	8½	ADT	ADT		...	15	759	12	11⅝	11¾	...
	42¾	30⅜	♣AFLAC	AFL	.52f	1.3	13	643	40⅜	39¾	39⅞	− ⅜
s	37¼	24	AGCO Cp	AG	.04	.1	6	1036	35⅞	35½	35½	− ¼
	24	12⅝	AL Pharma	ALO	.18	.8	dd	119	23¾	23⅜	23⅜	− ⅜
	22⅞	17	♣AMLI Resdntl	AML	1.72f	9.5	17	344	18⅝	18	18⅛	− ⅜
s▲	43⅛	31⅜	♣AMP	AMP	.92	2.1	23	7813	43⅜	42	43⅛	+ ⅞
	70	48⅛	AMR	AMR		...	23	8120	69⅜	68¼	68⅝	− ⅛
	51	41¼	ARCO Chm	RCM	2.50	5.3	13	478	46⅞	46½	46¾	+ ¼
	53¾	40	ASA	ASA	2.00	4.4	...	1038	45⅛	44½	45	+ ⅜
x	27¾	19¾	ATT Cap	TCC	.40	1.5	11	150	26⅛	25⅞	26	...

	52 Weeks Hi	Lo	Stock	Sym	Div	Yld %	PE	Vol 100s	Hi	Lo	Close	Net Chg
	4¾	3⅜	♣Aeroflex	ARX		...	6	170	3⅞	3¾	3⅞	+ ⅛
n	27	25	AetnaMIPS pfA		2.37	8.9	...	223	26⅞	26⅝	26¾	− ⅛
	59	42¼	AetnaLife	AET	2.76	4.8	11	2870	58¼	57⅜	58	+ ¾
	14¾	**8¼**	**♣AgnicoEgl**	**AEM**	**.10**	**.8**	**...**	**7632**	**12⅝**	**11¾**	**12⅝**	**+ 1**
	19¼	14⅝	AgreeRlty	ADC	1.80	12.1	...	106	15	14⅞	14⅞	− ⅛
x	22¾	15¼	Ahmanson	AHM	.88	4.1	14	4606	21⅝	21	21⅝	+ ½
x	26⅞	24½	Ahmanson pfB		2.40	9.3	...	124	26	25⅝	25⅞	+ ⅛
x	26	22⅛	Ahmanson pfC		2.10	8.3	...	226	25½	25⅜	25⅜	+ ⅛
x	52	39¾	Ahmanson pfD		3.00	6.1	...	122	49½	48¾	49½	+ 1
	35⅞	24	Ahold	AHO	.20e	.6	...	31	35⅞	35⅜	35⅝	+ ½
	3	15/32	vjAileen	AEE		...	...	78	⅝	9/16	9/16	− 1/16
	52¼	38¾	AirProduct	APD	.98	1.9	18	2111	50⅞	50¾	50⅞	+ ⅛
	38⅜	18	AirbornFrght	ABF	.30	1.5	13	1310	20¼	19¾	19⅞	− ⅛
	29⅞	19⅝	♣Airgas	ARG		...	26	1490	23½	22⅞	23	− ½
	17	10⅞	Airlease	FLY	1.88	13.2	11	118	14⅜	14⅛	14¼	− ⅛
	30⅝	23⅛	AirTouch	ATI		...	cc	11998	26⅝	25⅝	25¾	− ¾
	33¼	19¼	AK Steel	AKS		...	2	867	27½	27	27¼	− ¼
n	33⅝	24⅛	AK Steel pf		2.15	7.4	...	162	29	28⅞	28⅞	− ⅛
	25¼	22	AlaPwr pfA		1.90	7.6	...	24	25	24¾	25	+ ¼
	23	18	AlaPwr pfB		1.70	7.6	...	20	22½	22	22⅜	+ ⅜
	24⅞	20⅛	AlaPwr pfD		1.85e	8.4	...	10	22	22	22	...
	25	21⅞	AlaPwr pfH		1.90	7.6	...	10	25	25	25	+ ¼
	18	13⅛	AlaskaAir	ALK	.05j	...	18	1519	17	16⅞	16⅞	− ⅛
	22⅜	16⅛	♣AlbanyInt	AIN	.35	1.6	24	421	22⅛	22	22⅛	...

Source: *The Wall Street Journal*, Volume CXXXII No. 88, May 5, 1995, p. C3.

The quotes provide the price data for the previous day (i.e., May 4, 1994). The first two columns give the highest price and the lowest price for which the stock sold in the last 52 weeks. The highest price that the first stock listed, AAR, sold for in the last 52 weeks was \$15.875 per share (15⅞) and its lowest price in the last 52 weeks was \$11.875 per share (11⅞). These 52-week high and low figures do not include the current day's (May 4) prices. If a new 52-week high was reached on the day for which the quotes appear, an upward arrow will appear in the left margin as it does for AMP; if a new 52-week low was experienced, a downward arrow will appear.

The next two columns give the abbreviated name of the firm and its ticker symbol. If the stock is a preferred issue, the letters "pf" will appear after the abbreviated name, as is the case for AK Steel (second column). AK Steel has two listings. The first listing, "AK Steel," provides the quotes for the common stock while the second listing, "AK Steel pf," gives the quotes for the preferred stock. Some firms, such as Ahmanson, have more than one preferred stock issue, in which case each issue has a separate line.

The fifth column indicates the annual dividend that the firm is paying. AAR is paying an annual dividend of \$0.48 a share. Dividends are typically paid quarterly, so the common shareholders would receive \$0.12 a quarter for each share they own. The following column is the **dividend yield**. This number is calculated by dividing the annual dividend by the close price for the day. It measures the return that the investor will receive on the dividend income. Investors who are investing for high current income will tend to invest more in firms that pay high dividend yields. AAR's dividend yield is 3.5%.

The seventh column gives the **price-earnings (P/E)** ratio for the firm. This number indicates how much investors are paying for the stock relative to each dollar of earnings that the firm has. It is calculated by dividing the close price for the day by the most recent 12 months' earnings per share figure for the firm. A high P/E ratio means that investors are paying a high price for the stock relative to the current earnings of the firm. A low P/E ratio indicates that investors are paying a low price for the stock relative to the current earnings of the firm. AAR's P/E ratio of 24 means that for every dollar of earnings per share, investors are paying $24.00 for the stock of AAR. (Since the close price for the day is $13.875, as discussed below, AAR's earnings per share must be less than $1.00.)

The eighth column reports the number of shares of the stock that were traded on the day of the quotes. The volume is given in hundreds of shares, so 21,300 shares of AAR were traded on May 4, 1995. (If the volume had been only 87 shares, a "z" would have appeared before the number—i.e., z87—to indicate that the quote is not in hundreds.) Stocks which had an unusually heavy trading volume for the day will have their line of quotes underlined as does AgnicoEgl.

The next three columns report the highest price, the lowest price, and the close price for the stock on the day of the quotes. The highest price for which AAR sold on May 4, 1995 was $13.875 a share, the lowest price was $13.75, and the stock closed at $13.875 a share. The last column tells the reader that the close price is up $0.125 (⅛) from the previous day. Any stock for which the close price is at least 5% *higher* or *lower* than the close price of the previous day will have its line of quotes printed in bold print. AgnicoEgl had an unusually heavy trading volume *and* closed at a price that was at least 5% higher (since the change in the close is +$1.00) than the previous day's close price.

? According to Exhibit 1, what is the highest price for which the stock of ADT traded on May 4, 1995?

Answer: $12.00.

The highest price that the stock sold for on the day of the quotes is reported in the ninth column. For ADT, the highest price is listed as 12.

12.   In addition to using equity to finance their operations, firms also use debt financing. Long-term investments are typically financed using notes and bonds. These instruments are similar to each other, but notes usually have maturities of less than 10 years while bonds are issued to mature in 10 years or more. Both notes and bonds generally pay a **coupon**, or interest. The interest rate is referred to as the **coupon rate**. The annual amount of interest that the investor will receive can be determined by multiplying the coupon rate by the **face value** of the note or bond. The face value, also called the **maturity value** or **par value**, is the amount that the investor (otherwise known as a noteholder or bondholder) will receive when the debt instrument matures. The face value of most corporate bonds is $1,000 while the face value of most notes is $5,000. (Bonds with face values of less than $1,000 are called **baby bonds**.) Most domestic notes and bonds pay interest semiannually. If a $1,000 bond has a coupon rate of 10%, bondholders will receive $100 (0.10 × $1,000) in interest each year until the bond matures. If interest is paid semiannually, the bondholders will receive $50 every 6 months. At maturity, the investors will receive the $1,000 face value of the bond along with the last interest payment.

? IBM has a bond issue that matures in 1998. The bond has a face value of $1,000 and a 9% coupon rate. Interest is paid semiannually. How much interest does the bondholder receive every 6 months?

Answer: $45.

The coupon rate is the *annual* interest rate. The bondholders will receive 0.09 × $1,000 = $90 a year in interest. Therefore, the bondholders will receive a check for $45 every 6 months.

13. Most bonds today are **registered bonds**, which means that the name and address of the bondholder is registered with the issuing firm. The firm automatically sends the bondholder the interest payments when they are due and the face value when the bond matures. If the bond is a **bearer bond**, however, the issuing firm has no record of who owns the bond. The bondholder must clip coupons that are attached to the bond and turn the coupons in when they are due to be paid in order to receive his interest payments. (Most commercial banks will send the coupon in to the paying agent listed on the bond for collection for the bondholder, often giving the bondholder immediate credit in his account for the coupon payment.) When the bond matures, the bondholder must turn the bond in to the paying agent in order to receive the face value. If bearer bonds are stolen from the investor, the new "owner" will be able to receive the interest payments and the face value of the bond when due with no problem since there is no record of ownership.

[?] True or False: The holder of a registered bond must clip coupons attached to the bond and send them in to the paying agent in order to receive his interest payments.

Answer: False.

The issuing firm automatically sends the interest payments to the registered bondholders.

14. Bonds may sell for their face values, or they may sell for more or less than their face values. A bond that sells for its face value is said to be selling **at par**. A bond that is selling for *more than* its face value is said to be selling at a **premium**, and a bond that is selling for *less than* its face value is said to be selling at a **discount**. The coupon rate on most new bonds is set so that the bond will sell at par. This is accomplished by setting the coupon rate equal to the yield that existing investments of similar risk are offering. In this way, investors are earning their entire yield in the form of interest payments since they are receiving only the return of their original investment when the bond matures. If a 7%, $1,000 bond issued by the XYZ Corporation is selling for $1,000, a bondholder that buys it receives $70 in interest each year and $1,000 when the bond matures. The bondholder's annual return is $70/$1,000 = 7%.

As interest rates in the economy change, so will bond prices. Bond prices vary *inversely* with interest rates. Let us suppose that interest rates increase, so that investments that are similar in risk to the XYZ Corporation bond are now yielding 9%. If the XYZ Corporation's bond were to continue selling for $1,000, no one would buy it. The coupon rate on the bond does not change with interest rates, so investors would still be earning only 7% on it, and they could earn 9% elsewhere for the same risk. Market forces will drive the price of the bond *down*, so that the bond sells at a discount. An investor who purchases the bond at the discounted price receives capital gain income (the difference between the price he pays for the bond and its face value) in addition to the interest payments. The price of the bond will drop until the return, both interest and capital gains, will be the same as that offered by similar risk investments—in this example, 9%.

If, on the other hand, interest rates in the economy are falling, the prices of existing bonds will rise. Suppose that interest rates fall so that investments that are similar in risk to the bond of the XYZ Corporation are yielding only 5%. If the XYZ Corporation's bond were still selling for $1,000, every investor would want to buy it. By paying $1,000 for it, the investors would be receiving a 7% return, which is better than what they can earn on investments of similar risk. The demand for the bond will cause the price of the bond to increase, and the bond will sell for more than $1,000. Now the investor who buys the bond will have a capital loss when the bond matures since he has paid more than face value for the bond. This capital loss offsets part of the interest income, so that this bond's yield will drop. The price will be bid up, in fact, until the yield on this bond will be only 5%, the rate paid on similar risk investments.

? Pier 1 has a bond issue that matures in 2002. The coupon rate on the bond is 6⅞%. Interest rates have risen so that similar risk investments are yielding 8%. Would you expect to find the Pier 1 bonds selling at par, a discount, or a premium?

Answer: A discount.

Since similar risk investments are returning more than the coupon rate on the Pier 1 bonds, the Pier 1 bond prices have to fall so that the investors will receive capital gain income in addition to the interest income, bringing the total return up to 8%.

15.   Prices of corporate bonds that are traded on the national exchange floors are quoted daily in *The Wall Street Journal* as shown below:

Exhibit 2

Bonds	Cur Yld	Vol	Close	Net Chg.		Bonds	Cur Yld	Vol	Close	Net Chg.
CORPORATION BONDS Volume, $38,626,000						Actava 9½98	9.8	10	97	+ 1⅜
						AirbF 6¾01	cv	110	94¾	...
						AlaPw 9¼21	8.9	8	103½	− ¼
AK Stl 10¾04	10.2	33	105	+ ¼		AlskAr 6⅞14	cv	20	79	− ½
AMR 9s16	8.9	73	101	+ 1⅝		AlskAr zr06	...	31	44⅞	...
AMR 6½24	cv	11	99	− 1		Albnylnt 5¼02	cv	40	95	+ 1½
ATT 7½06	7.4	5	101⅛	+ ½		AlldC zr98	...	45	79¾	+ ¾
ATT 8.35s25	8.0	133	103¾	+ 1½		AlldC zr95	...	5	98¹¹/₃₂	+ 1/16
ATT 7¾07	7.5	225	103⅛	+ ¾		AlldC zr05	...	20	46⅜	+ ½
ATT 4¾98	5.0	10	94¼	+ ¼		AlldC zr07	...	140	39	+ ⅝
ATT 4⅜99	4.8	163	91½	− ⅛		AlldC zr09	...	10	32⅞	+ ¼
ATT 5⅛01	5.7	9	90½	...		Allwst 7¼14	cv	3	86	− ½
ATT 8⅝31	8.2	160	104⅝	+ 1¼		Ametek 9¾04	9.4	16	104	...
ATT 7⅛02	7.1	392	100⅜	+ ¾		Amsco 2002	cv	1	85½	+ 1
ATT 8⅛22	8.0	84	101¼	+ ⅝		Ancp 13⅞02f	cv	215	56¾	− ⅜
ATT 8⅛24	8.1	297	100¾	+ ¼		Anhr 8⅝16	8.4	15	103	...
ATT 4½96	4.6	5	98⁷/₁₆	− 1/16		AnnTaylr 8¾00	8.9	507	98	− ⅛
ATT 6¾04	6.9	88	97⅜	+ ⅞		Arml 11⅜99	11.2	50	102	...
Aames 10½02	10.3	20	102	+ 1		Ashlnd 6¾14	cv	21	98	+ 1
Actava 9⅞97	9.9	50	99¾	+ ¼		ARch 9⅛11	8.2	20	112	...

Source: *The Wall Street Journal*, Volume CXXXII No. 88, May 5, 1995, p. C22.

The first column gives the name of the issuer. The second listing shown is for a bond of the AMR Corporation, the parent company of American Airlines. The string of numbers next to the name indicates the coupon rate on the bond and the year in which the bond matures. The first number, which is followed by an "s" if space allows, is the coupon rate. The next two numbers are the last digits in the maturity year. The first AMR bond listed has a 9% coupon rate and will mature in 2016, the next year that ends in "16." In some cases, no coupon rate is given. The letters "zr" appear in its place as is the case for the second of the two Alaska Air (AlskAr) bonds listed. This indicates that the bond is a zero coupon bond. A zero coupon bond makes no periodic interest payments. Instead the bondholder buys the bond for substantially less than its face value and receives face value when the bond matures. The difference between the face value of the bond and the purchase price of the bond constitutes the investor's return. (The close price on the Alaska Air zero coupon bond indicates that the bond is selling for $448.75 per $1,000 face value. An investor who pays $448.75 for the bond today will receive no interim interest payments, but will receive $1,000 when the bond matures in 2006.)

The following column reports the **current yield** on the bond. The current yield is the yield on interest income only. It is calculated by dividing the annual interest by the close price of the bond on the day of the quotes. The AMR bond is offering an 8.9% return from interest income. If a bond is convertible (convertible bonds are discussed in a later frame), the letters "cv" appear in the current yield column as is the case with the Alaska Air bond that matures in 2014. Because zero coupon bonds pay no interest periodically, no current yield is calculated for those bonds.

The fourth column indicates the volume of these bonds that were traded on the day of the quotes. This column is given in thousands of dollars. This means that $73,000 of AMR bonds were traded on the given day. If each bond has a face value of $1,000, this translates to the fact that 73 of the bonds were traded. However, we cannot make this assumption blindly. While most bonds have a face value of $1,000, some are issued with other face values, such as $500 or $100.

The fifth column gives the close price of the bond on the day specified. The price is given per $100 of par value even though most bonds have a face value of $1,000. The AMR bonds closed at 101. This means that they closed at $101 for each $100 of par value. If an investor purchased a $1,000 bond at the close price, he would have paid $1,010 for it. (This ignores any interest that has accrued on the bond that the new buyer must pay the seller as well as transactions costs.)

The final column gives the change in the close price from the previous day's close. The AMR bond closed. This is also stated per $100 of par value. So the AMR bond closed up $1.625 per $100 or $16.25 per $1,000.

? What is the coupon rate on the Actava bond issue that matures in 1998?

Answer: $9\frac{1}{2}\%$.

The Actava bond that matures in 1998 is the second bond listed for the corporation. The coupon rate is given immediately before the maturity year in Exhibit 2. In this instance an "s" does not follow the coupon rate because of space limitations.

16.   Bonds may be **secured** or **unsecured**. Secured bonds are backed by one or more assets owned by the firm. If the firm fails to make the required payments on these bonds, the assets can be sold to satisfy the bondholders' claims. **Mortgage bonds** are backed by real estate owned by the firm. Some firms have **junior**, or **second mortgage bonds**. These bonds are backed by the same real estate as the **first mortgage bonds**, but have a lower priority. If the firm fails to make the required payments, the real estate that serves as security for the bonds will be sold, and the first mortgage bondholders will be paid in full, assuming that the sale of the property results in sufficient funds to do so. Any remaining proceeds from the sale will be divided among the junior mortgage bondholders. If the proceeds from the sale are not enough to pay their claims in full, these bondholders will then stand in line with the unsecured creditors to receive any additional funds due them. **Collateral trust receipts** are bonds that are backed by securities owned by the firm—i.e., stocks and bonds that it might own of another corporation. **Equipment trust receipts** are bonds that are backed by specific equipment owned by the firm.

A **debenture** is unsecured, long-term debt of a firm. Because debentures are riskier than secured bonds of the same corporation, these bonds will offer a higher yield. A **subordinated debenture** is unsecured debt that has junior priority. Subordinated debenture investors will have their claims satisfied only after all the debt claims that are senior to their bonds are satisfied.

? Which of the following bonds of the same issuer would you expect to offer the highest yield?

a. junior mortgage
b. equipment trust receipt
c. debenture
d. subordinated debenture

Answer: d.

Both junior mortgages and equipment trust receipts are backed by assets and are therefore less risky than unsecured debt of the same issuer. Subordinated debentures are junior in priority to debentures, so they are more risky than debentures. The riskier bonds must offer the higher returns.

17.   Like preferred stock, bonds may have a variety of features. **Convertible bonds** may be exchanged for shares of common stock. The **conversion ratio** specifies the number of shares of common stock for which each bond can be traded. The **conversion value** of the bond is, therefore, the market price of the common stock multiplied by the conversion ratio. At a minimum, the bond will sell for the higher of its conversion value or its straight value (i.e., the value of the bond if it were not convertible). The **conversion price** is defined as the amount of the bond's face value that is exchanged for each share of stock. If a $1,000 bond of the XYZ Corporation is convertible into 25 shares of common stock and the common stock is selling for $55 a share, the conversion ratio is 25, the conversion value is $1,375 ($55 × 25 = $1,375), and the conversion price is $40 ($1,000/25 = $40). Convertible bonds are usually unsecured debt issues.

? W & W, Incorporated, has a convertible bond issue that is convertible into 50 shares of the common stock of the corporation. Each bond has a face value of $1,000. The common stock of the firm is currently selling for $23 a share. What is the conversion value of the bonds?

Answer: $1,150.

The conversion value is the value that the investor would receive if he converted the bond to common stock. It is calculated by multiplying the conversion ratio by the current market price of the stock. 50 × $23 = $1,150.

18.   Bonds may also be **callable**, which means that the issuing firm has the right to buy the bonds back from the investors at a prespecified price. Like the call option on convertible preferred stock, this option can be used to force the bond investors to convert the bond into shares of common stock. The prespecified price (call price) may vary over time according to a predetermined schedule, and the exercise period may also be specified. Some bonds have a **deferred call**, meaning that several years must pass before the issuer can exercise its call option.

Bonds with **put options**, or **putable bonds**, permit investors to sell the bond back to the firm at a prespecified price. Put options on bonds were attractive to bond investors in the early 1980s when interest rates were volatile since investors who had invested in a low-yielding bond could sell the bond back to the issuer using this option and purchase another higher yielding bond with the proceeds received. Most of the time put options are only exercisable under given circumstances, such as an attempted takeover of the firm by another corporation. (These are referred to as **poison puts** since they are used to discourage hostile takeovers of the firm.)

Other bonds have **warrants** attached. Warrants are call options; they give the holder the right to buy the stock of the firm at a prespecified price, the **exercise price**, within a certain period of time, the **exercise period**. Unlike a normal call option, a warrant is written by the firm on whose stock the warrant is exercisable; a normal call option is written by another investor who may have no affiliation with the firm. The exercise period on the warrant may be as long as 5 or more years, whereas the exercise period on a normal call option is generally at most 9 months. Warrants may be **detachable** or **nondetachable**. An investor who owns a bond with a detachable warrant may keep the bond and sell the warrant if he so chooses. If the warrant is nondetachable, the bond must be sold with the warrant intact. In either case, the bondholder may choose to exercise the warrant while still retaining the bond. Unlike the circumstance with a convertible bond, the bondholder does not give up the bond when the warrant is exercised. Rather, the bondholder pays the strike price on the warrant and exchanges the warrant and the cash for shares of the stock, retaining ownership of the bond.

? A bond which has a provision that allows a firm to buy back the bond from its investors is called a
   a. callable bond.
   b. convertible bond.
   c. putable bond.
   d. bond with a detachable warrant.

Answer: a.

Although all of the options may result in the debt obligation of the firm being reduced, only one is at the option of the issuing firm, and that is the callable bond. With this option, the issuing firm can buy back the bonds from the investors at a prespecified price.

19. A bond's **indenture provision** specifies the precise terms of the bond. The denomination of the bond, the amount of the interest payments, and the payment due dates are indicated as well as any convertible, callable, or putable features. The indenture provision lists all of the rights that the investors have and all of the obligations of the issuer. Some bonds have **nonrefunding provisions** in their indenture provisions. A nonrefunding provision prohibits the bond issuer from buying back the bond using the proceeds from the sale of a new, lower coupon bond. This feature protects investors in times of falling interest rates. While the bond may be bought back using excess cash the firm may acquire, the firm may not float another bond issue in a period of falling interest rates and use the funds generated to retire a higher coupon bond issue.

Many bonds have **sinking fund** provisions. This provision mandates that the issuing firm put aside a specified amount of money each year that can be used to retire the debt. The money in the fund may be used to retire some of the bonds periodically, or it may accumulate so that there is a sufficient amount to pay the face value of the bonds at maturity. Like the nonrefunding provision, this provision provides protection for the bondholder since it provides assurance that the firm will have funds available to meet its debt obligations when they come due.

A **bond series** refers to several bond issues that have the same provisions but that are sold at different times; one blanket indenture provision covers all of them. This term should not be confused with **serial debt**. Serial debt refers to debt that is issued at the same point in time with differing maturities.

? A nonrefunding provision protects investors in times of _____ interest rates.

Answer: falling.

When interest rates fall, bond issuers would prefer to be able to retire existing higher coupon debt by issuing debt that has a lower coupon. This exposes investors to reinvestment rate risk since the investors would then have to reinvest the proceeds received at the new, lower rates in existence. A nonrefunding provision prohibits bond issuers from doing this.

20. Some of the bond provisions are accounted for in the **bond rating**. Bond ratings are done by financial services firms such as Standard & Poor's and Moody's. The bond rating reflects only the **default risk** of the bond, i.e., the risk that the bond issuer will be unable to meet the payments required by the bond issue. The highest rating granted by the rating agencies is triple A—"AAA" for Standard & Poor's and "Aaa" for Moody's. Any bond issue rated down to triple B—"BBB" for Standard & Poor's and "Baa" for Moody's—

is considered investment grade. That is, the bonds have only a moderate risk of default. Double B, Single B, Triple C, and lower rated bonds are progressively riskier. The greater the risk, the greater is the expected return.

? All else equal, which of the following bonds should offer investors the highest rate return?
   a. AAA rated bonds
   b. CCC rated bonds
   c. BB rated bonds
   d. A rated bonds

Answer: b.
Triple C rated bonds have the most default risk and must offer the highest return.

21.   Corporations are not the only issuers of long-term debt instruments. Governments also issue notes and bonds. The U.S. government issues **Treasury notes** and **Treasury bonds**. Like corporate notes and bonds, these differ with respect to maturity. Treasury notes are most often issued with maturities of 10 years or less and have a face value of $5,000. Treasury notes are usually not callable. Treasury bonds, on the other hand, generally have maturities of greater than 10 years and a face value of $1,000. It is common for them to have a call feature in their indenture provision. Bonds issued by the U.S. Treasury are considered to be free of default risk; financial analysts use the return on these instruments as proxies for what they call the **risk-free rate** of interest. This is because Treasury notes and bonds are backed by the "full faith and credit" (taxing power) of the U.S. government. Interest income earned on Treasury securities is fully taxable at the federal level, but is exempt from state and local taxes in most areas.

Treasury bond and note prices are presented daily in *The Wall Street Journal*. Exhibit 3 is a clipping of quotes for May 4, 1995:

Exhibit 3

Rate	Maturity Mo/Yr	Bid	Asked	Chg.	Ask Yld.
$5^{7}/_{8}$	May 95n	100:00	100:02	+ 1	2.57
$8^{1}/_{2}$	May 95n	100:02	100:04	....	1.95
$10^{3}/_{8}$	May 95	100:04	100:06	− 1	0.65
$11^{1}/_{4}$	May 95n	100:04	100:06	− 1	1.47
$12^{5}/_{8}$	May 95	100:06	100:10	....	0.00
$4^{1}/_{8}$	May 95n	99:28	99:30	....	5.03
$4^{1}/_{8}$	Jun 95n	99:24	99:26	....	5.34
$8^{7}/_{8}$	Jul 95n	100:18	100:20	....	5.37
$4^{1}/_{4}$	Jul 95n	99:20	99:22	....	5.55
$4^{5}/_{8}$	Aug 95n	99:21	99:23	+ 1	5.61
$8^{1}/_{2}$	Aug 95n	100:23	100:25	....	5.49
$10^{1}/_{2}$	Aug 95n	101:09	101:11	....	5.39
$3^{7}/_{8}$	Aug 95n	99:11	99:13	....	5.77
$3^{7}/_{8}$	Sep 95n	99:05	99:07	+ 1	5.87
$8^{5}/_{8}$	Oct 95n	101:05	101:07	+ 1	5.74
$3^{7}/_{8}$	Oct 95n	99:00	99:02	+ 1	5.89
$5^{1}/_{8}$	Nov 95n	99:18	99:20	+ 1	5.87
$8^{1}/_{2}$	Nov 95n	101:09	101:11	+ 1	5.84
$9^{1}/_{2}$	Nov 95n	101:26	101:28	+ 1	5.79
$11^{1}/_{2}$	Nov 95	103:03	103:07	....	5.14
$4^{1}/_{4}$	Nov 95n	99:01	99:03	+ 1	5.91
$4^{1}/_{4}$	Dec 95n	98:27	98:29	+ 1	6.00
$9^{1}/_{4}$	Jan 96n	102:03	102:05	....	6.01
4	Jan 96n	98:16	98:18	+ 1	6.03
$7^{1}/_{2}$	Jan 96n	101:00	101:02	+ 1	6.00
$4^{5}/_{8}$	Feb 96n	98:28	98:30	+ 1	6.05
$7^{7}/_{8}$	Feb 96n	101:10	101:12	+ 1	6.03
$8^{7}/_{8}$	Feb 96n	102:03	102:05	+ 1	5.99
$4^{5}/_{8}$	Feb 96n	98:27	98:29	+ 1	6.02
$7^{1}/_{2}$	Feb 96n	101:03	101:05	+ 2	6.02

Source: *The Wall Street Journal*, Volume CXXXII No. 88, May 5, 1995, p. C22.

The first column reports the coupon rate on the note or bond. The first debt instrument listed pays a coupon rate of $5^{7}/_{8}$%. As was the case with corporate debt instruments, the coupon rate is quoted as an annual rate, but interest is paid semiannually. The second column indicates the month and year in which the issue matures. An "n" following this information tells us that this is a Treasury note. If there is no "n," the quote is for a Treasury bond. The first listing is a quote for a Treasury note that matures in May 1995. The following two columns give the bid and the ask prices on the note. Treasury notes and bonds are sold exclusively over-the-counter. Dealers in government bonds buy and sell them out of their own inventory. Dealers quote a **bid price**, which is the price at which they are willing to buy the security from an investor. They also quote an **ask price**, which is the price at which they are willing to sell the security to an investor. The difference between the ask price and the bid price is called the **dealer's spread** and is a source of profits for the dealer. The bid and ask prices on Treasury notes and bonds are quoted in thirty-seconds and are quoted per $100 of par value. Dealers are offering to buy the $5\frac{7}{8}\%$ Treasury note that matures in May 1995 for $100 per $100 of par value. Since this is a Treasury *note*, it has a face value of $5,000, so dealers are offering to buy the note for $5,000. The ask price is $100\frac{2}{32}$ per $100, which translates to $100.0625 per $100 or $1,000.625 per $1,000. Dealers are willing to sell this Treasury note for $5,003.125 ($1,000.625 × 5 = $5,003.125). The dealer's spread is $3.125 per note.

The column following the ask price reports the change in the bid price from the previous day. The change in the bid price for this first listing is $\frac{1}{32}$ per $100 or $0.03125 per $100 or $0.3125 per $1,000. This is $1.5625 for a $5,000 note.

The last column gives the yield-to-maturity on the security, based on the ask price. Unlike the current yield that is quoted for corporate bonds, the yield-to-maturity is indicative of the yield received on both interest income and capital gains (or losses). It is the promised average annual yield that an investor will receive if he buys the note or bond at the ask price and holds it to maturity. The yield-to-maturity on this first Treasury note is 2.57%.

? For what price would you be able to buy the $11\frac{1}{2}\%$ Treasury bonds that mature in November 1995?

Answer: $1,032.1875.

The price at which an investor can purchase the bonds is the ask price. Exhibit 3 indicates that the ask price on these bonds is $103\frac{7}{32}$ or $103.21875 per $100 of par. Since this is a Treasury bond, it has a face value of $1,000. The quote translates to $1,032.1875 per $1,000 of face value.

22. **Treasury strips** are instruments sold by brokerage firms that are backed by the firms' investments in Treasury securities. A brokerage firm will buy an issue of a Treasury security. It will then sell off smaller increments of the interest and principal payments on the issue to individual investors. For example, if a brokerage firm were to buy a $100 million issue of 10-year, 10% Treasury bonds, it would be entitled to receive $10 million in interest payments each year ($5 million every 6 months since interest is usually paid semi-annually), and $100 million face value at maturity. The brokerage firm might then sell Joe Duke, an individual investor, five 6-year, $1,000 Treasury strips, which entitles Joe to receive $5,000 of the firm's $10 million in interest income 6 years from now. Joe receives no other payments. Treasury strips have slightly more risk than a direct investment in a Treasury security since a brokerage firm experiencing financial distress might default on its obligations. *The Wall Street Journal* quotes prices on Treasury strips as shown in Exhibit 4 (on the following page). The format is similar to the quotes on the Treasury notes and bonds presented in Exhibit 3 with two notable exceptions: (1) No coupon rate is listed since Treasury strips are actually zero coupon bonds, and (2) The second column indicates whether the instrument is a stripped coupon payment, "ci," or a stripped principal payment, "np" (if the underlying security is a Treasury note) or "bp" (if the underlying security is a Treasury bond).

Exhibit 4

U.S. TREASURY STRIPS

Mat.	Type	Bid	Asked	Chg.	Ask Yld.
May 95	ci	99:28	99:28	+ 2	5.75
May 95	np	99:28	99:28	+ 2	5.79
Aug 95	ci	98:14	98:14	+ 2	5.74
Aug 95	np	98:14	98:14	+ 2	5.80
Nov 95	ci	97:00	97:01	+ 2	5.92
Nov 95	np	97:00	97:01	+ 2	5.89
Feb 96	ci	95:16	95:17	+ 3	6.02
Feb 96	np	95:15	95:16	+ 3	6.05
May 96	ci	94:01	94:02	+ 3	6.11
May 96	np	94:00	94:01	+ 3	6.14
Aug 96	ci	92:24	92:25	+ 4	5.97
Nov 96	ci	91:04	91:06	+ 4	6.17
Nov 96	np	91:02	91:03	+ 5	6.24
Feb 97	ci	89:22	89:23	+ 5	6.21
May 97	ci	88:03	88:05	+ 6	6.35
May 97	np	88:03	88:05	+ 6	6.34
Aug 97	ci	86:23	86:25	+ 6	6.34
Aug 97	np	86:20	86:22	+ 6	6.38
Nov 97	ci	85:07	85:09	+ 6	6.42
Nov 97	np	85:06	85:08	+ 7	6.44
Feb 98	ci	83:25	83:27	+ 7	6.45
Feb 98	np	83:24	83:27	+ 7	6.46
May 98	ci	82:12	82:15	+ 8	6.49
May 98	np	82:12	82:15	+ 8	6.49

Source: *The Wall Street Journal*, Volume CXXXII No. 88, May 5, 1995, p. C22.

? What is the promised average annual return that an investor will earn if he purchases the August 1996 Treasury strip at the indicated ask price and holds the instrument until maturity?

Answer: 5.97%.

The promised average annual return is the yield-to-maturity, which is given in the last column.

23. Federal government agencies—such as the U.S. Postal Service, the Tennessee Valley Authority, the Federal Home Loan Bank, and the Federal National Mortgage Association—also issue bonds to support their specific operations. While these bonds are not backed by the full taxing power of the U.S. government, it is very unlikely that Congress would allow these agencies to default on their debt obligations. These agency issues, therefore, are considered by investors to have an implied guarantee of the U.S. government. The default risk is only slightly higher than that of a treasury issue.

Federal government agency bond quotes are listed in a separate table in *The Wall Street Journal*, a sample of which appears on the following page. The format for the federal agency securities quotes is identical to the quotes on Treasury notes and bonds.

? What coupon rate is the FNMA bond that matures in September 1995 paying?

Answer: 10.5%.

The coupon rate is given in the first column of Exhibit 5 on the following page.

24. State and local governments also issue notes and bonds. **Municipal bonds** are debt of state and local governments. The term "local governments" is not limited to cities; it includes counties, school districts, and any other local government entity that has taxing power. A **general obligation (GO)** bond is backed by the full faith and credit (taxing power) of the issuing government. A **revenue bond** is backed by the proceeds of a specific project. The revenue bond is the riskier of the two since, if the project does not generate sufficient revenues to pay the bondholders, the state or local government is prohibited by law from making up the difference out of general tax dollars. Revenue bonds are often issued to finance airports, toll bridges, turnpikes, and other such publicly used

Exhibit 5

FNMA Issues				
Rate	Mat.	Bid	Asked	Yld.
11.70	5-95	100:02	100:04	0.00
11.15	6-95	100:13	100:15	5.89
4.75	8-95	99:12	99:14	6.69
10.50	9-95	101:06	101:10	6.47
8.80	11-95	101:09	101:13	5.93
10.60	11-95	102:03	102:07	6.07
9.20	1-96	101:30	102:02	6.00
7.00	2-96	100:15	100:19	6.16
9.35	2-96	102:03	102:07	6.29
8.50	6-96	102:07	102:11	6.23
8.75	6-96	102:15	102:19	6.24
8.00	7-96	101:13	101:17	6.61
7.90	8-96	101:10	101:14	6.68
8.15	8-96	101:19	101:23	6.69
7.70	9-96	101:20	101:24	6.31
8.63	9-96	102:14	102:18	6.58
7.05	10-96	100:19	100:23	6.51
8.45	10-96	102:19	102:23	6.45
6.90	11-96*	100:07	100:11	0.00
7.70	12-96	101:26	101:30	6.39
8.20	12-96	102:18	102:22	6.42
6.20	1-97*	99:14	99:20	6.43
7.60	1-97	101:23	101:29	6.37
7.50	2-97*	101:16	101:22	5.19
7.05	3-97*	100:18	100:24	0.00
7.00	4-97*	100:13	100:19	0.00

Source: *The Wall Street
Journal*, Volume CXXXII
No. 88, May 5, 1995, p. C22.

properties. An **industrial revenue bond** is one issued by a state or local government with the proceeds being used to benefit a business venture, such as an industrial park. The revenues generated by the venture, such as the lease payments of the businesses located in the industrial park, are used to repay the bondholders. Interest income earned on municipal bonds is exempt from federal taxation. Due to this feature, the before-tax yield on municipal bonds is lower than similar risk corporate bonds on which interest income is fully taxable. Because of the number of state and local governments in the nation, it would be impossible for *The Wall Street Journal* to carry price quotes for every issue although the paper does carry a short list of prices for representative issues.

? Which of the following debt instruments generates interest income that is exempt from federal taxation?
   a. general obligation bond
   b. mortgage bond
   c. Treasury bond
   d. federal agency bond

Answer: a.
Only a municipal bond generates income that is exempt from federal taxation. A general obligation bond is a specific type of a municipal bond.

25. Governments and corporations also issue short-term debt to meet their short-term needs for funds. The federal government issues **Treasury bills**. Treasury bills are short-term debt obligations of the U.S. government with maturities of 3, 6, or 12 months. The minimum face value is $10,000, and the bills sell at a discount with no periodic interest payments. If a 3-month $10,000 Treasury bill is selling for $9,850, the investor who pays $9,850 receives no periodic interest payments but will receive $10,000 when the bill matures in 3 months.

Treasury bill prices are quoted on the basis of discount yields. A sample of Treasury bills quotes listed in *The Wall Street Journal* appears on the following page. The first column gives the maturity date of the issue. Following this column, the number of days to maturity is reported. The next columns give the dealers' bid and ask prices in terms of discount yields. To understand how these discount yields translate into prices, consider the quotes for the Treasury bill that matures on November 2, 1995. On the day of the

Exhibit 6

TREASURY BILLS

Maturity	Days to Mat.	Bid	Asked	Chg.	Ask Yld.
May 11 '95	3	5.34	5.24	− 0.02	5.32
May 18 '95	10	5.34	5.24	− 0.06	5.32
May 25 '95	17	5.38	5.28	+ 0.10	5.37
Jun 01 '95	24	5.46	5.36	− 0.12	5.45
Jun 08 '95	31	5.35	5.31	− 0.25	5.41
Jun 15 '95	38	5.47	5.43	− 0.13	5.54
Jun 22 '95	45	5.56	5.52	− 0.07	5.64
Jun 29 '95	52	5.51	5.47	− 0.06	5.59
Jul 06 '95	59	5.54	5.52	− 0.07	5.65
Jul 13 '95	66	5.55	5.53	− 0.07	5.66
Jul 20 '95	73	5.54	5.52	− 0.06	5.66
Jul 27 '95	80	5.57	5.55	− 0.07	5.70
Aug 03 '95	87	5.60	5.58	− 0.06	5.73
Aug 10 '95	94	5.61	5.59	− 0.07	5.75
Aug 17 '95	101	5.61	5.59	− 0.06	5.76
Aug 24 '95	108	5.63	5.61	− 0.05	5.79
Aug 31 '95	115	5.64	5.62	− 0.05	5.82
Sep 07 '95	122	5.65	5.63	− 0.03	5.84
Sep 14 '95	129	5.65	5.63	− 0.04	5.84
Sep 21 '95	136	5.65	5.63	− 0.05	5.83
Sep 28 '95	143	5.63	5.61	− 0.02	5.83
Oct 05 '95	150	5.65	5.63	− 0.05	5.86
Oct 12 '95	157	5.66	5.64	− 0.04	5.88
Oct 19 '95	164	5.66	5.64	− 0.05	5.87
Oct 26 '95	171	5.66	5.64	− 0.05	5.89
Nov 02 '95	178	5.64	5.62	− 0.06	5.88
Nov 16 '95	192	5.68	5.64	− 0.06	5.89
Dec 14 '95	220	5.69	5.67	− 0.06	5.93
Jan 11 '96	248	5.71	5.69	− 0.04	5.96
Feb 08 '96	276	5.72	5.70	− 0.04	5.98
Mar 07 '96	304	5.71	5.69	− 0.05	6.01
Apr 04 '96	332	5.73	5.71	− 0.06	6.05
May 02 '96	360	5.74	5.72	− 0.05	6.08

Source: *The Wall Street Journal*, Volume CXXXII No. 88, May 5, 1995, p. C22.

quotes, there were 178 days left until this bill matured. The discount yield figures are annualized numbers. In order to determine the dollar amount of the discount we must multiply the yield given by the fraction of the year left to maturity. A banker's year of 360 days is used in this calculation. This new yield is then multiplied by the face value of a Treasury bill. Subtracting the dollar discount from the face value of the Treasury bill gives us the actual price. To illustrate this, the price at which dealers are willing to purchase the November 2, 1995, Treasury bill, the bid price, is calculated below:

$$\text{Dollar amount of discount} = 178/360 \times 0.0564 \times \$10,000 = \$278.87$$

$$\text{Bid price} = \$10,000 - \$278.87 = \$9,721.13.$$

The column following the ask price quotations reports the change in the bid yield from the previous day. The last column gives us the annualized yield-to-maturity, based on the ask price. This figure differs from the discount ask yield in that a 365-day year is used to calculate the yield-to-maturity and the effects of compounding interest is also considered in the calculation. It must be stressed that this number is an annualized figure. An investor in the November 2, 1995, Treasury bill does not earn 5.88% for holding the bill for 178 days until it matures. However, the 178-day return is equivalent to 5.88% when annualized.

? Calculate the actual ask price on the November 2, 1995, Treasury bill.

Answer: $9,722.12.
The dollar amount of the discount is calculated as follows:
178/360 × 0.0562 × $10,000 = $277.88
The ask price is equal to $10,000 − $277.88 = $9,722.12.

26. Large corporations issue unsecured, short-term debt securities called **commercial paper**. The typical minimum face value of commercial paper is $100,000 although there is some issued with face values as low as $25,000. In order to avoid having to register the security with the Securities and Exchange Commission, which costs time and money, commercial paper usually has a maximum maturity of less than 270 days, with an average maturity of 5 months. Commercial paper sells at a discount from face value and pays no periodic coupons. The issuing firm can sell the paper directly to the investors, in which case the security is called **direct paper**, or it can use dealers to sell the issue to the public; the latter type of issue is referred to as **dealer paper**.

Bankers' acceptances are dual obligations of the writer of a draft and the bank on which the draft is drawn. This debt instrument is most often used in international trade. An importer writes a check as payment for goods to be received. A bank guarantees the check, indicating that it will make payment in the event that the importer defaults. The exporter can hold the security until it matures and receive the full face value for it, or he can sell the security in the financial markets at a discount from face value. Bankers' acceptances are similar to commercial paper. They are traded in the financial markets and sell at a discount from face value with no periodic interest payments. They also have maturities of less than 270 days.

Repurchase agreements (Repos) are short-term *secured* debt instruments. In this type of arrangement, the borrower sells a marketable security (often a Treasury bill) to the lender with an agreement to buy the security back within a short period of time (shorter than the maturity of the security being sold) for a prespecified higher price. The loan amount is less than the value of the security being sold, so the lender has very little risk. The amount by which the security's market price exceeds the loan amount (i.e., the price at which the borrower sold the security) is called the **haircut**. If the borrower defaults on the loan, the lender keeps the security. If the borrower upholds his end of the agreement, the lender receives a higher price for the security than the price at which he purchased the security from the borrower; the difference is the interest that the lender receives on his loan.

? A short-term, unsecured debt instrument issued by a large corporation is called
  a. a repurchase agreement.
  b. a revenue bond.
  c. a Treasury bill.
  d. commercial paper.

Answer: d.

A repurchase agreement is collateralized, not unsecured, debt. A revenue bond is issued by a state or local government, and a Treasury bill is short-term debt of the U.S. government. Commercial paper is defined as an unsecured, short-term debt obligation of a large corporation.

27.   Rather than investing in securities directly, an investor may choose to invest through an investment company. An investment company pools the money of all its investors and invests in a variety of securities according to a stated investment objective. Balanced funds invest in both common and preferred stock as well as bonds; bond funds invest exclusively in a range of bonds; government bond funds invest only in government bonds; aggressive growth funds invest in stocks that the fund manager believes will offer the maximum capital gains. There are funds that invest in foreign as well as domestic securities, and others that invest only in the securities of a single country like the Japan Fund offered by the Asia Management Company. If an investor wants to take advantage of tax-free securities, there are funds that invest only in municipal bonds. Regardless of an individual investor's investment objective, it is likely that he can find a fund that meets his goals.

There are two general types of investment companies. A **closed-end investment company** is so named because, like most corporations, it has a fixed number of shares. The shares are bought and sold on exchange floors, just like shares of any other corporation. The price is set by supply and demand for the fund's shares. Investors in closed-end companies incur brokerage costs when they buy and sell shares of the company. They also pay an annual management fee. An **open-end investment company** is more popularly known as a **mutual fund**. (Both open-end and closed-end investment companies are referred to as "funds," but only open-end companies are mutual funds.) Mutual funds have no fixed number of shares. If an investor wants to buy a share and no one wants to sell, the fund simply creates a new share. The shares are bought and sold through the investment company itself; they are not traded on exchange floors, so the investor does not have to pay a brokerage fee. The price at which mutual fund shares can be bought or sold is based on the **net asset value** of the fund. Net asset value is calculated by taking the total value of the assets owned by the company and subtracting any liabilities. The result is divided by the number of shares outstanding. If the mutual fund is a **no load fund**, investors can purchase shares of the fund at this price. If the mutual fund is a **load fund**, a sales charge is added to net asset value. The resulting figure is called the **offering price**, and investors can buy shares of the fund for this price. Regardless of whether the mutual fund is a load fund or a no load fund, the shareholders will also be charged a management fee annually and will pay their proportionate share of the commission costs incurred by the fund when the fund's manager buys and sells securities for the fund.

? Which of the following is a characteristic of a mutual fund?
  a. Shares may sell below net asset value.
  b. Shares are bought and sold through the fund.
  c. Shares are sold on exchange floors.
  d. The funds have a fixed number of shares that can be sold.

Answer: b.
Mutual fund shares are bought and sold through the fund itself. The shares will sell for at least net asset value, unlike shares of a closed-end company for which prices are set by supply and demand forces. Mutual funds are open-end companies and have no fixed number of shares.

28. The National Association of Securities Dealers (NASD), a self-regulatory body, has ruled that any sales charge, or load, that exceeds 8.5% of the offering price is excessive. If a fund does not offer dividend reinvestment plans wherein dividends received from the fund can be reinvested at net asset value, volume discounts, and other such services, the maximum allowable sales charge becomes 6.25%. The percentage load being charged can be calculated using the formula below:

$$\text{Percentage load} = \frac{\text{offering price} - \text{net asset value}}{\text{offering price}}.$$

For example, the Ohio tax-free bond mutual fund had an offering price of $12.05 and a net asset value of $11.57 on October 4, 1994. This represents a percentage load of ($12.05 − $11.57)/$12.05 = 3.9%.

? The United Bond fund had an offering price of $6.10 and a net asset value of $5.75 on October 4, 1994. What is the percentage load on this fund?

Answer: 5.7%.
The percentage load is ($6.10 − $5.75)/$6.10 = 5.7%.

29. By algebraically manipulating the equation introduced in the previous frame, we can calculate the offering price of a fund if we know its net asset value.

$$\text{Offering price} = \frac{\text{net asset value}}{1 - \text{percentage load}}$$

If a certain fund has a net asset value of $12.50, and the load is $8\frac{1}{2}$%, the offering price will be $12.50/(1 − 0.085) = $13.66.

? The Fidelity Magellan fund has a 3% load. If the net asset value is $68.03, at what price can an investor buy shares of the fund?

Answer: $70.13.
The investor can buy shares at the offering price. The offering price is equal to $68.03/0.97 = $70.13.

30. Investors may receive a reduced load depending on the amount of money they are investing. The different sales volume levels that permit investors to receive reduced sales charges are called **breakpoints**. These are usually listed in a fund's **prospectus**, a document that gives the investor financial data and other information, such as the investment objective of the fund and the specific securities in which the fund has invested. Many funds will allow an investor to pay a lower sales charge if he signs a **letter of intent**. By signing this document, the investor indicates that he plans on purchasing enough shares within the next 13-month period to meet one of the breakpoints. The fund will then allow all the purchases to be made as if that breakpoint had been met with the first purchase. If an investor fails to fulfil his end of the agreement, he will be required to pay the difference between the reduced sales charge and the load he would have had to pay had he not signed the letter. No other penalty is inflicted.

? An investor may be able to receive a reduced load even if his original purchase does not meet a breakpoint if he signs a
    a. prospectus.
    b. load agreement.
    c. letter of intent.
    d. balanced fund agreement.

Answer: c.
A letter of intent is a document whereby the purchaser signals his intention of buying enough shares within a 13-month period such that the total purchases would meet a breakpoint in the volume discount schedule.

31. In order to sell shares of a closed-end company, an investor would call his broker, just as he would to sell shares of any other publicly traded company. In order to sell shares of a mutual fund, the investor must contact the fund itself. The fund is legally required to redeem an investor's outstanding shares at the request of the shareholder. The fund will buy back the shares at net asset value, which is calculated each day at the end of the trading day. Some funds charge a **redemption fee**, however. Redemption fees are also known as **rear-end loads** and are generally equal to 1% to 2% of the net asset value of the fund. A mutual fund can still classify itself as a no load fund even if it has a redemption fee. The term "no load" means only that there is no *front end* sales charge.

? Jeff Gorman owns 1,000 shares of the Better Fund, which has a redemption fee of 1%. The net asset value of the fund was computed at the end of the trading day on Friday to be $19.21. If Jeff had requested to sell his shares on Friday, how much money would he receive?

Answer: $19,020.

The redemption fee is equal to $0.19 per share ($19.21 × 0.01). Therefore, an investor will receive only $19.02 per share. Since Jeff owns 1,000 shares, he will receive $19,020.

32.   Closed-end fund prices can be found daily by looking for the fund name on the exchange on which the fund is traded. They are listed along with the prices of stocks of all the other corporations. Open-end companies have their own special listing. Exhibit 7 is an example.

Exhibit 7

```
American Funds:
 A Bal p      S&B 13.08   13.88    ...   +10.2 +12.2 +11.3 B
 Amcp p       GRO 12.66   13.43    ...    +8.1 +11.1 +11.5 C
 AMutl p      G&I 22.20   23.55  +0.03   +11.5 +12.2 +11.0 D
 Bond p       BND 13.29   13.95  +0.06    +7.8  +7.5 +10.5 B
 CapIB p      EQI 33.48   35.52  +0.05    +7.5  +8.8 +12.7 B
 CapW p       WBD 16.63   17.46  +0.09   +11.5 +13.9 +11.6 A
 CapWGr pWOR 18.75        19.89  +0.10    +8.1  +9.6   NS ..
 Eupac p      ITL 22.19   23.54  +0.15    +5.0  +4.0 +12.0 A
 FdInv p      G&I 19.35   20.53  +0.01   +12.4 +13.9 +12.8 A
 Govt p       MTG 13.10   13.75  +0.04    +6.0  +5.9  +8.6 C
 Gwth p       GRO 28.92   30.68  -0.07   +13.3 +16.8 +13.0 B
 HiInMuni     HYM 14.86   15.60  +0.04    +8.1   NS    NS ..
 HI Tr p      BHI 14.08   14.78  +0.08   +10.7  +8.9 +13.5 C
 Inco p       EQI 14.39   15.27  +0.04   +11.1 +11.7 +12.1 B
 IntBd p      BIN 13.37   14.04  +0.03    +6.0  +6.0  +8.3 C
 ICA p        G&I 19.42   20.60    ...   +10.6 +11.5 +11.4 C
 LtdTEBd pIDM 14.06       14.76  +0.03    +5.2  +4.1   NS ..
 NEco p       GRO 14.49   15.37  +0.01    +5.5  +5.2 +13.2 B
 N Per p      WOR 15.73   16.69  +0.05    +9.5 +10.9 +12.7 A
 SmCp p       WOR 22.53   23.90  +0.03    +5.2  +7.8 +12.6 A
 TxEx p       GLM 11.70   12.28  +0.05    +7.5  +5.7  +8.3 B
 TECA p       MCA 15.46   16.23  +0.06    +8.0  +5.4  +8.3 B
 TEMd p       SSM 15.02   15.77  +0.06    +6.7  +5.1  +7.3 E
 TEVA p       SSM 15.57   16.35  +0.07    +7.1  +5.5  +7.7 D
 Wsh p        G&I 19.13   20.30  +0.06   +14.5 +16.3 +12.3 B
 A GthFd      GRO  7.93    8.41  +0.05    +8.5  +4.5 +12.7 B
 A Heritg     CAP  0.71   NL    -0.01   -16.5 -23.5  +5.1 E
 A HeritgGr   GRO  3.69   NL      ...    +7.6 +17.5   NS ..
Amer Natl Funds:
 Grth         GRO  4.25    4.51  -0.01   +11.5 +14.9 +11.4 C
 Inco         EQI 20.85   22.12  -0.06   +11.2 +11.8 +11.6 B
 Triflex      S&B 15.59   16.54  +0.01    +9.8 +11.5  +9.8 D
 API Gr fp    CAP 12.24   12.24  +0.09    +8.5 +12.2 +11.7 C
Am Perform:
 AggGro       SML 13.09   13.64  -0.04    +5.4   NA    NS ..
 Bond         BND  9.12    9.50  +0.04    +5.8  +5.5   NS ..
 Equity       GRO 11.25   11.72  -0.01   +11.9 +14.1   NS ..
 IntBd        BIN 10.15   10.46  +0.03    +4.6  +4.7   NS ..
 IntmTxF      IDM 10.41   10.73  +0.03    +6.3  +4.7   NS ..
AmSouth Funds:
 Balance      S&B 12.29   12.87  +0.02   +11.1 +10.9   NS ..
 Bond         BND 10.62   10.95  +0.05    +7.6  +7.2  +9.1 D
 Equity       CAP 15.87   16.62  -0.02   +13.6 +13.2 +12.1 C
 FlaTxF       IDM 10.16   10.47  +0.01    +4.9   NS    NS ..
 GvtIn        MTG  9.45    9.74  +0.04    +5.8  +6.4   NS ..
 LtdMat       BST 10.29   10.61  +0.02    +5.7  +5.6  +7.3 C
 RegEq        CAP 17.87   18.71  -0.09    +8.4  +9.2 +13.6 B
 AmUtlFd      SEC 21.06   NL    +0.05    +9.3  +9.5   NS ..
 Amway        GRO  7.43    7.66  +0.01    +8.0  +9.5 +10.9 D
 Analyt       EQI 12.01   12.01  -0.02    +8.6 +10.2  +8.0 E
 AnalytShTGvBST 9.82      9.82  +0.01    +4.7  +5.4   NS ..
 AnchrCa      MID 21.76   21.76  +0.05    +8.5 +12.2  +6.7 E
 AnchrInBd WBD 9.42       9.42  +0.05   +16.7   NA    NA ..
 AnthmGr p    G&I 11.57   NL    -0.04    +6.9  +9.7   NS ..
Aquila Funds:
 AZ TF        SSM 10.28   10.71  +0.02    +6.8  +5.0  +7.9 C
 CO TF        SSM 10.20   10.62  +0.02    +5.8  +4.3  +7.8 C
 HI TF        SSM 11.11   11.57  +0.02    +6.6  +4.6  +7.2 E
 KY TF        SSM 10.35   10.78  +0.01    +5.9  +4.8  +7.8 C
 Nrgnst TF SSM 9.65      10.05  +0.03    +8.0  +5.9   NS ..
 OR TF        SSM 10.34   10.77  +0.01    +6.2  +4.8  +7.6 D
 TxFUT        SSM  9.50    9.90  +0.03    +8.3  +5.9   NS ..
Aquinas:
 Balance      S&B 10.16   NL    +0.02    +8.5  +9.7   NS ..
 EqInc        EQI 10.75   NL    +0.01   +15.2 +14.9   NS ..
```

Source: *The Wall Street Journal*, Volume CXXXII No. 88, May 5, 1995, p. C18.

The bold print indicates the family of funds, under which individual funds with differing investment objectives are listed. For example, the American National family of funds offers a growth fund and an income fund among others. The first column gives the name of the fund, and the second column lists its investment objective. The classifications used by *The Wall Street Journal* are shown in Exhibit 8:

Exhibit 8

MUTUAL FUND OBJECTIVES

Categories used by The Wall Street Journal, based on classifications developed by Lipper Analytical Services Inc., and fund groups included in each:

STOCK FUNDS

Capital Appreciation (CAP): Capital Appreciation.
Growth & Income (G&I): Growth & Income, S&P 500 Index.
Growth (GRO): Growth.
Equity Income (EQI): Equity Income.
Small Company (SML): Small Company Growth
MidCap (MID): MidCap.
Sector (SEC): Health/Biotechnology; Natural Resources; Environmental; Science & Technology; Speciality & Miscellaneous; Utility; Financial Services; Real Estate; Gold Oriented.
Global (WOR): Global; Small Company Global.
International (non-U.S.) (ITL): International; European Region; Pacific Region; Japanese; Latin American; Canadian; Emerging Market; International Small Company.

TAXABLE BOND FUNDS

Short Term (BST): Adjustable Rate Mortgage; Ultrashort Obligation; Short U.S. Treasury; Short U.S. Government; Short Investment Grade.
Intermediate (BIN): U.S. Treasury; U.S. Government; Investment Grade Corporate.
General U.S. Taxable (BND): U.S. Treasury; General Bond; Target Maturity; Flexible Income; Corporate A-Rated; Corporate BBB-Rated.
High Yield Taxable (BHI): High Current Yield.
Mortgage (MTG): U.S. Government; GNMA; U.S. Mortgage.
World (WBD): Short World Multi-Market; Short World Single-Market; General World Income.

MUNICIPAL BOND FUNDS

Short Term (STM): Short Municipal Debt; Short term California; Other States Short Municipal Debt.
Intermediate (IDM): Intermediate Municipal Debt; Intermediate California Muni Debt; Intermediate Florida Muni Debt; Intermediate Massachusetts Muni Debt; Intermediate Michigan Muni Debt; Intermediate New York Muni Debt; Intermediate Ohio Municipal Debt; Intermediate Pennsylvania Muni Debt; Other States Intermediate Muni Debt.
General (GLM): General Municipal Debt.
California (MCA): California Municipal Debt.
Florida (MFL): Florida Municipal Debt.
Massachusetts (DMA): Mass. Municipal Debt.
New Jersey (MNJ): New Jersey Municipal Debt.
New York (DNY): New York Municipal Debt.
Ohio (MOH): Ohio Municipal Debt.
Pennsylvania (MPA): Pennsylvania Municipal Debt.
Single-State Municipal (SSM): All single-state municipal debt, except California, Florida, Massachusetts, New Jersey, New York, Ohio and Pennsylvania.
High Yield Municipal (HYM): High Yield Municipal Debt.
Insured, All Maturities, All Issuers (ISM): Insured Municipal Debt; California Insured Debt; New York Insured Debt.

STOCK & BOND FUNDS

Blended Funds (S&B): Flexible Portfolio; Global Flexible Portfolio; Balanced; Balanced Target Maturity; Convertible Securities; Income.

Source: *The Wall Street Journal*, Volume CXXXII No. 88, May 5, 1995, p. C18.

The following column gives the net asset value, which is calculated at the close of each day. The offering price is then given. If the fund is a load fund, this number will be higher than the net asset value. If it is a no load fund, the number will be the same as net asset value or the letters "NL" will appear in this column. The load on the American National growth fund is $0.26 ($4.51 − $4.25 = $0.26) per share. Investors must pay $4.51 per share to buy into the fund. If they sell their shares, they will receive $4.25, the net asset value, for the shares, assuming there is no redemption fee. (A redemption fee would be indicated by the letter "r" after the fund name.) On the other hand, in this same family of funds, the API Growth fund is a no load fund. Investors can buy shares of that fund at its net asset value, which is $12.24 a share. They will also receive $12.24 a share if they are selling their shares.

The column following the offering price indicates the change in net asset value from the previous day. The API growth fund increased $0.09 a share in net asset value. If you had purchased 100 shares of this fund the previous day, you gained $9.00.

The sixth column reports the total return—with interest, dividend, and capital gains or losses included—that investors have earned since the beginning of the year. Since the quotes shown in Exhibit 7 are for May 4, 1995, investors in the API growth fund have gained 8.5% on their investment since December 31, 1994.

The information provided in the seventh and eighth columns changes each day. On Mondays, *The Wall Street Journal* lists the maximum initial sales charge (i.e., load) and the total expense ratio, which is the fund's total operating expenses for the fiscal year divided by the fund's average net assets. The management advisory fee, which is usually around $1/2$% of net assets, comprises the largest part of the operating expenses. Most funds try to keep their operating expenses below 1% of the fund's net assets. This ratio is especially important to investors who are investing with the objective of augmenting their income from other sources since the fund must pay all of its operating expenses before it can distribute dividends or interest income to its investors.

On Tuesdays, the seventh and eighth columns report the total return for the last 4 weeks and the total return over the last year. On Wednesdays, these columns report the total return for the last 13 weeks and the annualized total return over the last 3 years as is shown in Exhibit 7. On Thursdays, the 26-week total return and the annualized total 4-year return is presented; on Fridays, the paper lists the 39-week total return and the annualized total return earned over the last 5 years.

The final column ranks the fund relative to other funds having the same investment objective. The ranking is given based on the total return for the longest time period listed for the day. The top 20% are given an "A" ranking, the next 20% a "B" ranking, the middle 20% a "C" ranking, the next 20% a "D" ranking, and performers in the bottom 20% are given an "E" ranking.

? Karen Shoemaker is considering buying shares of the Aquila Arizona tax-free bond fund (AZ TF). What would she have to pay for each share on May 4, 1995?

Answer: $10.71.
Karen will have to pay the offering price to buy shares of the fund.

31.   A money market mutual fund is a special type of mutual fund. By law, it can invest only in securities that mature in 1-year or less. (A **money market instrument** is defined as one with a maturity of less than or equal to 1 year.) Money market mutual fund quotations appear in *The Wall Street Journal* on Thursdays. A sample of quotes for February 8, 1995 appears on the following page. After the column containing the fund name, the average maturity of the instruments in which the fund invests is supplied. The annualized yield, based on the most recent 7-day return (not including capital gains or losses), is listed next. An investor can compare this to the annual rate she can earn on a bank savings account. While money market mutual funds are not federally insured as most bank accounts are, they are considered to be relatively safe since the monies are invested in short-term, high quality instruments such as Treasury bills, commercial paper, and negotiable certificates of deposit. Funds with higher returns listed may also invest in some lower grade commercial paper. In order to achieve higher returns, more risk must be incurred.

The last column reports the assets controlled by the fund in millions of dollars. This is indicative of the size of the fund. Some investors prefer to invest only in the larger money market mutual funds.

? Marsha Sailors believes that money invested in the AARP High Quality (AARP HQ) money market fund is as safe as money in the bank. If her bank is currently paying 4%, compounded annually on its savings accounts, which investment offers her the greater return?

Exhibit 9

MONEY MARKET MUTUAL FUNDS

The following quotations, collected by the National Association of Securities Dealers Inc., represent the average of annualized yields and dollar-weighted portfolio maturities ending Wednesday, February 8, 1995. Yields don't include capital gains or losses.

Fund	Mat.	Yld.	Assets
AALMny	24	4.69	68
AARP HQ	30	5.28	382
AFD ExRsv A	25	4.84	39
AFD ExResB	25	4.34	94
AIM MM C	25	5.20	274
AIM MMA	25	5.22	129
AVESTA Tr	41	5.32	51
AccUSGov	78	5.24	12
ActAsGv	42	5.26	541
ActAsMny	63	5.67	5106
AetnaAdvs	31	5.86	63
Aetna Sel	31	5.86	173
AlexBwn	47	5.52	1413
AlxBTr	48	5.12	535
AlgerMM	53	5.80	151
Alll TrResv	36	5.11	304
AlliaCpRs	28	4.98	2474
AliaGvR	28	4.92	2210
AlliMny	28	5.02	1946
AmAAdTrl	1	5.63	86
AmAAdMMI	47	5.96	1553
AmCRes	15	4.96	345
AmPerCsh	43	5.37	228
AmPerTrs	1	5.14	170
AmSouth Pr	42	5.43	508
AmSouth US	27	5.15	319
AmbMMF	28	5.41	317
AmbTreas F	38	5.15	260
AmbTreasl	38	5.00	62
AmbMMI	28	5.26	543
AmbMMA	28	5.16	41
AmbTreasA	38	4.90	2
Amcore Gv	11	5.30	131
AmAAdMMM	47	5.61	70
ArchUSTr	38	4.74	2
ArchFd	27	5.28	50

Fund	Mat.	Yld.	Assets
FidRetGov	37	5.55	1993
FidRetMM	32	5.64	3777
FidSpGov	38	5.54	738
FidSpMM	33	5.61	7595
FidSpUSTr	54	5.30	1687
59WallStTreas	33	4.97	110
59WallStMM	38	5.15	619
FnclRsv	34	5.43	657
FstAmerInstit	32	5.63	1572
FtBostInInst	87	6.16	457
First Muni	8	3.56	74
FstOmahaGv	63	5.18	95
FirPrTreasTr	62	5.52	117
First USGv	31	5.66	89
FtInvCs	40	5.41	122
FtPraGv	12	4.81	114
FtPraMM	22	5.21	119
First USTrs	29	5.47	44
CalvFtGv	37	5.20	227
FlexInst	44	5.86	42
FlexFd	44	5.67	148
Fortis A	42	5.24	93
ForumDATrs	38	5.36	33
Founders	44	5.26	164
FountSGv	42	5.52	165
FountSCP	37	5.54	245
FountSTO	36	5.36	304
FrnkIFT	34	5.88	280
FrankLate f	24	5.57	29
FrkUSTr	45	5.39	245
FrkIFTGS	20	5.75	273
FrkFdl b	20	5.07	138
FreeCsh	33	5.33	1114
FreeGv	46	5.01	249
FremntMM	45	5.80	302
FrkMny	34	5.22	1031

Fund	Mat.	Yld.	Assets
ML US Tr	39	4.72	64
MetLfSf E	26	5.24	164
MdIncTrGv	45	4.59	79
MdinInst	44	5.37	42
MileTrsOb	27	5.56	92
MonManGvt	47	4.60	16
Mon&ManPr	34	4.84	90
MonarchCash	28	5.72	62
MonarchCU	28	5.99	26
MonarchGvt	16	5.80	177
MonarchGU	16	6.07	30
MonarchTrsyInst	146	5.56	33
MonMMgt f	40	5.05	104
MonMkTrst	35	5.69	552
MonitorMMT	36	5.60	292
MonitorUST	33	5.36	253
MonitrMMI	36	5.50	45
MontGovRes	35	5.34	266
MS Mony	31	5.49	805
MunderC	22	5.45	285
NatnsPrTrA	54	5.84	3053
NCC Govtl	40	5.52	557
NCC GovtR	40	5.42	20
NCC MMR	28	5.58	179
NCC MMI	28	5.68	1114
NCC Treas	33	5.35	133
NYL Inst	27	5.51	55
NatnsPrinvB	54	5.58	132
NatnsTrinvA	28	5.16	106
NatnsPrinvA	54	5.39	668
NatnsGvMMTrA	34	5.55	452
NatnsTreTrA	28	5.53	3087
NatwMM	35	5.46	529
NeubCsh	48	5.36	309
NeubGvt	50	5.00	254
NewEngCMTUSG	37	5.04	63
NewEngCMT	46	5.26	663
Newpoint Gv	52	4.99	55
Nicholas	23	5.60	109
Northern	28	5.59	908
NorthernGvSI	42	5.78	53
NorthernMun	34	3.35	949
NorthernUSGv	37	5.59	247
NorwestCash	44	5.68	1456

Fund	Mat.	Yld.	Assets
STIUSGvIv	5	5.14	45
Safeco f	31	5.16	164
SalomonUST	6	4.53	20
SansomSt	31	5.64	414
SchbValAdv	40	5.73	4223
Schwabintl	39	5.58	66
SchwbRetir	35	5.35	51
SchwbGv	37	5.22	1882
SchbMM	38	5.33	11463
Schb UST	55	5.80	831
ScudCshin	30	5.37	1757
Scud UST	42	5.11	384
SecurityCsh	29	5.13	45
SelectGv	27	5.05	119
SeligmnCshA	25	5.27	203
SentinelUST	55	4.93	73
SevnSea f	39	5.68	2748
SvnSeaGv	27	5.57	359
1784InstUSTr	26	5.50	338
1784 USTreas	29	5.29	35
ShawPrmMMIn	22	5.25	188
ShmtPrTr	22	5.50	555
ShtTrmIncoA	24	4.87	569
ShTrInUS	19	5.00	465
SierraGlbA	77	5.43	95
SierraGovA	25	5.13	46
SmBarCash	50	5.50	18467
SmBarGvt	53	5.38	3779
SmBarRetir	42	5.37	1041
SoTrVicnTres	46	5.34	227
Stagecoach	26	5.53	2706
Stagecoachint	36	5.88	147
StarPrmeObl	17	5.09	105
StarTreas	24	5.04	332
StarbGovT	38	5.24	158
StarbMMT	35	5.48	152
SteinroeCRs	49	5.38	527
SteinroeGvt	45	5.11	104
Stepstninst	20	5.36	522
Stepstninv	20	5.16	112
StepstnTrinst	22	5.32	129
StepstnTrinv	22	5.07	145
Strong	49	6.24	937
StrongUST	48	4.70	53

Fund	Mat.	Yld.	Assets
DWSrNY	24	2.51	43
DelaTax	61	2.92	48
DryBasicMu	73	3.75	1013
DryCTMu	57	3.24	256
DreyCalTx	42	2.84	284
DrMI Mun	31	3.21	62
DrNJMun	72	3.15	769
DrNYTE	63	2.95	324
DRPA Mun	34	3.25	156
DreyTxEx c	43	3.10	1009
DryMAMun	41	3.14	152
DryOHMu	63	3.31	52
DryCATF	42	3.15	31
DryMATF	41	2.98	130
DryTxExR	43	3.06	232
EatnVn	73	3.66	48
EvgrnTE	45	3.51	389
FFB PA TF	56	3.69	45
FFB TF	45	3.15	106
FMNYSv	36	3.35	254
FMMNCsh	49	3.16	120
FMOHIns	51	3.37	74
FMPACsh	49	2.82	26
FMMASv	41	3.07	90
FMMABF	41	3.03	43
FMPASvc	49	3.22	239
FMMNin	49	3.56	239
FMCTSvc	47	3.08	236
FdOHMulI	51	3.07	157
FedTxF c	39	3.24	1195
FidCapRsMu	32	2.95	114
FidInTxEx	37	3.57	2074
FidCA	24	3.13	689
FidCT	46	2.99	313
FidDlyTE	39	3.20	447
FidMA	28	2.88	729
FidMI	28	3.12	221
FidNJ	54	3.11	428
FidNY	41	3.14	741
FidOH	26	3.16	112
FidSpCA	24	3.49	1177
FidSpCT	48	3.11	155
FidSpNJ	53	3.44	452
FidSpNY	40	3.25	567

Fund	Mat.	Yld.	Assets
NJDIvMun	56	2.92	106
NJ MuniSvc	46	3.11	27
NJ Mu Ins	46	3.21	86
NorthernCA	37	3.61	122
NorwestMunIv	26	3.33	43
NuvCal	43	3.21	156
NuvnMas	46	3.06	68
NuvNY	32	2.99	31
NuvnTFRs	34	3.05	346
NuvTxEx	43	3.28	744
OneGrMunA	37	3.08	48
OneGrOH A	38	2.98	60
OneGrOHMu	38	3.23	40
OneGrMuni	37	3.33	503
OvrExp	39	2.93	283
PA DailyMuni	57	3.35	41
PNCMunil	42	3.57	34
PNCMuniS	42	3.27	200
PNC NCI	22	3.39	93
PNC OH S	29	3.18	45
PNC PA I	28	3.41	188
PNC PA S	28	3.11	148
PcfCptlTFCsh	44	3.12	160
PcHorCA	36	3.09	273
PcHrzHorPH	39	3.07	486
PWRMA CA	46	3.18	311
PW KP CT	33	2.45	26
PW KP CalT	33	2.94	147
PW KP NJ	22	2.61	36
PW KP NY	16	2.58	58
PW KP TxE	37	2.91	488
PWRMA NY	43	3.02	195
PW RM Tx	43	3.23	1584
ParkTFInvA	39	2.95	43
ParkTxFInst	39	3.05	93
PierpontTE	52	3.27	1116
PillarTE A	40	3.16	42
PilotSTTxDP	32	3.51	408
PilotSTTEP	37	3.20	233
PiperTF	47	2.90	195
PorticoTE	42	3.21	72
PrincrTE	36	3.05	101
PIFMnNY	42	3.46	214
PIFMuni	46	3.50	780

Source: *The Wall Street Journal*, Volume XCV No. 28, February 9, 1995, p. C 25.

Answer: The AARP High Quality money market fund.
The annualized return on the AARP High Quality fund is 5.28%, which is higher than the bank rate.

34. While closed-end fund prices are reported daily in *The Wall Street Journal* under the exchange on which the fund is traded, a special column on closed-end prices is presented on Thursdays. In this column both the market price of the fund and its net asset value are reported. The amount by which the fund is selling above (at a premium) or below (at a discount) its net asset value is given as a percentage. Some market watchers look for closed-end companies that are selling at large discounts from their net asset values. By their analysis, these funds should be selling for prices that are closer to their net asset value and are therefore underpriced. (This trading rule should not be blindly followed, of course; there may be a very good reason that the fund is trading at so low a price.) Additionally, the return earned by the fund over the last 52 weeks is given. An example of this table is shown on the following page. Consider the Equus II fund in Exhibit 10. The fund's shares are traded on the American Stock Exchange, as shown in the second column. The net asset value of the fund on the day of the quotes is $19.63 (column 3), but it is selling on the exchange floor for only $12.75 a share (column 4). This is a 35% discount from its net asset value (column 5). However, note that the annual return over the last 52 weeks was a negative 24.6% (column 6).

? For what price could an investor buy shares of the Blue Chip Value fund on the day of the quotes?

Answer: $6.25 a share.
The price that the investor pays for a closed-end fund is given in the column labelled "market price."

Exhibit 10

Fund Name	Stock Exch	NAV	Market Price	Prem /Disc	52 week Market Return
General Equity Funds					
Adams Express	N	18.64	16⅛	−13.5	−2.2
Alliance All-Mkt	N	19.96	16¾	−16.1	N/A
Baker Fentress	N	17.75	14½	−18.3	−4.8
Bergstrom Cap	A	98.51	86	−12.7	−1.3
Blue Chip Value	N	7.21	6¼	−13.3	−11.1
Central Secs	A	17.06	16⅛	− 5.5	10.0
Charles Allmon	N	10.08	8½	−15.7	−9.3
Engex	A	9.72	6⅞	−29.3	−36.0
Equus II	A	19.63	12¾	−35.0	−24.6
Gabelli Equity	N	9.65	9¾	+ 1.0	0.7
General American	N	22.77	19¼	−15.5	−1.1
Inefficient Mkt	A	11.95	9½	−20.5	−10.4
Jundt Growth	N	15.13	14	− 7.5	4.1
Liberty All-Star	N	9.60	9	− 6.3	−8.7
Morgan FunShares -c	O	7.56	7	− 7.4	N/A
Morgan Gr Sm Cap	N	10.38	9	−13.3	−6.0
NAIC Growth -c	C	11.76	9¾	−17.1	−12.6
Royce Value	N	12.50	11½	− 8.0	−2.5
Salomon SBF -a	N	13.35	11¼	−15.7	−5.0
Source Capital	N	39.70	39¼	− 1.1	−5.0
Spectra	O	13.94	11	−21.1	−2.5
Tri-Continental	N	24.16	20⅜	−15.7	−3.9
Z-Seven	O	17.18	17½	+ 1.9	−5.2
Zweig	N	10.21	11	+ 7.7	−9.6
Specialized Equity Funds					
Alliance Gl Env	N	10.97	8⅝	−21.4	−13.8
C&S Realty	A	8.18	8⅞	+ 8.5	1.2
C&S Total Rtn	N	12.62	13¼	+ 5.0	−2.0
Centrl Fd Canada -c	A	4.60	4⁷⁄₁₆	− 3.5	−20.9
Counsellors Tand	N	15.48	13⅝	−12.0	−6.8
Delaware Gr Div	N	12.83	12⅜	− 3.5	−6.9
Delaware Grp Gl	N	13.01	12¼	− 5.8	N/A
Duff&Ph Util Inc	N	7.72	8⅝	+11.7	2.7
Emer Mkts Infra	N	12.18	10⅛	−16.9	−34.4
Emer Mkts Tel	N	17.98	17½	− 2.7	−29.7
First Financial	N	10.34	10½	+ 1.5	24.2
Gabelli Gl Media	N	7.59	7⅝	+ 0.5	N/A
Global Health	N	13.37	10⅞	−18.7	−1.1
Global Privat	N	13.66	11¾	−14.0	N/A
H&Q Health Inv	N	16.69	14⅞	−10.9	−14.2
H&Q Life Sci Inv	N	10.93	9¾	−10.8	−19.6
J Hancock Bank	N	20.38	19⅛	− 6.2	N/A
Nations Bal Tgt	N	9.36	7⅞	−15.9	N/A
New Age Media	N	13.58	11½	−15.3	−17.1

Source: *The Wall Street Journal*, Volume XCV No. 25, February 6, 1995, p. C10.

Apply It

1. The maximum number of shares a firm can issue is called its _____ shares while the number of shares that are held by investors is referred to as the firm's _____ shares. (Frame 1)

2. The H & W Corporation has 500,000 shares outstanding and a six-member board of directors. Four of the board seats are up for election. If the firm allows cumulative voting, how many shares would you have to control to ensure that your favorite candidate wins a seat? (Frame 2)

3. Win Diep owns 5,000 shares of the Xanadu Company. There are 1 million shares outstanding. If Xanadu is planning to issue 200,000 new shares and Win has preemptive rights, how many of the new shares will he have the opportunity to purchase? (Frame 4)

4. The Caleb Corporation is selling new shares through a rights offering. Owners of the rights can buy the new shares for $30. The shares are currently selling on the market for $36. Five rights are required to buy one new share. What is the value of one right? (Frame 4)

5. On January 10, 1995, the board of directors of the Kerr-McGee Corporation announced that it would pay dividends of $0.38 a share to its shareholders of record as of Friday, March 3, 1995. The dividends were to be paid on Monday, April 3, 1995. What is the latest day an investor could buy this stock and still receive the announced dividend payment? (Frame 5)

6. The Trimac Corporation paid dividends of $800,000 to its common shareholders during 1994. The firm had $4 million in net income that year, and 1 million common shares outstanding. Trimac has no preferred stock. Calculate the firm's dividend per share and the dividend payout ratio. (Frame 6)

7. If a firm with 6 million shares outstanding does a 3:2 stock split, how many shares will be outstanding after the split? (Frame 7)

8. If a firm with 1,000,000 shares outstanding and a market price of $0.25 per share were to do a 1:100 reverse split, what would the price per share be after the split? (Frame 8)

9. An issue of preferred stock is selling for $60 a share. The par value of the stock is $80, and the dividend is 6%. What is the dividend per share? (Frame 9)

10. All else equal, which type of preferred stock would you expect to sell for the higher price—cumulative or noncumulative? (Frame 9)

11. An issue of the preferred stock of the Hypothetical Corporation is selling for $108 a share. Each share of the stock is convertible into three shares of common stock. The preferred stock is also callable at par value, which is $100. At present, the common stock has a market value of $36 a share. If Hypothetical issues a call on its preferred stock, should a preferred shareholder accept the call or convert her shares to common stock? (Frame 10)

12. Refer to Exhibit 1 in Frame 11 to answer the following questions:
    a. At what price did the stock of ADT close on May 4, 1995? (Frame 11)
    b. How many shares of ABM Industries were traded on May 4, 1995? (Frame 11)

13. Refer to Exhibit 2 in Frame 15 to answer the following questions:
    a. How much will investors in the ATT bonds that mature in 2002 receive every 6 months in interest? (Frames 12 and 15)
    b. What is the current yield on the Ametek bonds? (Frame 15)
    c. What special feature do the Amsco bonds have? (Frame 15)
    d. What price will an investor in the ATT bonds that mature in the year 2,004 pay for each $1,000 bond? (Frame 15)

14. A $1,000 bond of the AmU Corporation pays a 9% coupon. Interest rates on similar risk investments have recently risen to 11%. Will the AmU bond sell at a discount, a premium, or par? (Frame 14)

15. Which of the following debt instruments is unsecured—a collateral trust receipt, a debenture, or a repurchase agreement? (Frames 16 and 26)

16. A $1,000 bond of the Kanger Corporation is convertible into 25 shares of the firm's

common stock. The stock of the company is currently selling for $50 a share. What is the conversion value of the bond? (Frame 17)

17. All else being equal, which of the following bonds would offer the highest return—a callable bond, a convertible bond, or a putable bond? (Frame 18)

18. If a firm issues debt at a single point in time that has different maturities, the debt is referred to as _____. (Frame 19)
   (a bond series/serial debt)

19. Refer to Exhibit 3 in Frame 21 to answer the following:
   a. For what price are dealers willing to sell the 11½% Treasury bonds that mature in November of 1995? (Frame 21)
   b. If an investor buys the Treasury notes that mature in December 1995 for the ask price and holds the notes to maturity, what is her promised average annual yield? (Frame 21)

20. What is a Treasury strip? (Frame 22)

21. Refer to Exhibit 5 in Frame 23 to answer the following:
   a. For what price are dealers willing to buy the FNMA bond that matures in January 1996? (Frame 23)
   b. What is the coupon rate on the FNMA bond that matures in January 1996? (Frame 23)

22. What special feature of municipal bonds is attractive to investors? (Frame 24)

23. Refer to Exhibit 6 in Frame 25 to answer the following:
   a. For what price are dealers willing to buy the May 2, 1996, Treasury bills? (Frame 25)
   b. What is the yield-to-maturity on the February 8, 1996, Treasury bills? (Frame 25)

24. Which of the following is not a short-term debt instrument—Treasury bill, equipment trust receipt, commercial paper? (Frame 26)

25. Which type of investment company is better known as a mutual fund? (Frame 27)

26. A certain mutual fund has assets of $24 million and liabilities of $2 million. There are 5 million shares outstanding.
   a. What is the net asset value of the fund? (Frame 27)
   b. If the fund has a 5% load, what is the offering price? (Frame 29)

27. Refer to Exhibit 7 in Frame 32 to answer the following:
   a. What is the percentage load on the American Funds Bond Fund? (Frames 28 and 32)
   b. For what price could an investor sell his shares in the American Funds ICA Fund, assuming no redemption fee applies? (Frames 7 and 32)
   c. If an investor had purchased 50 shares of the American National Income Fund on the day prior to the day of the quotes, how much money would he have gained or lost in the 1-day holding period? (Frame 32)

28. An investor in a mutual fund may be able to receive a reduced sales charge if he signs a letter of _____. (Frame 30)

29. True or False: A fund that is advertised as a no load fund will have neither a front-end nor a rear-end load. (Frame 31)

30. True or False: A money market mutual fund will invest primarily in shares of common stock. (Frame 33)

31. Refer to Exhibit 10 from Frame 34 to answer the following:
  a. For what price can an investor buy shares of the Z-Seven closed-end investment company? (Frame 34)
  b. Is the Spectra Fund selling at a discount or a premium from its net asset value? (Frame 34)

Apply It Answers

1. The maximum number of shares that a firm can issue is called its **authorized** shares while the number of shares that are held by investors is referred to as the firm's **outstanding** shares.

2. Using the equation given in Frame 2, we can calculate the number of shares as follows:

$$\text{Shares needed} = \frac{(1)(500,000)}{4+1} + 1 = 100,001 \text{ shares.}$$

3. Win currently owns 0.5% of the stock of Xanadu (5,000/1,000,000 = 0.5%). Preemptive rights allows him to maintain his percentage ownership in the firm, so he will be allowed to purchase 0.5% of the new shares, or 1,000 shares, calculated as follows: $0.005 \times 200,000 = 1,000$ shares.

4. The price at which the existing owners can buy the new shares is the subscription price. Using the equation given in Frame 4, we can calculate the value of a right as follows:

$$R = \frac{\$36 - \$30}{5+1} = \$1.00.$$

5. The stock goes ex-dividend four business days prior to the date of record. Since the record date is on a Friday, the stock will trade ex-dividend on Monday, February 27, 1995. This means that an investor must have purchased it prior to February 27, 1995, in order to receive the announced dividend payment. Friday, February 24, 1995, was the last trading day that an investor could purchase the stock and be entitled to the dividend.

6. The dividend per share is simply the total dividends divided by the number of shares outstanding. The dividend per share is $0.80 ($800,000/1,000,000 = $0.80). The dividend payout ratio is the dividends divided by the earnings available to common shareholders. This number is the net income minus any preferred dividends, but since

Trimac has no preferred stock, all of the net income is available to the common shareholders. The dividend payout ratio is, therefore, 20% ($800,000/$4,000,000 = 20%).

7. The shares that will be outstanding after the split can be found by multiplying the existing shares by the split ratio.

$$6,000,000 \times {}^3\!/_2 = 9,000,000 \text{ shares}$$

8. A reverse split decreases the number of shares outstanding and increases the price per share. The new price per share can be found by dividing the existing price by the split ratio (or multiplying by the reciprocal of the ratio).

$$\$0.25 \times 100 = \$25.00$$

9. The dividend per share is found by multiplying the percentage dividend by the par value of the stock.

$$0.06 \times \$80 = \$4.80$$

10. Cumulative preferred stock should sell at a higher price than noncumulative since cumulative preferred shareholders receive any missed dividend payments whereas noncumulative preferred shareholders would not.

11. If the preferred shareholder converted his shares to common stock, he would receive three shares. Since the current value of the common stock is $36 a share, this makes the conversion value of the preferred shares $108 (3 × $36 = $108). Since this is higher than the amount that he will get if he accepts the call ($100), he should convert the stock.

12. a. The close price is found in the next to the last column: $11.75.
    b. The volume is given in hundreds of shares: 39,500 shares.

13. a. The coupon rate on the ATT bonds that mature in 2002 is $7^1\!/_8\%$. This is an annual rate. Investors receive 0.07125 × $1,000 = $71.25 each year in interest. Since interest is paid semiannually, they will receive $71.25/2 = $35.625 every 6 months.
    b. 9.4%.
    c. The letters "cv" instead of a current yield quote mean that the bonds are convertible.
    d. The bonds closed at $97^3\!/_8$ for every $100 of par. An investor will pay $973.75 for a $1,000 bond.

14. The bond will sell at a discount. Since investors who pay face value for a new bond with similar risk to the AmU bond will receive a return of 11%, the price of the 9% bond must fall so that it, too, is returning 11%—partly in interest income and partly in capital gains.

15. A debenture is defined as a long-term, unsecured debt instrument.

16. The conversion value is calculated by multiplying the conversion ratio by the current market price of the common stock.

$$25 \times \$50 = \$1,250$$

17. If all the other bond features were the same, the callable bond would have to offer the highest return since it is the only debt instrument of the three listed that gives the issuing firm an option—i.e., the right to buy the bond back from the investors. Convertible bonds and putable bonds give the investors options, so they can offer lower returns.

18. If a firm issues debt at a single point in time that has different maturities, the debt is referred to as **serial debt**.

19. a. The price at which dealers are willing to sell the bonds is the *ask price*. The quotes are in 32nds, so the bonds are selling for $103⁷/₃₂ per $100 of par. This translates to $103.21875. A $1,000 bond will sell for $1,032.1875.

    b. If the investor holds the bonds to maturity, she should earn the yield-to-maturity, which is quoted to be 6.00%.

20. A Treasury strip is a zero-coupon bond that is sold by brokerage houses. The proceeds that the brokerage houses use to pay the bond investors are derived from earnings that the brokerage houses receive on an investment that they have made in a Treasury security.

21. a. The price at which dealers are willing to buy a bond is the *bid price*. The quotes are in 32nds, so dealers are willing to buy the bond at $101³⁰/₃₂ per $100 of par. This translates to $101.9375. A $1,000 bond will sell for $1,019.375.

    b. The coupon rate is found in the first column. It is 9.20% for the January 1996 issue.

22. Municipal bonds are the only investments that pay interest that is exempt from federal taxation.

23. a. The price at which dealers are willing to buy the bills is the *bid price*. Treasury bill bid and ask prices are quoted as discount yields. The bid discount on the May 2, 1996, issue is 5.74%. This is an annual figure, however, but the bill matures in 360 days, as indicated in column two. The dollar amount of the discount is calculated below:

$$Discount = 360/360 \times 0.0574 \times \$10,000 = \$574.00.$$

The bid price is the face value less this discount.

$$Bid\ price = \$10,000 - \$574 = \$9,426$$

    b. The yield-to-maturity is given in the last column. It is 5.98% for the February 8, 1996, issue.

24. The equipment trust receipt is the only instrument listed that is a long-term debt instrument.

25. An open-end investment company is also known as a mutual fund.

26. a. The net asset value is calculated by subtracting the liabilities from the assets of the fund and then dividing by the number of shares outstanding.

$$Net\ asset\ value = (\$24,000,000 - \$2,000,000)/5,000,000 = \$4.40$$

b. Using the equation provided in Frame 27, the offering price is calculated as follows:

$$\text{Offering price} = \frac{\$4.40}{1 - 0.05} = \$4.63.$$

27. a. The percentage load is found by subtracting the net asset value from the offering price and then dividing by the offering price. The net asset value of the American Funds Bond Fund is $13.29. The offering price is $13.95. The percentage load is calculated below:

$$\text{Percentage load} = \frac{\$13.95 - \$13.29}{\$13.95} = 4.7\%.$$

b. An investor will always sell the shares back to the fund at net asset value if there is no redemption fee. The net asset value of the ICA Fund is $19.42.

c. The American National Income Fund is down $0.06 a share from the previous day as indicated in column 5. An investor who had purchased 50 shares would have lost $3.00 ($50 \times \$0.06 = \$3.00$).

28. An investor in a mutual fund may be able to receive a reduced sales charge if he signs a letter of **intent**.

29. False. A fund can advertise itself as a no load fund so long as it does not have a front-end load. It may or may not have a rear-end load.

30. False. By law, money market mutual funds can only invest in securities that have short-term maturities. This eliminates common stocks since stocks have no maturity date.

31. a. Investors must pay the market price for the fund. This is given in the fourth column as $17.50 per share.

b. The market price of the Spectra Fund is $11. This is a discount from the net asset value of the fund, which is $13.94. Column five indicates that this is a discount of 21.1%.

OPTIONS AND FUTURES

This module will introduce you to options and futures contracts. The basic terminology of each is discussed, and common trading strategies utilizing these instruments are presented. Sample *Wall Street Journal* quotations for each instrument are presented, along with their interpretations.

Equations introduced in this module

$$\text{Rate of return} = \frac{\text{selling price} - \text{purchase price}}{\text{purchase price}}$$

1. An **option contract** is an agreement to buy or sell an underlying asset within a specified time period for a price specified today. The specified time period is referred to as the **exercise period**. The prespecified price is known as the **strike price** or the **exercise price**. There are two types of options. A **call option** gives the investor the right to *buy* the underlying asset at the strike price; a **put option** gives the investor the right to *sell* the underlying asset at the strike price. An investor pays a price, referred to as the **option premium**, for the option. The **option writer**, or the **option seller**, is simply another investor. The option writer receives the option premium and in return must stand ready to sell the underlying asset for the prespecified price if he has written a call option or to buy the underlying asset for the prespecified price if he has written a put option. The option writer *does not have an option*; only the investor who has purchased the option can decide whether the option will be exercised. The owner of the option can choose to exercise his option (i.e., buy or sell the underlying asset, depending on whether it is a call option or a put option) within the exercise period, or he can elect to let his option expire.

Suppose that in February 1996 Meg Bodnar pays $125 for a call option on AT&T stock that has a strike price of $50 and expires in March 1996. The standard option contract gives Meg the right to buy 100 shares of the stock at the strike price At the time she purchased the option AT&T was selling for $51 a share. Now suppose that, prior to expiration of the option, AT&T is selling for $55 a share. Meg has the right to exercise her option or to let it expire. (In reality, Meg has a third choice—she can sell her option—but we will leave that discussion to a later frame.) If she exercises her option, she will pay $50 a share for 100 shares of AT&T stock. An investor who wrote the call option and received the $125 option premium *must* sell the stock to Meg at this strike price. Since AT&T is worth more than the $50 strike price, Meg should choose to exercise her option.

? If AT&T stocks were selling for $48 a share immediately prior to expiration, what should Meg do?

Answer: Meg should let her option expire.

If Meg exercises her option, she can buy 100 shares of AT&T for the $50 a share strike price. Since she could buy AT&T for $48 a share on the exchange floor, she should not choose to pay $2 more a share for the stock.

2. Now suppose that in February 1996, Meg had purchased a put option on Aclaim stock for $75. The option has a strike price of $15 and expires in March 1996. This option gives Meg the right to sell 100 shares of Aclaim stock for $15 a share. The option writer receives the $75 option premium and *must* purchase the shares of Aclaim from Meg for $15 a share if she chooses to exercise her option. If Aclaim stock is selling for $15.50 prior to expiration, Meg should choose to let her option expire since she can sell the stock on the exchange floor for $15.50, but will only receive $15 a share if she exercises her put option. In this case, the option writer is $75 (the amount of the option premium) richer. Regardless of whether they have written a call or a put option, option writers make money when options are left to expire.

? If, just prior to expiration, Aclaim stock was selling for $14.875 a share, what should Meg do?

Answer: If Aclaim is selling for $14.875 a share, Meg should exercise her option. In doing so, she will receive $15 a share for the stock. If she sold the stock through her broker, she would receive only $14.875 a share.

3. Call options are worth more as the price of the underlying asset increases. As the example in Frame 1 illustrated, when the market price of the stock exceeds the strike price on the option, the option is valuable. The option holder can exercise the option and purchase the stock for a price that is below market. The option holder can also *sell* his option. The minimum price for which the call option should sell is the difference between the market price of the stock and the strike price of the option. This is referred to as the **intrinsic value** of the option. Therefore, if an option to buy Biogen stock has a strike price of $30 when the stock is selling on the exchange floor for $39.75, the intrinsic value of the standard option contract is $975. (Since a standard option contract is for 100 shares and the intrinsic value per option share is $39.75 − $30 = $9.75, the intrinsic value of the contract is 100 × $9.75 = $975.) In the event that the market price of the stock is less than the strike price of the option, the intrinsic value of the option is zero; the intrinsic value is never a negative number. If an option has time remaining before expiration, the option will also have a **time value**. This is because there is time left for the market value to rise even higher relative to the strike price of the option. In this case, the option will sell for more than its intrinsic value. The longer the time to expiration, the greater will be the value of the option.

When the market price of the stock is greater than the strike price on a call option, the option is said to be **in the money**. If the market price of the stock is less than the strike price on the call option, the option is said to be **out of the money**. Finally, if the market price of the stock is approximately equal to the strike price on the option, the option is said to be **at the money**.

? Meg is considering purchasing a call option on Cisco stock. The option has a strike price of $40 and expires in July 1996. The option premium is $250 for the standard option contract. Currently (February 1996), the stock is selling for $36.375 on the exchange floor. What is the intrinsic value of this option? Why is the option selling for more than its intrinsic value?

Answer: The intrinsic value is 0, the option does not mature until July 1996.
Since the stock is selling for less than the strike price of the option, the option has no intrinsic value. However, the option contract is selling for a positive price, i.e., $250, because it has approximately 5 months until it expires. During this time, it is possible that the price of Cisco stock will rise above the strike price. This is what investors in this call option are betting on and why they are willing to pay $250 for the option.

4.   It follows from the preceding discussion that the investor in a call option is hoping that the price of the underlying asset will increase. Assume that in February 1996, Meg purchased a call option on Bethlehem Steel that had a strike price of $17.25 and matured in July 1996. The call option cost Meg $125, and Bethlehem Steel was selling for $16.00 a share at the time of her purchase. If Meg had wanted to buy Bethlehem Steel stock, she could have done so for a price ($16) that was cheaper than the strike price of her option ($17.25). Of course, the direct investment in the stock of Bethlehem Steel would require more money. One hundred shares would cost Meg $1,600. A call option can offer a large return on a relatively small dollar investment. The investor's losses are limited to the price of the call. While this *is* a loss of 100% of the investor's investment, the dollar amount may be much smaller than if the investor had invested directly in the stock.

Let us suppose that Bethlehem Steel stock increases to $20 a share prior to July 1996. If Meg had purchased 100 shares of the stock for $1,600, she could now sell the shares for $2,000. This is a rate of return of 25%, calculated as follows:

$$rate\ of\ return = \frac{selling\ price - purchase\ price}{purchase\ price}$$

$$= \frac{\$2,000 - \$1,600}{\$1,600} = 25\%.$$

If instead, Meg had purchased the call option, she would have paid $125. She could now sell the option, assuming she does not actually want to hold the stock of Bethlehem Steel stock, for at least its intrinsic value. Since the strike price on the option is $17.25, the intrinsic value is $2.75 ($20.00 − $17.25 = $2.75) per option share, or $275 for the standard option contract. The rate of return on her investment is calculated below:

$$\text{rate of return} = \frac{\$275 - \$125}{\$125} = 120\%.$$

Of course the dollar amount of her gain is less than had she invested directly in the stock. Ignoring brokerage fees, she would have realized a gain of $400 ($2,000 − $1,600 = $400) if she had purchased the stock. The dollar amount of the gain she received from investing in the option is $150 ($275 − $125 = $150).

On the other hand, assume that the price of Bethlehem Steel stock had decreased to $14 a share. If Meg had purchased the stock, she would have a loss of $200 ($1,600 − $1,400 = $200), while the most she could lose when investing in the option is the $125 cost of the option. As was noted above, however, this is 100% of her investment. The loss associated with the investment in the stock itself is only a negative $12\frac{1}{2}\%$ return as calculated below:

$$\text{rate of return} = \frac{\$1,400 - \$1,600}{\$1,600} = -12.5\%.$$

? In February 1996, Joe West purchased a call option on Bally stock for $137.50. The option had a strike price of $7.50 and expired in April 1996. Prior to expiration, Bally was selling for $9.25 a share. Assuming that Joe does not want to purchase the stock, should he sell his option or let it expire? What is his minimum rate of return on this investment?

Answers: Sell it; 27.3%.
Since the strike price on the option is less than the current market price of the stock, the option has value, so Joe should sell the option. At a minimum, he can sell the stock for its intrinsic value, which is $1.75 per option share or $175 for the option contract. This is a rate of return of 27.3% as calculated below:

$$\text{rate of return} = \frac{\$175.00 - \$137.50}{\$137.50} = 27.3\%.$$

5. The writer, or seller, of a call option wins if the value of the stock remains stable or decreases. If either of these situations occurs, the option holder will let her option expire and the writer keeps the premium. The option seller may or may not own the underlying stock. If he owns the stock on which he has written the option, he is said to have sold a **covered option**. If he does not own the stock, he will have to buy it if the option holder chooses to exercise her option. He is said to have sold a **naked**, or **uncovered option**. Writing a covered option is a relatively conservative investment strategy. If the price of the stock remains stable, the option premium that the seller receives augments the dividend income of his portfolio; if the price of the stock drops, the option premium that the seller receives serves to offset his loss on the stock that he owns; and even if the stock price increases and he is forced to sell the stock, he will often be selling it for a higher price than that for which he originally bought the stock, in which case the option seller realizes a gain, although not as much as he might have experienced had the stock not been called away from him.

Suppose that in February 1996, Meg purchases 100 shares of stock of the Chiron Corporation for its current market price of $66 per share. At the same time Meg writes an April call on Chiron with a $70 strike price, receiving the option premium of $225. The option premium can be thought of as extra income or it can be considered to be downside protection on her investment in Chiron, since the net price of her purchase is now $6,375, or $63.75 per share. (The 100 shares cost her $6,600, but she received $225 for writing the option.) If the price of the stock increases to $71 by April 1996, and the stock is called away from her, she will still have a gain of $625, ignoring dividends. She will receive $7,000 for her shares of the stock, which is a $400 gain, and she also earned the option premium of $225. The rate of return on her two-month investment is $625/$6,600 = 9.5%.

[?] In February 1996, Joe West purchased 100 shares of the Cisco Corporation for $36.50 per share. At the same time, Joe wrote a July call on Cisco with a $40 strike price and received the option premium of $250. In July 1996, Cisco was selling for $42 a share and the stock was called away from Joe. Ignoring dividends, what rate of return did Joe earn on this investment?

Answer: 16.4%.

Joe realized a $350 gain on the sale of the stock ($4,000 − $3,650 = $350). He also earned $250 for selling the option, so his total dollar gain was $600 on an investment of $3,650. This is a rate of return of 16.4% ($600/$3,650 = 16.4%).

6. Investors purchase put options when they expect the price of the underlying asset to fall. Some investors own the stock and buy the put as an insurance policy. If the price of the stock falls, they have locked in the price at which they can sell it. Other investors do not own the stock, but are placing a bet that the stock price will decline. If it does, these put holders can sell their puts for at least their intrinsic values. The intrinsic value of a put is found by subtracting the market value of the stock from the strike price on the put. If the strike price on the put is higher than the market value of the stock, the holder of the put makes money since the put gives her the right to sell the stock at a price that is greater than its market value. If the strike price is less than or equal to the market value of the stock, the intrinsic value of the put is zero. Like call options, put options also have a time value. The longer the time to expiration, the greater the value of the put. A *put option* is **in the money** if the strike price on the put is greater than the market price of the stock, and it is **out of the money** if the strike price is less than the market price. These are the exact opposite definitions from those for call options. When the strike price is approximately equal to the market price of the stock, the put option, like the call option, is said to be **at the money**.

[?] The stock of AGCO Corporation is currently selling for $27.875 a share. Meg has purchased an August 1996 put on the stock for $350. The strike price on the put is $30. Is this an "out of the money" put or an "in the money" put?

Answer: In the money.

Since Meg has the right to sell shares of AGCO for $30 a share (the strike price on the put) when the market price of the stock is only $27.875, the put is "in the money."

7. Suppose Meg had previously purchased 100 shares of AGCO stock for $25 a share. Let us consider several scenarios, the first of which is that AGCO stock is selling for $22 a share prior to August 1996, and Meg had purchased the put described in the previous frame. Meg can use her put to sell the shares for $3,000 ($30 × 100 = $3,000). She paid $2,500 for the stock and $350 for the put option for a total investment of $2,850. Her gain on this investment is $3,000 − $2,850 = $150. This represents a rate of return of 5.3% ($150/$2,850 = 5.3%). However, had she not purchased the put, she would have been able to sell her shares for only $22 a share. This is a loss of $300 ($2,200 − $2,500 = −$300), which translates to a return of negative 12% (−$300/$2,500 = −12%). In this instance, her purchase of the "insurance policy" paid off.

What if, prior to August 1996, the shares of AGCO were selling for $35 a share? If Meg had purchased the put option, she would let it expire since she can sell her shares for $35 a share on the exchange floor rather than exercise her put option to sell them for $30 a share. Her gain will be less than what it would have been had she not purchased the put. Her total investment in the stock and the put option is still $2,850, so she has a gain of $650 ($3,500 − $2,850 = $650), which translates to a return of 22.8% ($650/$2,850 = 22.8%). Had she not invested in the put, her total investment would be only $2,500, making her gain $1,000 ($3,500 − $2,500 = $1,000), which is a return of 40% ($1,000/$2,500 = 40%).

? In February 1996, Joe West purchased 100 shares of Chrysler Corporation for $45.375 a share. Because he was concerned about the volatility of the profits of the company, he simultaneously purchased an April 1996 put with a $45 strike price for $187.50. Joe decided that this strategy would limit his losses should Chrysler's stock go down rather than increase in value as he had hoped. By April 1996, Chrysler was selling for $40 a share. What rate of return did Joe receive from this investment? What rate of return would Joe have received had he *not* purchased the put?

Answers: − 4.8%, −11.8%.
Since Joe purchased the put, his total investment is comprised of $4,537.50 for the purchase of the shares and $187.50 for the purchase of the option, which totals to $4,725. The put option allows him to sell the shares for $4,500, however, so his loss is $4,500 − $4,725 = − $225. This translates to a rate of return of − 4.8% (−$225/$4,725 = − 4.8%). Had Joe not purchased the put, his investment would be only the cost of the shares, $4,537.50. However, he can sell the shares only for the going market price of $40 a share, or $4,000. His loss is −$537.50 ($4,000 − $4,537.50 = −$537.50). The rate of return is −11.8% (−$537.50/$4,537.50 = −11.8%).

8. As was mentioned in a previous frame, some investors who purchase puts do not own the underlying stock and are only betting that the price of the stock will fall so that they can sell their put options for a profit. For example, in February 1995 the stock of Bank of America was selling for $46.375. On the same day, a March 1995 put option on the stock with a $50 strike price was selling for $412.50. If, prior to the expiration date of the March 1995 option, the stock price drops to $44 a share, the investor who bought the put option can sell the put for at least its intrinsic value of $600 ($5,000 − $4,400 = $600). This is a profit of $187.50 ($600 − $412.50 = $187.50), which represents a return of 45.5% ($187.50/$412.50 = 45.5%). Of course, if the stock price of Bank of America increases to $49 prior to expiration, the intrinsic value of the put will be only $100 ($5,000 − $4,900 = $100), and the put investor will have a loss of $312.50 ($100 − $412.50 = − $312.50), or a return of −75.8% (−$312.50/$412.50 = −75.8%). If the stock price increases to $52 a share, which is greater than the strike price on the put, the put option will be worthless and the put holder will lose 100% of his investment.

? Marie Gonzales purchased a March 1995 put option on Best Buy stock for $400. The strike price of the option was $30 a share. Best Buy was selling for $26.50 a share when Marie purchased her option. Immediately prior to expiration of the option, Best Buy was selling for $28 a share. What is Marie's gain or loss on this investment?

Answer: Marie lost $200.
When the stock of Best Buy is selling for $28 a share, the intrinsic value of the put option is $200 ($3,000 − $2,800 = $200). If the option is about to expire, there is no time value on the option, so the most Marie can sell the option for is $200. Since she had paid $400 for it, she has lost $200 (ignoring brokerage fees).

9.   The writer, or seller, of a put option is required to purchase the stock from the put option owner at the strike price on the option if the option owner decides to exercise his option. The seller of a put option is betting that the price of the underlying stock will rise and that the option holder will let his option expire. In this case, the option writer profits by the amount of the option premium that he received for writing the option.

Suppose that Meg Bodnar wrote a July 1996 put with a $40 strike price on the stock of Cisco Corporation, receiving the option premium of $500. At the time Meg sold the put, Cisco was selling for $36.50 per share. If Cisco stock increases in value to $45 a share, or any price in excess of the $40 strike price, prior to the expiration date on the option, the owner of the option will let it expire. The owner will not force Meg to purchase the stock for $40 a share when he can get $45 if he sells the stock on the exchange floor. Meg's profit is the $500 she received for writing the put.

As another example, assume that Cisco's stock price is only $38.50 a share prior to expiration of the put. In this case the put holder will require that Meg purchase the stock from him for $40 a share. Meg's investment in the stock will be $4,000. However, this is partially offset by the $500 that she received for selling the put, making the net price she has to pay for the stock $3,500. Since the stock is selling on the market for $38.50 a share, Meg still makes a profit of $350 ($3,850 − $3,500 = $350).

On the other hand, if Cisco's stock price drops to $32 a share prior to expiration, Meg will have lost money. Again, the put holder will force Meg to purchase the shares for the strike price of $40 a share and, again, the net cost of the shares for Meg is $3,500 since the price at which she must buy the shares is partially offset by the option premium that she received when she sold the put. However, in this case Meg can sell the shares for only $3,200, which is a loss of $300 ($3,200 − $3,500 = −$300).

? In February 1996, Joe West wrote a July put on the stock of Chiron Corporation. The put had a strike price of $65 a share, and Joe received the option premium of $400. At the time Joe wrote the put, Chiron was selling for $66 a share, but prior to the expiration date on the put, the stock price was $68 a share. What is Joe's profit or loss on this transaction?

Answer: $400.

If Chiron's stock is selling for $68 a share, the owner of the put will not force Joe to buy the stock from him for the strike price of $65 a share. The put holder will instead let the option expire, and Joe keeps the option premium of $400.

10.   Until 1973, the purchase and sale of options contracts was limited to the over-the-counter market. Investment firms that were members of the Put and Call Association served as intermediaries between the buyers and the writers. Through them, investors negotiated specific put and call options on given stocks. Because there was not an active resale market for the options, investors were typically locked into their positions until their options expired. The **Chicago Board Options Exchange (CBOE)** was created in April 1973. It was initially the only trading floor on which existing options could be bought and sold. The establishment of the CBOE created a central marketplace for options trading, with regulatory power and disclosure requirements. A clearing corporation was also introduced to serve as the guarantor of every option that traded on the CBOE, which allowed option buyers and sellers to terminate their positions whenever they wished. The clearinghouse takes the opposite position to every trade. If an investor wants to buy an option, the clearinghouse stands as the seller; if an investor wants to write an option, the clearinghouse becomes the buyer.

Expiration dates were standardized, as were strike prices. Most options expire in January, April, July, and November; others expire in February, May, August, and November. The actual date of expiration is the Saturday following the third Friday of the expiration month, but trading in the option ceases at the close of the market on the third Friday of the month. For most stocks, strike prices are established in $5 increments, e.g.,

$30, $35, $40. An odd strike price, e.g., $17.50, means that the stock was split sometime after the option was sold. When a stock splits, the strike prices on the options are adjusted. If a stock that had been selling for $40 a share split 2:1, its new price would be $20. If an option on that stock had a strike price of $35, it, too, would be split 2:1, and the new strike price would be $17.50.

Options are now traded on the two major exchanges—the New York Stock Exchange and the American Stock Exchange—and on some of the regional exchanges in addition to the CBOE. Price quotes are presented daily in *The Wall Street Journal*, an example of which appears below:

Exhibit 1

			–Call–		–Put–	
Option/Strike		Exp.	Vol.	Last	Vol.	Last
ADT	12 1/2	Jun	40	1/4	...	...
AGCO	30	Mar	37	1 1/8	20	2 5/8
27 7/8	30	May	61	2 1/8	...	...
27 7/8	30	Aug	1	3 3/8	50	3 1/2
ALC Cm	25	Mar	85	3 3/4	...	...
28 1/8	30	Feb	30	3/16	...	...
28 1/8	30	Mar	30	1 1/16	...	...
A M R	50	Feb	60	7 1/4	...	...
57 1/4	55	Feb	85	2 3/16	10	1/8
57 1/4	60	Feb	105	1/8	3	3
57 1/4	60	Mar	125	15/16	3	3 5/8
A S A	45	Feb	184	1/4	34	1 3/16
44 1/2	45	Mar	65	15/16	10	1 11/16
AST Rs	10	May	29	6 1/4	...	...
15 7/16	12 1/2	Feb	100	3 1/2	...	...
15 7/16	12 1/2	May	74	3 5/8	...	...
15 7/16	15	Feb	1042	7/8	45	3/8
15 7/16	15	Mar	1595	1 1/4	50	11/16
15 7/16	15	May	196	2 1/8	38	1 1/4
15 7/16	15	Aug	20	3	30	2 1/4
15 7/16	17 1/2	Feb	696	1/4	...	...
15 7/16	17 1/2	Mar	264	9/16	30	2
15 7/16	17 1/2	May	247	1 1/16	10	2 1/2
AT&T	45	Jul	135	7 3/4	...	...
51 7/8	50	Feb	974	1 7/8	329	1/8
51 7/8	50	Mar	121	2 1/4	58	3/8
51 7/8	50	Apr	275	2 5/8	128	11/16
51 7/8	50	Jul	22	3 1/2	31	1 1/8
51 7/8	55	Mar	40	3/16	...	...
51 7/8	55	Apr	271	3/8	...	...
51 7/8	55	Jul	293	1	...	...
AbbeyH	20	May	100	8 7/8	...	...
28 1/2	30	Feb	34	3/8	10	1 1/2
Abbt L	35	Feb	234	1/2	2	7/16
35	35	Mar	711	1 3/16	10	7/8
35	35	May	102	1 3/4	27	1 3/8
Aclaim	12 1/2	Feb	82	2 9/16	...	...
15 3/8	12 1/2	Jul	...	...	40	3/8
15 3/8	15	Feb	508	11/16	160	3/8
15 3/8	15	Mar	352	1 1/8	20	3/4
15 3/8	15	Apr	121	1 5/8	20	1 1/8
15 3/8	15	Jul	37	2 7/16	...	...
15 3/8	17 1/2	Apr	79	7/16	...	...
15 3/8	17 1/2	Jul	129	1 1/16	...	...
Actava	7 1/2	Mar	40	2 1/2	...	...
...	10	Mar	61	1 1/16	...	...
...	10	Jun	415	1 9/16	30	1 1/8
Acuson	17 1/2	Apr	...	...	55	3 7/8
AdobeS	25	Feb	10	4 3/4	100	1/16
29	30	Apr	20	2 1/8	33	2 5/8
A M D	30	Feb	356	1 3/8	160	1/4
31 1/8	30	Mar	100	2 3/8	30	7/8
31 1/8	35	Feb	40	1/16	...	...
31 1/8	35	Mar	45	5/16	...	...
AdvTLb	15	Mar	...	...	65	5/8
Aetna	55	Apr	100	1	...	...
Agnico	10	Mar	30	3/8	...	...
9 5/8	10	May	60	11/16	...	...
9 5/8	12 1/2	May	60	3/16	...	...
Ahman	20	Jul	34	7/16	...	...
AliasR	20	Feb	60	6 7/8	...	...
27 15/16	20	Mar	85	7	...	...
27 15/16	22 1/2	Feb	30	4 1/2	...	...
27 15/16	22 1/2	Mar	35	4 5/8	...	...
12 1/2	15	Apr	164	3/8	...	...
12 1/2	15	Jul	48	7/8	...	...
Bally	7 1/2	Feb	210	13/16	...	...
8 1/4	7 1/2	Mar	37	1 1/16	...	...
8 1/4	7 1/2	Apr	165	1 3/8	5	3/8
8 1/4	7 1/2	Jul	36	1 11/16	...	...
8 1/4	10	Mar	80	3/16	...	...
8 1/4	10	Apr	30	5/16	...	...
8 1/4	10	Jul	100	11/16	...	...
BalyGm	7 1/2	Mar	...	...	30	7/16
BncOne	25	May	30	4 1/2	...	...
BkBost	25	Feb	93	4 5/8	...	...
29 5/8	30	Feb	37	3/8	200	3/4
BankAm	40	Apr	...	...	32	1/4
46 3/8	45	Mar	14	2 1/8	111	7/8
46 3/8	45	Apr	22	2 9/16	325	1 3/16
46 3/8	50	Mar	...	...	206	4 1/8
BkrsLH	20	Feb	60	1	...	...
20 7/8	22 1/2	Aug	50	1 3/4	...	...
BkrsTr	55	Mar	...	...	100	1/4
62 5/8	60	Feb	100	2 3/4	...	...
62 5/8	60	Jul	...	...	50	3
62 5/8	65	Feb	170	1/2	25	2
BanySy	15	Mar	...	...	50	7/16
BarNbl	30	Feb	87	1 5/8	5	7/16
ABrrck	20	Feb	24	1 1/16	70	1/16
21 1/8	20	Apr	85	2	300	11/16
21 1/8	22 1/2	Feb	190	1/8	10	1 1/2
21 1/8	22 1/2	Mar	244	9/16	...	...
21 1/8	22 1/2	Apr	660	15/16	25	2
21 1/8	22 1/2	Jul	151	1 1/2	...	...
BattlM	10	Feb	93	1/16	...	...
9 3/8	10	Mar	99	3/8	...	...
9 3/8	10	Apr	251	7/16	20	1 3/16
9 3/8	12 1/2	Apr	72	1/8	...	...
BausLm	30	Mar	500	4 3/4	...	...
34 1/8	35	Feb	80	1/16	...	...
Baxter	25	Aug	...	...	150	1/2
28 7/8	30	Mar	...	...	35	1 11/16
BayNtw	25	Feb	20	6 3/8	36	1/16
31 1/8	30	Feb	934	1 5/8	...	...
31 1/8	30	Mar	69	2 5/8	3	1 1/16
31 1/8	30	Jun	68	4 5/8	37	2 1/2
31 1/8	30	Sep	...	...	40	3 1/4
31 1/8	35	Feb	89	1/8	...	...
BellAtl	55	Apr	52	1	...	...
BellSpt	17 1/2	Feb	40	13/16	10	9/16
BellSo	60	Jul	63	2 1/4	...	...
BergB o	19	Mar	50	6	...	...
24 3/4	21 3/8	Mar	40	3 7/8	20	3/8
24 3/4	23 3/4	Mar	30	2 1/2	...	...
BergBr	25	Feb	119	7/8	50	3/4
BestBuy	22 1/2	Mar	30	4 1/2	...	...
26 1/2	25	Feb	10	1 5/8	70	1/4
26 1/2	25	Mar	10	2 1/2	79	1
26 1/2	30	Feb	...	...	162	3 1/2
26 1/2	30	Mar	21	1/2	79	4
26 1/2	40	Jun	12	5/16	62	13 3/8
Beth S	17 1/2	Jul	100	1 1/4	...	...
BetzLb	45	Mar	...	...	40	5/8
45 3/8	45	Apr	...	...	36	1 1/8
Biogen	30	Apr	...	...	110	3/8
39 3/4	35	Feb	21	5 3/4	136	1/8
39 3/4	35	Mar	10	5 1/4	45	7/8

Source: *The Wall Street Journal*, Volume XCV No. 29, February 10, 1995, p. C12.

The first column of the quotes lists the name of the company whose stock serves as the underlying asset for the option. If more than one option exists on the stock, the price at which the stock closed on the exchange floor is listed below the name of the company for as many options as are listed. For example, Exhibit 1 is a clipping of quotes for February 9, 1995. AMR stock closed at $57.25 a share on February 9, 1995, as indicated by the numbers directly under the name of the company.

The second column lists the strike prices on the various options that are available, and the third column reports the month in which the option expires. There are four option combinations being traded on AMR stock. One has a $50 strike price and expires in February 1995; another has a $55 strike price and expires in February 1995; and two have strike prices of $60, expiring in February 1995 and March 1995, respectively. The fourth and fifth columns report the volume of trading and the option premium for the call options with the specified strike price and expiration month, while the sixth and seventh columns present the volume and option premium figures for put options with the specified strike price and expiration month. The option premiums are quoted per option share. The standard option contract is for 100 shares, so the actual cost to the investor is 100 times the premium listed.

Consider, as examples, the options that can be purchased on AMR that have a $60 strike price and expire in February 1995. An investor can purchase a call for $0.125 per option share, or $12.50 for the standard option contract. This is relatively inexpensive because it is an "out of the money" call. The strike price of $60 is greater than the price at which AMR closed on the New York Stock Exchange on the same day—$57.25. You might also note that the following call option, with a $60 strike price and a *March 1995* expiration, is selling for slightly more than this one—$15/16 translates to $0.9375 per option share. The March call option has more *time value*. The February 1995 put option is selling for $3 an option share, or $300. The put option is more expensive than the call option in this example because the put option is "in the money." The holder of the put can sell the stock for the $60 strike price when the market price of the stock is only $57.25. As was the case with the call options, the put option that is listed with a $60 strike price and that expires in *March* is selling for a higher price—$3.375 per option share—due to the greater time value.

? According to Exhibit 1, how much would an investor who wanted to buy a March option to sell AMD stock for $30 a share have to pay for the standard option contract?

Answer: $87.50.
An option to sell is a put option. The put option that is listed with a $30 strike price, expiring in March, has a price of $7/8 per option share. This translates to $0.875 per option share. A standard option contract for 100 shares would cost $87.50.

11. Although call options and put options were originally designed for the stocks of individual companies, investors can now purchase calls and puts on various stock market indexes, such as the S&P 500. If an investor believes the stock market will rise in general, he might buy a call on the S&P 500. If the market does go up as he anticipates and he exercises his option, he does not get one share of each of the stocks that make up the S&P 500. Index options are settled in cash based on the intrinsic value of the option at expiration. If the market falls, the intrinsic value of the index option will be zero, and the holder of the call will let his option expire.

The buyer of a put option on a stock market index is betting that the stock market will fall. If he is correct, his profit will be based on the intrinsic value of the index option at expiration. Some investors, large portfolio managers included, buy stock index puts if they anticipate a decline in the market but do not want to sell their holdings in the stocks since by doing so they would be triggering a taxable gain. If the market does fall, the profit that is received by exercising the put option helps to offset the losses on the portfolio.

Options can also be purchased on debt instruments, such as U.S. Treasury bonds, and on foreign currencies. These options are used in the same way that individual stock options and stock index options are used: (1) to hedge an existing position in the asset by offsetting a potential loss in the asset's value with a gain on the option position, or (2) to bet on the direction that the value of the asset will take without taking an actual position in the asset.

? An investor who wants to bet that the stock market will rise should purchase a _____ option on an index option.

Answer: call.
A call option on a market index will increase in value as the stock market rises since the value of the market index will then increase relative to the strike price on the option.

12.   A futures contract is similar to an option in that an investor agrees to buy or sell the underlying asset at a future time for a prespecified price. Unlike an options contract, a futures contract legally binds both the purchaser and the seller. Neither has the ability to let the contract simply expire. The purchase and delivery of the underlying asset in a futures contract takes place on a specific date, *not* at any point within an exercise period. The investor who purchases the futures contract is said to be taking a **long position**, while the seller of the futures contract is taking a **short position**. Unlike the situation with calls and puts, for every long position there must be a short position. The investor in the long position is committing to buy the underlying asset on the future date at the prespecified price, and the investor in the short position is committing to sell the underlying asset on the future date for that price. If either investor decides he does not want to remain in the commitment, he must do a **reversing trade**. In other words, if the investor had agreed to buy 5,000 bushels of corn in May 1996, he must call his futures broker and enter a short position in May 1996 corn. The short position will cancel out his long position. On the other hand, if the investor had agreed to sell 5,000 bushels of corn in May 1996, he would have to call his futures broker and enter a long position in May 1996 corn in order to cancel out his short position.

An investor who wants to lock in the price at which he can buy an underlying asset for a prespecified price would take a _____ position in a futures contract on that asset.

Answer: long.
An investor who wishes to buy the asset in the future will take a long position, which commits him to buy the asset at the prespecified price unless he does a reversing trade.

13.   Whether the investor is entering the futures contract in the long or the short position, he must deposit a **margin**, or good faith deposit, with his futures broker. This margin is usually between 10% and 20% of the value of the contract. If one futures contract for corn is for 5,000 bushels, and the price is $3 a bushel, the value of the contract is $3 \times 5,000 = $15,000$. If the margin required is 10%, the investor would have to deposit $1,500 with his broker. Each day futures contracts are *marked to market*, which means that each investor's account is adjusted for any gains or losses that the investor realized due to price changes. For example, suppose an investor enters a futures contract on February 27, 1996 to purchase corn in May 1996 (i.e., entered a long position) at $3 a bushel. Now assume that on February 28, 1996 the price of corn for May delivery has risen to $3.05 a bushel. Every investor who has purchased a futures contract on May corn must now pay $3.05 a bushel if he takes delivery of the corn in May; every investor who has sold a futures contract on May corn will now receive $3.05 a bushel when he delivers the corn in May. However, because the investor who entered the contract to purchase the corn in May had agreed the day before to pay $3 a bushel for the corn, he will be paid the 5 cents a bushel difference at the close of trading on February 28. The computer will add $0.05 \times 5,000 = $250 to his account. The computer will *deduct* the 5 cents a bushel difference from all the investors who agreed on the previous day to deliver the corn for $3.00 a bushel in May. That is, $250 will be deducted from the accounts of all the *short positions*. Now suppose that the following day, March 1, the price of corn for May delivery has fallen to $3.02 a bushel. All the May corn contracts will be remarked at $3.02. The long positions will now pay $3.02 in May if they take delivery of the corn, and the short positions will receive $3.02 when they make delivery. The long positions now have to pay 3 cents less in May, and the short positions agree to accept 3 cents less. Since this is a *decrease* from the previous day's price, the difference of $150 ($0.03 × 5,000 = $150) will be *deducted from* the long position accounts and *added to* the short position accounts. In summary, if the price increases, short positions pay the long positions the difference today; if the price decreases, long positions pay the short positions the difference today. The price at which the contracts are marked to market is known as the **settlement price**, which is the day's average closing price for the contracts.

? Because of reports of an exceptionally good growing season, you expect the price of orange juice to fall in the near future. If the price does drop, investors who have taken a _____ position in a futures contract for orange juice will profit.

Answer: short.

When the price of an asset for future delivery falls, futures contracts are marked to market at the new, lower price. Since investors who have committed to deliver the orange juice at a higher price will now receive a lower price when they deliver the juice, the difference will be paid them today.

14. There are two general types of investors in the futures market. The **hedger** enters a futures contract in order to lock in a price at which he can buy or sell the asset at some future date. The **speculator** is placing a bet on the direction that the value of the underlying asset will take. Consider first the Midwest Farm Corporation (MFC), which produces corn as its primary crop. In February, MFC wants to lock in a selling price for its corn when it harvests it in September. September corn is selling for $2.515 a bushel in the futures market, and Midwest takes a short position in the contract (or *sells* a futures contract for September corn), thereby agreeing to deliver the corn in September for $2.515 a bushel. One corn contract is for 5,000 bushels, so the value of the contract is $2.515 × 5,000 = $12,575. This is the amount that MFC will receive when it delivers 5,000 bushels of corn in September regardless of any interim price changes. If the required margin is 20%, MFC must deposit $2,515 with the broker. For simplicity's sake, we will assume that the price of September corn changes only three times between February and September. (While it will simplify the discussion greatly, this assumption is totally unrealistic; daily price fluctuations are the norm.) We will assume that on March 16th, the settlement price on September corn changes to $2.550 a bushel. Since this is an *increase* of 3½ cents a bushel from the previous price, the short positions must pay the long positions the difference, and the contracts will now have the new price of $2.550. Because MFC is in the short position, its account will be reduced by $175 ($0.035 × 5,000 = $175). MFC's brokerage account is now reduced to $2,340 ($2,515 − $175 = $2,340).

We will assume the next price change occurs on May 29th. This time the contracts are marked to market at $2.650 a bushel. This is a price *increase* of 10 cents a bushel over the previous price, so again the short positions must pay the long positions; this time $500 is deducted from the short accounts ($0.10 × 5,000 = $500). MFC's account balance is now $1,840 ($2,340 − $500 = $1,840).

We will now assume that the last of the three price changes to occur before the delivery date specified on the contract occurs on August 10th. The settlement price on this day is $2.625 per bushel. This is a price *decrease* from the previous price, so long positions pay the short positions the difference of 2½ cents a bushel or $125 ($0.025 × 5,000 = $125). MFC's balance is now $1,965 ($1,840 + $125 = $1,965). Since we have assumed that no other price changes will occur prior to delivery, MFC will receive $13,125 when it delivers the corn in September ($2.625 × 5,000 = $13,125). However, the firm *lost* money on its futures contract. MFC's initial deposit was $2,515, but it now has only $1,965 in the account. The loss of $550 offsets the gain on the sale, making the net profit $12,575, which is the price MFC locked in when it entered the futures contract.

[?] In April, the Purple Dinosaur Frozen Food Corporation (PDFF) entered a long position in a corn futures contract in order to lock in the price that it would have to pay for corn the following December. (One contract = 5,000 bushels.) The price of December corn at that time was $2.70 per bushel. The last price at which December corn sold prior to the December delivery date was $2.75 per bushel. How much did PDFF have to pay for the 5,000 bushels of corn when it was delivered? Did PDFF have a profit or loss on its futures position?

Answers: $13,750; PDFF had a profit on its futures position.
When the corn was delivered, PDFF had to pay the price that existed on the contract at that time—$2.75 a bushel. This made the total cost $13,750 ($2.75 × 5,000 = $13,750). However, PDFF's gain on its futures contract offset the actual cost of the corn. Since the price of the corn increased by 5 cents a bushel, PDFF's profit on the futures contract was $250 ($0.05 × 5,000 = $250). This gain reduced the total cost to $13,500, or $2.70 per bushel ($13,500/5,000 = $2.70).

15. Both the Midwest Farm Corporation and the Purple Dinosaur Frozen Food Corporation wanted to lock in a future price for the corn. Ms. Annie Tanks, on the other hand, has no corn to sell and has no need for the corn—at least not 5,000 bushels of it. However, having grown up in Ohio, she believes that the weather conditions will result in a poor corn crop and that corn prices will rise due to the short supply. If Ms. Tanks is a betting woman, she can bet on the increase in the corn prices by taking a *long* position in a futures contract (or *buying* a corn futures contract). Since she thinks the prices will rise, she will want to take the position that gets paid if this occurs, and short positions pay the long positions in the event of a price increase. Assume that Ms. Tanks placed her bet on the same day that MFC entered its short position, at $2.515 a bushel. Ms. Tanks must also deposit a 20% margin with her broker, so her initial account balance is $2,515. When the price increases to $2.550 a bushel on March 16th, Ms. Tanks account will be increased by the same amount that MFC's account decreased—$175, or 3½ cents a bushel. Her account balance is now $2,690. If Ms. Tanks is not greedy, she can call her broker at this time and enter a short position in September corn, thereby closing out her position. Before brokerage costs, she has gained $175. If Ms. Tanks *is* greedy or believes that the price of September corn will increase more, she can continue to hold her position. If she does so, her account balance will increase again on May 29th when the price of September corn increases to $2.650 a bushel. This time $500 will be added to her account, making the new balance $3,190. At this point she can again choose to do a reversing trade to close out her position or she can continue. If she closes out her position at this time, she will have earned $675 before brokerage fees. Since Ms. Tanks is only a speculator, she must make certain that she does a reversing trade at some point or she will end up as the proud owner of 5,000 bushels of corn.

[?] Cassandra Salem has a premonition that the price of copper will decrease sharply over the next 6 months. Although she has no interest in buying or selling copper, she would like to make money on this premonition. If her premonition is correct, she will make money by _____ a futures contract on copper.

Answer: selling.
If the price decreases, the long positions pay the short positions, so Ms. Salem should take the position that will be paid if her premonition comes true. Entering a short position is the same as selling a futures contract on copper.

16. The commodities on which futures contracts are traded can be divided into eight major groups: grains and oilseeds, livestock and meat, food and fiber, metals and petroleum, wood, debt instruments, foreign currencies, and stock market indicators. The examples that we have been using have involved corn futures, which fall into the grains and oilseeds group. The futures market on debt instruments is relatively new and has grown rapidly since the mid-70s. The volatility of interest rates led investors to use these contracts in order to hedge their positions. A **short hedge** refers to the sale of a financial futures contract to hedge against a position that the investor currently holds in the financial instrument, while a **long hedge** is used to guard against adverse price movements that are related to the actual purchase of bonds in the future. As was the case with corn futures, the hedger wants to establish a position in the futures market that will get paid if his fears are realized. For example, a short hedge might be used by a bond dealer who wishes to minimize the risk of price changes on the bonds he holds in his portfolio. He would sell bond futures contracts for approximately the value of his portfolio. If interest rates rise, bond prices will fall. His bond portfolio loses value but, in the futures market, long positions pay the short positions when prices fall, so his loss on the portfolio is offset by a gain on the futures contracts.

Long hedges are used more infrequently. One instance in which it is sometimes used is when a bond portfolio manager is expecting to receive cash for maturing securities in the near future but fears that interest rates might fall prior to the cash inflow. He can lock in the current rate by buying bond futures contracts for approximately the value of the expected inflow. If interest rates do fall as he expects, bond prices will rise, and he will have a gain on his futures contracts.

? Francesca Berrera is negotiating a $100,000 mortgage to purchase a new home. She is concerned that mortgage interest rates will increase prior to closing on the house. If she wanted to hedge using a futures contract to protect herself, should she buy or sell a futures contracts on General National Mortgage Association (GNMA) bonds?

Answer: She should sell a futures contract on GNMA bonds.
Francesca wants to hedge against an increase in interest rates. If interest rates do increase, bond prices will fall, so she should take the position in the futures market which will pay her if bond prices fall. When prices fall, the short positions get paid.

17. Futures contracts trade on exchange floors in a manner similar to that in which stocks are traded, but futures contracts trade on their own exchanges and many of the trading practices differ from that of stocks. One significant difference is that while stock prices are free to fluctuate without limit, futures contracts have an established daily limit for price fluctuations. The limit depends upon the commodity on which the contract is written. Once the price has reached its limit, trading in the contracts ceases for the day. There are also differences in the unit of trading. Stocks are normally traded in round lots, which for most issues is 100 shares. The units of trading differ among the various commodities. For example, one corn contract is for 5,000 bushels, whereas one sugar contract is for 112,000 pounds.

While the amount of money that an investor in the futures market deposits with his broker is called a margin, it is not the same as a margin transaction in the stock market. A margin transaction in the stock market is one in which the investor puts up some of his own money, the margin, and borrows the remainder of the investment money from his broker. The margin associated with trading of futures contracts is simply a good-faith deposit. Because a futures contract is basically a deferred delivery agreement, payment for the commodity is not made until the delivery date on the contract. The good-faith deposit is used to adjust the accounts when the contracts are marked to market each day. The investors are required to maintain a minimum amount of margin, just as they must in stock transactions. The maintenance margin for most futures contracts is 75% of the initial margin. A **margin call**, i.e., a call for more cash, will be triggered when the money in an investor's account falls to the level of the maintenance margin as a result of the daily account adjustments.

Stock market transactions are regulated by the Securities and Exchange Commission (SEC), while the futures market is governed by a totally separate organization, the **Commodity Futures Trading Commission (CFTC)**. Exchanges on which futures contracts are traded must obtain approval from the CFTC prior to introducing a new futures contract. Larger traders are required to file periodic reports on their trading activities.

Commissions on futures trading are paid only after a contract is settled—i.e., delivery and payment for the commodity has been made. No brokerage commission is charged when the contract is initiated. Commissions on futures contracts are also smaller as a percentage of the total value of the contract than commissions charged on stock transactions.

? Which of the following is *not* a difference between trading in stocks and trading in futures contracts?
   a. Stocks are traded on exchange floors, but futures contracts are traded only over the counter.
   b. The stock market is regulated by the SEC, while the futures market is regulated by the CFTC.
   c. Stock prices can fluctuate without limits, but a daily limit is placed on price fluctuations for each futures contract.
   d. Commissions on futures contracts are paid only after delivery and payment for the commodity has been made; commissions on stock transactions must be paid at the time the stock is purchased and again when it is sold.

Answer: a.
Both stocks and futures contracts trade on exchange floors.

18.   An example of futures quotations from the *Wall Street Journal* is shown on the following page in Exhibit 2. The exchange on which the futures contract is traded is given in parenthesis beside the name of the commodity on which the futures contract is being traded. Corn futures are traded on the CBT, or Chicago Board of Trade, exchange. Next, the size of one contract is given. One futures contract in corn is an agreement to purchase or sell 5,000 bushels of corn. The last item in bold print designates the units in which the quotes are given.

Corn futures contracts are written for a number of delivery dates. For each delivery date, the price at which the contract opened, the highest price for the day, and the lowest price for the day are presented. The fifth column reports the settlement price which, as previously noted, is the price at which contracts are marked to market daily. The change from the previous day's settlement price is given in the following column. To determine how much one position has to pay the other, multiply this number by the size of the contract (in this case, 5,000 bushels). The last three columns report the highest price at which the contract sold since its introduction, the lowest price at which the contract sold since its introduction, and the **open interest**, which is the number of contracts that remain active—i.e., have not been closed out by investors doing a reversing trade. The open interest is quoted for one day prior to the day of the quotes. For example, Exhibit 2 contains the quotes for Thursday, February 9, 1995; the open interest column is the number of contracts that had not been closed out as of *February 8, 1995.*

The corn contract for September delivery opened at $2.5125 per bushel (251¼ cents per bushel). The highest price at which it sold on February 9, 1995 was $2.5175 and the lowest price was $2.5025. The settlement price was $2.515, and this was unchanged from the previous day's settle price. (Therefore, no accounts needed to be adjusted.) The highest price at which September corn sold since the contract was introduced to the market was $2.705 and the lowest price was $2.38. There were 11,346 contracts that remained outstanding on February 8, 1995.

Exhibit 2

Thursday, February 9, 1995

Open Interest Reflects Previous Trading Day

	Open	High	Low	Settle	Change	Lifetime High	Lifetime Low	Open Interest
GRAINS AND OILSEEDS								
CORN (CBT) 5,000 bu.; cents per bu.								
Mar	232½	234	231½	233¾	....	282½	220½	88,848
May	239¾	242	239½	241½	....	285	228	74,512
July	245½	247¼	244¾	247	+ ¼	285½	232½	71,424
Sept	251¼	251¾	250¼	251½	....	270½	238	11,346
Dec	254	256½	254	256	....	263	235½	56,211
Mr96	261½	262¾	261½	262¼	− ¼	263½	249½	6,299
May	266½	266½	266¼	266½	− ¼	267½	259½	178
July	267½	268¾	267½	268½	− ¼	270	254	3,137
Dec	254½	255½	254½	255	− ¼	258	239	1,661
Est vol 35,000; vol Wed 33,522; open int 313,630, −336.								
OATS (CBT) 5,000 bu.; cents per bu.								
Mar	118½	119¾	118¼	119¼	+ ½	152¾	116½	7,260
May	123¼	125	123¼	124¼	+ ¾	151	122¼	3,794
July	128¼	129½	128¼	129½	+ ¾	142½	127½	2,325
Sept	133	133¾	133	133¾	+ ¾	142½	132	114
Est vol 1,000; vol Wed 1,991; open int 13,573, −49.								
SOYBEANS (CBT) 5,000 bu.; cents per bu.								
Mar	551½	557	550¾	554¼	+ 1½	705	544½	53,317
May	561	566	560	563¾	+ 2	705½	553¼	32,649
July	567½	573	567	571¼	+ 2	706½	559¼	31,052
Aug	570¼	575	570¼	574	+ 1¾	612	562¾	3,747
Sept	572	576	572	575	+ 2½	615	564¾	2,508
Nov	580	584¼	579¾	582½	+ 1¾	645	573¼	17,215
Ja96	588½	592	588½	591	+ 2¼	616	582¾	1,014
July	606	608	606	607½	+ 1	636¼	599½	300
Nov	593	594½	592	594	+ 1¾	611	585	534
Est vol 35,000; vol Wed 24,063; open int 142,406, −1,440.								
SOYBEAN MEAL (CBT) 100 tons; $ per ton.								
Mar	154.90	155.70	154.10	154.40	− .70	207.50	153.50	32,385
May	158.20	159.30	157.60	158.10	− .30	207.00	156.60	23,865
July	162.30	163.50	161.70	162.40	....	206.00	160.30	18,638
Aug	164.30	165.00	163.70	164.50	+ .10	182.60	162.40	6,015
Sept	165.80	166.30	165.80	166.20	....	182.70	164.40	4,148
Oct	167.50	168.40	167.30	167.70	+ .20	181.80	166.20	7,505
Dec	170.70	171.80	170.30	171.00	+ .30	185.20	169.30	8,118
Ja96	172.20	172.80	172.10	172.20	+ .20	185.50	171.00	199
Est vol 14,000; vol Wed 12,191; open int 100,874, +285.								
SOYBEAN OIL (CBT) 60,000 lbs.; cents per lb.								
Mar	26.63	26.94	26.63	26.89	+ .23	28.45	22.91	34,624
May	25.98	26.22	25.95	26.19	+ .22	28.05	22.85	25,042
July	25.53	25.76	25.53	25.74	+ .18	27.85	22.76	16,932
Aug	25.30	25.48	25.30	25.47	+ .16	27.20	22.73	4,597

Source: *The Wall Street Journal*, Volume XCV No. 29, February 10, 1995, p. C14.

? How much did the short positions in March oats have to pay the long positions at the close of the day on February 9, 1995?

Answer: $25.00.

The change in the settlement price is ½ cents ($0.005) per bushel. Multiplying this by 5,000 bushels gives us $25.00.

19. Futures options are option contracts (calls and puts) for which the underlying asset is a futures contract. The owner of a call option has the right to buy a futures contract at a specified price during the exercise period if he chooses to exercise his option; the owner of a put option has the right to sell a futures contract at a specified price during the exercise period. The options expire at the same time as the underlying futures contract. If the owner of a call option chooses to exercise his option, he receives a long position in the futures contract; the investor who exercises a put option assumes a short position in the futures contract. An example of quotes on futures options is shown on the following page. Consider the options on the corn futures. There are six different strike prices ranging from $2.10 per bushel to $2.60 per bushel. The expiration dates are in March, May, and July. An investor can buy a call option on a March futures contract with a $2.40 strike price for $0.04125 per bushel, or $206.25 ($0.04125 × 5,000 = $206.25). If, immediately prior to the March expiration date, corn is selling for $2.38 a bushel, the investor in the call option will let his option expire. If, however, at some point during the exercise period March corn is selling for $2.45 a bushel, the investor could exercise his option, assuming a long position

Exhibit 3

Thursday, February 9, 1995.

AGRICULTURAL

CORN (CBT)
5,000 bu.; cents per bu.

Strike Price	Calls–Settle Mar	May	Jly	Puts–Settle Mar	May	Jly
210	23 3/4	31 1/2	37	1/8	1/8	1/8
220	13 3/4	21 1/2	27	1/8	3/8	7/8
230	4 1/8	12 1/2	18 1/2	1/2	1 1/4	2 1/4
240	1/4	6	12 1/2	6 1/2	4 3/4	5 5/8
250	1/8	2 1/2	8 1/4	16 1/4	11 1/2	11 1/8
260	1/8	7/8	5 1/4	26 1/4	....	18 1/2

Est vol 8,000 Wed 5,357 calls 3,023 puts
Op int Wed 112,540 calls 75,631 puts

SOYBEANS (CBT)
5,000 bu.; cents per bu.

Strike Price	Calls–Settle Mar	May	Jly	Puts–Settle Mar	May	Jly
500	....	....	....	1/8	1/4	7/8
525	29 1/4	39 1/4	48 1/2	1/8	3/4	3 1/4
550	6 5/8	19	29 1/4	2 3/8	5 1/4	9
575	1/8	6 1/4	16 1/4	20 3/4	17 1/2	20 1/2
600	1/8	2	9 1/4	45 3/4	38	38 1/2
625	1/8	3/4	5 7/8	70 3/4	....	59 1/4

Est vol 6,500 Wed 3,495 calls 2,211 puts
Op int Wed 72,946 calls 33,902 puts

SOYBEAN MEAL (CBT)
100 tons; $ per ton

Strike Price	Calls–Settle Mar	May	Jly	Puts–Settle Mar	May	Jly
145	....	....	17.40	....	....	.65
150	4.55	8.60	....	.20	.65	1.05
155	.80	4.90	9.25	1.50	1.75	2.00
160	.15	2.20	6.10	5.65	4.00	3.75
165	.05	1.00	3.80	10.60	7.80	6.40
170	.05	.60	2.50	15.60	12.15	9.85

Est vol 500 Wed 362 calls 108 puts
Op int Wed 11,637 calls 9,047 puts

SOYBEAN OIL (CBT)
60,000 lbs.; cents per lb.

Strike Price	Calls–Settle Mar	May	Jly	Puts–Settle Mar	May	Jly
25	1.900	1.450	1.370	.010	.250	.690
26	.930	.790	.930	.070	.650	1.200
27	.160	.420	.670	.330	1.240	1.900
28	.020	.250	.520	1.130	....	2.710
29	.005	.130	.390	2.120	....	....
30	.005	.080	....	....	....	....

Est vol 750 Wed 593 calls 449 puts
Op int Wed 11,471 calls 15,826 puts

WHEAT (CBT)
5,000 bu.; cents per bu.

Strike Price	Calls–Settle Mar	May	Jly	Puts–Settle Mar	May	Jly
350	19 1/2	17 1/2	9 1/2	1/4	5 1/2	20
360	10 1/2	11 1/2	7	1 1/4	9 1/2	27
370	4 1/4	7 5/8	5 1/4	4 3/4	15 1/4	35
380	1 1/2	5	3 3/4	12	22 1/2	43 1/2
390	3/8	3 1/4	2 3/4	21 1/8	30 3/4	52 1/2
400	1/8	2 1/8	2	30 5/8	39 1/2	61 1/2

Source: *The Wall Street Journal*, Volume XCV No. 29, February 10, 1995, p. C14.

in the futures contract at $2.40 a bushel. He will earn a profit by then selling the futures contract at the current price of $2.45. His gain on the futures contract is $250 ($0.05 × 5,000 bushels), making his net profit from the transaction $43.75 ($250.00 – $206.25 = $43.75).

? How much must an investor pay for a put option on a July corn futures contract with a $2.50 strike price?

Answer: $562.50.

The listing quotes the July corn futures put at 11 1/8 cents per bushel. Multiplying this by 5,000 bushels gives an option premium of $562.50.

Apply It

1. Christy Dupke purchased a March put on IBM stock for $25 at the same time that she purchased the stock for $75 7/8 per share. The put had a strike price of $75. If IBM

increases in price to $80 a share prior to expiration, should Christy exercise her put or let it expire? What is her gain or loss on this transaction? (Frames 2 and 7)

2. Which should cost more—a July put on Texaco with a strike price of $65 or a July call on Texaco with a strike price of $65—if Texaco is currently selling for $62⅞? (Frames 3 and 6)

3. You are expecting airline stock prices to fall in 1996. If you want to capitalize on this gut feeling, what kind of option would you purchase on Delta Airlines? (Frame 4)

4. The writer of a call option is expecting the stock price to move in what direction? (Frame 5)

5. If you are expecting the stock market to increase in 1996, would you buy a put or a call on the S&P 500 index? (Frame 11)

6. In February 1995, a July call on Federal Express stock that had a $65 strike price was selling for $312.50. At the time of expiration of the call, the stock was selling for $63. What was the gain or loss experienced by the writer of this option, assuming he wrote a naked call? (Frame 5)

7. Having read about a recent trade embargo against major oil producing countries, you expect crude oil prices to increase significantly. If you wish to invest in a futures contract based on these expectations, would you buy or sell oil futures? Why? (Frame 15)

8. Is the seller of a put expecting the price of the underlying asset to increase or decrease? (Frame 9)

9. An American exporter is expecting to receive a payment in German marks. The exporter is concerned that the value of the mark will fall relative to the dollar prior to receiving the payment. He would like to hedge his position. How can he use a futures contract to do this? (Frame 14)

10. Roy Blount purchased an April call on Quaker Oats stock for $350. The call had a strike price of $32.50. Immediately prior to expiration, the stock was selling for $38, and Roy sold his option for its intrinsic value. What rate of return did Roy receive? (Frame 4)

11. Assume you own some shares of Texaco and expect its stock price to drop slightly in the near future. You do not want to sell your shares since you want Texaco in your long-term portfolio; furthermore, you do not expect a substantial decline, so it would not be worth all the brokerage fees for you to sell the stock and repurchase it later. Would it be appropriate to sell a call option or a put option on Texaco at this time? (Frame 5)

12. In February 1995, Terry Lewis purchased a July call on Motria stock for $950. The call option had a strike price of $55. Immediately prior to expiration, Motria was selling for $65. Should Terry exercise his option or let it expire? (Frame 1)

13. J.T. Plunkert purchased a March put option on Sybase stock for $600. The option has a $50 strike price. Just prior to expiration, Sybase was selling for $43 a share, and J.T. was able to sell the put for its intrinsic value. What rate of return did J.T. earn on this transaction? (Frame 8)

14. Annette sold a March put on Gap stock for $200. The strike price on the option was $35. Prior to expiration, Gap was selling for $34.00. What was Annette's profit or loss on this transaction? (Frame 9)

15. Refer to Exhibit 4 below to answer the following questions: (Frame 10)

Exhibit 4

71	90	Feb	...	...	42	18 5/8
Compaq	30	Feb	200	5 3/8	...	...
35 3/8	30	Mar	400	5 5/8	12	3/16
35 3/8	30	Apr	27	6 1/4	24	7/16
35 3/8	30	Jul	...	...	77	1 1/16
35 3/8	35	Feb	1273	1	727	5/8
35 3/8	35	Mar	153	1 7/8	1150	1 3/16
35 3/8	35	Apr	998	2 3/4	374	1 7/8
35 3/8	35	Jul	122	4 1/8	231	2 3/4
35 3/8	40	Feb	153	1/16	590	4 5/8
35 3/8	40	Mar	872	5/16	1	4 1/2
35 3/8	40	Apr	748	13/16	46	5 1/8
35 3/8	40	Jul	330	2 1/16	182	5 3/4
35 3/8	45	Mar	130	1/16	...	...
35 3/8	45	Apr	106	1/4	1	9 1/2
35 3/8	45	Jul	59	1	...	...
35 3/8	50	Apr	81	1/16	...	...
CmprsL	7 1/2	Feb	100	1 1/4	30	3/16

Source: *The Wall Street Journal*, Volume XCV No. 27, February 8, 1995, p. C16.

a. For what price can an investor buy an option to sell Compaq stock for $35 a share that expires in July?
b. For what price can an investor buy an option to buy Compaq stock for $45 a share that expires in April?
c. How much will the seller of an April put on Compaq with a $35 strike price receive for the option?

16. Refer to Exhibit 5 below to answer the following questions:
a. If the margin requirement is 10%, how much must an investor in a May coffee futures contract deposit with his broker if he enters the contract at the settlement price listed? (Frames 13 and 18)

Exhibit 5

FOOD AND FIBER

COCOA (CSCE) – 10 metric tons; $ per ton.								
Mar	1,322	1,324	1,308	1,316 –	1	1,605	1,077	20,074
May	1,346	1,352	1,336	1,346	....	1,612	1,111	25,226
July	1,374	1,375	1,361	1,368 –	2	1,600	1,225	10,348
Sept	1,390	1,392	1,383	1,392 +	1	1,611	1,263	3,613
Dec	1,419	1,413	1,401	1,412 +	1	1,633	1,290	4,534
Mr96	1,422	1,422	1,422	1,434 +	1	1,676	1,350	6,576
May		....	....	1,454 +	1	1,642	1,390	4,620
July		....	....	1,469 +	1	1,595	1,410	2,558
Sept		....	....	1,490 +	1	1,549	1,445	1,889
Dec	1,480	1,501	1,489	1,514 +	1	1,572	1,489	490
Est vol 13,411; vol Mon 14,763; open int 79,928, –360.								
COFFEE (CSCE) – 37,500 lbs.; cents per lb.								
Mar	154.80	155.65	153.60	154.00 +	.10	244.00	78.90	13,267
May	156.80	157.50	155.40	155.95 +	.25	244.40	82.50	11,233
July	158.30	158.85	156.60	157.00 –	.20	245.10	85.00	5,510
Sept	159.40	159.50	157.50	157.55 –	.95	238.00	89.00	3,317
Dec	159.75	159.75	157.25	157.25 –	1.00	242.00	151.00	3,399
Mr96	158.00	158.00	158.00	156.25 –	1.00	203.50	151.35	315
Est vol 6,397; vol Mon 8,709; open int 37,100, +1,707.								
SUGAR – WORLD (CSCE) – 112,000 lbs.; cents per lb.								
Mar	13.85	13.96	13.81	13.86 +	.12	15.83	10.56	48,458
May	13.74	13.85	13.73	13.80 +	.10	15.87	10.57	48,067
July	13.00	13.12	13.00	13.05 +	.13	15.21	10.57	33,137
Oct	12.58	12.70	12.58	12.64 +	.11	14.25	10.57	34,029
Mr96	12.26	12.38	12.26	12.32 +	.08	13.39	10.88	9,551
May	12.27	12.27	12.27	12.26 +	.09	13.25	11.56	2,358
July		....	....	12.08	....	12.91	11.75	2,269
Oct	11.85	11.85	11.85	11.88 +	.05	12.50	11.85	457
Est vol 30,355; vol Mon 45,224; open int 178,326, +2,675.								
SUGAR – DOMESTIC (CSCE) – 112,000 lbs.; cents per lb.								
Mar	22.67	22.67	22.50	22.59 –	.05	22.80	21.60	1,117
May	22.72	22.72	22.67	22.71 –	.01	22.77	21.81	4,329

Source: *The Wall Street Journal*, Volume XCV No. 27, February 8, 1995, p. C14.

b. What is the maintenance margin that an investor in the May coffee futures contract must keep if it is equal to 75% of the initial margin? (Frames 17 and 18)

c. How much did investors who were short in March 96 sugar pay the long positions at the conclusion of the day of the quotes? (Frames 13 and 18)

17. In January, Hannah Sisernos purchased a March put futures option on wheat. The option had a strike price of $3.70 per bushel. Each futures contract is for 5,000 bushels. In February, March wheat was selling for $3.65 per bushel, and Hannah decided to exercise her option. What is her profit on this transaction? (Frame 19)

Apply It Answers

1. Christy should let her option expire. The put option gives her the right to sell IBM stock for $75 a share. If she sells it on the open market, she can get $80 a share for it. She will have a gain of $387.50 on the transaction, calculated as follows:

Sell 100 shares of IBM @ $80	$ 8,000.00
Price paid for 100 shares of IBM	−$ 7,587.50
Price paid for option	−$ 25.00
Net gain	$ 387.50

2. The put should cost more since it is an "in the money" put with an intrinsic value of $212.50 [($65.00 − $62.875) × 100]. The call is "out of the money" and has an intrinsic value of zero since the strike price on the option is greater than the current market price of Texaco. The time value for both options is the same since both expire in July.

3. You should purchase a put option on Delta Airlines. If the market price of the stock falls as you expect, the strike price on the option should be greater than the price of the stock. You can then sell the put for its intrinsic value, at a minimum.

4. The writer of a call is expecting the price of the stock to decrease. If the price falls, the option holder will not exercise his option to buy the stock at a higher price, and the writer keeps the option premium.

5. If you are expecting the stock market to increase in 1996, you should buy a call on the S&P 500 Index. As the value of the index rises above the strike price on the call, the call option becomes more valuable.

6. Since the call option had a $65 strike price and the stock was selling for $63 when the option expired, the option holder will not exercise the option. The writer's gain will be the $312.50 he received as the option premium.

7. You should buy (take a long position in) oil futures. When prices increase, the long positions get paid.

8. The seller of a put option is expecting the price of the underlying asset to increase. If this occurs, the put holder will not exercise his option. He will, instead, sell his stock at the market price, and the option seller keeps his option premium.

9. He should take a short position in deutschemark futures. If the mark does fall relative to the dollar, he will have locked in a higher exchange rate that he will be able to get when he receives the payment.

10. Roy's dollar gain is $200, as calculated below:

Price paid for option	−$350
Intrinsic value of call	$550 [($38.00 − $32.50) × 100]
Net gain	$200

This is a rate of return of 57% ($200/$350 = 57%).

11. You should sell a call option in this situation. If the price does fall as you anticipate, the option holder will let the call expire rather than force you to sell him the stock for a higher price. The option premium received will help to offset losses received from the decline in the stock value.

12. If Terry exercises his option, he can purchase 100 shares of Motria stock for $55 a share. Since Motria is currently selling for $65 a share, Terry can buy it at a substantial discount. He should exercise his option.

13. J.T.'s dollar gain is $100, as calculated below:

Price paid for the option	−$600
Intrinsic value of the put	$700 [($50 − $43) × 100]
Net gain	$100

This is a rate of return of $16\frac{2}{3}$% ($100/$600 = $16\frac{2}{3}$%).

14. Since Gap was selling for less than the strike price of $35 prior to expiration, the put holder will exercise his put, forcing Annette to purchase 100 shares of Gap at $35 a share. Annette can turn around and sell the shares in the open market for $34 a share. Her net profit is $100, calculated as follows:

Payment received for writing the put	$ 200
Price she must pay for the stock	−$3,500
Price at which she can sell the stock	$3,400
Net profit	$ 100

(This does, of course, ignore all commissions.)

15. a. $275. An option to sell Compaq is a put option. The July put listed with a $35 strike price has an option premium of 2\frac{3}{4}$ per option share, so the option will cost $275 ($2.75 × 100).

 b. $25. An option to buy Compaq is a call option. The April call listed with a $45 strike price is selling for $$\frac{1}{4}$ per option share, so the option will cost $25 ($0.25 × 100).

 c. $187.50. The seller of the put receives the option premium. The option premium reported for the April put that has a $35 strike price is 1\frac{7}{8}$ per option share, or $187.50 for the option contract ($1.875 × 100).

16. a. $5,848.125. Based on the settlement price, the value of the contract is $58,481.25 ($1.5595 × 37,500 pounds). The required margin is 10% of this, and 0.10 × $58,481.25 = $5,848.125.

 b. The maintenance margin is 75% of $5,848.125, which is $4,386.09.

 c. $89.60. The change in the settlement price from the previous day is 0.08 cents per bushel (column 6). Since this is an increase, short positions must pay the long positions $0.0008 × 112,000 pounds = $89.60.

17. $250. Since the option has a strike price that is greater than the current market price, the intrinsic value of the put is $0.05 per bushel ($3.70 − $3.65). The futures position is for 5,000 bushels, so $0.05 × 5,000 = $250. This is Hannah's net profit if she exercises her option and does a reversing trade to close out her futures position.

SECURITY MARKETS, REGULATION, AND MARKET INDICATORS

This module provides an introduction to the terminology and logistics involved in securities trading. Both the market for new issues and the market for existing issues are discussed. Players, arenas, transaction types, and market regulations are introduced. Market indicators and their usefulness are also addressed.

Equations introduced in this module

$$\text{Margin} = \frac{\text{investor's equity}}{\text{total value of portfolio}}$$

$$\text{Net profit} = \text{selling price} - \text{purchase price} - \text{interest expense}$$

$$\text{DJIA} = \frac{\sum_{i=1}^{30} \text{price}_i}{\text{adjusted divisor}}$$

$$\text{S \& P 500 Index} = \frac{\sum_{i=1}^{500} (\text{price}_i \times \text{shares outstanding}_i)_{\text{today}}}{\sum_{i=1}^{500} (\text{price}_i \times \text{shares outstanding}_i)_{\text{base period}}} \times 10$$

1.   Securities markets can be divided into two principal groups, the **primary market** and the **secondary market**. The primary market is the market for new issues while the secondary market is the market for existing issues that are being traded among investors. A new issue of common stock, a new Treasury bill sold at a Monday auction, and a new 15-year corporate bond are all examples of primary market instruments. Shares of common stock that have previously been owned by another investor, a 3-month Treasury bill with 1 month remaining to maturity, and a 15-year corporate bond that has 5 years left to maturity are examples of secondary market instruments.

We can further divide both the primary market and the secondary market into subgroups. The **stock market** is the market for equity issues, i.e., preferred and common stock, while the **bond market** is the market for debt issues. The **capital market** refers to the market for long-term securities, i.e., securities that have greater than 1 year to maturity, and the **money market** is the market for securities that have less than or equal to 1 year to maturity. A 5-year note, a 10-year bond, and preferred and common stock are all capital market instruments. Commercial paper and Treasury bills are examples of money market instruments.

? A new issue of common stock can be classified in which of the following two categories?
   a. the primary market and the money market
   b. the secondary market and the stock market
   c. the secondary market and the capital market
   d. the primary market and the capital market

Answer: d.
Since it is a new issue, it is classified as a primary market transaction. Because common stock has no maturity, it is a long-term security and, therefore, will trade in the capital markets.

2.   Investment bankers are players in the primary market. A firm that wishes to issue a new security may negotiate terms with an investment banking firm. (The firm may or may not already be publicly held. If a firm is selling its stock to the public for the first time, the issue is referred to as an **initial public offering** or an **IPO**.) The investment banker can advise the firm on the size and timing of the issue as well as on the type of security that the market might best accept at that particular time. The investment banker also handles all of the red tape involved in issuing the new security. This includes filing a **registration statement** with the Securities and Exchange Commission. A registration statement contains the financial statements of the firm and other information that allows an investor to judge the quality of the issue. The investment banker is obligated to practice **due diligence**, which means that it must verify the information that the issuing firm provides in its registration statement, even to the extent of investigating the issuing firm's corporate charter, past financial statements, corporate minutes, patents, and customers. A 20-day cooling period during which the securities can be neither advertised nor sold follows the filing of the registration statement.

The **prospectus**, an abbreviated registration statement, must be given to prospective investors when the security is offered for sale. SEC approval of an issue does *not* mean that the security is a sound investment; it means only that a rational investor has been provided with enough information to judge the quality of the issue for himself.

A registration statement is not required for all new securities; some issues are exempt from registration requirements. These include government securities, securities offered by government-regulated agencies, issues that are sold to investors who live in only one state (**intrastate offerings**), short-term securities that have less than 270 days to maturity, and issues that are less than $1.5 million in face value. (The latter are exempt under Regulation A of the Securities Act of 1933, and are called "Reg A" issues. They require a simpler "offering circular" rather than a full-blown prospectus.)

? Which of the following securities is exempt from the SEC registration requirements?
a. a new issue of common stock for Texaco
b. a bond issued by the state of Colorado
c. a bond issued by IBM
d. an issue of preferred stock that has a par value of $2 million

Answer: b.
A bond issued by a government body need not be registered with the SEC.

3. The investment banking firm may **underwrite** the issue for the firm. This means that the investment banker purchases the issue from the issuing firm and resells the issue to the public. The issuing firm receives its money up front, and the investment banker bears the risk if the security has been incorrectly priced or if market forces effect an adverse price change between the time that the investment banker purchases the issue and the time that it resells the issue to the public. The investment banker's profits come from the **underwriting spread**, which is the difference between what it has paid the issuing firm for the securities and the price that it can receive for the securities when it resells them to the public.

In most cases, the underwriting is a **negotiated underwriting**, which means that the issuing firm approaches one investment banking firm and the terms of the issue are settled between them. Other times, the underwriting may be **competitive**. In this situation, the issuing firm announces to the investment banking industry that it plans to issue so much of a certain type of security and asks for bids from interested investment bankers. Some government regulated firms, such as public utility firms, are required to engage only in competitive underwriting agreements.

If an issue is deemed too risky, investment banking firms may be unwilling to underwrite the issue. Alternatively, the investment banker might offer to enter a **best efforts agreement** with the issuing firm. Under this type of agreement, the investment banker merely acts as a matchmaker for the securities. The investment banker does not purchase the issue from the issuing firm, but instead agrees to do its *very best* to sell the issue for the firm. In return, the investment banker receives a fee for its services. Any securities that do not sell are simply returned to the issuing firm. Because a best efforts agreement can sometimes leave the issuing firm worse off than before if the entire issue does not sell, the firm and the investment banker may agree to a best efforts, **all-or-nothing commitment**. If this is the agreement, the securities will not be issued unless the entire issue sells. The prospectus will warn investors that the issue will be withdrawn if it is not fully subscribed to within so many days (say, 30 days).

? The investment banking firm bears the risk if the securities do not sell in a(n)
a. underwriting agreement.
b. best efforts agreement.
c. all-or-nothing commitment.
d. None of the above; the investment banking firm is never exposed to risk.

Answer: a.
In an underwriting agreement, the investment banking firm actually purchases the issue from the issuing firm and is fully exposed to any risk associated with the issue.

4. In a negotiated underwriting agreement, the investment banking firm that negotiates the terms with the issuing firm is often referred to as the **lead underwriter** or the

managing house. The lead underwriter will then typically contact other investment bankers and form an **underwriting syndicate**. Each investment banker in the syndicate purchases a portion of the issue. In this way, no single investment banking firm has a large cash flow drain, and the risk is spread among many investment bankers if the issue fails to sell at the set price. For example, an issue may be for $10 million. A $10 million cash outflow would be difficult for a single investment banker to handle, but if this amount is divided equally among 25 investment bankers, each firm needs to come up with only $400,000 cash. As a second example, consider the effect of an unexpected increase in interest rates on the price of a new bond issue. When interest rates increase, bond prices fall. There have been instances in which an issue was sold to the public at a loss of several hundred thousands of dollars. If an issue lost, say, $600,000 due to this phenomenon and there were 25 underwriting firms, each firm would lose only $24,000.

Each member of the underwriting syndicate will contact other investment bankers, brokers, and dealers to help it sell the issue. This becomes known as the **selling group**. The members of the selling group who do not belong to the underwriting syndicate receive a commission for the part of the issue that they sell to the public. The sale cannot take place until the SEC has approved of the registration statement and the 20-day cooling period has passed. While the securities cannot even be advertised for sale during this period, the underwriters are allowed to circulate what is referred to as a **red herring prospectus** in an effort to gauge investor interest. This is an incomplete, preliminary prospectus that has not been approved by the SEC, a fact which must be prominently stated on the front cover of the prospectus in red ink, hence the term "red herring." It is not until a few days before the end of the cooling period that the public offering price is actually set. Since the investment bankers will suffer losses if they are unable to sell the issue for the expected price, the bankers wait until the last minute in order to have more complete knowledge of the economic conditions at the time that the securities are introduced to the market.

? Which of the following steps in the underwriting process will occur last?
a. An underwriting syndicate is formed.
b. The selling group is organized.
c. The public offering price is set.
d. A red herring prospectus is circulated to the public.

Answer: c.
The underwriters will wait until the very last minute to set the public offering price so that they have the most current information when doing so.

5. Once a new issue is entirely sold, it can be sold among investors in the secondary market. Brokers and dealers are the major players in this market. There is a fine distinction between the two. A **broker** is simply a matchmaker. He matches buyers and sellers and receives a commission for doing so. A **dealer**, on the other hand, buys and sells securities out of his own inventory. He earns the **dealer's spread**, which is the difference between the price at which he will sell a security (the **ask price**) and the price at which he will buy the security (the **bid price**). Since he actually owns the securities, he also earns interest and dividend income on his portfolio. Sometimes a broker may act as a dealer in a particular transaction; that is, he may be selling a client a security that he owns, or he may be purchasing the security for himself. If such is the case, he must inform his client of the situation.

? Which is exposed to more risk—a broker or a dealer?

Answer: A dealer.
Because the dealer actually owns the securities, he will suffer if the securities lose value. The broker stands to lose only a commission if he cannot sell the securities.

6.   Secondary market transactions take place in one of two general types of arenas—organized exchange floors or the over-the-counter market. In the United States, there are two major organized exchanges, the New York Stock Exchange (NYSE) and the American Stock Exchange (AMEX). The New York Stock Exchange, founded in 1817, is the larger of the two and lists larger, sounder firms. The American Stock Exchange is a newer exchange, founded in 1910 as the New York Curb Market Association (its current name was adopted in 1953), and has been more innovative in its listing of securities. It listed foreign securities, warrants, and options well before the New York Stock Exchange. Most of the firms listed on the AMEX are smaller and younger than those listed on the NYSE, and AMEX has tended to emphasize foreign securities, with these securities constituting about 15% of the total volume of the trading done on the AMEX. Although firms may elect to be listed on both major exchanges, none do. Firms must pay a fee to be listed on an exchange, and since the majority of the trading takes place on the New York Stock Exchange, firms that can meet its listing requirements find that it is not worth it to be listed on both exchanges.

In addition to the two major exchanges, there are seven dominant regional exchanges—the Midwest Stock Exchange (Chicago), the Pacific Stock Exchange (San Francisco), the Philadelphia Exchange, the Boston Stock Exchange, the Spokane Stock Exchange, the Honolulu Stock Exchange, and the Intermountain Stock Exchange (Salt Lake City). The three largest regional exchanges, the Midwest, the Pacific, and the Philadelphia, account for approximately 90% of the trading volume that is conducted on all the regional exchanges. Regional exchanges exist for two basic reasons: (1) to provide firms that cannot meet the listing requirements of either of the two major exchanges a floor on which their securities can trade, and (2) to provide brokers who cannot afford a seat on a major exchange a place to conduct trades. Most of the trading done on the regional exchanges consists of **dual listings**, i.e., stocks that are also listed on one of the two major exchanges. For example, General Motors is listed on the NYSE as well as on several of the regional exchanges.

❓ Which of the following statements about regional exchanges is true?
  a. Unlike trades on the major exchanges, trades on the regional exchanges are negotiated, rather than done by auction.
  b. Most of the trading done on regional exchanges is in stocks that are also traded on a major exchange.
  c. Most of the trading done on regional exchanges is in foreign securities.
  d. Brokers do not need to own a seat to conduct a trade on a regional exchange.

Answer: b.
One of the two major reasons that regional exchanges exist is so that brokers who cannot afford a seat on a major exchange can conduct trades, and most of the volume of trading on regional exchanges consists of dual listings.

7.   All organized exchanges have some characteristics in common. First, they provide a central marketplace on which trades are conducted. These trades are done by auction. The auctioneer is the **specialist** who is a member of the exchange and has applied to the exchange to become a dealer in assigned stocks. Most specialists belong to a specialist unit that shares the workload and the risk of the stocks assigned to the unit. The specialist must buy and sell stocks out of his own inventory when the supply and demand for the stock will not provide for a continuous market in the assigned stocks. When a broker receives an order to buy or sell a stock from a client, he relays the order to the exchange floor and a **commission broker**, who is employed by the broker's firm, proceeds to the specialist unit in that stock to complete the trade. Technological innovations have helped with increasing trading volume. For example, **Super Dot** is an electronic order-routing system that allows a firm that is a member of the NYSE to transmit an order directly to the specialist unit at which the security is traded or to the member firm's booth. After the order is filled, a report is returned directly to the office that placed the order over the same system.

Member firms are firms that own seats on the exchange. Only firms that own seats on an exchange can conduct trades on that exchange. Each exchange has a limited number of seats available (the NYSE has 1,366 seats), and the price of the seats is set by supply and demand. Seats on the NYSE have at times sold for over $1 million, but seats on the regional exchanges are much cheaper.

Each exchange also has a set of listing requirements. Only firms that meet these requirements can have their shares traded on that exchange. These requirements involve the amount of pretax income, the number of publicly held shares, the market value of the shares, the minimum number of shareholders, and the value of the net tangible assets that the firm has. The NYSE has the most stringent listing requirements of all of the organized exchanges. A listed firm that falls short of the listing requirements of the exchange on which it is traded at some future point in time can be delisted.

? ABC Brokers owns a seat on the American Stock Exchange. Can it conduct a trade on the New York Stock Exchange?

Answer: No.
In order to conduct a trade on an exchange, a firm must own a seat on that exchange.

8. Unlike the organized exchanges, the over-the-counter market (OTC) does not consist of a central marketplace. Instead, it is composed of geographically dispersed security dealers who enter bid and ask prices and are linked via a sophisticated computerized network. Securities that are not traded on an organized exchange are traded OTC. In addition, even securities that are listed on an exchange can be traded in the OTC market. This is known as the **third market**.

Because there is no central marketplace, the OTC market is not an auction market; instead, it is referred to as a negotiated market. Theoretically, at least, the investor can negotiate the price with the dealer who is making a market in the security. One of the computerized quotation systems on which security dealers enter their bid and ask quotes is **NASDAQ (The National Association of Securities Dealers Automated Quotation System)**. The most actively traded OTC stocks make up NASDAQ's **National Market Issues**. The OTC has the largest number of equity issues traded although the NYSE still dominates it in the total market value of the trading that is conducted. The OTC market is not limited to stocks. All types of securities, including bonds, warrants, and options are traded over-the-counter. In fact, *most* corporate bonds and *all* government bonds are traded only in the OTC market.

There are no listing requirements for the OTC market. Technically, a security can be traded as long as two investors are willing to make a market in it. There are, however, listing requirements for a security to be traded over the NASDAQ system. No seat need be purchased in order to conduct a trade in the over-the-counter market. Anyone wishing to make a market in a security can do so. However, dealers who wish to enter bid and ask quotes on the NASDAQ system must subscribe to the system, and they must pass tests before they can do so.

? Which of the following statements regarding the over-the-counter market is true?
a. Only penny stocks are traded over-the-counter.
b. The OTC market trades are conducted via an auction process.
c. Only bonds and other debt instruments are traded over-the-counter.
d. Stocks that are listed on exchange floors are also traded in the OTC market.

Answer: d.
The third market is defined as over-the-counter trading of listed stocks.

9.   Regardless of whether the security is listed on a major exchange, a regional exchange, or is traded exclusively over-the-counter, to conduct a trade, an investor simply has to call a broker and place an order to buy or sell a specific security. The most common type of order is a **market order**, which is an order to buy or sell the security at the prevailing price. If the investor wishes instead to specify a maximum price at which she is willing to purchase the stock or a minimum price at which she is willing to sell the stock, she will place a **limit order**. If no one is willing to buy or sell at the prespecified price or better, the investor's broker will leave the order with the specialist who will fill the order when and if the stock hits that price. The investor may specify a time period during which she wishes the limit order to remain on the books. For example, a **good until cancelled (GTC)** order is theoretically left on the books indefinitely. (In reality, the limit orders are cleared from the books periodically, and the investor would have to actively request that the order remain on past the clean-up period.) If a time limit is not specified, the order is considered to be a **day order**, and it is cancelled at the end of the trading day.

   Orders can be of different sizes. A **round lot** for most stocks consists of 100 shares, so an order to buy or sell 300 shares would be an order to buy or sell 3 round lots. An **odd lot** is an order for less than 100 shares. Institutional traders deal in **block trades**, which is a trade consisting of 10,000 or more shares.

[?] An order to buy or sell at the prevailing price is called a _____ order.

Answer: market.
This is the definition of a market order.

10.   Another type of order that an investor can place is called a **short sale**. This is an order to sell stock that the investor *does not own*. The investor's broker borrows the stock out of another client's portfolio and sells it, depositing the proceeds from the sale in the short seller's account (along with a good-faith deposit that is required of the short seller) until the short seller covers her position (i.e., buys the stock on the open market and returns it to the lender). The short seller is betting that the stock will drop in value. To illustrate, if an investor short sells 100 shares of GAP stock at $35 a share, the broker will deposit the $3,500 proceeds in the investor's account along with the short seller's good-faith deposit of say, $1,800. If the short seller is right in believing that GAP will drop in value, she can buy the stock back at a lower price and return. For instance, if GAP drops to $30 a share, the short seller will pay $3,000 for 100 shares. Her gross profit will then be $500. (We are ignoring commissions and earnings that could have been made on the $1,800 good-faith deposit, which will earn no interest.) This is a return of 27.8% ($500/$1,800). On the other hand, if GAP does not drop in value, but instead increases in price, the short seller may be forced to purchase the stock at a higher price in order to return it and cut her losses. If GAP increases in value too much, the broker will do a margin call, meaning that he will contact the investor and require that she deposit more good faith money into her account if she wishes to keep her short position open. While there is no time limit to how long a short position may be kept open, the short seller is responsible for any dividends that are paid during the period. In addition, no interest is earned on the proceeds from the sale or the good-faith deposit, so the short seller has an opportunity loss as long as the short position remains uncovered.

[?] Jack Thomas short sold 100 shares of IBM stock at $70 a share. He was required to deposit a margin of $3,500 with his broker when he entered the short position. Jack covered his position when IBM fell to $63 a share. Ignoring commissions and opportunity losses, what was his gain on this transaction and what rate of return did he earn?

Answers: $700, 20%.
Jack received $7,000 in his account when he sold the shares. He was able to repurchase

the shares for $6,300, giving him a gain of $700. His investment was the $3,500 that he deposited with his broker, so the return on that investment is $700/$3,500 = 20%.

11. Investors can borrow part of their investment money. This is known as a **margin transaction**. The **margin** refers to the amount of cash (or near-cash assets) that the investor must have on deposit with his broker. The initial margin requirement is set by the Board of Governors of the Federal Reserve System. It is currently 50% in 1995, which means that investors can borrow up to 50% of their investment funds. Brokerage firms may require a higher initial margin, but they may *not* require less than 50%.

$$\text{margin} = \frac{\text{investor's equity}}{\text{total value of portfolio}}$$

Suppose Mario's broker requires a 60% initial margin and Mario wants to invest in a portfolio that has a total value of $30,000. Then Mario will have to deposit $18,000 with his broker, borrowing the remaining $12,000 from him. This can be calculated as follows:

$$\frac{\text{investor's equity}}{\$30,000} = 0.60$$

$$\text{investor's equity} = 0.60(\$30,000) = \$18,000.$$

? Ann Marie wishes to invest in 100 shares of a stock that is selling for $60 a share. If her broker requires a 55% initial margin, how much cash must Ann Marie put up?

Answer: $3,300.

The total value of Ann Marie's portfolio is $60 × 100 = $6,000. She will need to deposit 55% of this with her broker, and 0.55 × $6,000 = $3,300.

12. If the value of the portfolio falls after the investor has purchased it, his equity position is eroded. The equity position is allowed to drop only to the point of the **maintenance margin**, which is set by the exchange floors. (In 1995, the NYSE maintenance margin requirement is 25%, but brokerage firms may require more than this.) If the equity position falls below the maintenance margin, a **margin call** is triggered. The broker calls the investor and requests that he deposit additional money. If the investor neglects to do so, the broker will sell the portfolio in order to pay off the loan that was made to the investor.

If Mario's $30,000 portfolio falls in value to $16,000 and his broker requires a maintenance margin of 35%, Mario will get a margin call. Note that the portfolio has lost $14,000 in value ($30,000 − $16,000), which means that Mario has only $4,000 left in equity ($18,000 − $14,000 = $4,000). This is only 25% of the total value of his portfolio ($4,000/$16,000). His equity needs to be 35% of the portfolio value, or $5,600 (0.35 × $16,000 = $5,600). Since he still has $4,000 on deposit with his broker, his margin call will be for $1,600 ($5,600 − $4,000). If he fails to deposit this additional amount, his broker will sell his portfolio, using the proceeds to repay the $12,000 loan plus interest.

? Ann Marie's broker has a maintenance margin requirement of 25%. If Ann Marie's portfolio loses $2,500, will she get a margin call? If so, for how much?

Answers: Yes, for $75.

If the portfolio loses $2,500, the total value of the portfolio is now only $3,500($6,000 − $2,500). Ann Marie's equity has dropped by this amount to $800 ($3,300 − $2,500). She currently has only 22.8% in equity ($800/$3,500 = 22.8%). She is required to have 25% of the total value of the portfolio or $875 (0.25 × $3,500). Therefore, she must deposit an additional $75 with her broker.

13. Investors can use margin transactions to earn a much higher return on their own money than is otherwise possible, but they can also lose much more than had they invested only their available cash. Suppose Erin Irish has $10,000 to invest in a stock that is selling for $50 a share and the initial margin requirement is 50%. Erin can borrow an additional $10,000 from her broker and invest $20,000. If she does so, she can purchase 400 shares of the stock; if she uses only her available cash, Erin can purchase only 200 shares.

Suppose her broker charges 10% on borrowed funds. If the shares double in value to $100 a share, Erin's net profit on 400 shares can be calculated as follows:

$$\text{net profit} = 400(\$100) - 400(\$50) - 0.10(\$10,000) = \$19,000.$$

This is a rate of return on her investment of 190% ($19,000/$10,000). If Erin had *not* borrowed any money and had purchased only 200 shares, her net profit would be $10,000.

$$\text{net profit} = 200(\$100) - 200(\$50) = \$10,000$$

This is a rate of return of only 100% ($10,000/$10,000).

On the other hand, if the shares had dropped in value to $25 a share and Erin had used the available margin to buy 400 shares, her net loss is $11,000.

$$\text{net loss} = 400(\$25) - 400(\$50) - 0.10(\$10,000) = -\$11,000$$

This is a return on her investment of −110% (−$11,000/$10,000). Had she used only her available cash to invest her loss would be $5,000.

$$\text{net loss} = 200(\$25) - 200(\$50) = -\$5,000$$

This is a return on her investment of −50% (−$5,000/$10,000).

? Sam Deutsch's broker has an initial margin requirement of 60%. Sam purchased 500 shares of a $30 stock using all the margin available to him. Subsequently, the shares increased in value to $40 a share. If his broker charged 8% interest, what was Sam's net profit on the transaction, and what was his rate of return?

Answers: $4,520, 50.2%.

The total value of Sam's portfolio is 500($30) = $15,000. Since the initial margin requirement is 60%, Sam must deposit $9,000 with his broker (0.60 × $15,000) and can borrow the remaining $6,000 from him. The interest on $6,000 at 8% is $480(0.08 × $6,000). His net profit is 500($40) − 500($30) − $480 = $4,520. Sam's investment is $9,000, so the return on his investment is $4,520/$9,000 = 50.2%.

14. After the 1929 stock market crash, the U.S. government instituted a number of regulations for the securities industry. The first of these was the **Securities Act of 1933**. This act focuses on the primary market and requires full and fair disclosure of information regarding new security issues in an attempt to prevent fraud. It is this act that instituted the registration requirements previously mentioned. All securities except those that are exempt must file a registration statement with the SEC before they can be offered for sale or delivered after sale either through the mail or interstate commerce. Exempt securities include private offerings, U.S. government securities, municipal securities, securities issued by carriers that are regulated by the Interstate Commerce Commission, and securities issued by nonprofit organizations. The 1933 act also requires that the prospectus must be supplied to prospective investors prior to or with any solicitation of an order for individual securities or for mutual fund shares.

Sections 11 and 12 of the Securities Act of 1933 specify penalties for failure to carry out the provisions of the act. Any broker, dealer, or representative who offers to sell or who sells a security in violation of the registration or prospectus requirements or who engages in fraud in order to sell a security can be held civilly liable for damages. Section 17 of the act provides for criminal liability in the event that fraud exists. Furthermore, the antifraud provisions apply to securities that are exempt from SEC registration as well as to registered securities.

? Carolyn is a registered representative with a well-known family of mutual funds. In selling one of the funds, Carolyn forgets to give her buyer a prospectus on the fund. Which of the following statements is true?
   a. Carolyn can be held civilly liable under the Securities Act of 1933.
   b. Since there was no attempt on her part to defraud her client, Carolyn would not be subject to any penalty.
   c. Carolyn can be held criminally liable under the Securities Act of 1933.
   d. Since mutual funds are not covered under the Securities Act of 1933, there is no liability in this case.

Answer: a.
The sale of mutual fund shares falls under the Securities Act of 1933, and Carolyn is liable for failing to carry out the provisions of the act. Since Carolyn merely forgot to give her buyer a prospectus and was not engaging in fraudulent activity, she would be only civilly liable.

15.   The Securities Act of 1933 empowered the SEC to make rules and regulations in order to implement the provisions of the law. One such rule is **Rule 134**, which establishes the rules for **tombstone advertisements**. These ads are not considered a prospectus. The content of the ad is limited to the name of the issuer, the title of the security and the amount offered, a brief indication of the type of business in which the issuing firm is engaged, and the name and address of a place where a prospectus can be obtained. Advertisements conforming to these specifications need not be accompanied by a prospectus.

Rule 135A is similar to Rule 134 and applies to investment companies. Essentially this rule states that advertisements that do not specifically refer by name to the securities held by a particular investment company, to the investment, or to any nonexempt security will not be considered an offer to sell and, therefore, need not be accompanied by a prospectus. **Rule 156** also applies to investment companies. It establishes guidelines for the sales literature of these companies. It makes it unlawful to use any sales literature that is materially misleading, i.e., which contains an untrue statment or an omission of a material fact. The rule further stipulates that a statement can be considered misleading due to a lack of necessary explanations, qualifications or limitations, due to the way in which past or future investment performance is represented, or due to the way in which an investment company or its management is represented. Sales literature is defined by the rule to include any communication, whether in writing, or on radio or television.

? Which of the following would not be included in a tombstone advertisement?
   a. the name of the issuer
   b. the name and address of a place where a prospectus can be obtained
   c. the title of the security
   d. the expected return on the security

Answer: d.
The information supplied in a tombstone advertisement is limited to the name of the issuer, the title of the security and amount offered, the general type of business of the issuer, and the name and address where a prospectus can be obtained.

16.   The **Securities Exchange Act of 1934** regulates the secondary market activities. It established rules for the operation of the exchange floors and the over-the-counter markets. This act established the **Securities and Exchange Commission (SEC)**, which is composed of five members appointed by the president of the United States with Senate approval. (Prior to the establishment of the SEC, the provisions of the 1933 Act were administered by the Federal Trade Commission.) Once established, the SEC was given the responsibility of administering all of the federal securities laws.

The 1934 Act prohibits fraudulent and manipulative practices in the sale of existing securities. Creating misleading impressions for the purpose of price manipulation, making misleading statements about a security, and price-fixing are violations of this act. False impressions regarding the trading activity of a security are sometimes done through a **wash sale**, wherein one individual purchases and sells the same stock at approximately the same time, or through a **matched order**, which is a transaction that does not involve a true ownership change. Both of these practices are illegal.

Section 13 of the 1934 Act requires that the issuing firm send copies of an annual report to its investors before an annual meeting at which directors are to be elected. The report must include financial statements for the past 2 years (only *one* is required of investment companies). Section 15 deals with registration requirements and provides for the registration of both the securities exchanges and the securities listed on the exchanges. It also requires that any broker or dealer who uses mail or interstate commerce for any transaction in a security other than on a national securities exchange be registered with the SEC. Since December 1983, all brokers and dealers are required to be members of a national securities association. Practically speaking, this means the broker or dealer must be a member of the **National Association of Securities Dealers (NASD)**, the only national securities association registered with the SEC to date.

Section 17 of the Act requires that brokers and dealers keep certain records. For one, personnel files for each registered representative must be kept. These files must contain information regarding the representative's employment history, education, arrest record, disciplinary action, etc. The SEC examiner can demand access to the required records. Failure to keep the requisite records can result in the revocation of registration.

Directors, officers, and the principal stockholders of a corporation are referred to as insiders, and the 1934 Securities Exchange Act has special requirements and prohibitions regarding this group. Each insider must file a report with the SEC indicating his holdings in the corporation and must file additional reports any time he buys or sells his corporation's securities. Insiders are prohibited from engaging in certain trading activities involving their company, such as short sales. These rules have been established to protect the investor who is not privy to the private information available to this select group from losing money due to insider trading activity.

The **Maloney Act of 1938** is an amendment to the Securities Exchange Act of 1934. It provides for SEC registration of national securities associations and for the establishment of standards for such organizations. As previously mentioned, the National Association of Securities Dealers is registered under this act.

? Since 1983, all brokers and dealers

a. must be members of an organized exchange.
b. must be members of NASD.
c. must report all of their personal trading activity to the SEC.
d. None of the above are requirements.

Answer: b.
Since December 1983, all brokers and dealers must belong to a registered national securities association, and NASD is the only registered association.

17. The **Investment Company Act of 1940** provides for the registration and regulation of investment companies. These companies must be registered with the SEC. The definition of an investment company is given as any issuer "engaged primarily. . .in the business of investing, reinvesting or trading in securities." Any company that holds investment securities that have a value of greater than 40% of the company's total assets is an investment company. An investment company must also have more than 100 shareholders.

The 1940 Act requires that no more than 60% of the members of the board of directors of an investment company can be "interested persons." Interested persons are defined to include officers, employees, and investment advisors of the company, any interested person of the investment advisor, any person who has acted as a counsel for the company within the last 2 fiscal years, and any broker or dealer who is registered with the SEC. In addition, a majority of the board of directors may not have a direct connection with a regular broker of the company or its principal underwriter, be investment bankers, or be directors or officers of a bank.

Under Section 12 of the Investment Company Act, registered investment companies are prohibited from purchasing any security on margin or engaging in a short sale of any security in violation of SEC rules or regulations. However, at present there are no SEC laws that prohibit investment companies from engaging in these transactions, so many companies do.

The investment policies of an investment company must be stated in its registration statement and its prospectus. The 1940 Act requires that a majority vote of the shareholders be obtained before the investment policies can be changed. The public offering price of investment company securities is set forth in the prospectus, and this price must be maintained in transactions between dealers and customers. In other words, a dealer cannot discount the public offering price in an effort to stimulate sales; nor can he arbitrarily increase the offering price of a fund that is selling well.

A registered investment company must also have a net worth of at least $100,000 before it can make a public offering of securities. Open-end investment companies (mutual funds) are prohibited from issuing bonds and preferred stock under the Act, but closed-end companies are under no such restriction. Open-end companies may, however, borrow money from a bank if it provides at least 300% collateral asset coverage.

Dividends paid by investment companies must come from accumulated undistributed net income or current income. If the payment comes from any other source, a written disclosure of the source must accompany the payment. Investment companies *are* allowed to make loans unless the company's policy prohibits it, and most funds *do* have policies that either forbid or restrict loans. (Bond purchases are not considered making loans under this definition.)

? Open-end investment companies
a. are not subject to SEC registration requirements.
b. are not permitted to pay dividends.
c. may change their investment policies only if the majority of the board of directors of the company approve of the change.
d. are not permitted to issue preferred stock or bonds.

Answer: d.
Open-end investment companies, or mutual funds, must be registered with the SEC and are permitted to pay dividends. They may change their investment policies only if a majority of their *shareholders* approve of the change. They are *not*, however, allowed to issue senior securities—i.e., preferred stock or bonds.

18. The National Association of Securities Dealers, the only association registered under the Maloney Act, is the over-the-counter market's self-regulatory agency. The NASD has four stated purposes as set forth in its Certificate of Incorporation:

1. "To promote through cooperative effort the investment banking and securities business, to standardize its principles and practices, to promote therein high standards of commercial honor, and to encourage and promote among members observance of Federal and State securities laws."

2. "To provide a medium through which its membership may be enabled to confer, consult, and cooperate with governmental and other agencies in the solution of problems affecting investors, the public and the investment banking and securities business."

3. "To adopt, administer, and enforce rules of fair practice and rule to prevent fraudulent and manipulative acts and practices, and in general to promote just and equitable principles of trade for the protection of investors."

4. "To promote self-discipline among members, and to investigate and adjust grievances between the public and members and between members."

Membership in the NASD is open to any broker or dealer who is regularly engaged in any type of investment banking activity or securities business in the United States. Persons who have been suspended or expelled from a national securities exchange or a registered securities organization, whose registration has been revoked or denied by the SEC, who have been convicted of a felony or misdemeanor involving the purchase or sale of securities in the last 10 years, or who have been convicted of a felony or misdemeanor involving embezzlement, misappropriation of funds, or abuse or misuse of a fiduciary relationship within the past 10 years will be barred from membership. NASD membership includes the advantages of price concessions, discounts and other privileges, so denial of membership would impose severe economic sanctions on a securities firm, making it difficult for it to continue operations.

The NASD requires an individual who is actively engaged in the management of a member firm's investment banking or securities business to register as a principal. Other employees, such as those who solicit orders or sell securities for a firm, must be registered with the NASD as representatives. Employees who only perform clerical duties, deal only in commodities or exempted securities, or who only transact business on a national securities exchange on which they are registered are not subject to NASD registration requirements. Principals must pass an NASD examination that qualifies them for that category. Representatives must be of good character and must also pass a qualifying NASD exam. If a registered representative's association with an NASD member firm is terminated, the NASD must be notified in writing within 30 days. Registration may not be transferred from one member firm to another; instead, the employee must terminate her membership with the first member firm and reregister under her new employer. If a representative is no longer employed by a member firm, she cannot maintain her registration by merely paying an annual fee.

? Which of the following employees of an NASD member firm would not have to be registered with the NASD?
   a. a salesperson
   b. a financial planner
   c. a receptionist
   d. a supervisor

Answer: c.
Because the receptionist only performs clerical duties, she would be exempt from registration requirements.

19. The National Association of Securities Dealers has established Rules of Fair Practice in accordance with the NASD By-Laws. The Rules apply to all NASD member firms and to everyone associated with a member. Violations of the rules can result in suspension or expulsion of the member firms. The Rules require that a member who is recommending a purchase, sale, or exchange of any security has reasonable grounds for believing that his recommendation is suitable for the specific customer based on the member's knowledge of the customer's other security holdings, his financial situation, and his needs. Recommendations of speculative low-priced securities without regard to suitability, excessive trading activity on a customer's account, fraudulent activity, recommendations for purchases without regard to the customer's financial situation, and trading in shares of mutual funds are all considered to be activities in violation of the Rules of Fair Practice. (Since 1985, a broker can grant loans so that customers can buy mutual fund shares. Mutual fund shares are considered marginable securities.)

The Rules also require that fees charged by member firms for services be reasonable and nondiscriminatory. Members are prohibited from using manipulation, deception, or fraud to stimulate the purchase or sale of securities. They are also prohibited from improperly using a customer's securities or funds. They may not borrow or lend a customer's securities without written permission, nor may they guarantee a customer's account against loss. A regular customer has the right to inspect information concerning the member firm's financial condition as contained in the member's most recent balance sheet.

When the NASD receives a complaint against a member or a person associated with a member, a Code of Procedure is followed. The complaint is first reviewed by the District Business Conduct Committee. If the matter is not satisfactorily settled by this group, it is taken to the NASD Board of Governors, which performs the function of an appeals and review body. If a violation is upheld, the member or person associated with the member can be censured, fined up to $15,000, suspended or expelled from membership, barred from associating with other members, and/or given any other penalty that is deemed appropriate.

? Under the Rules of Fair Practice, can a brokerage firm charge a long-standing customer a reduced commission on a transaction when it charges a new customer the regular commission for a trade involving the same amount of investment dollars?

Answer: No.
The Rules of Fair Practice require that any charges for services performed must not unfairly discriminate between customers.

20.   The **Securities Investor Protection Act** was passed in 1970. The Act established the **Securities Investor Protection Corporation (SIPC)**, which is a federally chartered, nonprofit membership corporation that provides protection for the customers in the event of the insolvency of a member firm. All registered brokers and dealers and members of the national securities exchanges are automatically members of the SIPC unless they are exempt. Brokers and dealers who deal exclusively with mutual funds are among those who are exempt, but they may elect to belong to the SIPC anyway. Members of the SIPC pay assessment fees. The SIPC guarantees that clients of an insolvent firm will be paid up to $500,000 to cover unreturned cash and/or securities. Only $100,000 in cash will be repaid, however.

? The funding used to reimburse customers of insolvent brokerage firms is provided by
a. the U.S. government.
b. member firms.
c. the national exchanges.
d. the taxpayers.

Answer: b.
Member firms pay assessments which fund the SIPC.

21. Individual states also regulate securities businesses that operate within their borders. State securities laws are referred to as **blue sky laws**, so named because one legislator argued for laws that would prevent securities' dealers from promising investors the "blue sky." Most state laws contain antifraud provisions that prohibit fraudulent and deceitful practices. State laws also govern the activities of brokers and dealers. Some states have registration requirements for these individuals; others restrict the fees that can be charged for services. State registration requirements also may exist for nonexempt securities. Compliance with the Securities Act of 1933 does not exempt a security from state registration regulations.

State laws may restrict the investments that institutional investors operating within their boundaries may make. For example, commercial banks may be prohibited from investing in any bond that is rated less than triple B. Additionally, some states regulate the conduct of a trustee who is investing in trust funds. At least 40 states judge the conduct of a trustee by what is known as the Prudent Man Rule. In other words, the trustee is expected to use prudence, discretion, and intelligence in choosing investments for the portfolio he is supervising.

? A new stock issue of the Novice Corporation has been approved by the SEC for sale to the public. Is this sufficient to allow it to be sold in all states, or must it also be approved by individual states that have their own security registration requirements?

Answer: SEC approval does not exempt the security from state registration requirements. It must also meet registration requirements of the individual states.

22. Investors look to market indicators to gauge how the market in general is performing and also for a benchmark by which to judge the performance of their own portfolios. There are a variety of market indicators, however, and investors should understand the differences among them.

Market indicators can be defined by three characteristics: sample, weighting, and computational procedure. We can differentiate them in terms of sample size, sample source, and the breadth of the sample. Some indicators are price-weighted; others are value-weighted; and still others are equally weighted. They may be computed as an arithmetic average, a geometric average, or an index. We will use these criteria to discuss the differences among the major indicators.

Probably the best known market indicator is the Dow Jones Industrial Average (DJIA). This indicator is calculated by adding the prices of 30 blue chip industrial stocks that trade on the NYSE and dividing by an adjusted divisor. Since only prices are used, it is a price-weighted indicator. The DJIA is a simple arithmetic average, with the divisor adjusted for stock splits.

$$\text{DJIA} = \frac{\sum_{i=1}^{30} \text{price}_i}{\text{adjusted divisor}}$$

This indicator has been the target of a great deal of criticism throughout the years for three reasons:

1. Because the indicator is calculated using only 30 out of over 5,000 stocks that are publicly traded and those 30 are blue chip stocks that trade on the NYSE, critics feel that it is not very representative of the market as a whole.
2. Because it is price-weighted, a change in the price of a higher priced stock will cause the DJIA to fluctuate by a greater amount than a change in the price of a lower priced stock.

3. Because only the price is included in the calculation, there is a downward bias in the DJIA when a stock is split. This reduces the price of one of the 30 stocks and causes the DJIA to drop, all else remains the same.

Dow Jones has responded to this criticism more recently and now publishes an equity market index as well. The new index is market-value weighted, using price and shares outstanding in its calculation, and the sample size is much larger and includes stocks that trade on both major exchanges and over-the-counter.

? Should an investor who invests mainly in small stocks use the DJIA as a benchmark by which to judge her portfolio? Why or why not?

Answer: No.
The DJIA is calculated using the prices of 30 well-known firms that trade on the NYSE. Small stocks may or may not be performing in a similar fashion.

23. When academicians talk about the "market portfolio," they generally use the S&P 500 as a proxy for this portfolio. The S&P 500 Index differs from the DJIA in that it uses 500 stocks in its sample. These stocks trade on the NYSE, the AMEX, and in the OTC market and include industrial stocks, transportation stocks, utility stocks, and financial stocks. (Dow Jones also produces a utility average that is composed of 15 stocks and a transportation average that uses 20 stocks in addition to the industrial average. They then report a composite average using all 65 stocks, but this is not as popular as the DJIA.) The S&P 500 is market-value weighted, which means that it uses "price × shares outstanding" for each of the 500 stocks. It is calculated as an index. This calculation involves summing the current market values of each of the 500 stocks and dividing by the summation of the market values that existed during some base period. The result is then multiplied by an arbitrary index value, typically a multiple of 10. For example, the S&P 500 base period value is the average summation of the market values from 1941 to 1943 and the index value used is 10. Because it is market-value weighted, investors can compare the percentage change in the index to the return that their own portfolios have earned. They are unable to make this comparison with a price-weighted indicator.

$$S \& P \ 500 \ Index = \frac{\sum_{i=1}^{500}(price_i \times shares \ outstanding_i)_{today}}{\sum_{i=1}^{500}(price_i \times shares \ outstanding_i)_{base \ period}} \times 10$$

Other popular market indicators that are market-value weighted and use the index computational procedure are the NYSE Composite Index, which differs from the S&P 500 Index in that it uses all the stocks that trade on the New York Stock Exchange; the AMEX Composite Index, which uses all the stocks that trade on the American Stock Exchange; the NASDAQ Composite Index, which uses all domestic common stocks that are listed on NASDAQ; and the Wilshire 5000 Equity Index, which uses all the NYSE and AMEX stocks plus the most active stocks trading in the OTC market and is, therefore, the broadest-based domestic equity index. An investor should choose whichever of these indicators is most comparable to his portfolio as a benchmark. An investor whose portfolio consists solely of small stocks might elect to use the Russell 2000 Index, which is yet another market-value weighted index that is made up of 2,000 relatively small stocks of publicly traded companies.

An equally weighted indicator assumes that an equal amount of money is invested in each of the stocks in the indicator. Therefore, if there are 100 stocks used to calculate the indicator, each one has a weight of $1/100$. Neither price nor market value is important.

The best known equally weighted indicator is the Value Line Composite Average. This indicator is calculated as a geometric average and uses 1,700 stocks that are traded on the NYSE, the AMEX, and in the OTC market.

? How does the S&P 500 Index differ from the NYSE Composite Index?

Answer: While the S&P 500 Index uses 500 stocks that trade on the NYSE, the AMEX, and in the OTC market, the NYSE Composite Index uses only stocks that trade on the New York Stock Exchange in its calculation. Furthermore, they use all the stocks that trade on the NYSE, not just 500 stocks.

 Apply It

1. What is the difference between the primary market and the secondary market? (Frame 1)

2. What is the difference between the money market and the capital market? (Frame 1)

3. In which case does an investment banker take more risk—an underwriting agreement or a best efforts agreement? (Frame 3)

4. Matt Dimino is considering investing in a new bond of the Shaky Company. He is particularly attracted by the extremely high yield and feels that the investment will nevertheless be a safe one since the SEC has had to approve the registration statement prior to the issue's being sold to the public. What advice would you give Matt? (Frame 2)

5. What is meant by an underwriting syndicate? (Frame 4)

6. You are considering the purchase of a municipal bond issue that sells over-the-counter. Will you be able to buy it at the bid price or the ask price? (Frame 5)

7. What are the two major reasons that regional exchanges exist? (Frame 6)

8. How does the NYSE differ from the AMEX? (Frame 6)

9. What is a commission broker? (Frame 7)

10. How does the OTC market differ from organized exchanges? (Frame 8)

11. How does a market order differ from a limit order? (Frame 9)

12. Sarah Ray sold 100 shares of Egghead, Incorporated, short at $11 a share. She was required to deposit a margin of $600 with her broker when she entered the transaction. Subsequently, Egghead dropped in value to $9\frac{1}{4}$ a share. What was Sarah's return on the transaction? (Frame 10)

13. Lao Tsu wants to invest in a portfolio that will cost $100,000. If the initial margin requirement is 55%, how much cash will he need? (Frame 11)

14. Dan Summers invested in a portfolio that had a value of $20,000. The initial margin requirement was 60%, and Dan borrowed the maximum amount allowed. The maintenance margin requirement is 40%. If the value of the portfolio drops to $15,000, will there be a margin call? If so, for how much? (Frame 12)

15. Tracy Teufel invested in a portfolio that had a value of $36,000. The initial margin requirement was 50%, and Tracy borrowed the maximum amount allowed. The maintenance margin requirement is 35%. If the value of the portfolio drops to $23,000, will there be a margin call? If so, for how much? (Frame 12)

16. Eric Fontaine purchased 200 shares of a stock that was selling for $42 a share. The initial margin requirement was 50%, and Eric borrowed the maximum amount allowed. The interest rate on the loan was 10%. Subsequently, the stock increased in value to $50 a share. What was Eric's return on his investment? (Frame 13)

17. You own a portfolio that is composed solely of stocks that trade over-the-counter. Which market indicator would be the best benchmark by which to judge your portfolio's performance? (Frame 23)

18. How does the DJIA differ from the S&P 500 Index? (Frames 22 and 23)

19. Frank's broker has been trying to convince Frank to purchase part of a new issue of municipal bonds issued by Cowtown to build a new airport. According to the broker, the bonds are offering exceptionally high yields and yet are virtually riskless. The bonds are being sold over-the-counter and are exempt from SEC registration requirements. Is Frank's broker in violation of any securities laws? (Frames 18 and 19)

20. What types of securities need not be registered with the SEC? (Frame 14)

21. A radio advertisement for a certain mutual fund indicated that the fund had offered an annual return of 15% for the past 5 years and implied that investors could expect a return of this magnitude in the next year. Unfortunately, the fund only earned its investors a 5% return in that year. When challenged, the fund representatives argued that investors had nothing in writing that guaranteed a 15% return. Is the fund in violation of any securities laws? (Frame 15)

22. A new bond issue is being advertised by its underwriting syndicate in *The Wall Street Journal*. The advertisement announces the issuing firm and indicates the type of business in which the firm is engaged, the total amount being raised by the bond issue, and a name and address that a potential investor can write to in order to obtain a prospectus. The issue has not yet received SEC approval, however. Is the underwriting syndicate in violation of any securities laws? (Frame 15)

23. Which major federal law regulates trading activities that take place on the exchange floors and in the over-the-counter markets? (Frame 16)

24. Mark Mayhem is president of his company, the shares of which trade OTC. Mark recently purchased another 5,000 shares in his company through his broker. Is this a violation of securities laws? (Frame 16)

25. Is it currently a violation of securities laws for a mutual fund to do a short sale? (Frame 17)

26. Judy Mitchell was recently hired by Everyman's Funds to give sales seminars to prospective clients. Must Judy be registered with the NASD to perform this service? (Frame 18)

27. If Judy Mitchell decides to accept a position with Janus Funds, can she transfer her NASD registration from her current employer (Everyman's Funds) to Janus? (Frame 18)

28. Cassie Eckert has recently acquired a client who is a retired widow. The widow has communicated to Cassie that her primary investment objective is preservation of capital. In other words, the widow would like to be able to live off the income of her investments and not erode the principal. The widow is also concerned about risk and prefers to invest in securities that are either risk-free or of extremely low risk. Cassie recommends a mutual fund that invests only in new firms that are expected to have high growth potential. Is Cassie in violation of any securities laws? (Frame 19)

29. An investor had $800,000 in cash and securities on deposit with a brokerage firm that became insolvent. The firm was a member of the SIPC. What can the investor expect in the way of reimbursement from the SIPC? (Frame 20)

30. To what does the term "blue sky laws" refer? (Frame 21)

Apply It Answers

1. The primary market refers to the market for new issues while the secondary market is the market in which issues are bought and sold among investors.

2. The money market is the market for securities that have less than or equal to 1 year to maturity while the capital market is the market for securities that have greater than 1 year to maturity.

3. The investment banker takes more risk in an underwriting agreement since he purchases the issue outright from the issuing firm. If the issue does not sell, the investment banker bears the loss. In a best efforts agreement, if the issue does not sell, the securities are simply returned to the issuing firm.

4. SEC approval merely means that enough information is supplied for a rational investor to judge the quality of the issue for himself. The investment can be extremely risky, and in this case probably is, given the abnormally high yield.

5. An underwriting syndicate is a group of investment banking firms that has each purchased a portion of a particular issue with the intention of reselling the securities to the public.

6. The ask price is the price at which over-the-counter dealers are offering the bond for sale.

7. Regional exchanges exist so that brokers who cannot afford a seat on a major exchange can conduct trades and also so that companies that cannot meet the listing requirements of a major exchange can have their securities traded on an exchange floor.

8. The NYSE is the larger of the two exchanges. It lists older, sounder companies, has more stringent listing requirements, and has more expensive seats than the AMEX. Considerably more trading volume is done on the NYSE than on the AMEX.

9. A commission broker is an employee of a brokerage firm that owns a seat on an exchange floor. The commission broker conducts the actual trades for the customers of his brokerage firm.

10. The OTC market has no physical location, whereas organized exchanges do. Trades on the organized exchanges are done in an auction market; trades in the over-the-counter market are negotiated. The OTC has no listing requirements and no seats that must be purchased as all organized exchanges do.

11. A market order is an order to buy or sell a security at the prevailing price. A limit order is an order to buy or sell a security at a specified price or better.

12. 29.2%. Sarah received $1,100 from the short sale of Egghead. She subsequently was able to purchase the stock for $925 to cover her short position. This is a profit of $175. Her investment was her $600 margin requirement, so the return on this investment was $175/$600 = 29.2%.

13. If the initial margin requirement is 55%, Lao will need $0.55 \times \$100,000 = \$55,000$.

14. No. Since the initial margin requirement was 60%, Dan had to deposit $12,000 cash with his broker ($0.60 \times \$20,000$). If the portfolio drops in value to $15,000, Dan has lost $5,000 ($20,000 – $15,000). His brokerage account now has $7,000 in it ($12,000 – $5,000). This is a margin of 46.7%, as calculated below, which is greater than the maintenance margin requirement.

$$\text{Margin} = \frac{\text{equity}}{\text{total value of portfolio}} = \frac{\$7,500}{\$15,000} = 46.7\%$$

15. Yes. There will be a margin call for $3,050. Since the initial margin requirement was 50%, Tracy had to deposit $18,000 with her broker ($0.50 \times \$36,000$). If the portfolio drops in value to $23,000, Tracy will lose $13,000 ($36,000 – $23,000), which makes her cash position $5,000 ($18,000 – $13,000). Her margin would then be at 21.7%, which is less than the 35% required maintenance margin ($5,000/$23,000 = 21.7%). She needs $0.35 \times \$23,000 = \$8,050$ in order to meet the maintenance margin requirement. Since Tracy still has $5,000 in her account, the margin call will be for $3,050 ($8,050 – $5,000).

16. 28.1%. Eric purchased the stock for $8,400 ($200 \times \$42$), but he was able to borrow half of the investment money, or $4,200. Since the interest rate was 10%, his interest expense was $420. When the stock increased in value to $50 a share, Eric's net gain was $10,000 – $8,400 – $420 = $1,180. This is a return on his $4,200 investment of 28.1% ($1,180/$4,200 = 28.1%).

17. The NASDAQ Composite Index, since it consists of most of the stocks that trade over-the-counter.

18. The DJIA uses only 30 blue chip industrial stocks that trade on the NYSE in its calculation, whereas the S&P 500 Index uses 500 stocks—utilities, transportation stocks,

and financial stocks as well as industrial. These stocks trade on the NYSE, the AMEX, and in the OTC market. DJIA is a price-weighted indicator, while the S&P 500 Index is value-weighted. Lastly, the DJIA is calculated as an arithmetic average, and the S&P 500 Index is calculated using the index method.

19. Yes. The municipal bonds are being sold over-the-counter and the NASD Rules of Fair Practice are designed to prevent misrepresentations and fraudulent behavior on the part of its members. A municipal bond that is offering high yields cannot also be "virtually riskless," so Frank's broker is in violation of the NASD Rules of Fair Practice.

20. Exempt securities include private offerings, securities issued by the U.S. government, municipal securities, securities issued by carriers that are regualted by the ICC, and securities issued by nonprofit organizations.

21. Yes. Rule 156 of the Securities and Exchange Commission establishes guidelines for sales literature of investment companies and applies to any type of communication, written or oral. Since funds cannot promise investors that past performance is indicative of what can be expected in the future, the fund's advertisement was misleading. This is in violation of Rule 156.

22. No. The advertisement described contains no more information than is allowed in a tombstone advertisement as established by Rule 134 of the Securities and Exchange Commission. This type of advertisement is permitted prior to approval of the registration statement by the SEC.

23. The Securities Exchange Act of 1934 is the major federal law that regulates the activities in the secondary market.

24. No. As president of the company, Mark is considered an insider and must report this trade to the SEC, but he is permitted to buy and sell shares of his company.

25. No. According to the Investment Company Act of 1940, investment companies are prohibited from doing a short sale or a margin transaction *in violation of SEC rules or regulations.* Currently, the SEC has no rules that restrict these types of transactions for investment companies.

26. Yes. Since Judy is, in effect, soliciting orders for Everyman's, she must be registered as a representative with the NASD.

27. No. Judy must first terminate her membership with Everyman's and then reregister under Janus Funds.

28. Yes. Cassie has no reason to believe that her recommendation is suitable for the widow based on her knowledge of the widow's needs. In fact, the recommendation is very *unsuitable.* The fund that Cassie has recommended is high risk (new firms), and will probably not provide much current income in the form of dividends to the widow since the firms that the fund invests in will be reinvesting for growth. The widow needs investments that provide her with current income on which to live, and she has indicated a high degree of risk aversion to Cassie.

29. Up to $100,000 of the cash will be reimbursed. Of the remaining $700,000, the investor can expect to receive only $400,000 once the securities of the firm are liquidated. The SIPC insures the accounts for a maximum of $500,000.

30. Blue sky laws refer to state securities regulations.

THE TIME VALUE OF MONEY

This module will introduce you to the concept of time value of money, which is a major building block on which the study of finance is based. You will learn how to calculate the future value of money deposited today, given that you know the interest rate and the length of time, as well as the amount needed today (the present value) in order to obtain an amount in the future. You will also learn to determine the future value and the present value of a series of payments, the interest rate being paid or received, and the number of periods that money must be left on deposit in order to obtain a desired future amount. The difference between an annual percentage rate and an effective annual rate is discussed, and the calculations for each are explained.

Equations introduced in this module

$$FV = PV \times (1+i)^n$$

$$PV = FV \times \frac{1}{(1+i)^n}$$

$$FV = PV \times e^{in}$$

$$APR = \text{interest rate per period} \times \text{number of periods in a year}$$

$$EAR = (1 + \text{interest rate per period})^{\text{number of periods in a year}} - 1$$

$$FVIFA = \sum_{t=1}^{n}(1+i)^{n-t} = \frac{(1+i)^n - 1}{i}$$

93

$$\text{FV of an ordinary annuity} = \text{payment}(\text{FVIFA}_{i\%,n})$$

$$\text{FV of an annuity due} = \text{payment}(\text{FVIFA}_{i\%,n} - 1)$$

$$\text{PVIFA} = \sum_{t=1}^{n} \frac{1}{1+i)^t} = \frac{1 - \dfrac{1}{(1+i)^n}}{i}$$

$$\text{PV of an ordinary annuity} = \text{payment}(\text{PVIFA}_{i\%,n})$$

$$\text{PV of a perpetuity} = \frac{\text{payment}}{i}$$

1. The concept of time value of money is one of the cornerstones on which most financial theory is based. The time value of money says that a dollar received today is worth more than a dollar received tomorrow. This is true because a dollar received today can be invested to earn interest. Interest can be thought of from two standpoints: (1) the compensation that an investor receives for lending his money, and (2) the price that a borrower must pay for credit. The interest paid by a borrower compensates the lender for his **opportunity cost**, which is the return that the lender could have earned on an alternative investment of similar risk. Stated differently, the interest rate compensates the lender for both the cost of not having the funds available to invest elsewhere and his risk, which refers to the uncertainty regarding the receipt of future cash flows. The amount that is invested today is referred to as the **principal,** or the **present value**. The amount that the lender will receive in the future is referred to as the **future value**, and it includes both the return of the principal to the lender as well as the interest earned.

? Jake Zeek deposited $1,000 in a savings account that paid 5% interest. One year later, his account balance was $1,050. The $1,000 is the _____, and the $1,050 is the _____. The $50 is the _____ Jake earned and compensates Jake for his _____ cost.

Answers: Principal or present value, future value, interest, opportunity.
The amount deposited today is referred to as the principal or the present value, and the amount to be received in the future is referred to as the future value. The future value includes the return of the $1,000 to Jake plus $50 in interest. The interest compensates Jake for not having the funds available to spend elsewhere as well as the risk that he may not receive the promised amount. This is the opportunity cost.

2. Simple interest is interest paid on the principal only. If Jake deposits $1,000 into an account that pays 5% simple interest and leaves the $1,000 in for 2 years, he will earn $1,000 × 0.05 = $50.00 in interest the first year and $1,000 × 0.05 = $50.00 in interest the second year, so his total interest earned in the 2 years will be $50.00 + $50.00 = $100.00.

? If Jake deposits $500 into an account that pays 6% simple interest, how much interest will he have earned after 3 years?

Answer: $90.
Each year Jake will earn interest on the principal only. The annual interest earned will be 0.06 × $500 = $30.00, so his total interest earned will be 3 × $30.00 = $90.00.

3. Most accounts pay **compound interest**, which means that interest is also paid on the interest that has accumulated in the account. If Jake deposits $1,000 into an account that pays 5%, compounded annually, and leaves the principal and any accumulated interest in for 2 years, he will earn $1,000 × 0.05 = $50.00 the first year and $1,050 × 0.05 = $52.50 the second year, so his total interest earned will be $50.00 + $52.50 = $102.50. The future value of an amount deposited today when interest is compounded can be determined more easily by the equation

$$FV = PV(1 + i)^n,$$

where FV is the future value; PV is the present value or principal; i is the interest rate per period; and n is the number of periods. In the above example, PV = $1,000, i = 5%, and n = 2, so FV = $1,000(1.05)^2 = $1,102.50. $1,000 is the principal value, and $102.50 is the total interest earned.

? If Jake deposits $500 into an account that pays 6% interest and leaves the principal and any accumulated interest in for 4 years, how much will he have in the account at the end of 4 years?

? How much interest did he earn?

Answers: $631.25, $131.25.
FV = $500(1.06)^4 = $500(1.2625) = $631.25. Therefore, he will have $631.25 in his account at the end of 4 years.
Since the principal was $500, he earned $631.25 − $500.00 = $131.25 in interest.

4. In order to make the computation easier, a table of future value interest factors ($FVIF_{i\%,n}$) has been developed (see Appendix A-1). The future value interest factor for a given interest rate and a given number of compounding periods is simply equal to $(1 + i)^n$. Therefore, $FVIF_{3\%,7} = (1.03)^7 = 1.2299$.

? What is the future value interest factor for 22%, 5 periods?

? If Jake deposits $2,000 into an account that pays 22%, compounded annually, and leaves both the principal and accumulated interest in for 5 years, how much will Jake have in the account at the end of that time?

Answers: 2.7027, $5405.40.

$$FVIF_{22\%,5} = (1.22)^5 = 2.7027$$

If Jake deposits $2,000 in an account and leaves it in the account for 5 years, he will accumulate FV = $2,000(2.7027) = $5,405.40.

5. The process of finding a future value when a present value is known is called **compounding**. Sometimes it is necessary to determine what the present value of dollars to be received in the future is. This process is referred to as **discounting**. As with any algebraic equation, if all but one of the variables is unknown, the equation can be solved for the missing variable. For example, if Jake wants to know how much he must set aside today in an account that pays 8% compounded annually to ensure that he will have $10,000 in 3 years, he will be looking for the PV in the equation FV = PV(1 + i)^n. An algebraic manipulation of this equation reveals that

$$PV = \frac{FV}{(1+i)^n} = FV \times \frac{1}{(1+i)^n}.$$

Therefore, $PV = \$10,000 \times 1/(1.08)^3 = \$10,000(0.7983) = \$7,983.00$. If Jake deposits $7,938 in an account that pays 8%, compounded annually, he will have $10,000 in the account at the end of 3 years.

? Jake wants to have $12,000 accumulated in 5 years to meet a loan balloon payment. (That is, Jake is required to make a principal repayment of $12,000 on the loan at the end of 5 years.) If he can earn 5%, compounded annually, on his money, how much must he set aside today?

Answer: $9,402.00.

$$PV = \$12,000 \times \frac{1}{(1.05)^5}$$
$$= \$12,000(0.7835) = \$9,402.00$$

6.   There is a table that provides the present value interest factors ($PVIF_{i\%,n}$) for numerous interest rates and compounding periods (see Appendix A-2). The present value interest factor is the reciprocal of the future value interest factor, or $1/(1 + i)^n$. Therefore, $PVIF_{6\%,10} = 1/(1.06)^{10} = 0.5584$.

? What is the present value interest factor for 26%, 2 years?

? How much must Jake deposit today in an account that pays 26%, compounded annually, if he wants to have $6,000 in the account at the end of 2 years?

Answers: 0.6299, $3,779.40.
The present value interest factor for 26%, 2 years is calculated as $1/(1.26)^2 = 0.6299$. Therefore, we can calculate the amount Jake needs to deposit today as $PV = \$6,000(PVIF_{26\%,2}) = \$6,000(0.6299) = \$3,779.40$.

7.   If we know both the present value and the future value, we can determine what effective annual rate of interest we are paying (or receiving) as well, by solving for "i" in the equation. For example, assume that Jake can borrow $8,000 today but must pay back $12,167 at the end of 3 years. The present value is $8,000, the future value is $12,167, and the number of periods is 3, so using the formula $FV = PV(1 + i)^n$,

$$\$12,167 = \$8,000(1+i)^3$$

$$(1+i)^3 = \frac{\$12,167}{\$8,000}$$

$$1+i = \sqrt[3]{\frac{\$12,167}{\$8,000}}$$

$$\text{so } i = \sqrt[3]{\frac{\$12,167}{\$8,000}} - 1 = 15\%.$$

? Jake can borrow $3,000 today from his Uncle Sly, but must pay Uncle Sly back $4,320 at the end of 2 years. What effective annual rate is Uncle Sly charging Jake?

Answer: 20%.
The present value is $3,000 and the future value is $4,320, so

$$\$4{,}320 = \$3{,}000(1+i)^2$$

$$(1+i)^2 = \frac{\$4{,}320}{\$3{,}000}$$

$$1+i = \sqrt{\frac{\$4{,}320}{\$3{,}000}}$$

$$i = \sqrt{\frac{\$4{,}320}{\$3{,}000}} - 1 = 20\%.$$

8. If a calculator that determines root values higher than square roots is not available, the time value tables can be used to determine the approximate interest rate. For example, if Jake can borrow $2,500 today, but must pay back $3,800 in 4 years, then $3,800 = $2,500(1 + i)^4$, which we can also write as $\$3{,}800 = \$2{,}500 \times \mathrm{FVIF}_{i\%,4}$, since $\mathrm{FVIF}_{i\%,4} = (1 + i)^4$. Solving for $\mathrm{FVIF}_{i\%,4}$, $\mathrm{FVIF}_{i\%,4} = \$3{,}800/\$2{,}500 = 1.5200$.

We can now look at the future value interest factor table (Appendix A-1) across the four periods row for the factor closest to 1.5200. The factor for 11%, 4 periods is 1.5181 and the factor for 12%, 4 periods is 1.5735, so the effective interest rate is between 11% and 12%. It is much closer to 11%, however.

? Use the time value tables to determine what the effective annual interest rate is if Jake borrows $20,000 today and must pay back $25,000 at the end of 5 years.

Answer: i is between 4% and 5%.
The present value is $20,000 and the future value is $25,000, so $25,000 = $20,000 \times \mathrm{FVIF}_{i\%,5}$; therefore, $\mathrm{FVIF}_{i\%,5} = \$25{,}000/\$20{,}000 = 1.2500$. Looking across the 5 period row, the factor for 4% is 1.2167 and the factor for 5% is 1.2763. 1.2500 lies between these two factors, so the interest rate is between 4% and 5%.

9. It is also possible to determine the number of periods it will take to accumulate a certain amount of money, given that the principal and the interest rate are known. Assume that Jake deposits $1,500 today in an account that pays 10%, compounded annually, and he would like to know how long it will take for the account balance to be $5,000. In this case, the present value is $1,500 and the future value is $5,000, so $5{,}000 = \$1{,}500(1.10)^n$. Therefore, $(1.10)^n = \$5{,}000/\$1{,}500 = 3.3333$. To solve this for "n", we must use natural logarithms as follows:

$$n \ln(1.10) = \ln 3.3333$$

$$n = \ln 3.3333/\ln 1.10 = 1.2040/0.0953 = 12.6 \text{ years.}$$

? If Jake deposits $2,000 at 5%, how long will it take for the account balance to be $10,000?

Answer: 33 years.

$$\$10{,}000 = \$2{,}000(1.05)^n$$
$$(1.05)^n = \$10{,}000/\$2{,}000 = 5.000$$

$$n \ln(1.05) = \ln 5.000$$

$$n = \ln 5.000/\ln 1.05 = 1.6094/0.0488 \approx 33 \text{ years.}$$

10. Many times interest is compounded more frequently than once a year. It may be compounded twice a year (semiannually), four times a year (quarterly), twelve times a year (monthly), or any other number of times annually. The original formula, $FV = PV(1 + i)_n$, still applies. Remember that "i" is the interest rate per period (whatever the period length is) and "n" is the number of compounding periods. Therefore, if Jake deposits $1,000 into an account that pays 8%, compounded semiannually, and leaves the principal and accumulated interest in the account for 6 years, the interest rate per period is 4%, and the number of compounding periods is 12, since interest is paid twice a year. So $FV = \$1,000(1.04)^{12} = \$1,000 \times FVIF_{4\%,12} = \$1,000(1.6010) = \$1,601.00$.

❓ Suppose Jake deposits $5,000 into an account that pays 12% interest, compounded monthly. How much will he have in the account at the end of 3 years?

❓ If Jake needs to have $4,000 saved at the end of 4 years and he can earn 8%, compounded quarterly, how much must he set aside today?

Answers: $7,154.00, $2,913.60.
In the first question since interest is compounded monthly, the monthly rate is 12%/12 = 1%. There are 36 months in 3 years, so the number of compounding periods is 36. Therefore, $FV = \$5,000(1.01)^{36} = \$5,000 \times FVIF_{1\%,36} = \$5,000(1.4308) = \$7,154.00$.
In the second question, we are looking for the principal, or present value. The interest rate per period is 8%/4 = 2%, and the number of quarters in 4 years is 16. Therefore, $PV = \$4,000 \times 1/(1.02)^{16} = \$4,000 \times PVIF_{4\%,16} = \$4,000(0.7284) = \$2,913.60$.

11. Sometimes interest is compounded continuously, which means that interest is compounded at the smallest possible time intervals. The future value is then calculated as $FV = PV \times e^{in}$, where e is the constant 2.71828, i is the stated annual rate, and n is the number of years. If Jake were to deposit $1,000 into an account that paid 8%, compounded continuously, and he left the principal and accumulated interest in the account for 2 years, he would have $FV = \$1,000 \times e^{(0.08 \times 2)} = \$1,000 \times (2.71828)^{0.16} = \$1,000(1.1735) = \$1,173.50$ in the account at the end of 2 years.

❓ If Jake deposits $500 into an account that pays 3%, compounded continuously, and leaves the principal and the accumulated interest in for 5 years, how much will he have at the end of that time?

Answer: $580.90.

$$FV = \$500 \times e^{(0.03 \times 5)}$$
$$= \$500 \times (2.71828)^{0.15}$$
$$= \$500(1.1618) = \$580.90$$

12. Similarly, if Jake needs to accumulate $3,000 by the end of 3 years and he can earn 4%, compounded continuously, on his money, we can solve for the amount he needs to set aside today in the following fashion:

$$\$3,000 = PV \times e^{(0.04 \times 3)}$$
$$PV = \$3,000/e^{0.12}$$
$$= \$3,000/(2.71828)^{0.12}$$
$$= \$3,000/1.1275 = \$2,660.75.$$

❓ If Jake needs to have $10,000 accumulated at the end of 8 years, and he can earn 6%, compounded continuously, on his money, how much must he set aside today?

Answer: $6,187.74.

$$\$10,000 = PV \times e^{(0.06 \times 8)}$$
$$PV = \$10,000/e^{0.48} = \$10,000/(2.71828)^{0.48} = \$10,000/1.6161 = \$6,187.74$$

13.   In the previous examples, the interest rate that is specified is called the stated annual rate, or the **annual percentage rate (APR)**. The APR is equal to the interest rate per period times the number of compounding periods in a year. Therefore, if a finance company indicates that it charges 1.8% monthly, this is an APR of 21.6% (1.8% × 12 = 21.6%).

The **effective annual rate (EAR)** is equal to the annual percentage rate (APR) if interest is compounded annually. If interest is compounded more than once a year, the effective annual rate will be greater than the annual percentage rate and is calculated as follows:

$$EAR = (1 + \text{interest rate per period})^{\text{number of periods in a year}} - 1.$$

So in the finance company example, while the APR is 21.6%, the EAR = $(1.018)^{12} - 1$ = 23.9%.

? If a bank states that it pays 4%, compounded monthly, on its savings account deposits, the APR is _____ and the EAR is _____.

Answers: 4%, 4.07%.
The APR is the stated rate of 4%. The interest rate per period is 4%/12 = 0.3333%, and there are 12 compounding periods in a year, so the EAR = $(1.003333)^{12} - 1$ = 4.07%.

14.   Many times, instead of making a lump-sum deposit or withdrawal, we make a series of equal deposits or withdrawals. This series of equal payments is called an **annuity**. If the payments occur at the end of the period, it is an **ordinary annuity**. If the payments occur at the beginning of the period, it is an **annuity due**.

? Jake pays his car insurance premiums in 4 equal installments. The first installment was due when he took out the policy. This is an example of a (an) _____.

Answer: annuity due.
The payments occur at the beginning of each period.

15.   The future value of an annuity can be determined by adding up the future values of each payment. For example, if Jake makes 3 end-of-period deposits of $100, and we want to know how much he will have in his account at the end of the third year if he can earn 4% on his money, we can calculate it by finding the future value of the 3 lump-sums.

A useful visual aid in solving more complex problems is a time line, which depicts the timing of the cash inflows and/or outflows. Each mark on the time line represents the end of a period, so we can plot Jake's cash flows as follows:

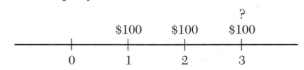

The "?" indicates that we are looking for the value of the cash flows at the end of the third period. Note that the first $100 deposit will earn interest for only 2 periods, the second will earn interest for 1 period, and the third will not have earned any interest. Therefore, using the formula $FV = PV(1 + i)^n$,

$$FV = \$100(1.04)^2 + \$100(1.04)^1 + \$100(1.04)^0$$

$$FV = \$100(FVIF_{4\%,2}) + \$100(FVIF_{4\%,1}) + \$100$$

$$FV = \$100(1.0816) + \$100(1.0400) + \$100 = \$312.16.$$

To cut down on the number of computations, we can use the distributive property of algebra and factor out the $100 in the first step. This gives us

$$FV = \$100[(1.04)^2 + (1.04)^1 + (1.04)^0].$$

There is a table of factors that sums up these lump-sum factors (see Appendix A-3). The factors are called the future value interest factors of an annuity ($FVIFA_{i\%,n}$), and each factor sums up the future value interest factors beginning with $(1 + i)^0$ and ending with $(1 + i)^{n-1}$, where n is the number of periods. Using mathematical shorthand, this can be written as follows:

$$FVIFA = \sum_{t=1}^{n}(1+i)^{n-t}.$$

Our problem can, therefore, be solved in the following manner:

$$FV = \$100\sum_{t=1}^{3}(1.04)^{3-t}$$

$$FV = \$100(FVIFA_{4\%,3})$$

$$FV = \$100(3.1216) = \$312.16.$$

? If Jake makes six end-of-period deposits of $500 and can earn 5% on his money, how much will he have in his account at the end of the sixth period?

Answer: $3,400.95.

$$FV = \$500\sum_{t=1}^{6}(1.05)^{6-t}$$

$$FV = \$500(FVIFA_{5\%,6})$$

$$FV = \$500(6.8019) = \$3,400.95$$

16.   If tables are unavailable, we can calculate the future value interest factor of an annuity by adding up the future value interest factors beginning with $(1 + i)^0$ and ending with $(1 + i)^{n-1}$. While this is not difficult so long as the number of periods is reasonably small, it can be quite cumbersome for larger numbers of periods. However, there is an algebraic formula for calculating the sum of a finite series that makes the calculation more manageable:

$$FVIFA_{i\%,n} = \sum_{t=1}^{n}(1+i)^{n-t} = \frac{(1+i)^n - 1}{i}.$$

Therefore, the

$$\text{FVIFA}_{4\%,3} = \frac{(1.04)^3 - 1}{0.04} = 3.1216.$$

? What is the future value interest factor of an annuity for 63%, 10 periods?

Answer: 208.5657.

$$\text{FVIFA}_{63\%,10} = \frac{(1.63)^{10} - 1}{0.63} = 208.5657.$$

17.   If Jake had made the deposits at the *beginning* of each period, we would be working with an annuity due, and the time line would be labelled as follows:

Again, we could find the future value at the end of the third period by finding the future value of each payment and summing all of the future values. Note that in this case, the first $100 deposit will earn interest for three periods, the second deposit will earn interest for two periods, and the last deposit will earn interest for one period.

$$\text{FV} = \$100(1.04)^3 + \$100(1.04)^2 + \$100(1.04)^1$$

$$= \$100(\text{FVIF}_{4\%,3}) + \$100(\text{FVIF}_{4\%,2}) + \$100(\text{FVIF}_{4\%,1})$$

$$= \$100(1.1249) + \$100(1.0816) + \$100(1.0400)$$

$$= \$112.49 + \$108.16 + \$104.00 = \$324.65$$

Unfortunately, the future value interest factor of an annuity table is designed for *ordinary* annuities. However, we can still use the tables by remembering that $\text{FVIFA}_{i\%,n} = (1 + i)^0 + (1 + i)^1 + \ldots + (1 + i)^{n-1}$. If we use the distributive property of algebra on the above problem, we get $\text{FV} = \$100[(1.04)^3 + (1.04)^2 + (1.04)^1]$. Since we need to pick up $(1.04)^3$ in the summation, and the future value interest factors of annuities sum the future value interest factors *up to* $(1 + i)^{n-1}$, we will need to use the future value interest factor of an annuity for *one more period*, i.e., $\text{FVIFA}_{4\%,4}$. However, this will sum $(1.04)^0 + (1.04)^1 + (1.04)^2 + (1.04)^3$. Note that in our problem we do not have a deposit that earns interest for no periods; therefore, we do not want to include $(1.04)^0$ in our sum. Since any number raised to the zero power is equal to one, we can simply subtract "1" from our summation. So, we can solve this annuity due problem using the time value tables in the following manner:

$$\text{FV} = \$100(\text{FVIFA}_{4\%,4} - 1)$$

$$= \$100(4.2465 - 1) = \$324.65.$$

? If Jake makes six beginning-of-period deposits of $500 and can earn 5% on his money, how much will he have in his account at the end of the sixth period?

Answer: $3,571.00.

Since this is an annuity due, if we use the tables we must look up the factor for one additional period. We must also subtract "1" from the factor since none of the deposits earn interest for zero periods.

$$FV = \$500(\text{FVIFA}_{5\%,7} - 1)$$

$$= \$500(8.1420 - 1) = \$3,571.00$$

18.   We sometimes want to determine what the current value of a series of future payments is. In this case, we are looking for the present value of the annuity. As in the example given for the future value of an annuity, the present value of an annuity can be determined by adding up the present values of each payment. For example, if Jake has a trust fund that will pay him $5,000 at the end of each of the next 5 years and he wants to know for how much he should sell the rights to this trust fund, he can find the present value of each of the $5,000 payments by using the formula

$$PV = FV \times \frac{1}{(1+i)^n},$$

and add up the present values.

? Draw a time line depicting Jake's cash flows.

Answer:

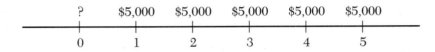

19.   If Jake can earn 4% on his money, the present value of his trust fund is, therefore,

$$PV = \$5,000 \times \frac{1}{(1.04)^1} + \$5,000 \times \frac{1}{(1.04)^2} + \$5,000 \times \frac{1}{(1.04)^3} + \$5,000 \times \frac{1}{(1.04)^4} + \$5,000 \times \frac{1}{(1.04)^5}$$

$$= \$5,000(\text{PVIF}_{4\%,1}) + \$5,000(\text{PVIF}_{4\%,2}) + \$5,000(\text{PVIF}_{4\%,3}) + \$5,000(\text{PVIF}_{4\%,4}) + \$5,000(\text{PVIF}_{4\%,5})$$

$$= \$5,000(0.9615) + \$5,000(0.9246) + \$5,000(0.8890) + \$5,000(0.8548) + \$5,000(0.8219) = \$22,259.00.$$

Again, we can use the distributive property of algebra and factor out the $5,000. This gives us

$$PV = \$5,000[\frac{1}{(1.04)^1} + \frac{1}{(1.04)^2} + \frac{1}{(1.04)^3} + \frac{1}{(1.04)^4} + \frac{1}{(1.04)^5}].$$

We have another table that gives us the sum of various lump-sum present value factors. These are called the present value interest factors of an annuity ($\text{PVIFA}_{i\%,n}$). (See Appendix A-4.) These factors add up the lump-sum present value factors beginning with $1/(1+i)^1$ and ending with $1/(1+i)^n$, where n is the total number of periods. Using mathematical shorthand, this can be written as

$$PVIFA = \sum_{t=1}^{n} \frac{1}{(1+i)^t}.$$

The above problem can therefore be set up in the following manner:

$$PV = \$5,000 \sum_{t=1}^{5} \frac{1}{(1.04)^t}$$

$$= \$5,000(\text{PVIFA}_{4\%,5})$$

$$= \$5,000(4.4518) = \$22,259.00.$$

? Jake would like to know how much he must have accumulated to be able to receive $50,000 a year at retirement if he can earn 8% on his money and he expects to live for 25 years after retirement. Draw a time line depicting these cash flows and determine how much Jake will need before he can retire.

Answer: $533,740.

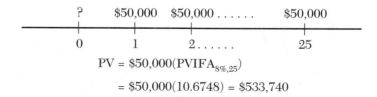

$$PV = \$50,000(PVIFA_{8\%,25})$$

$$= \$50,000(10.6748) = \$533,740$$

20.   If tables are not available, we can calculate the present value interest factor of an annuity in a manner similar to the calculation of the future value of an annuity factor.

$$PVIFA_{i\%,n} = \sum_{t=1}^{n}\frac{1}{(1+i)^t} = \frac{1-\dfrac{1}{(1+i)^n}}{i}$$

Therefore, $PVIFA_{4\%,5}$ can be calculated as

$$\frac{1-\dfrac{1}{(1.04)^5}}{0.04} = 4.4518.$$

? Calculate the present value interest factor of an annuity for 27%, 31 periods.

Answer: 3.7015.

$$PVIFA_{27\%,31} = \frac{1-\dfrac{1}{(1.27)^{31}}}{0.27} = 3.7015.$$

21.   If Jake's first trust fund payment will be paid today and at the beginning of each year for a total of five payments, we have an annuity due, and the time line is as follows:

?
$5,000 $5,000 $5,000 $5,000 $5,000

0   1   2   3   4   5

Note that we could find the present value of the four $5,000 payments occuring in the future by using the present value interest factor of a 4-year annuity and add to that the $5,000 payment that is already in current dollars as follows:

$$PV = \$5,000\sum_{t=1}^{4}\frac{1}{(1.04)^t} + \$5,000$$

$$= \$5,000(PVIFA_{4\%,4}) + \$5,000$$

$$= \$5,000(3.6299) + \$5,000 = \$23,149.50.$$

? If Jake plans to begin his retirement immediately, drawing his first $50,000 payment today, how much must he have in his account?

Answer: $576,440.00.

The $50,000 payment he draws today is already in current dollars, so we must discount back the 24 payments that occur in the future and add it to the payment he receives today.

$$PV = \$50,000(PVIFA_{8\%,24}) + \$50,000$$
$$= \$50,000(10.5288) + \$50,000 = \$576,440.00$$

22. Many times we may want to know how much we have to set aside each period in order to accumulate a certain amount in the future. For example, suppose that Jake wants to have $1,000,000 accumulated when he retires and that he expects to retire in 20 years. If we assume that he sets aside the same amount at the end of each year and that he can earn 8% on his money, the time line can be drawn as follows:

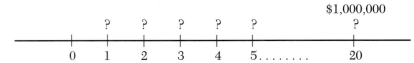

Note that we know the future value of the payments, but we need to find the payments. We can use the relationship $FV = payment(FVIFA_{i\%,n})$ to solve for the payment as follows:

$$\$1,000,000 = payment(FVIFA_{8\%,20})$$
$$payment = \$1,000,000/FVIFA_{8\%,20}$$
$$= \$1,000,000/45.7620 = \$21,852.19.$$

? How much would Jake have to set aside at the end of each year if he could earn 10% on his money and did not plan to retire for 25 years?

Answer: $10,168.07.

$$\$1,000,000 = payment(FVIFA_{10\%,25})$$
$$payment = \$1,000,000/FVIFA_{10\%,25}$$
$$= \$1,000,000/98.3471 = \$10,168.07$$

23. There are other times when we know the present value of the payments, but wish to know the payments. For example, if Jake were going to buy a $15,000 car and planned to put $5,000 down and finance the rest at 12%, he would make equal payments on the loan each month for the specified time of the loan. The first payment would be due one month after he signed the loan agreement, so the time line for a 4-year loan would appear as follows:

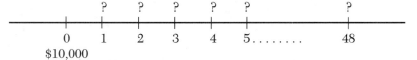

Note that there are 48 periods since the payments are made each month for 4 years. Note also that the amount of the loan is $10,000 since that is the amount that Jake is borrowing today. We know the present value and want to find the payments. The relationship is $PV = payment(PVIFA_{i\%,n})$. The interest rate is 12%, but remember that this is the stated annual rate. The monthly rate is 12%/12 = 1%. We can solve for the payment as follows:

$$\$10,000 = payment(PVIFA_{1\%,48})$$

$$payment = \$10,000/PVIFA_{1\%,48}$$

$$= \$10,000/37.9740 = \$263.34.$$

? If Jake had instead had a 3-year loan, what would his monthly payments be?

Answer: $332.14.

$$\$10,000 = payment(PVIFA_{1\%,36})$$

$$payment = \$10,000/PVIFA_{1\%,36}$$

$$= \$10,000/30.1075 = \$332.14$$

24.   Sometimes we expect the equal payments to continue indefinitely, in which case we are dealing with a **perpetuity**. An example of this is preferred stock dividends. These dividends are typically fixed and will be paid "forever." The present value of a perpetuity is equal to the payment divided by the interest rate. (This can be derived mathematically from the basic equation

$$PV = FV \times \frac{1}{(1+i)^n},$$

but the derivation is beyond the scope of this book.) For instance, if an issue of preferred stock pays a $7.00 a share dividend and the relevant interest rate is 10%, the present value of the dividends is $7.00/0.10 = $70.00.

? If a perpetual bond offers an interest payment of $50 a year indefinitely and the relevant interest rate is 8%, what is the present value of these interest payments?

Answer: $625.

$$PV = \$50/0.08 = \$625.00$$

25.   Oftentimes there are situations in which we have uneven payment streams. For example, suppose Jake's daughter Judy is in college and is also trying to establish a savings plan. For the next 2 years while she's still in college, she believes she can save $500 a year by giving up her Twinkies at lunch. After she gets a job using her newly earned sheepskin, she hopes to save $1,200 a year. If she wants to know how much she will have saved at the end of 5 years if she can earn 5% on her money, she must find the future value of these uneven payment streams. The time line for the payments is as follows:

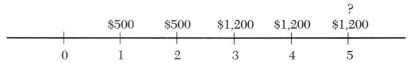

We can begin to solve this problem by finding the future value of the two $500 payments by using the future value interest factor of an annuity.

$$FV = \$500(FVIFA_{5\%,2})$$

$$= \$500(2.0500) = \$1,025$$

This is the future value of the two payments at the end of the second period. Since Judy will be leaving the money in the account until the end of the fifth year, we need to determine what the $1,025 will grow to by the end of year 5. We can do this by finding the future value in 3 years of the $1,025 as a lump sum.

$$FV = \$1,025(1.05)^3$$
$$= \$1,025(FVIF_{5\%,3})$$
$$= \$1,025(1.1576) = \$1,186.54$$

Next we need to determine how much the three $1,200 payments will accumulate to by the end of year 5. We can do this by finding the future value of a 3-year ordinary annuity.

$$FV = \$1,200(FVIFA_{5\%,3})$$
$$= \$1,200(3.1525) = \$3,783.00$$

Finally, we can add this to the $1,186.54 that the two $500 payments accumulated to by the end of the fifth year.

$$\$1,186.54 + \$3,783.00 = \$4,969.54$$

Judy will have $4,969.54 in her account by the end of the fifth year.

? If Judy believes that she can save only $300 a year for the 2 remaining years she is in school and $1,600 for the following 6 years, how much will she have in her account at the end of 8 years, assuming she can earn 5% on her money?

Answer: $11,707.20.
A time line depicting the cash flows is as follows:

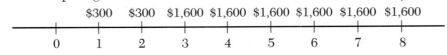

Step 1:   Find the future value at the end of year two of the two $300 deposits. The two payments are an annuity, so we can find the future value of the two period annuity as follows:

$$FV = \$300(FVIFA_{5\%,2})$$
$$= \$300(2.0500) = \$615.00.$$

Step 2:   Determine what the value of the $615.00 will be at the end of year 8, which is 6 years from the end of year 2, if it is left in the account. The $615.00 is a lump sum, so we use the lump-sum future value interest factor to find the future value at the end of year 8.

$$FV = \$615(FVIF_{5\%,6})$$
$$= \$615(1.3401) = \$824.16$$

Step 3:   Determine the value of the six $1,600 deposits at the end of year 8. The six payments are a 6-year ordinary annuity.

$$FV = \$1,600(FVIFA_{5\%,6})$$
$$= \$1,600(6.8019) = \$10,883.04$$

Step 4:   Find the total value in the account at the end of the eighth year.
We do this by adding the future value of the $615.00 to the future value of the
$1,600 6-year annuity.

$$\$10{,}883.04 + \$824.16 = \$11{,}707.20$$

26.   Jake is trying to decide whether to purchase an item with $3,050 cash today, or make
the following payments:

Year	Payment
1	$500
2	$500
3	$1,000
4	$1,000
5	$600

He can earn 5% on his money. In this situation we know if Jake pays cash today, the item
will cost him $3,050. In order to compare this to the payments, we need to convert the
future payments to current dollars by finding the present value of them. We could discount each payment back individually and sum the present values as follows:

$$PV = \$500 \times \frac{1}{(1.05)^1} + \$500 \times \frac{1}{(1.05)^2} + \$1{,}000 \times \frac{1}{(1.05)^3} + \$1{,}000 \times \frac{1}{(1.05)^4} + \$600 \times \frac{1}{(1.05)^5}.$$

While this is not too cumbersome when we are working with only five payments, it
becomes more so as the number of periods increases. The ability to use annuity factors
would be helpful. To demonstrate how annuity factors can be used, we will first use the
distributive property of algebra to factor out payments. This gives us the following:

$$PV = \$500[\frac{1}{(1.05)^1} + \frac{1}{(1.05)^2}] + \$1{,}000[\frac{1}{(1.05)^3} + \frac{1}{(1.05)^4}] + \$600[\frac{1}{(1.05)^5}].$$

The sum of $1/(1.05)^1$ and $1/(1.05)^2$ is given by the present value interest factor of an annuity for 5%, two periods. In order to get the sum of only $1/(1.05)^3$ and $1/(1.05)^4$, we can use
the present value interest factor for an annuity for 5%, four periods, which sums $1/(1.05)^1$
$+ 1/(1.05)^2 + 1/(1.05)^3 + 1/(1.05)^4$, and subtract the present value interest factor of an annuity for 5%, two periods to eliminate the first two terms, $1/(1.05)^1$ and $1/(1.05)^2$, from the
sum. The last payment of $600 is a lump-sum payment, not an annuity, and therefore we
use the present value interest factor (PVIF) for 5%, five periods to discount it back. Using
the factors, we can solve the problem as follows:

$$PV = \$500(PVIFA_{5\%,2}) + \$1{,}000(PVIFA_{5\%,4} - PVIFA_{5\%,2}) + \$600(PVIF_{5\%,5})$$
$$= \$500(1.8594) + \$1{,}000(3.5460 - 1.8594) + \$600(0.7835) = \$3{,}086.40.$$

Since the present value of the payments is greater than the cash needed to pay for the item
today ($3,050), Jake should pay cash.

? Jake has won a sweepstakes. He has the choice of receiving $1.5 million today or
accepting the following payments over the next 10 years, with the first payment to be made
at the end of this year:

Year	Payment
1	$100,000
2	$100,000
3	$100,000
4	$200,000
5	$200,000
6	$200,000
7	$200,000
8	$250,000
9	$250,000
10	$400,000

Assuming that these payments are guaranteed and no additional risk is involved, if Jake can earn 6% on his money, which is the better deal?

Answer: Jake is better off taking the $1.5 million today.

To answer this question, we need to find the present value of the payments in order to compare it to the amount offered today.

$$PV = \$100,000(PVIFA_{6\%,3}) + \$200,000(PVIFA_{6\%,7} - PVIFA_{6\%,3})$$

$$+ \ \$250,000(PVIFA_{6\%,9} - PVIFA_{6\%,7}) + \$400,000(PVIF_{6\%,10})$$

$$= \$100,000(2.6730) + \$200,000(5.5824 - 2,6730)$$

$$+ \ \$250,000(6.8017 - 5.5824) + \$400,000(0.5584) = \$1,377,365$$

Since this is less than $1,500,000, he is better off taking the money today.

Apply It

1. Why is the amount that accumulates in an account over a given period of time greater if compound interest is paid than if simple interest is paid? (Frames 2 and 3)

2. Which of the following methods of calculating interest will allow you to accumulate the most in a savings account in a given period of time? (Frame 13)
   a. 5%, compounded annually
   b. 5%, compounded semiannually
   c. 5%, compounded monthly

3. A credit card company is advertising an APR of 6% on balances transferred from other credit cards. Furthermore, no payments need be made for one full year. If interest is charged monthly, what is the monthly rate and what is the effective annual rate? (Frame 13)

4. Jaime would like to take a 3-year world tour. He estimates that he will need $30,000 a year. How much does Jaime need to have saved in order to make his first $30,000 withdrawal today if his account earns 8% annually? (Frame 21)

5. Juan has inherited some money and has decided to set aside $5,000 today in a special vacation account. If Juan leaves the money in the account for 4 years and earns a 10% annual rate on his money, how much will he have accumulated at the end of 4 years? (Frame 3)

6. Tang has decided to start saving for her retirement. If she can save $200 a month for the next 20 years in an account that pays 12%, compounded monthly, how much will she have accumulated at the end of 20 years? Assume she makes her first deposit at the end of this month. (Frames 15 and 16)

7. Josie wants to retire at the end of this year. She has calculated that she will need $40,000 a year to maintain her current standard of living. If Josie hopes to live for 30 years after retirement and plans to draw her first payment at the end of this year, how much must she have accumulated today if she can earn 8% annually on her savings? (Frame 18)

8. Mary and John are the proud parents of a new baby girl. They want to open an account that will accumulate to $21,000 by her twenty-first birthday. If they can earn 6% on the account, how much must they set aside today to accomplish this goal? (Frame 5)

9. Carlos has received $2,500 from some contract work he recently completed. He has decided to put the money in a separate account. When the account has grown to $5,000, he plans to surprise his wife with a new living room set. If Carlos earns 8% on his money, how long will his wife have to wait for this surprise? (Frame 9)

10. You purchased some stock 3 years ago for $32 a share. The stock paid no dividends, but it is currently selling for $48 a share. What is your annual rate of return? (Frames 7 and 8)

11. Joan has accumulated $250,000 in her retirement account. If she hopes to live for 25 more years, how much can she withdraw from her account each year if the account earns 7% a year in interest and she makes her first withdrawal at the end of this year? (Frame 23)

12. Given the same time period, what happens to each of the following as the interest rate increases? Why? (Frames 5, 15, and 18)
    a. present value of $1 to be received in the future
    b. future value of an annuity
    c. present value of an annuity

13. Given the same interest rate, what happens to each of the following as the number of periods increases? Why? (Frames 3, 5, and 18)
    a. present value of $1 to be received in the future
    b. future value of a dollar
    c. present value of an annuity

14. Bill just received his first paycheck and has decided to open a savings account with $125 today. He hopes to continue saving $125 each month. If he can earn 12%, compounded monthly, on his money, how much will he have accumulated at the end of 10 years? (Frame 17)

15. Tony is the beneficiary of a trust fund that will make the following payments to him:

Year 1:	$1,000
Years 2 and 3:	$2,000
Years 4, 5, and 6:	$5,000

The payments will be made at the end of each year. Tony also has the option of taking the money in a lump sum today. If Tony can earn 8% on his money, what is the lowest lump-sum settlement that he should accept? (Frame 26)

16. Hans wishes to have $40,000 accumulated 6 years from now when his daughter starts college. If he can earn 6% on his money, how much must he save each year to achieve this goal, assuming he makes end-of-year deposits? (Frame 22)

17. Cindy just turned 40 and has decided to open a special savings account to enable her to afford a face lift, a tummy tuck, and an Alaskan cruise when she turns 50. She believes that she can save $2,000 a year for the next 3 years while her children are finishing college. After that, she hopes to save $5,000 a year. How much will she have saved by her 50th birthday if she earns 5% on her money? (Frame 25)

18. Pierre has just finished paying off his mortgage and has decided to continue making those same monthly payments to himself. Beginning next month, he will deposit $1,000 each month into an account that pays 12% interest, compounded monthly. How much will he accumulate at the end of 10 years? (Frame 15)

19. If you were to deposit $2,000 into an account that paid 12% annually for your newborn child, at what age would your child become a millionaire? (Frame 9)

20. Your Uncle Solomon has agreed to lend you $10,000 today to help you finance your last 2 years of college. However, he expects you to repay $12,000 2 years after you graduate (i.e., 4 years from today). What effective annual rate are you paying? (Frame 7)

Apply It Answers

1. When interest is compounded, you earn interest on your interest. When simple interest is paid, you earn interest only on your original deposit.

2. You will accumulate the most in the account that pays 5%, compounded monthly, since you will earn interest each month and will then earn interest on the interest. You could also look at the effective annual rates offered by each of the alternatives listed. The EAR of 5%, compounded annually, is just 5%. The EAR of 5%, compounded semiannually is $(1.025)^2 - 1 = 5.06\%$. The EAR of 5%, compounded monthly, is $(1.004167)^{12} - 1 = 5.12\%$.

3. The monthly rate is 6%/12 = 0.5%, so the EAR = $(1.005)^{12} - 1 = 6.17\%$.

4.

```
              ?
        $30,000  $30,000  $30,000
     +----+--------+--------+--------+
     0    1        2        3
```

Note that this is an annuity due, and we are looking for the present value.

$$PV = \$30,000(PVIFA_{8\%,2}) + \$30,000$$

$$= \$30,000(1.7833) + \$30,000 = \$83,499$$

5. This is the future value of a lump sum.
$$FV = \$5,000(FVIF_{10\%,4})$$

$$= \$5,000(1.4641) = \$7,320.50$$

6. This is the future value of an annuity, but interest is compounded 12 times a year, so the interest rate per period is 1% and the number of periods is 240. Since tables do not contain this factor, we must use the formula

$$FVIFA_{i\%,n} = \frac{(1+i)^n - 1}{i}$$

to calculate the factor before we can solve the problem.

$$FVIFA_{1\%,240} = \frac{(1.01)^{240} - 1}{0.01} = 989.2554$$

Then FV = $200(FVIFA_{1\%,240}) = \$200(989.2554) = \$197,851.00.

7. This is the present value of an ordinary annuity.

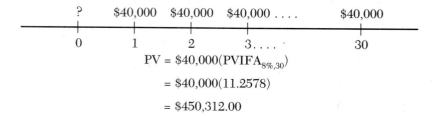

```
  ?      $40,000  $40,000  $40,000 . . . .        $40,000
  |         |        |        |                      |
  0         1        2        3. . . .              30
```

$$PV = \$40,000(PVIFA_{8\%,30})$$
$$= \$40,000(11.2578)$$
$$= \$450,312.00$$

8. This is the present value of a single lump-sum deposit.

$$PV = \$21,000(PVIF_{6\%,21})$$
$$= \$21,000(0.2942)$$
$$= \$6,178.20$$

9. In this case we are looking for the number of periods.

$$FV = PV(1 + i)^t$$
$$\$5,000 = \$2,500(1.08)^t$$
$$t \ln(1.08) = \ln 2$$
$$t = \ln 2/\ln 1.08 = 0.6931/0.0770 \approx 9 \text{ years}$$

10. Here we want to find the interest rate, given that we know the present value, the future value and the time period.

$$\$48 = \$32(1+i)^3$$
$$(1+i)^3 = \frac{\$48}{\$32}$$
$$(1+i) = \sqrt[3]{\frac{\$48}{\$32}}$$
$$i = \sqrt[3]{\frac{\$48}{\$32}} - 1 = 14.5\%$$

11. In this problem we are looking for the payment given that we know the present value of the payments.

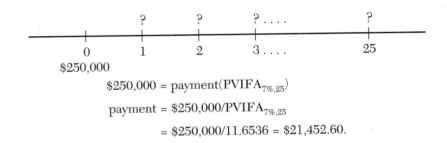

$$\$250,000 = payment(PVIFA_{7\%,25})$$

$$payment = \$250,000/PVIFA_{7\%,25}$$

$$= \$250,000/11.6536 = \$21,452.60.$$

12. As the interest rate increases, the present value of $1 to be received in the future decreases, since an amount deposited today will earn more interest and, therefore, the amount that is needed today to obtain $1 in the future is less. The future value of an annuity will be higher since each payment will earn interest at a higher rate. The present value of an annuity decreases as the interest rate increases since, again, as the interest rate we can earn rises, the amount we must have in an account today to make a series of equal withdrawals will be less.

13. As the number of periods increases, the present value of $1 to be received in the future is less, since the amount we deposit today will earn interest for a longer number of periods. The future value of $1 will increase since the dollar will earn interest for more periods. The present value of an annuity will also increase since there are more payments involved.

14. This is the future value of an annuity due. The interest rate is compounded more than once a year, so the interest rate per period is 12%/12 = 1%. The number of periods is 120.

	$125	$125	$125		?
	0	1	2.		120

Since the first payment earns interest the full 120 periods, we need to use the future value interest factor of an annuity for 121 periods, since the factors are calculated based on end-of-period payments. This factor can be calculated using the formula

$$FVIFA_{i\%,n} = \frac{(1+i)^n - 1}{i}.$$

So,

$$FVIFA_{1\%,121} = \frac{(1.01)^{121} - 1}{0.01} = 233.3391$$

and

$$FV = \$125(FVIFA_{1\%,121} - 1)$$

$$= \$125(233.3391 - 1)$$

$$= \$125(232.3391) = \$29,042.39.$$

15. In this case we are dealing with an uneven stream of payments. Note that the first payment of $1,000 is a lump sum and is discounted back using a lump-sum factor.

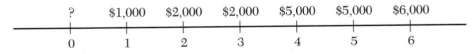

$$PV = \$1,000(PVIF_{8\%,1}) + \$2,000(PVIFA_{8\%,3} - PVIFA_{8\%,1})$$
$$+ \$5,000(PVIFA_{8\%,6} - PVIFA_{8\%,3})$$
$$PV = \$1,000(0.9259) + \$2,000(2.5771 - 0.9259) + \$5,000(4.6229$$
$$- 2.5771) = \$14,457.30$$

16. Here we know the future value of the payments and want to find the payments.

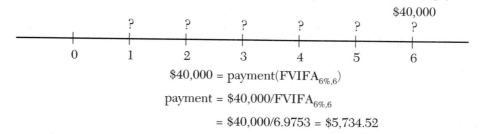

$$\$40,000 = payment(FVIFA_{6\%,6})$$
$$payment = \$40,000/FVIFA_{6\%,6}$$
$$= \$40,000/6.9753 = \$5,734.52$$

17. This is a problem involving the future value of an uneven stream of payments. We first find the future value of the $2,000 as a 3-year annuity. That is the future value at the end of the third year, however, so we must find the value of that amount given that it is left in the account to earn interest for 7 more years. To that we add the future value of the $5,000 7-year annuity.

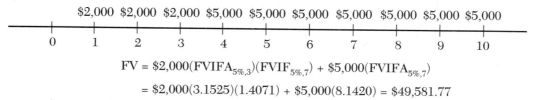

$$FV = \$2,000(FVIFA_{5\%,3})(FVIF_{5\%,7}) + \$5,000(FVIFA_{5\%,7})$$
$$= \$2,000(3.1525)(1.4071) + \$5,000(8.1420) = \$49,581.77$$

18. This is the future value of an ordinary annuity. Interest is compounded monthly, however, so the interest rate per period is 1% and the number of periods is 120. The future value interest factor of the annuity is

$$FVIFA_{1\%,120} = \frac{(1.01)^{120} - 1}{0.01} = 230.0387.$$

The future value of the annuity is, therefore,

$$FV = \$1,000(FVIFA_{1\%,120})$$
$$= \$1,000(230.0387) = \$230,038.70.$$

19. In this case we are looking for the number of periods.

$$FV = PV(1 + i)^t$$
$$\$1,000,000 = \$2,000(1.12)^t$$
$$(1.12)^t = \$1,000,000/\$2,000 = 500$$
$$t \ln(1.12) = \ln 500$$
$$t = \ln 500/\ln 1.12 = 6.2146/0.1133 = 54.8 \approx 55 \text{ years old}$$

20. In this case we are trying to find the interest rate.

$$FV = PV(1+i)^t$$

$$\$12,000 = \$10,000(1+i)^4$$

$$(1+i)^4 = \frac{\$12,000}{\$10,000} = 1.2000$$

$$(1+i) = \sqrt[4]{1.2000}$$

$$i = \sqrt[4]{1.2000} - 1 = 1.0466 - 1 = 4.66\%$$

STOCK AND BOND VALUATION

In this module, you will learn how to apply the concepts of time value of money (Module 5) in order to determine the prices at which stocks and bonds should be selling. You will also become familiar with some of the terminology involved with investing in these types of securities, including the different types of returns associated with them and how to calculate these returns. (For a more thorough coverage of the specific types of instruments available, see Module 2.)

Equations introduced in this module

$$\text{Bond price} = \text{coupon}\,(\text{PVIFA}_{\text{ytm,n}}) + \text{maturity value}(\text{PVIF}_{\text{ytm,n}})$$

$$\text{Approximate YTM} = \frac{\text{coupon} + \dfrac{\text{face value} - \text{price}}{\text{number of years before maturity}}}{\dfrac{\text{price} + \text{face value}}{2}}$$

$$\text{Current yield} = \frac{\text{annual interest income}}{\text{price}}$$

$$\text{Price (preferred stock)} = \frac{\text{dividend}}{\text{R}}$$

$$\text{Rate of return (preferred stock)} = \text{R} = \frac{\text{dividend}}{\text{price}}$$

115

$$\text{Price (common stock)} = PV = \frac{\text{dividend}_1}{(1+R)^1} + \frac{\text{dividend}_2}{(1+R)^2} + \frac{\text{dividend}_3}{(1+R)^3} + \cdots$$

$$\text{Price (common stock assuming constant growth)} = \frac{\text{dividend}_1}{R-g}$$

$$\text{Dividend}_1 = \text{Dividend}_0(1+g)$$

$$\text{Rate of return (common stock)} = \frac{\text{dividend}_1}{\text{price}} + g$$

$$\text{One - year holding period return} = \frac{\text{what you get} - \text{what you paid}}{\text{what you paid}}$$

1.   The price of any financial asset is determined by calculating the present value of its expected future cash flows. The interest rate that is used to translate the expected future cash flows into current dollars must compensate the investor for his risk. Therefore, it can be thought of as the rate of return that an investor could earn on an investment of similar risk or, alternatively, what investors require as a rate of return on the investment. Therefore, if we are attempting to determine the price of a Treasury security, we discount the expected cash flows at what is referred to as the risk-free rate. The risk-free rate compensates the investor for any expected losses in purchasing power (due to inflation) as well as for simply lending the government the money. (U.S. government instruments are considered to be free of **default risk**, which is the risk that the debt will not be repaid as scheduled. For a more complete discussion of these securities, refer to Module 2.)

For example, suppose Marshall Ryan is interested in buying a 12-month Treasury bill that has a maturity value of $10,000. Mr. Ryan requires a 6% return. Treasury bills sell at a discount, which means that they sell for less than their face value and do not make periodic interest payments. The price that Mr. Ryan should pay is the present value of the $10,000 to be received at the end of the year.

$$\text{Price} = \$10{,}000 \times 1/(1.06)^1$$

$$= \$10{,}000(\text{PVIF}_{6\%,1})$$

$$= \$10{,}000(0.9434) = \$9{,}434.00$$

If Mr. Ryan pays more than $9,434.00 for the bill, he will not be earning 6% on his money.

? If Mr. Ryan wants an 8% return, what is the maximum price he should pay for the Treasury bill?

Answer: $9,259.00.

$$\text{Price} = \$10{,}000 \times 1/(1.08)^1$$

$$= \$10{,}000(\text{PVIF}_{8\%,1})$$

$$= \$10{,}000(0.9259) = \$9{,}259.00$$

2.   Unlike Treasury bills, Treasury notes and bonds, as well as notes and bonds issued by corporations, typically pay interest periodically. The annual interest rate is referred to as the **coupon rate**, and the dollar amount of the interest payment is referred to as the **coupon**. Treasury notes usually have a face value, or maturity value, of $5,000, and

Treasury bonds usually have a face value of $1,000. The dollar amount of the coupon is equal to the coupon rate times the face value of the security.

Suppose we want to determine the price of a 15-year, $1,000 face value Treasury bond that pays a 7% coupon, and the risk-free rate is 6%. In this case the coupon payments are $0.07 \times \$1,000 = \$70$ each year, and we receive the $1,000 face value at maturity. We can depict these cash flows as follows:

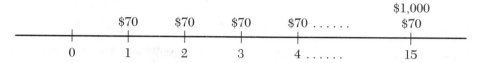

We can discount back the coupon payments as an ordinary annuity and the face value as a lump sum.

$$\text{Price} = \text{PV} = \$70(\text{PVIFA}_{6\%,15}) + \$1,000(\text{PVIF}_{6\%,15})$$
$$= \$70(9.7122) + \$1,000(0.4173) = \$1,097.15$$

So $1,097.15 is the maximum price an investor who wants a 6% return on this investment should pay. This bond is said to be selling at a **premium**, which means that it is selling for more than its face value. This will occur when the coupon rate on the bond is higher than the required rate of return. If it had sold for par (i.e., its face value), everyone would rush to buy this bond since it would be offering a 7% return when 6% is sufficient to compensate investors for the risk they are taking. This demand for the bond will push the price up until the bond is yielding only 6%.

? What is the annual amount of interest that an investor who buys a $5,000, 5-year Treasury note that pays an 8% coupon will earn?

? If the investor requires a 10% return on the note, what is the maximum price he should be willing to pay for it?

Answers: $400, $4,620.82.

The interest is equal to the coupon rate times the face value of the note, so $0.08 \times \$5,000 = \$400$. The price is simply the present value of the expected future cash flows, calculated as follows:

$$\text{Price} = \$400(\text{PVIFA}_{10\%,5}) + \$5,000(\text{PVIF}_{10\%,5})$$
$$= \$400(3.7908) + \$5,000(0.6209) = \$4,620.82.$$

3. Most notes and bonds, both government and corporate, pay interest semiannually, and this must be taken into account when determining the price. For example, suppose Mr. Ryan is considering purchasing an issue of bonds of the Greyhound Corporation. The bonds pay a 10% coupon, with interest paid semiannually, have a $1,000 face value, and mature in 6 years. Since similar-risk bonds are yielding 12% annually, Mr. Ryan requires at least a 12% yield on the Greyhound bonds as well. The bonds pay $0.10 \times \$1,000 = \$100$ in interest each year. Since interest is paid semiannually, Mr. Ryan will receive $50 in interest every 6 months for 6 years, as well as the $1,000 face value at maturity. When we discount these cash flows back, we must also use an equivalent semiannual opportunity cost. Since similar bonds are yielding 12%, the 6-month yield is 6%. (In reality, this is an approximate 6-month yield, but further discussion is beyond the scope of this guide.) The number of 6-month periods in 6 years is 12, and the maximum price that Mr. Ryan should pay for these bonds is calculated as follows:

$$\text{Price} = \$50(\text{PVIFA}_{6\%,12}) + \$1,000(\text{PVIF}_{6\%,12})$$
$$= \$50(8.3838) + \$1,000(0.4970) = \$916.19.$$

Note that in this case, the bond is selling for less than its face value of $1,000. This bond is said to be selling at a **discount,** or for less than its face value. This occurs when the coupon rate is less than the required rate of return. If an investor were to pay face value for this bond, he would get a return of 10%, which is the coupon rate. But similar risk instruments are paying 12%, so the price of this bond will fall until the investor receives a 12% return on this bond as well—part of the return is from interest income and part of it is from capital gains. (**Capital gains** is the difference between the purchase price of the bond and the amount that the investor receives when the bond matures.)

? Mr. Ryan is also considering the purchase of some Viacom bonds that mature in 12 years and have an 8% coupon. The bonds pay interest semiannually and have a $1,000 face value. Mr. Ryan requires a 12% return on these bonds as well. What is the maximum price Mr. Ryan should pay for these bonds?

Answer: $749.02.

$$\text{Price} = \$40(\text{PVIFA}_{6\%,24}) + \$1,000(\text{PVIF}_{6\%,24})$$
$$= \$40(12.5504) + \$1,000(0.2470) = \$749.02$$

4. The equivalent annual discount rate that is used to determine the price of a bond is the bond's **yield-to-maturity**. This is the promised average annual yield that an investor will receive if he buys the bond at that price and holds the bond to maturity. So the yield-to-maturity on the Greyhound bonds in the example above is 12%.

? What is the yield-to-maturity on the Viacom bonds?

Answer: 12%.
12% is the annual rate we used to discount back the cash flows. This is the yield an investor can expect to receive if he buys the bonds at the price calculated and holds them to maturity.

5. Sometimes we know the price of a bond and its expected future cash flows, but we want to determine the yield-to-maturity on the bond. Since the yield-to-maturity is the discount rate that makes the price equal to the expected future cash flows, we can use the equation

$$\text{Price} = \text{coupon}(\text{PVIFA}_{ytm,n}) + \text{maturity value}(\text{PVIF}_{ytm,n})$$

where n = number of years to maturity and ytm = yield-to-maturity, and solve it for the yield-to-maturity. For example, if we observe a $1,000 bond that matures in 10 years and pays a 10% coupon, with interest paid annually, selling for $1,134.20, the equation becomes

$$\$1,134.20 = \$100(\text{PVIFA}_{ytm,10}) + \$1,000(\text{PVIF}_{ytm,10}).$$

Unfortunately, this is an equation with two unknown quantities, PVIF and PVIFA. (It can also be thought of as a 10th-degree equation, with ytm as the unknown quantity. This is a more mathematically correct description.) Therefore, we must either use a financial calculator to solve for the yield-to-maturity, or we must use trial and error. To use trial and error, we simply try various values for the ytm to determine which value will make the price equal to the discounted expected future cash flows. Since the bond is selling at a premium, we know that its yield is less than the coupon rate on the bond, so we might try 7% as follows:

$$\$100(PVIFA_{7\%,10}) + \$1,000(PVIF_{7\%,10})$$
$$= \$100(7.0236) + \$1,000(0.5083) = \$1,210.66.$$

Since the price we got when we used 7% is higher than the current price of the bond ($1,134.20), the discount rate of 7% is too low. (Remember that the higher the discount rate, the lower is the present value of the cash flows.) So we might try 9%:

$$\$100(PVIFA_{9\%,10}) + \$1,000(PVIF_{9\%,10})$$
$$= \$100(6.4177) + \$1,000(0.4224) = \$1,064.17.$$

Now the price we have calculated is lower than the actual price of the bond, indicating that 9% is too high. Since the discount rate must be between 7% and 9%, we can try 8%:

$$\$100(PVIFA_{8\%,10}) + \$1,000(PVIF_{8\%,10})$$
$$= \$100(6.7101) + \$1,000(0.4632) = \$1,134.21.$$

There is only a penny difference, so 8% is the correct yield-to-maturity.

? A $1,000 bond that matures in 12 years and pays a 6% coupon, with interest paid annually, is selling for $785.18. Is its yield-to-maturity going to be higher or lower than the coupon rate?

? Write the equation that you will use to determine the yield-to-maturity.
Using 7%, 8%, 9%, and 10% as trials, determine which is the correct yield-to-maturity.

Answers: Higher, $785.18 = \$60(PVIFA_{ytm,12}) + \$1,000(PVIF_{ytm,12})$, 9%.
The yield-to-maturity is higher than the coupon rate since the bond is selling at a discount. Therefore, the investor will receive capital gains in addition to the interest income. Since the bond pays a 6% coupon annually, the interest payments are $60 each year, and the face value will be paid at maturity.

Trials:
Using 7%:
$60(7.9427) + $1,000(0.4440) = $920.56, so 7% is too low.
Using 8%:
$60(7.5361) + $1,000(0.3971) = $849.27, so 8% is also too low.
Using 9%:
$60(7.1607) + $1,000(0.3555) = $785.14. Since there are only pennies difference, 9% is the correct yield-to-maturity, and we need not even try 10%.

6. There is a formula that can be used to approximate the yield-to-maturity on a bond.

$$\text{Approximate YTM} = \frac{\text{coupon} + \dfrac{\text{face value} - \text{price}}{\text{number of years before maturity}}}{\dfrac{\text{price} + \text{face value}}{2}}$$

Using the previous example of the 10%, 10-year, $1,000 bond that was selling for $1,134.20, we can approximate its yield as follows:

$$\text{Approximate YTM} = \frac{\$100 + \dfrac{\$1,000 - \$1,134.20}{10}}{\dfrac{\$1,134.20 + \$1,000}{2}} = 8.1\%.$$

? Use the approximation formula to determine the yield-to-maturity on the $1,000, 6%, 12-year bond that was selling for $785.18.

Answer: 8.7%.

$$\text{Approximate YTM} = \frac{\$60 + \dfrac{\$1,000 - \$785.18}{12}}{\dfrac{\$1,000 + \$785.18}{2}} = 8.7\%$$

7.   If the bond pays interest semiannually, we can solve for the yield-to-maturity in the same manner, but bear in mind that the rate we get will be the semiannual rate. We can find the effective annual rate by using the formula $(1 + i_s)^2 - 1$, where i_s is the semiannual rate. (We can get an approximate annual rate by simply doubling the semiannual rate, but then we ignore the effect of compounding.) For example, if in our first example, the 10%, $1,000 bond with 10 years to maturity had paid interest *semiannually* and sold for $1,135.90, the equation would be $1,135.90 = \$50(\text{PVIFA}_{ytm,20})$ + $\$1,000(\text{PVIF}_{ytm,20})$, since the bond pays $50 interest every 6 months and there are twenty 6-month periods in 10 years.

In this case, we know that the semiannual yield is less than the semiannual coupon rate since the bond sells for a premium, so we might use 3% as a first trial as follows:

$$\$50(\text{PVIFA}_{3\%,20}) + \$1,000(\text{PVIF}_{3\%,20})$$

$$= \$50(14.8775) + \$1,000(0.5537) = \$1,297.58.$$

Since $1,297.58 is greater than the actual price, 3% is too low, so we will try 4%.

$$\$50(\text{PVIFA}_{4\%,20}) + \$1,000(\text{PVIF}_{4\%,20})$$

$$= \$50(13.5903) + \$1,000(0.4564) = \$1,135.92$$

Since this is within pennies of the price of the bond, 4% is the semiannual yield, and the effective annual yield-to-maturity is $(1.04)^2 - 1 = 8.16\%$.

? A $1,000, 8% coupon bond with 7 years to maturity is selling for $901.00. Write the equation that can be used to find the yield-to-maturity.

? Is the semiannual yield going to be higher or lower than the coupon rate?

? Use trial and error to determine the semiannual yield.

? What is the effective annual yield-to-maturity?

Answers: $901 = \$40(\text{PVIFA}_{ytm,14}) + \$1,000(\text{PVIF}_{ytm,14})$, higher, 5%, 10.25%.
Since the bond pays interest semiannually, it will pay $40 every 6 months, and there are fourteen 6-month periods in 7 years. It will also pay the face value at maturity.
Since the bond is selling at a discount, the investors are receiving a yield that is higher than the coupon rate.

**Possible trials: (You may have selected other
interest rates to try initially.)**
Using 6%:
$40(9.2950) + $1,000(0.4423) = $451.60, so 6% is too
  high.
Using 5%:
$40(9.8986) + $1,000(0.5051) = $901.04, so 5% is the
  semiannual yield-to-maturity.
  $(1.05)^2 - 1 = 10.25\%.$

---

8. Sometimes when brokers refer to the yield on a bond, they are not referring to the yield-to-maturity, but to the **current yield**. While the yield-to-maturity is the total return, with both capital gains or losses and interest income taken into account, that is promised to investors providing that the investor holds the bond to maturity, the current yield is the yield on interest income only. The current yield is calculated as follows:

$$\text{Current yield} = \frac{\text{annual interest income}}{\text{price}}.$$

In our first example of the 10%, 10-year bond that sold for $1,134.20, we calculated the yield-to-maturity to be 8%. The current yield is $100/$1,134.20 = 8.8%.

? What is the current yield on the 6%, $1,000 bond that sold for $785.18?

Answer: 7.6%.
The current yield is equal to $60/$785.18 = 7.6%.

9. The value of preferred stock is also equal to the present value of its expected future cash flows. Preferred stock typically pays a fixed dividend and has no maturity date, so to find the present value of the cash flows, we find the present value of a perpetuity.

$$\text{Price} = \text{PV} = \frac{\text{dividend}}{R}$$

where R is the required rate of return. Therefore, if Mr. Ryan requires a 9% return on his investment in the preferred stock of Armco Corporation, which pays a dividend of $2.10 per share, the maximum price he should pay is calculated as follows:

$$\text{Price} = \$2.10/0.09 = \$23.33.$$

? Armco has another issue of preferred stock that pays a dividend of $4.50. Because this issue has different, riskier terms than the issue described above, Mr. Ryan requires a 10% return on this issue. What is the maximum price he should pay?

Answer: $45.

$$\text{Price} = \$4.50/0.10 = \$45.00$$

10. Since the price of preferred stock is equal to its fixed dividend divided by the rate of return, we can easily find the return on an issue of preferred stock by solving the equation
Price = dividend for R:
          R

$$R = \frac{\text{dividend}}{\text{price}}.$$

For example, if Mr. Ryan were to pay $73.50 for an issue of preferred stock that pays a dividend of $5.25 per share, his annual rate of return is $5.25/$73.50 = 7.1%.

? If Mr. Ryan buys an issue of preferred stock that pays a $3.75 per share dividend for $37.25, what is his annual return on this investment?

Answer: 10.1%.

$$i = \$3.75/\$37.25 = 10.1\%$$

11.   The price of common stock is also equal to the present value of its expected future cash flows. Unlike preferred stock and bonds, however, common stock payments are not fixed and, unlike bonds, common stock has no maturity. Theoretically, the value of a share of common stock could be expressed in the following manner:

$$\text{Price} = \text{PV} = \frac{\text{dividend}_1}{(1+R)^1} + \frac{\text{dividend}_2}{(1+R)^2} + \frac{\text{dividend}_3}{(1+R)^3} + \ldots$$

where dividend$_t$ is the dividend payment for the t–th year. Since the dividends are expected to continue indefinitely, you can imagine how difficult it will be to predict the dividend to be paid 20 years from today, let alone 50 or 100 years into the future.

There are, fortunately, a couple of ways to circumvent the problem. The first method depends on a constant growth assumption. If we can assume that dividends will grow or decline at a constant rate indefinitely, the above equation boils down to the following:

$$\text{Price} = \frac{\text{dividend}_1}{R-g},$$

where R is the required rate of return, g is the constant growth rate and dividend$_1$ is the *expected dividend next year*. Note that it is *not* the current year's dividend. If we only know the current year's dividend, dividend$_0$, we can extrapolate the expected future dividend by multiplying today's dividend by 1 plus the growth rate; i.e.,

$$\text{Dividend}_1 = \text{dividend}_0(1 + g).$$

? The Twoboys Company paid a dividend of $0.50 per share this year. Dividends are expected to grow at a constant rate of 7% indefinitely. What is the expected dividend for next year?

Answer: $0.535.

$$\text{Dividend}_1 = \$0.50(1.07) = \$0.535$$

12.   If Mr. Ryan is considering purchasing a share of Twoboys stock and requires a 16% return on his investment, we can calculate the maximum price he should pay in the following manner:

$$\text{Price} = \frac{\text{dividend}_1}{R - g}$$

$$= \frac{\$0.535}{0.16 - 0.07} = \$5.94$$

? Suppose Mr. Ryan is also considering the purchase of stock in the Asman Corporation. Asman paid a dividend of $1.00 a share this year. Dividends are expected to grow at a constant rate of 5%, and Mr. Ryan requires a 14% return on his investment. What is the maximum price Mr. Ryan should pay for this stock?

Answer: $11.67.

The expected dividend next year is $1.00(1.05) = $1.05. The price is calculated as follows:

$$\text{Price} = \frac{\$1.05}{0.14 - 0.05} = \$11.67.$$

13.   The equation,

$$\text{Price} = \frac{\text{dividend}_1}{R - g}$$

is often referred to as the constant growth model, or the Gordon growth model after the man who formulated it. It can provide us with insight into what factors determine a stock's price, namely expected future dividends, the expected growth rate of those dividends, and the investor's required rate of return. Note that the price does not depend on the amount of time that the investor plans to hold this investment before selling it.

If we manipulate the equation algebraically to solve for the required rate of return, R, we get the following:

$$\text{Price}(R - g) = \text{dividend}_1$$

$$R - g = \frac{\text{dividend}_1}{\text{Price}}$$

$$R = \frac{\text{dividend}_1}{\text{Price}} + g.$$

In this form, we can see that the return a stock offers can be broken down into two components. Dividend$_1$/Price, is called the dividend yield, and it is the return that comes from dividend income only. The "g" represents the capital gains yield, or the return due to price appreciation. Two different firms may both offer the same total return, but one firm, say one that is in a mature industry and expects low, no, or negative growth, may give the investor his total return in dividend income, whereas a second firm, one that is growing rapidly, may pay no dividends, and instead offer its return in the form of capital gains. Yet a third firm, a moderate growth company, might offer part of the return in capital gains and part in dividend income. Different investors have different preferences for the type of return they want and will invest accordingly. This is referred to as the **clientele effect**.

For example, assume that the Moderate Corporation is expected to pay a dividend of $1.20 per share and currently sells for $48. If investors require a 10% return on this firm's stock, then the expected capital gains must be 7.5%, as calculated below, or no one would be buying the stock at the given price of $48.

$$R = \frac{dividend_1}{Price} + g$$

$$10\% = \frac{\$1.20}{\$48.00} + g$$

$$0.10 = 0.025 + g$$

$$g = 0.10 - 0.025 = 0.075 = 7.5\%$$

? If the Moderate Corporation is expected to pay a $0.75 per share dividend, is expected to grow at a rate of 5%, and is currently selling for $10 a share, what is its dividend yield, its capital gains yield, and its total return?

Answers: 7.5%, 5%, 12.5%.
The dividend yield is $0.75/$10.00 = 7.5%. The capital gains yield is the growth rate of 5%, and the total return is the sum of these two yields, which is 12.5%.

14.   Obviously, not all firms' futures are such that we can assume constant growth indefinitely. Also, note that our constant growth equation becomes invalid if the growth rate "g" is greater than the required rate of return "R." We would then get a negative number as a price, which makes no sense if the firm is growing so fast, at what is sometimes referred to as a supernormal rate. Nor can the equation be used if g = R since we would then have a zero in the denominator, and division by zero is undefined in mathematics.
   When it is inappropriate to use the constant growth formula for whatever reason, we can estimate a holding period, (this is for convenience only; remember that a stock's price does not depend on the holding period) forecast the dividends to be paid during that time, and forecast a selling price at the end of the holding period. (This forecasted selling price implicitly incorporates expected future dividends from that point in time.) We can then discount these values back at the required rate of return. For example, assume that Mr. Ryan is considering investing in the Thrice Corporation. He expects dividends to be $0.90, $1.03, and $1.05 in the first 3 years, respectively. At the end of the third year, he expects the stock to be selling for $28. If he requires a 12% return on this investment, the maximum price he should pay can be calculated as follows:

$$Price = PV = \frac{\$0.90}{(1.12)^1} + \frac{\$1.03}{(1.12)^2} + \frac{\$1.05}{(1.12)^3} + \frac{\$28.00}{(1.12)^3}$$

$$= \$0.90(PVIF_{12\%,1}) + \$1.03(PVIF_{12\%,2}) + \$1.05(PVIF_{12\%,3}) + \$28.00(PVIF_{12\%,3})$$

$$= \$0.90(0.8929) + \$1.03(0.7972) + \$1.05(0.7118) + \$28.00(0.7118) = \$22.30.$$

? Mr. Ryan is also considering buying some stock in the Forerunner Corporation. He plans to hold the stock for 4 years, during which time he expects to receive dividends of $0.75, $0.95, $1.00, and $1.10, respectively. He believes the stock will sell for $42 at the end of 4 years. If he wants to earn 14% on this investment, what is the maximum price he should pay for the stock?

Answer: $27.58.

$$Price = \$0.75(PVIF_{14\%,1}) + \$0.95(PVIF_{14\%,2}) + \$1.00(PVIF_{14\%,3})$$

$$+ \$1.10(PVIF_{14\%,4}) + \$42.00(PVIF_{14\%,4})$$

$$= \$0.75(0.8772) + \$0.95(0.7695) + \$1.00(0.6750)$$

$$+ \$1.10(0.5921) + \$42.00(0.5921) = \$27.58$$

15. Next, let us assume that Mr. Ryan is considering purchasing stock in Takeoff Corporation, which is currently growing at a fast rate of 30% annually. Mr. Ryan expects the firm to continue growing at this rate for the next 2 years, at which time its patent protection runs out. He then feels Takeoff will grow at a constant rate of 10% indefinitely. Takeoff currently pays a dividend of $0.30 a share, and Mr. Ryan requires a 16% return on his investment.

In this problem, we can easily get the first 2 years' cash flows as follows:

$$\text{Dividend}_1 = \text{Dividend}_0(1 + g) = \$0.30(1.30) = \$0.39$$
$$\text{Dividend}_2 = \text{Dividend}_1(1 + g) = \$0.39(1.30) = \$0.51.$$

It is at the end of year 2 that the firm is expected to grow at a constant rate of 10%. We can use this information to determine the price at that point in time by utilizing the constant growth model,

$$\text{Price} = \frac{\text{dividend}_1}{R - g}.$$

Since we are determining the price at the end of year 2, we need to use the next expected dividend, dividend_3, in the model.

$$\text{Dividend}_3 = \text{dividend}_2(1 + g) = \$0.51(1.10) = \$0.56$$

Note that "g" is now 10%. The price at the end of year 2 is, therefore,

$$\text{Price}_2 = \frac{\text{dividend}_3}{R - g} = \frac{\$0.56}{0.16 - 0.10} = \$9.33.$$

We now have the next 2 years' expected dividends and the selling price at the end of 2 years as depicted on the time line below.

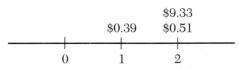

In order to determine what Mr. Ryan should pay for the stock today, we must discount back these cash flows to time zero.

$$\text{Price}_0 = \frac{\$0.39}{(1.16)^1} + \frac{\$0.51}{(1.16)^2} + \frac{\$9.33}{(1.16)^2}$$
$$= \$0.39(0.8621) + \$0.51(0.7432) + \$9.33(0.7432) = \$7.65$$

? Mr. Ryan is also considering purchasing stock in the GNU Corporation, which is currently growing at a rate of 22% annually. Mr. Ryan anticipates that this growth rate will continue only for 4 more years, at which point he expects the firm to continue growing at 11% indefinitely. Mr. Ryan expects the next dividend to be $0.50 per share, and he requires a 13% return on this investment. What is the maximum price he should pay for this stock?

Answer: $47.95.

First it is necessary to determine the dividends for years 1 through 4 as follows:

$$\text{Dividend}_1 = \$0.50$$
$$\text{Dividend}_2 = \$0.50(1.22) = \$0.61$$
$$\text{Dividend}_3 = \$0.61(1.22) = \$0.74$$
$$\text{Dividend}_4 = \$0.74(1.22) = \$1.34$$

Next, we can find the dividend at the end of the fifth year, which is the year that the constant growth is expected to commence, and use it to determine an expected selling price at the end of year 4.

$$\text{Dividend}_5 = \$1.34(1.11) = \$1.49$$

$$\text{Price}_4 = \frac{\text{dividend}_5}{R-g} = \frac{\$1.49}{0.13-0.11} = \$74.50$$

To find the price that Mr. Ryan should pay today, we now discount back the dividends for years 1 through 4 and the expected selling price at the end of 4 years.

$$\text{Price}_0 = \frac{\$0.50}{(1.13)^1} + \frac{\$0.61}{(1.13)^2} + \frac{\$0.74}{(1.13)^3} + \frac{\$1.34}{(1.13)^4} + \frac{\$74.50}{(1.13)^4}$$

$$= \$0.50(0.8850) + \$0.6(0.7831) + \$0.74(0.6931)$$

$$+ \$1.34(0.6133) + \$74.50(0.6133) = \$47.95$$

16. As another example, assume that Mr. Ryan expects dividends for the SC Corporation to grow at an annual rate of 3% for the next 3 years and then expects the firm to reach maturity and have a zero growth rate. SC paid a dividend this year of $2.00 a share, and Mr. Ryan requires a 10% return on his investment. In this case, the dividend cash flows are as follows:

$$\text{Dividend}_1 = \$2.00(1.03) = \$2.06$$
$$\text{Dividend}_2 = \$2.06(1.03) = \$2.12$$
$$\text{Dividend}_3 = \$2.12(1.03) = \$2.18$$

Since from this point on, the firm is expected to cease growing, the selling price at the end of year 3 will be the present value of a perpetuity because the $2.18 dividend is expected to continue at that same level indefinitely. Recall that the present value of a perpetuity is simply the perpetual cash flow divided by the required rate of return. So, $\text{Price}_3 = \$2.18/0.10 = \$21.80$. The price that Mr. Ryan should pay today is the present value of all of these cash flows, discounted back to time zero.

$$\text{Price}_0 = \frac{\$2.06}{(1.10)^1} + \frac{\$2.12}{(1.10)^2} + \frac{\$2.18}{(1.10)^3} + \frac{\$21.80}{(1.10)^3}$$

$$= \$2.06(0.9091) + \$2.12(0.8264) + \$2.18(0.7513) + \$21.80(0.7513) = \$21.64$$

? Mr. Ryan is considering investing in a stock that paid a dividend of $0.80 a share this year. He expects this dividend to grow at a rate of 15% for the next 2 years, at which point he expects the growth to stop and dividends to remain constant. If Mr. Ryan requires a 9% return on his investment, what is the maximum price he should pay for the stock?

Answer: $11.63.

The expected dividends in years 1 and 2 are as follows:

$$\text{Dividend}_1 = \$0.80(1.15) = \$0.92$$
$$\text{Dividend}_2 = \$0.92(1.15) = \$1.058.$$

Since dividends are expected to remain constant from this point on, the expected price at the end of year 2 is $1.058/0.09 = $11.76. We discount this back along with the expected dividends for years 1 and 2 to determine the price that Mr. Ryan should pay for the stock today.

$$\text{Price}_0 = \frac{\$0.92}{(1.09)^1} + \frac{\$1.058}{(1.09)^2} + \frac{\$11.76}{(1.09)^2}$$

$$= \$0.92(0.9174) + \$1.058(0.8417) + \$11.76(0.8417) = \$11.63$$

17. Regardless of whether we are referring to stock or bond investments, we can calculate a 1-year **holding period return** by using the following equation:

$$HPR = \frac{\text{what you get} - \text{what you paid}}{\text{what you paid}}.$$

Note that the "what you get" should include any interest or dividend income as well as the selling price of the security. This formula is valid *only* when calculating a 1-year return since future dividends, interest, and selling prices would need to be discounted back further if we were considering a longer holding period. As it is, this 1-year formula is a bit inaccurate since dividends on stock are normally paid quarterly and interest on bonds is typically paid semi-annually, but the formula does not consider these timing elements. It assumes all cash flows occur at the end of the year. As an example, let us assume that Mr. Ryan purchased a bond 1 year ago for $1,000. The bond paid a 6% coupon. After receiving the interest payments, Mr. Ryan sold the bond for $1,090. We can calculate his holding period return as follows:

$$HPR = \frac{(\$60 + \$1,090) - \$1,000}{\$1,000} = 15\%.$$

 Assume Mr. Ryan purchased some shares of a stock for $1,200. He received dividends of $30.00 over the year, and then sold the stock for $1,125. What was his holding period return?

Answer: −3.75%.

$$HPR = \frac{(\$1,125 + \$30) - \$1,200}{\$1,200} = -3.75\%$$

Apply It

1. If a bond is selling at a premium, is its yield-to-maturity going to be greater than or less than its coupon rate? Why? (Frame 2)

2. What does it mean when a security is said to be selling at a discount? (Frame 1)

3. An investor is considering buying a $1,000, 5% coupon bond, with 8 years remaining to maturity. Interest is paid semiannually.
   a. What is the maximum price he should pay for the bond if he requires a 10% return? (Frame 3)
   b. What is his current yield? (Frame 8)
   c. What return will the investor receive if he holds this bond to maturity? (Frame 4)

4. An investor is considering investing in an issue of preferred stock that pays a $4.50 annual dividend.
   a. If he requires a 7% rate of return, what is the maximum price he should pay for the stock? (Frame 9)
   b. If the stock is selling for $60 a share, what return will an investor receive on this investment? (Frame 10)

5. Pierre is considering investing in a firm that currently pays a dividend of $1.10. The dividends are expected to grow at a rate of 8% annually in the foreseeable future.
   a. If Pierre requires a 12% return on this investment, what is the maximum price he should pay for the stock? (Frame 11)
   b. If he pays the price determined in part (a), what is his dividend yield? (Frame 13)

6. Selena is considering investing in a stock that currently pays a $0.50 dividend. The dividend is expected to grow at a rate of 12% annually for the next 4 years. Afterwards, the growth rate is expected to be 5% indefinitely. If Selena wishes to get a 16% return on this investment, what is the maximum price she should pay? (Frame 15)

7. Jack Merryman is considering investing in a stock that is expected to pay dividends of $1.00 and $2.00 for the next 2 years, respectively, at which point dividends are expected to remain constant. What is the maximum price he should pay for the stock if he requires a 12% return? (Frame 16)

8. Otto Deutsch wants to purchase a 9%, $1,000 bond that matures in 5 years and pays interest annually.
   a. If he wants an 11% return on this investment, what is the maximum price he should pay for the bond? (Frame 2)
   b. After 1 year, Mr. Deutsch needs to sell this bond. Similar risk bonds are yielding 10% at that time. What price can he expect to receive for the bond? (Frame 2)
   c. If Otto purchased the bond for the price calculated in part (a) and sells it for the price calculated in part (b), what is his holding period return? (Frame 17)
   d. If instead of selling the bond, Otto had held the bond to maturity, what would his average annual return have been? (Frame 4)

9. Julie bought a zero coupon bond of the ABC Corporation for $550. The bond has a face value of $1,000 and matures in 10 years. What is her yield-to-maturity? (Frame 5)

Apply It Answers

1. The yield-to-maturity will be less than the coupon rate since the investor will not receive as much as he paid for it when the bond matures. The capital loss will offset some of the return from interest income.

2. When a security is selling at a discount, it means that it is selling for less than its maturity value.

3. a. Since interest is paid semiannually, the interest paid every 6 months is $25, and there are 16 periods in 8 years. The semiannual opportunity cost is 5%.

$$\text{Price} = \$25(\text{PVIFA}_{5\%,16}) + \$1,000(\text{PVIFA}_{5\%,16})$$

$$= \$25(10.8378) + \$1,000(0.4581) = \$729.05$$

   b. The current yield is the annual interest payment divided by the price, so current yield = $50/$729.05 = 6.9%.
   c. If the investor holds the bond until maturity, he will earn the yield-to-maturity, which is the interest rate that equated the price with the expected future cash flows. In this case, the semiannual rate was 5%. This is equivalent to $(1.05)^2 - 1 = 10.25\%$ annually.

4. a. The price of preferred stock is the present value of its perpetual dividend payments, so Price = $4.50/0.07 = $64.29.

   b. The investor's return is the dividend divided by the price he paid, so $4.50/$60 = 7.5%.

5. a. It is first necessary to determine the expected dividend for next year, given that we know the current dividend.

   $$\text{Dividend}_1 = \$1.10(1.08) = \$1.19$$

   Now, using the constant growth model, we can calculate the price as follows:

   $$\text{Price} = \frac{\$1.19}{0.12 - 0.08} = \$29.75.$$

   b. The dividend yield is the annual dividend divided by the price, so Pierre's dividend yield is $1.19/$29.75 = 4%.

6. We first need to determine the dividends in the years prior to the point at which the firm starts growing at a constant rate.

   $$\text{Dividend}_1 = \$0.50(1.12) = \$0.56$$
   $$\text{Dividend}_2 = \$0.56(1.12) = \$0.63$$
   $$\text{Dividend}_3 = \$0.63(1.12) = \$0.71$$
   $$\text{Dividend}_4 = \$0.71(1.12) = \$0.80$$

   We also need to determine the dividend in year 5 in order to use it to calculate the expected selling price at the end of year 4.

   $$\text{Dividend}_5 = \$0.80(1.05) = \$0.84$$

   Using this in the constant growth model, we get a selling price at the end of year 4 of

   $$\text{Price}_4 = \frac{\$0.84}{0.16 - 0.05} = \$7.64.$$

   Discounting the expected dividends and the expected selling price at the end of year 4 gives us the price at which the stock should sell today.

   $$\begin{aligned}
   \text{Price} &= \$0.56(\text{PVIF}_{16\%,1}) + \$0.63(\text{PVIF}_{16\%,2}) \\
   &\quad + \$0.71(\text{PVIF}_{16\%,3}) + \$0.80(\text{PVIF}_{16\%,4}) + \$7.64(\text{PVIF}_{16\%,4}) \\
   &= \$0.56(0.8621) + \$0.63(0.7432) + \$0.71(0.6407) \\
   &\quad + \$0.80(0.5523) + \$7.64(0.5523) = \$6.07
   \end{aligned}$$

7. Since dividends are expected to remain constant at $2.00, we can find the expected selling price at the end of year 2 by using the formula for the present value of a perpetuity as follows:

   $$\text{Price}_2 = \$2.00/0.12 = \$16.67.$$

   We then discount back the 2 years of dividend payments along with the expected selling price at the end of year 2 to determine the price today.

   $$\begin{aligned}
   \text{Price} &= \$1.00(\text{PVIF}_{12\%,1}) + \$2.00(\text{PVIF}_{12\%,2}) + \$16.67(\text{PVIF}_{12\%,3}) \\
   &= \$1.00(0.8929) + \$2.00(0.7972) + \$16.67(0.7972) = \$15.78
   \end{aligned}$$

8. a. The bond pays $90 interest each year for 5 years and $1,000 at maturity. Discounting these expected cash flows back, we get

$$\text{Price} = \$90(\text{PVIFA}_{11\%,5}) + \$1,000(\text{PVIF}_{11\%,5})$$
$$= \$90(3.6959) + \$1,000(0.5935) = \$926.13.$$

b. The price that an investor is willing to pay for the bond is dependent upon that investor's expected future cash flows and his required rate of return. The new investor expects to receive $90 in interest each year for the next *4* years and $1,000 at maturity, which is 4 years from now. He will require a 10% return since that is what similar risk investments are yielding, so his expected future cash flows will be discounted back at that rate.

$$\text{Price}_{\text{year 1}} = \$90(\text{PVIFA}_{10\%,4}) + \$1,000(\text{PVIF}_{10\%,4})$$
$$= \$90(3.1699) + \$1,000(0.6830) = \$968.29$$

c. Otto will have received $90 in interest in addition to the $968.29 proceeds from the bond sale.

$$\text{HPR} = \frac{(\$90 + \$968.29) - \$926.13}{\$926.13} = 14.3\%$$

d. If Otto holds the bond until maturity, his average annual return is the yield-to-maturity on the bond, which is the discount rate that equated the price he paid with his expected future cash flows. That rate was 11%.

9. The yield-to-maturity is the discount rate that equates the price paid to the expected future cash flows. Since this bond has only one expected future cash flow, i.e., $1,000 at maturity, we can solve for the yield-to-maturity as follows:

$$\$1,000 = \$550(1 + \text{ytm})^{10}$$

$$(1 + \text{ytm})^{10} = \frac{\$1,000}{\$550}$$

$$1 + \text{ytm} = \sqrt[10]{\frac{\$1,000}{\$550}}$$

$$\text{ytm} = \sqrt[10]{\frac{\$1,000}{\$550}} - 1 = 6.2\%.$$

EXPECTED RETURN AND RISK

In this module you will learn how to calculate the expected return for a given probability distribution. You will also learn how to calculate the variance, the standard deviation, and the coefficient of variation, all of which are measures of the risk, or the uncertainty, surrounding an expected return. You will learn how these concepts apply to investment selection so that you can use them in structuring an investment portfolio that will maximize your return for a given level of risk. The Capital Asset Pricing Model, which describes the relationship between expected returns and systematic risk levels, is introduced as a tool to be used in investment analysis.

Equations introduced in this module

$$\text{Expected value} = (\text{probablity}_1 \times \text{outcome}_1) + (\text{probability}_2 \times \text{outcome}_2)$$
$$+ \ldots (\text{probability}_n \times \text{outcome}_n)$$

$$\text{Variance} = \sigma^2 = p_1(o_1 - \bar{o})^2 + p_2(o_2 - \bar{o})^2 + p_3(o_3 - \bar{o})^2 + \ldots$$

$$\text{Standard deviation} = \sigma = \sqrt{p_1(o_1 - \bar{o})^2 + p_2(o_2 - \bar{o})^2 + p_3(o_3 - \bar{o})^2 + \ldots}$$

$$\text{Coefficient of variation} = \frac{\text{standard deviation}}{\text{expected value}}$$

$$\text{Expected value (portfolio)} = \bar{r}_{pf} = wt_1\bar{r}_1 + wt_2\bar{r}_2 + wt_3\bar{r}_3 + \ldots$$

$$\text{Variance (two security portfolios)} = \text{wt}_1^2\sigma_1^2 + \text{wt}_2^2\sigma_2^2 + 2\text{wt}_1\text{wt}_2\sigma_{1,2}$$

$$= \text{wt}_1^2\sigma_1^2 + \text{wt}_2^2\sigma_2^2 + 2\text{wt}_1\text{wt}_2\rho_{1,2}\sigma_1\sigma_2$$

$$\text{Correlation coefficient} = \rho_{1,2} = \frac{\sigma_{1,2}}{\sigma_1\sigma_2}$$

$$R_j = \text{rfr} + \beta(\bar{r}_m - \text{rfr})$$

1. Finance is not an exact science. When we seek to determine the price of a financial asset, we use *expected* dividends and *expected* interest and *expected* future selling prices. When we try to determine whether a firm should undertake a particular project, we consider the *expected* cash flows from that project. We can calculate the expected value of a given variable by considering the likelihood of that variable having various values in the future. These likelihoods are otherwise referred to as *probabilities*. As a simple example, let us assume that you believe that there are only three scenarios that affect the future stock price of Carmaker Corporation (i.e., a recession, an improved economy, or an unchanged economy), and being somewhat of a pessimist, you believe that there is a 40% chance that the country will enter a recession within the year, a 10% chance that the economy will improve, and a 50% chance that the economy will remain unchanged. The current price of Carmaker Corporation is $50 a share, but you believe it will drop to $38 a share by the end of the year if we do have a recession. However, if the economy improves, you think the stock will sell for $63 a share by the end of the year, and if the economy remains stable, you estimate the year-end stock price will be $58. We can summarize these expectations as follows:

State of Nature	Probability	Stock Price in One Year
Recession	0.4	$38.00
Improved Economy	0.1	$63.00
Stable Economy	0.5	$58.00

The above table provides a **probability distribution** for the stock prices of Carmaker. Under our assumptions, all the possible outcomes and the probability of each is listed. The **range** of outcomes is from $38 to $63. The average value, also called the **expected value** or **mean**, can be found by weighting each outcome by its probability and adding the results. We can express this in formula form as follows:

$$\text{Expected value} = (\text{probability}_1 \times \text{outcome}_1) + (\text{probability}_2 \times \text{outcome}_2)$$

$$+ \ldots + (\text{probability}_n \times \text{outcome}_n).$$

So the expected value of the above probability distribution is equal to 0.4($38) + 0.1($63) + 0.5($58) = $50.50. The expected value is a middle value, but it is not necessarily the most likely outcome. Note that $58 is the most likely price 1 year from now since it has the highest probability of occurrence, that is, 50%. One commonly used mathematical notation to indicate expected value is a letter with a line over it, so since, in this case, we have calculated an expected price, we might use the following notation: $\bar{p} = \$50.50$.

? Russell Jacob believes that the future stock price of Compute Inc. depends solely on the success of their new product VoiceTech. If VoiceTech is successful, Russell believes that Compute's stock price will double by the end of the year, from $20 a share to $40. On the other hand, if VoiceTech bombs, he believes the price of the stock will drop to as low as $12 a share. He feels that VoiceTech has a 70% chance of success and a 30% chance of failure. What is Compute's expected stock price in 1 year?

Answer: $31.60.

The probability distribution can be depicted in tabular form as follows:

State of Nature	Probability	Stock Price in 1 Year
VoiceTech is a success	0.7	$40.00
VoiceTech is a failure	0.3	$12.00

$$\text{Expected price} = \bar{p} = 0.7(\$40.00) + 0.3(\$12.00) = \$31.60.$$

2. Let us suppose that there were two stocks to choose from, both of which were currently selling for $20 a share, and both of which had an expected price 1 year from today of $31.60. Would both be equally attractive? Not necessarily. It depends on how uncertain the expected price is in each case. This uncertainty is the **risk** associated with each investment. In the English language, risk has a negative connotation but, in finance, risk only refers to the uncertainty of the future outcome. The price in 1 year could be lower *or* higher. The news could be good or bad. We measure this risk by calculating the **standard deviation** of the returns. The standard deviation is the square root of another risk measure known as the **variance**. The variance, however, is expressed in units squared whereas the standard deviation shares the same unit measure as the expected return, so it is more commonly used. Both measure the degree of dispersion of the outcomes associated with the states of nature from the expected outcome.

In calculating the standard deviation, we first take the difference between the outcome associated with the state of nature and the expected outcome, or

$$(\text{outcome}_i - \text{expected outcome}) \text{ or, abbreviating,} (o_i - \bar{o}).$$

Next, we square the difference as follows:

$$(\text{outcome}_i - \text{expected outcome})^2 \text{ or } (o_i - \bar{o})^2.$$

We must then weight this result by multiplying it by the probability associated with that state of nature.

$$\text{probability}_i(\text{outcome}_i - \text{expected outcome})^2 \text{ or } p_i(o_i - \bar{o})^2$$

We then add the results together. This number is the **variance**, often designated as σ^2.

$$\sigma^2 = p_1(o_1 - \bar{o})^2 + p_2(o_2 - \bar{o})^2 + p_3(o_3 - \bar{o})^2 + \ldots$$

As stated earlier, the variance is in units squared; to find the standard deviation, we take the square root of this number. The symbol used for standard deviation is σ.

$$\sigma = \sqrt{p_1(o_1 - \bar{o})^2 + p_2(o_2 - \bar{o})^2 + p_3(o_3 - \bar{o})^2 + \ldots}$$

In the Carmaker example, we determined the expected future price to be $50.50. The variance and the standard deviation of the future stock price can be calculated as follows:

$$\sigma^2 = 0.4(\$38.00 - \$50.50)^2 + 0.1(\$63.00 - \$50.50)^2 + 0.5(\$58.00 - \$50.50)^2$$
$$= 106.25 \text{ dollars squared}$$
$$\sigma = \sqrt{106.25 \text{ dollars squared}} = \$10.31.$$

❓ Calculate the variance and the standard deviation of the future stock price of VoiceTech.

Answer: $\sigma^2 = 43.512$ dollars squared, $\sigma = \$6.60$.

$\sigma^2 = 0.7(\$40.00 - \$31.60)^2 + 0.3(\$12.00 - \$31.60)^2 = 164.64$ dollars squared

$\sigma = \sqrt{43.512 \text{ dollars squared}} = \$12.83$

3. Which one is riskier, Carmaker or VoiceTech? You might be tempted to answer Carmaker since it has the larger standard deviation, but it also has the larger expected future stock price. In order to determine which is riskier when the expected values are different, we can calculate a number called the **coefficient of variation**. The higher the coefficient of variation, the greater is the risk. It is a relative measure of variability and is calculated by dividing the standard deviation by the expected value. In other words, it is a measure of risk per percent of expected return. We can express this in formula form as follows:

$$CV = \frac{\text{standard deviation}}{\text{expected value}} = \frac{\sigma}{\overline{o}}.$$

The coefficient of variation for Carmaker is, therefore, equal to $\$10.31/\$50.50 = 0.204$.

? Calculate the coefficient of variation for VoiceTech. Which is riskier, VoiceTech or Carmaker?

Answers: 0.209, VoiceTech.

$$CV = \$6.60/\$31.60 = 0.209$$

This is slightly higher than the coefficient of variation for Carmaker, so VoiceTech is slightly riskier.

4. While we assumed that only three states of nature would affect the future stock price of Carmaker and only two would affect the future stock price of VoiceTech, in reality it is obvious that many more events play a part in determining these future prices. For example, a car manufacturing firm is affected not only by economic conditions in general, but also by the current import/export tax laws as well as many other conditions too numerous to mention. When this occurs, we actually have a **continuous probability distribution**, the best known of which is the **normal distribution**, which results in a bell-shaped curve. Research has shown that stock prices follow a normal distribution over the long-run. Whenever a set of observations, such as stock prices, are normally distributed, it has been found that 68.2% of the time the *actual* outcome will lie within one standard deviation of the mean, or expected value; 95.5% of the time the actual outcome will lie within two standard deviations of the mean; and 99.7% of the time the actual outcome will lie within three standard deviations of the mean. Therefore, if the stock prices of the Melden Corporation are normally distributed, and the mean price is $50 with a standard deviation of $5, then 95.5% of the time the actual price will be between $40 and $60, which is $50 ± 2 standard deviations or $50 ± $10.

? The Geomiss Corporation has an average stock price of $48 with a standard deviation of $4. The stock prices are normally distributed. Within what range will the future price of Geomiss fall 99.7% of the time?

Answer: $36 to $60.
Since the prices are normally distributed, the actual price will be within three standard deviations of the mean 99.7% of the time. Three standard deviations is $12. So the price will be $48 ± $12, which is between $36 and $60.

5. The variance, standard deviation, and coefficient of variation of a probability distribution are all measures of *total* risk. Total risk is comprised of unsystematic risk and systematic risk. **Unsystematic risk** is risk unassociated with the "system" and can be thought of as company-specific risk. It is the risk that is unique to the company itself, such as the risk associated with death of a CEO, a patent on a successful new product (remember that in finance risk is not necessarily bad), or an employee strike. On the other hand, **systematic risk** is risk that all firms face to one degree or another. It is the risk of the market in general, such as the risk associated with inflation, recession, or war. While not all firms are affected to the same extent by these events, all *are* affected. We can diversify away a firm's unsystematic risk by holding a portfolio of securities. A **portfolio** simply means holding more than one security. The more securities that are held, the more risk is diversified up to a point. A study by Eugene Fama indicated that most of the unsystematic risk can be diversified in the first five well-chosen securities, and that a well-diversified portfolio can be constructed with anywhere from 15 to 20 well-chosen securities. The expected return on a portfolio of securities can be simply calculated as the weighted average of the expected returns of each security in the portfolio, weighted by the amount invested in each security. We can express this as follows:

$$\bar{r}_{pf} = wt_1\bar{r}_1 + wt_2\bar{r}_2 + wt_3\bar{r}_3 + \ldots$$

For example, suppose that Russell Jacob is interested in investing in two stocks, Stock M and Stock E. He plans to invest 40% of his money in Stock M, which has an expected return of 18%, and 60% in Stock E, which has an expected return of 22%. The expected return on his portfolio can be calculated as follows:

$$\bar{r}_{pf} = 0.4(18\%) + 0.6(22\%) = 20.4\%.$$

? Mr. Jacob is also considering Stock F and Stock R instead of Stock M and Stock E. Stock F is expected to return 10% and Stock R is expected to return 14%. If he were to invest 25% in Stock F and 75% in Stock R, what is his expected return on the portfolio?

Answer: 13%.

$$\bar{r}_{pf} = 0.25(10\%) + 0.75(14\%) = 13\%$$

6. Unfortunately, the risk of a portfolio is not simply a weighted average of the individual risks of the securities. The *comovement* of the securities must be considered. The degree to which two securities move together is measured statistically by calculating the covariance (often symbolized as $\sigma_{1,2}$) of the returns of the two securities. If the covariance is a positive number, the two securities' returns tend to move together; i.e., if one security's return has increased, the second security's return has also probably increased. If the covariance is a negative number, the two securities' returns tend to move in opposite directions; i.e., if the first security's return has increased, the second security's return has probably decreased. If the covariance is zero, there is no relationship between the returns of the two securities, meaning that you cannot predict the movement of the second by observing the movement of the first. The variance of a portfolio can be expressed as follows:

$$\sigma_{pf}^2 = wt_1^2\sigma_1^2 + wt_2^2\sigma_2^2 + 2wt_1wt_2\sigma_{1,2}$$

where wt_i is the weight invested in security i, σ_i^2 is the variance of security i, and $\sigma_{1,2}$ is the covariance of the two securities.

The problem with covariance is that it can be any number, so a covariance of +252 indicates only that the two securities' returns tend to move together, but not how much of the time. A more useful number is the **correlation coefficient** (symbolized as $\rho_{1,2}$).

The correlation coefficient is equal to the covariance of the two securities' returns divided by the product of their standard deviations, or

$$\rho_{1,2} = \frac{\sigma_{1,2}}{\sigma_1 \sigma_2}.$$

The correlation coefficient is a standardized covariance; its values lie between −1 and +1. Therefore, if the correlation coefficient of two securities' returns is +0.9, we know not only that the two securities' returns tend to move together, but also that they move together *most of the time* since +0.9 is very close to +1.

? What would a correlation coefficient of zero indicate?

Answer: A correlation coefficient of zero indicates that there is no relationship between the two securities' returns.

A correlation coefficient of zero indicates the same thing that a covariance of zero indicates. Note from the equation for the correlation coefficient that it will be zero only when the covariance is zero.

7.   Solving the correlation coefficient equation for the covariance, we get $\rho_{1,2} = \sigma_{1,2} \sigma_1 \sigma_2$. Substituting the right side of this equation into the equation for the variance of a portfolio in the place of covariance results in the following formula:

$$\sigma_{pf}^2 = wt_1^2 \sigma_1^2 + wt_2^2 \sigma_2^2 + 2wt_1 wt_2 \rho_{1,2} \sigma_1 \sigma_2.$$

Let us consider the portfolio of stocks M and E again. Stock M had an expected return of 18%, and Russell had invested 40% of his money in that stock. He invested the rest in Stock E, which had an expected return of 22%. Suppose the standard deviation of the returns of Stock M is 2%, and that of Stock E is 3.5%. Further assume that the correlation coefficient of the two stocks' returns is 0.85. We now have all the information necessary to calculate the risk of the portfolio.

$$\sigma_{pf}^2 = (0.4)^2 (2\%)^2 + (0.6)^2 (3.5\%)^2 + 2(0.4)(0.6)(0.85)(2\%)(3.5\%)$$

$$= 7.906 \text{ percent squared}$$

$$\sigma_{pf} = \sqrt{7.906} = 2.81\%$$

? Suppose the standard deviation of the returns of Stock F is 1.5% while that of Stock R is 4%. The correlation coefficient of the returns of the two stocks is 0.7. Assuming 25% is invested in Stock F and 75% in Stock R, what is the risk of the portfolio as measured by the standard deviation?

Answer: 3.27%.

$$\sigma_{pf}^2 = (0.25)^2 (1.5\%)^2 + (0.75)^2 (4\%)^2 + 2(0.25)(0.75)(0.7)(1.5\%)(4\%)$$

$$= 10.716 \text{ percent squared}$$

$$\sigma = \sqrt{10.716} = 3.27\%$$

8.   The single most important factor that determines the risk of the portfolio is the correlation between the pairs of the securities' returns in the portfolio. Consider the following portfolio consisting of equal investments in two securities with the same expected rate of return and the same variance.

	Weight (wt)	Expected return ($\bar{r}$)	Variance (σ^2)
Stock 1	0.5	8%	2 percent squared
Stock 2	0.5	8%	2 percent squared

Note that the expected return of this portfolio is 8%.

$$\bar{r}_{pf} = 0.5(8\%) + 0.5(8\%) = 8\%$$

The variance of the portfolio can be calculated as follows:

$$\sigma^2_{pf} = (0.5)^2(2) + (.5)^2(2) + 2(.5)(.5)\rho_{1,2}(\sqrt{2})(\sqrt{2}).$$

(Note that since the variance of each stock is 2, the standard deviation of each is the square root of 2.)

Let us first consider the case when the correlation coefficient for the two securities' returns is +1.0. The securities' returns are said to be **perfectly positively correlated**. The variance of the portfolio becomes

$$\sigma^2_{pf} = (0.5)^2(2) + (0.5)^2(2) + 2(0.5)(0.5)(1.0)(\sqrt{2})(\sqrt{2}) = 2 \text{ percent squared.}$$

Is an investor any better off investing in the portfolio than he would have been had he invested all of his funds in just one of the two? The answer is no. He is getting the same expected return, 8%, that he would have gotten by investing in just one of the securities, and the risk (2 percent squared) is the same. If two securities' returns are perfectly positively correlated *no risk diversification takes place*.

Next, consider the case when the correlation coefficient is zero. The last term of the equation is equal to zero, so the variance of the portfolio becomes

$$\sigma^2_{pf} = (0.5)^2(2) + (0.5)^2(2) + 0 = 1 \text{ percent squared.}$$

Now the investor would be better off than he would have been had he invested all of his funds in just one of the two securities. He is getting the same expected return of 8%, but he has reduced his risk in half. Some risk diversification has taken place.

? Calculate the variance of the portfolio when the correlation coefficient is −1.0. Is the investor any better off investing in the portfolio than if he had invested all of his funds in either Stock 1 or Stock 2?

Answers: 0, yes.

$$\sigma^2_{pf} = (0.5)^2(2) + (0.5)^2(2) + 2(0.5)(0.5)(-1.0)(\sqrt{2})(\sqrt{2}) = 0$$

In this case the investor's expected return is still 8% and he has diversified his risk entirely away, so he is definitely better off investing in the portfolio than he would have been by investing all of his funds in one of the two stocks.

9. When the correlation coefficient is −1.0, the securities' returns are said to be **perfectly negatively correlated** and all risk is diversified. Unfortunately, it is virtually impossible to find two securities with this characteristic. However, some risk diversification takes place so long as the two securities are *not* perfectly positively correlated. Too, the more securities in the portfolio, the more irrelevant their individual risk levels become, and the more important is the correlation between each pair of securities' returns. This can be better seen by considering the formulae for the variance of a three-security portfolio and that of a four-security portfolio. Note that as another security is added to the portfolio, only one individual risk term is added, but several correlation coefficient terms are added.

$$\text{variance}_{\text{three-security portfolio}} = (wt_1)^2(\sigma_1)^2 + (wt_2)^2(\sigma_2)^2 + (wt_3)^2(\sigma_3)^2$$
$$+ 2(wt_1)(wt_2)(\rho_{1,2})(\sigma_1)(\sigma_2) + 2(wt_1)(wt_3)(\rho_{1,3})(\sigma_1)(\sigma_3)$$
$$+ 2(wt_2)(wt_3)(\rho_{2,3})(\sigma_2)(\sigma_3)$$

$$\text{variance}_{\text{four-security portfolio}} = (wt_1)^2(\sigma_1)^2 + (wt_2)^2(\sigma_2)^2 + (wt_3)^2(\sigma_3)^2 + (wt_4)^2(\sigma_4)^2$$
$$+ 2(wt_1)(wt_2)(\rho_{1,2})(\sigma_1)(\sigma_2) + 2(wt_1)(wt_3)(\rho_{1,3})(\sigma_1)(\sigma_3)$$
$$+ 2(wt_1)(wt_4)(\rho_{1,4})(\sigma_1)(\sigma_2) + 2(wt_2)(wt_3)(\rho_{2,3})(\sigma_2)(\sigma_3)$$
$$+ 2(wt_2)(wt_4)(\rho_{2,4})(\sigma_2)(\sigma_4) + 2(wt_3)(wt_4)(\rho_{3,4})(\sigma_3)(\sigma_4)$$

We define the most well-diversified portfolio of risky assets as the **market portfolio**. Since this is a well-diversified portfolio, all of the **unsystematic** risk, or company-specific risk, is diversified away. The remaining risk is the **systematic** risk. If an investor holds a well-diversified portfolio, the relevant risk to consider when choosing another security for the portfolio is the security's systematic risk, which is a measure of how the security's returns varies with the market. A measure of this systematic risk is called **beta**. Beta measures the comovement of a security's returns with the market. A beta of 1.0 means that the security has the same risk as the market and should, therefore, offer the same return as the market portfolio. A beta of 0.5 indicates that the security is half as risky as the market portfolio. Its expected return will, therefore, be lower than that of the market. (It is *not* half the return of the market portfolio, however, as is discussed later in this module.) Similarly, a beta of 2.0 indicates that the security is twice as risky as the market; a beta of 0 indicates a risk-free security; and a negative beta would be associated with a security that has returns that tend to move opposite the market, i.e., when the market is up, we might expect that security to have negative returns and vice versa. Betas are not stable numbers; they can and do change, so they must be estimated on a regular basis. The betas for most firms fall between 0.0 and 2.0 when measured over the long-run.

? Assume the market portfolio is expected to return 14%. If Russell had invested in a stock that had a beta of 0.7, would you expect that stock to return more than 14%, less than 14%, or 14%?

Answer: Less than 14%.
With a beta of 0.7, the stock is less risky than the market portfolio and is therefore expected to return less.

10. Since the marginal investor in securities is the institutional investor, and institutional investors hold well-diversified portfolios, it stands to reason that the market will not reward an investor for holding diversifiable risk. Prices are determined by the marginal investors. A relationship between the nondiversifiable risk, i.e., systematic risk, and the return an investor can expect on a security if the market is in equilibrium has been developed. It is the **Capital Asset Pricing Model**. The relationship between the systematic risk of a security, as measured by its beta, and the expected equilibrium return on the security, which we will designate as R_j, has been found to be linear. Remembering that two points determine a line, we can easily draw a graph of the Capital Asset Pricing Model. We know that at a beta of zero, the security should return the risk-free rate (rfr), and at a beta of 1.0 the security should return the expected return on the market ($\bar{r}_m$). Therefore, the graph will appear as in the figure on the following page.

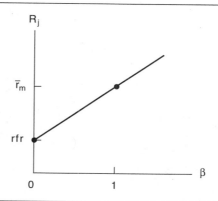

This graph is referred to as the **Security Market Line**. You might recall from your first algebra course that the equation of a straight line is y = mx + b, where m is the slope of the line (rise over run) and b is the y-intercept. In our example above, the independent variable (x) is beta, and the dependent variable (y) is the expected equilibrium rate of return, R_j. The slope, using the two points shown on the graph, is $(\bar{r}_m - rfr)/(1 - 0) = \bar{r}_m - rfr$. The y-intercept is the point at which the line crosses the y-axis, rfr. The equation is, therefore, $R_j = (\bar{r}_m - rfr)\beta + rfr$. This equation *is* the Capital Asset Pricing Model. It is usually written in the form $R_j = rfr + \beta(\bar{r}_m - rfr)$. In this form it is easier to see that every security must return at least the risk-free rate, rfr. In addition, the security must earn a risk premium, calculated as $\beta(\bar{r}_m - rfr)$, based on its relevant risk, the systematic risk. The term $(\bar{r}_m - rfr)$ is called the **market risk premium** since it is the amount that the market portfolio has to offer over and above the risk-free rate to get investors to invest in the market. If a security is correctly priced according to its risk, it should plot on the Security Market Line. If a security plots *above* the Security Market Line, it is returning more than is required for its risk level and is considered to be underpriced. If it plots *below* the Security Market Line, it is earning too low a return for its risk level and is overpriced. We would not expect either of these scenarios to be long-standing since, if a security is underpriced, the demand will be great and will push the price up and the return down; on the other hand, if a security is overpriced, the demand will be weak, and the price must fall, which will increase the return. Therefore, the Capital Asset Pricing Model (CAPM) can be used as a benchmark for what a security *should* return if it is correctly priced. In applying the CAPM, we generally use a Treasury security rate as a proxy for the risk-free rate since Treasury securities are viewed to be free of default risk. The maturity of the Treasury security chosen should match the investment horizon. The expected return on the S&P 500 Index is typically considered to be a proxy for the expected return on the market portfolio. Since this is sometimes the most difficult number to estimate, the *average* market risk premium is sometimes used in the equation. That is, analysts will often take the difference between the average return on the market over a given time period and the average return on a Treasury security over that same time period and use the result as the market risk premium instead of trying to forecast what the S&P 500 will return in the future.

Assume that Russell is considering investing in a stock that has a beta of 0.7. The relevant risk-free rate is 4.5% and the S&P 500 is expected to return 12%. If the stock is correctly priced, then Russell can expect to earn R_j = 4.5% + 0.7(12% − 4.5%) = 9.75%. This can be illustrated graphically as shown on the following page.

? One year later, Mr. Jacob is considering a stock that has a beta of 1.2. The relevant risk-free rate is now 6% and the market risk premium is 9%. What should Mr. Jacob require as a minimum rate of return on this investment?

Answer: 16.8%.

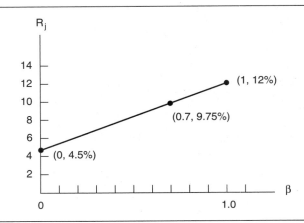

In this case, $(\bar{r}_m - rfr)$ is 9%, so $R_j = 6\% + 1.2(9\%) = 16.8\%$. Since the CAPM is the benchmark for what the security *should* return based upon its systematic risk, this is also the minimum return that an investor should require for taking on this level of risk.

11. The expected equilibrium rate of return can also be determined for a portfolio by using the portfolio beta in the Capital Asset Pricing Model. The portfolio beta is simply the weighted average of the betas of the securities in the portfolio. A portfolio beta is more stable than betas of individual securities; therefore, the CAPM is usually a better predictor of the return on a portfolio of securities than it is for an individual security.

Assume that Mr. Jacob invests 20% of his funds in Stock A, which has a beta of 0.75, 30% of his funds in Stock B, with a beta of 0.24, and 50% of his funds in Stock C, which has a beta of 0.60. If we want to determine what his expected portfolio equilibrium rate of return is, we must first find the beta of his portfolio as follows:

$$\beta_{pf} = 0.2(0.75) + 0.3(0.24) + 0.5(0.60) = 0.522.$$

If we know that the risk-free rate is 5% and the expected return on the S&P 500 is 12%, we can then use CAPM to determine his expected equilibrium rate of return:

$$R_j = 5\% + 0.522(12\% - 5\%) = 8.65\%.$$

? Assuming that the risk-free rate is 5% and the expected return on the S&P 500 is 12%, determine what Mr. Jacob should require as a minimum rate of return on the following portfolio of securities:

Security	Weight	Beta
Stock A	0.6	0.80
Stock B	0.3	1.00
Stock C	0.1	1.50

Answer: 11.51%.

$$\beta_{pf} = 0.6(0.8) + 0.3(1.0) + 0.1(1.5) = 0.93$$
$$R_j = 5\% + 0.93(12\% - 5\%) = 11.51\%$$

☞✎ **Apply It**

1. The probability distribution of the returns of BrightLights, Inc. has been estimated as follows:

State of Nature	Probability	Return
1	0.3	15%
2	0.4	10%
3	0.1	−3%
4	0.2	5%

   a. What is the expected return on BrightLights stock? (Frame 1)
   b. What is the standard deviation of the returns on BrightLights stock? (Frame 2)

2. The probability distribution of the returns of LoudMusic, Inc. has been estimated as follows:

State of Nature	Probability	Return
1	0.2	7%
2	0.6	16%
3	0.2	0%

   a. What is the expected return on LoudMusic stock? (Frame 1)
   b. What is the standard deviation of the returns on LoudMusic stock? (Frame 2)

3. Use the coefficient of variation to determine which is riskier, BrightLights or LoudMusic. (Frame 3)

4. You invest in 200 shares of Canso Corporation, which sells for $20 a share and has an expected return of 12% with a standard deviation of 3% and a beta of 1.1, and 600 shares of Darnit Corporation, which sells for $10 a share and has an expected return of 18% with a standard deviation of 5% and a beta of 1.3. The correlation coefficient of the returns of the two firms is 0.4.
   a. What is the expected return on your portfolio? (Frame 5)
   b. What is the risk of your portfolio as measured by its standard deviation? (Frame 7)
   c. What is the beta of your portfolio? (Frame 11)
   d. If the relevant risk-free rate is 5% and the market risk premium has averaged 8.5% in the last three decades, what is the minimum rate of return you should require on your investment in this portfolio? (Frame 11)
   e. Based on the information provided in part (d), sketch a graph of the Security Market Line and indicate the point at which your portfolio plots if your expectations in part (a) are met. (Frame 10)
   f. Is your portfolio overpriced, underpriced, or correctly priced? Explain. (Frame 10)

5. Why is systematic risk the relevant risk? (Frame 9)

6. What three factors determine the risk of a portfolio? (Frame 6)

7. Would a portfolio invested in five airline company stocks and four hotel stocks be well-diversified? Why or why not? (Frame 8)

8. What would you consider to be the single biggest factor in selecting stocks to form a well-diversified portfolio? Explain your reasoning. (Frame 9)

9. A mutual fund advertises that it has consistently had a return that beats the return on the S&P 500. You discover that the average beta of portfolio of stocks in which the fund is invested is 1.4. Are you impressed by the advertisement? Why or why not? (Frame 9)

10. Consider the following information regarding Stock Alpha and Stock Gamma:

State of Nature	Probability	Alpha	Gamma
1	0.3	10%	−3%
2	0.5	8%	14%
3	0.2	2%	6%

a. What is the expected return on Stock Alpha? (Frame 1)
b. What is the expected return on Stock Gamma? (Frame 1)
c. What is the standard deviation of the returns on Stock Alpha? (Frame 2)
d. What is the standard deviation of the returns on Stock Gamma? (Frame 2)
e. If the relevant risk-free rate is 3.5% and the expected return on the market is 11%, what is the expected return on Stock Alpha if its estimated beta is 0.5? (Frame 10)
f. If the relevant risk-free rate is 3.5% and the expected return on the market is 11%, what is the expected return on Stock Gamma if its estimated beta is 0.8? (Frame 10)
g. Based on your previous calculations, which stock, if either, would you recommend to an investor? Explain your rationale. (Frame 10)

Apply It Answers

1. a. $\bar{r} = 0.3(15\%) + 0.4(10\%) + 0.1(-3\%) + 0.2(5\%) = 9.2\%$
   b.
$$\sigma = \sqrt{0.3(15-9.2)^2 + 0.4(10-9.2)^2 + 0.1(-3-9.2)^2 + 0.2(5-9.2)^2}$$
$$= \sqrt{28.76} = 5.36\%$$

2. a. $\bar{r} = 0.2(7\%) + 0.6(16\%) + 0.2(0\%) = 11\%$
   b.
$$\sigma = \sqrt{0.2(7-11)^2 + 0.6(16-11)^2 + 0.2(0-11)^2}$$
$$= \sqrt{42.4} = 6.51\%$$

3. Coefficient of variation$_{BL}$ = 5.36/9.2 = 0.58
   Coefficient of variation$_{LM}$ = 6.51/11 = 0.59
   LoudMusic is slightly more risky than BrightLights.

4. a. Total investment in Canso = $20 × 200 shares = $4,000
   Total investment in Darnit = $10 × 600 shares = $6,000
   Therefore, 40% of your funds are invested in Canso and 60% are invested in Darnit.
   $\bar{r}_{pf} = 0.4(12\%) + 0.6(18\%) = 15.6\%$
   b.
$$\sigma^2_{pf} = \sqrt{(0.4)^2(3)^2 + (0.6)^2(5)^2 + 2(0.6)(0.4)(0.4)(3)(5)}$$
$$= \sqrt{13.32} = 3.65\%$$

c. $\beta_{pf} = (0.4)(1.1) + (0.6)(1.3) = 1.22$

d. $R_{pf} = 5\% + 1.22(8.5\%) = 15.37\%$

e.

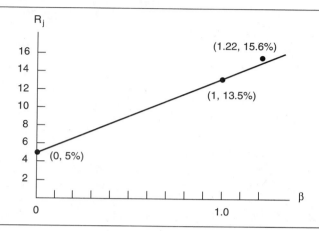

f. The portfolio is underpriced. Based on your analysis, you expect it to return 15.6% (from part (a)). The Capital Asset Pricing Model indicates that it should have to return only 15.37% to adequately compensate an investor for the risk. Therefore, you expect to it return more than the requisite amount, which means it is underpriced. You can also observe in part (e) that, based on your expectations, the portfolio plots *above* the Security Market Line.

5. Systematic risk is the relevant risk because it is the only risk investors are rewarded for holding. Since the marginal investor is the institutional investor and institutional investors hold well-diversified portfolios, the returns on investments are based on the assumption that the investor is investing in a well-diversified portfolio, which is one in which all the unsystematic risk has been diversified away.

6. The three factors that determine a portfolio's risk are the weight invested in each security, the individual risk of each security, and the comovements of the returns of the securities in the portfolio.

7. No. Even on an intuitive level it is obvious that the returns on airline company stocks and the returns on hotel stocks will be very highly correlated. Therefore, not much risk will be diversified away. An investor should choose firms that seem to be in unrelated industries so that the returns will be either uncorrelated or have a very low or a negative correlation.

8. The comovements of the returns of the securities is the biggest single factor to consider in selecting stocks to form a well-diversified portfolio. As more stocks are added to a portfolio, the individual risks of the securities become a negligible factor in determining the portfolio risk, while the correlations between each pair of securities' returns become an increasingly large factor.

9. You should not be impressed. If the beta of the portfolio is 1.4, the portfolio is riskier than the S&P 500. It *should* be offering a higher return to compensate the investors for the greater risk they are taking.

10. a. $\bar{r}_A = 0.3(10\%) + (0.5)(8\%) + 0.2(2\%) = 7.4\%$

b. $\bar{r}_C = 0.3(-3\%) + 0.5(14\%) + 0.2(6\%) = 7.3\%$

c.

$$\sigma_A = \sqrt{0.3(10-7.4)^2 + 0.5(8-7.4)^2 + 0.2(2-7.4)^2}$$
$$= \sqrt{8.04} = 2.84\%$$

d.

$$\sigma_G = \sqrt{0.3(-3-7.3)^2 + 0.5(14-7.3)^2 + 0.2(6-7.3)^2}$$
$$= \sqrt{54.61} = 7.39\%$$

e. $R_A = 3.5\% + 0.5(11\% - 3.5\%) = 7.25\%$

f. $R_G = 3.5\% + 0.8(11\% - 3.5\%) = 9.5\%$

g. Based on the given probability distribution, Stock Alpha is expected to return 7.4%. The Capital Asset Pricing Model indicates that it need only return 7.25% to compensate investors for their risk. Stock Alpha is, therefore, underpriced. Based on the probability distribution, Stock Gamma is expected to return 7.3%, but the Capital Asset Pricing Model indicates that it should be returning 9.5% to compensate investors for its risk level, so Stock Gamma is overpriced. Thus, Stock Alpha would be the one to recommend to investors.

ANALYSIS OF FINANCIAL STATEMENTS

This module provides a brief review of the income statement and the balance sheet. You will then learn the basic ratios that are calculated to analyze these statements in order to determine the financial strength of the firm. An emphasis is placed on the interpretation of the ratios. Common-size analysis is also introduced.

Equations introduced in this module

$$\text{Current ratio} = \frac{\text{current assets}}{\text{current liabilities}}$$

$$\text{Quick ratio} = \frac{\text{current assets} - \text{inventory}}{\text{current liabilities}}$$

$$\text{Inventory turnover} = \frac{\text{cost of goods sold}}{\text{inventory}}$$

$$\text{Average collection period} = \frac{\text{accounts receivable}}{\text{average daily sales}}$$

$$\text{Fixed asset turnover} = \frac{\text{sales}}{\text{net fixed assets}}$$

$$\text{Total asset turnover} = \frac{\text{sales}}{\text{total assets}}$$

$$\text{Debt ratio} = \frac{\text{total debt}}{\text{total assets}}$$

$$\text{Debt/equity ratio} = \frac{\text{total debt}}{\text{total equity}}$$

$$\text{Alternative debt/equity ratio} = \frac{\text{long-term debt}}{\text{total equity}}$$

$$\text{Equity multiplier} = \frac{\text{total assets}}{\text{total equity}}$$

$$\text{TIE} = \frac{\text{operating profit}}{\text{interest expense}}$$

$$\text{FCCR} = \frac{\text{EBIT} + \text{lease payments}}{\text{interest expense} + \text{lease payments} + \dfrac{\text{sinking fund payment} + \text{preferred dividends}}{1 - \text{tax rate}}}$$

$$\text{Gross profit margin} = \frac{\text{gross profit}}{\text{sales}}$$

$$\text{Operating profit margin} = \frac{\text{EBIT}}{\text{sales}}$$

$$\text{Net profit margin} = \frac{\text{net income}}{\text{sales}}$$

$$\text{ROA} = \frac{\text{net income}}{\text{total assets}} = \frac{\text{net income}}{\text{sales}} \times \frac{\text{sales}}{\text{total assets}}$$

$$\text{ROE} = \frac{\text{net income available for common shareholders}}{\text{common shareholders' equity}} = \frac{\text{net income} - \text{preferred dividends}}{\text{common shareholders' equity}}$$

$$\text{ROTE} = \frac{\text{net income}}{\text{preferred} + \text{common equity}} = \frac{\text{net income}}{\text{sales}} \times \frac{\text{sales}}{\text{total assets}} \times \frac{\text{total assets}}{\text{total equity}}$$

$$\text{EPS} = \frac{\text{net income} - \text{preferred dividends}}{\text{common shares outstanding}}$$

$$\text{DPS} = \frac{\text{total dividends declared}}{\text{common shares outstanding}}$$

$$\text{Dividend payout ratio} = \frac{\text{dividends}}{\text{distributable earnings}}$$

$$\text{P/E ratio} = \frac{\text{market price per share}}{\text{earnings per share}}$$

1. The two main financial accounting statements are the income statement and the balance sheet. The **income statement** accounts for the revenues and expenses of the firm *over a period of time* while the **balance sheet** gives a picture of the financial position of a firm *at a specific point in time*. The most recent two annual income statements of the hypothetical International Motor Corporation (IMC) are presented on page 147.

International Motor Corporation

Income Statement (in millions)

for the years ending December 31,

	1995	1996
Sales	$60,000	$75,000
−Cost of goods sold	52,000	61,000
Gross profit	$ 8,000	$14,000
−Selling and general administrative expenses	6,000	8,000
Operating profit	$ 2,000	$ 6,000
−Interest expense	1,400	1,300
Earnings before tax	$ 600	$ 4,700
−Taxes	300	2,350
Earnings after tax	$ 300	$ 2,350
−Preferred dividends	13	13
Earnings distributable to common shareholders $	287	$ 2,337

The gross profit is found by subtracting the cost of goods sold from the revenues that a firm receives. It indicates how much a firm has left after it has paid the direct costs associated with the good or service that it sells. The operating profit is so named because it represents the profits that the firm has earned from the general operations. It includes expenses of the firm that are not directly related to the product or service being sold, e.g., secretarial salaries and utilities and depreciation expenses that are not part of the cost of goods sold. Interest and dividend income or expense are not included in this calculation. The operating profit is also referred to as "earnings before interest and taxes" or EBIT. Interest expense is then subtracted from the operating profit and any interest or dividend income would be added to operating profit to obtain earnings before tax (EBT). Taxes are calculated based on the earnings before tax. We have assumed that IMC pays taxes at a flat rate of 50% in this example. After taxes are subtracted, we obtain earnings after tax, or net income. If there is no preferred stock, this is the amount of money that the firm has earned for its owners, the common shareholders. The firm may pay any or all of it out in dividends or it may choose to retain some or all of it to reinvest in the business. In the event that preferred stock does exist, the preferred shareholders must be paid their dividends before the common shareholders receive anything.

? The Golden Mining Company had net sales of $8.5 million in 1995. The cost of goods sold was $3.7 million, and other operating expenses were $2.8 million. The firm also had interest expense of $543,000 and interest income of $378,000. The tax rate is 40%. Prepare an income statement for Golden Mining Company.

Answer:

Golden Mining Company

Income Statement

for the year ending December 31, 1995

Sales	$8,500,000
−Cost of goods sold	3,700,000
Gross profit	$4,800,000
−Other operating expenses	2,800,000
Operating profit	$2,000,000
−Interest expense	543,000
+Interest income	378,000
Earnings before tax	$1,835,000
−Taxes	734,000
Earnings after tax	$1,101,000

2.   The balance sheet records the assets that a firm has and the manner in which those assets are financed, i.e., the liability (debt) and equity (stock) accounts. This financial statement gives a snapshot of the firm at a single point in time. By the time an investor receives the annual report of the firm, most of the accounts on the balance sheet will have changed. The most recent two balance sheets for International Motor Corporation are presented below:

International Motor Corporation

Balance Sheet (in millions)

as of December 31,

	1995	1996		1995	1996
Assets			*Liabilities*		
Cash	$ 3,080	$ 6,100	Accounts payable	$ 3,600	$ 4,600
Accounts receivable	2,800	6,900	Notes payable	1,180	1,250
Inventory	6,200	6,600	Accruals	5,600	6,211
Total current assets	$12,080	$19,600	Total current liabilities	$10,380	$12,061
Net plant, property,			Long-term debt	6,500	7,000
and equipment	$23,087	$19,200	Total liabilities	$16,880	$19,061
Total assets	$35,167	$38,800	*Equity*		
			Preferred stock	$ 284	$ 284
			Common stock(at par)	521	521
			Paid-in-surplus	1,930	1,930
			Retained earnings	15,552	17,004
			Total equity	$18,287	$19,739
			Total liabilities and		
			equity	$35,167	$38,800

Current assets are those assets that are considered to be quickly converted to cash, within one year or one operating cycle. The current assets for a typical firm consist of cash, marketable securities (IMC has none), accounts receivable, which are sales made to customers on credit, and inventory. **Long-term assets** are the equipment, land, and buildings that the firm owns. These are shown net of accumulated depreciation. Note that this account is less in 1996 than in 1995. This indicates that IMC did not purchase new equipment in an amount that was greater than or equal to the depreciation expense on the old equipment.

On the other side of the balance sheet are the liability and equity accounts. The liability accounts represent the debt of the firm. **Current liabilities** are debt obligations that are due within 1 year or 1 operating cycle. The most common current liability accounts are the accounts payable, which represents money that the firm owes its suppliers; notes payable, which is short-term debt that is due within 1 year; accruals, which are bills for services that have been received by the firm but that the firm has yet to pay, such as employee wages, utilities, and taxes, and the current portion of any long-term debt that may be due. **Long-term debt** is debt that is due in more than 1 year.

The equity accounts include preferred stock, if any exists. **Preferred stock** typically pays a fixed dividend and usually has no voting rights associated with it. Preferred shareholders have priority over common shareholders in that they receive any monies due them first. Common equity can be listed in as many as three separate accounts. If the common stock has a par value, which is simply an arbitrary number, there will be a common stock at par account, in which the par value of the outstanding shares is recorded, and a paid-in-surplus account, which indicates the amount that the shares sold for *over* their par value. Some common stock has no par value, in which case a single common stock account is used to record the total price for which the outstanding shares were sold. Regardless of whether there is a par value or not, the retained earnings account is also included as a common equity account. This represents the accumulated earnings of the firm that were not paid out as dividends to the common shareholders and instead were reinvested in the firm. The basic equation of accounting is that total assets must equal total liabilities and equity.

? Which of the following is *not* a current liability account?
a. accounts payable
b. accrued wages
c. accrued taxes
d. accounts receivable

Answer: d.

Accounts receivable represents money that is owed the firm by its customers and is, therefore, a current asset account.

3. Looking at the raw numbers on the income statement and balance sheet of a firm is often not very revealing. For example, the total debt of IMC has increased between 1995 and 1996, but the debt was used to finance assets that were used to generate profits, so is the firm in better or worse financial shape in 1996 than it was in 1995? Financial ratios can be calculated to determine answers to questions such as this.

A ratio is simply a fraction. You may recall that the top number of a fraction is called the numerator while the bottom number is called the denominator. A fraction will increase if the numerator increases or if the denominator decreases. The fraction will decrease if the numerator decreases or if the denominator increases. These basic facts will be helpful to keep in mind when evaluating the ratios of a firm.

? One ratio that is commonly calculated is the debt ratio, which is calculated as total debt/total assets. Which of the following events will cause the debt ratio to decrease, all else equal?
a. A firm issues new bonds and uses the proceeds to buy a new plant.
b. A firm sells its inventory for a profit.
c. A firm buys inventory for cash.
d. A firm buys inventory on credit.

Answer: b.

The debt ratio of a solvent firm must be less than 1.0 since total debt would not exceed total assets. If we begin with a fraction that is less than one and increase both the numerator and the denominator by the same amount, the fraction will increase. Therefore, in both a and d, the debt ratio will increase. (Many times students believe that the fraction should be unchanged, but remember that we are *adding* a number to both the numerator and the denominator; we are not multiplying or dividing by the number in which case the fraction would indeed be unchanged. To convince yourself of this, assume that the original debt ratio was $5/10$. Next assume that the firm purchases $10 of inventory on credit, so we add $10 to both the numerator and the denominator, making the fraction $15/20$, which is greater than $5/10$.) If inventory is purchased for cash, one total asset account (cash) is decreased, but a second total asset account (inventory) is increased by the same amount, so the denominator of the fraction is unchanged, and the transaction does not involve any of the accounts in the numerator (total debt). However, when inventory is sold for a profit, the inventory account decreases, while cash (or accounts receivable if the sale was a credit sale) increases by *more than* the decrease in the inventory account since inventory is carried at cost. The result is an increase in total assets. The denominator of the fraction has increased, so the value of the fraction decreases.

4. Different ratios are calculated to study different aspects of a firm's financial condition. A firm's short-term creditors may be most interested in the liquidity ratios of a firm, which measure the firm's ability to meet its short-term debt obligations. A shareholder may be most interested in the firm's profitability ratios. Nevertheless, no ratio should be studied in isolation for the true picture of the firm's financial condition is only revealed when the interrelationships between the ratios are considered. Ratios utilize numbers on the accounting statements, and these numbers can be easily manipulated to make a single ratio or set of ratios look better, but the problems will be revealed elsewhere in the ratio analysis. Consider, for example, the current ratio, which is calculated as current assets/current liabilities and measures a firm's liquidity. If a firm has obsolete inventory but wants to keep its liquidity ratio looking good, it may choose not to write off the inventory, which would cause current assets, and therefore the ratio, to decrease. However, the problem will be revealed when the inventory turnover ratio is calculated. The inventory turnover ratio is calculated in one of two ways: Sales/inventory or cost of goods sold/inventory. If obsolete inventory remains on the books, the denominator of these fractions will be artificially high resulting in a low inventory turnover ratio.

The choice of an inventory valuation method can also affect some of the ratios. Two of the common methods used are LIFO and FIFO. LIFO stands for "last in, first out," meaning that the last units purchased are considered the first units to be sold, so their value is included in the "cost of goods sold" account on the income statement, with the value of the first units purchased remaining as the "inventory" balance on the balance sheet. FIFO stands for "first in, first out." When this method is used, the value of the first units purchased is included in the "cost of goods sold" account while the value of the more recent purchases remains as "inventory." For example, consider a firm that purchased three units of inventory for $2 each and later purchased five units of inventory for $3 each, and assume that it sells four units. If the firm uses the LIFO method, its cost of goods sold will be $4 \times \$3 = \$12$, and its inventory balance will consist of the remaining unit that was purchased for $3 and the three units that were purchased for $2, so its value will be [$3 + (3 \times \$2)]$, or $9. On the other hand, if FIFO had been used, the cost of goods sold would be $9, since the first three units sold would be the first ones purchased at $2 each and the last unit sold would be one of the $3 units. The inventory balance would consist of the remaining four units purchased at $3 each, so it would be $12.

? If a firm makes its purchases during a period of inflation (i.e., rising prices), which method of inventory valuation—FIFO or LIFO—will result in a higher inventory turnover ratio?

Answer: LIFO.

During a period of inflation, the last units purchased will be the most expensive, so the most expensive inventory will be considered the first units sold, leaving the cheaper units as "inventory" on the balance sheet. The inventory balance will thus be lower when LIFO is used than if FIFO had been used. A lower number in the denominator of the ratio results in a higher ratio.

5. The first set of ratios that we will consider are the **liquidity ratios** which, as was previously mentioned, are designed to measure a firm's ability to handle its short-term debt obligations. The first of these is the current ratio.

$$\text{Current ratio} = \frac{\text{current assets}}{\text{current liabilities}}$$

It can be interpreted as follows: how much the firm has in quick-cash assets (i.e., current assets) for every dollar of short-term debt obligations (i.e., current liabilities). The current ratio for IMC for 1995 is, therefore, $12,080/$10,380 = 1.16. For every dollar of short-term debt, IMC has $1.16 in assets that can be quickly converted to cash. Whether this is good or bad depends on the average current ratio for the industry. Too high a current ratio compared to the industry average is just as bad as one that is too low since investment in liquid assets does not offer as high a return as investment in long-term assets. Sometimes it is more appropriate to compare a firm's ratios with one or more peers in the industry than with the industry as a whole since some industries have a lot of diversity among its firms. For example, consider the restaurant industry, which runs the gamut from fast food restaurants to low-priced, individually owned restaurants, to family-oriented chains, to gourmet dining establishments.

? We can also compare this year's ratio to IMC's current ratios in previous years to determine whether IMC's liquidity position is improving or deteriorating. Calculate IMC's current ratio for 1996. Has it improved or deteriorated?

Answers: 1.63, improved.
Current ratio = $19,600/$12,061 = 1.63. Since IMC has more quick-cash assets to cover its short-term debt obligations in 1996 than it had in 1995, its liquidity position has improved.

6. As was indicated in a previous frame, some of the current assets may not be as liquid as creditors would like. For example, the inventory may be obsolete or damaged and, ergo, unsalable. If this is a concern, creditors may prefer to measure a firm's liquidity by using the quick ratio, which is also known as the acid test. The **quick ratio** measures how many dollars of current assets, excluding inventory, that a firm has to cover its short-term debt obligations.

$$\text{Quick ratio} = \frac{\text{current assets} - \text{inventory}}{\text{current liabilities}}$$

The quick ratio for IMC for 1995 is ($12,080 − $6,200)/$10,380 = 0.57. This means that for every dollar of short-term debt, IMC has only $0.57 in assets that can quickly be converted to cash if inventory is not considered.

? Calculate the quick ratio for IMC for 1996. Has it improved or deteriorated since 1995?

Answers: 1.08, improved.
The quick ratio for 1996 is ($19,600 − $6,600)/$12,061 = 1.08. In 1996, IMC has $1.08 in assets that can be quickly converted to cash for every dollar of short-term debt, so this is an improvement over the previous year.

7. This improvement in the quick ratio may indicate that IMC is turning over its inventory more quickly. We can verify this by calculating the inventory turnover ratio, which is one of the **asset management ratios**, so named because this set of ratios is designed to identify problems in any area of asset management. While the inventory turnover ratio is sometimes calculated by dividing sales by inventory, many analysts prefer to calculate the ratio as follows:

$$\text{Inventory turnover} = \frac{\text{cost of goods sold}}{\text{inventory}}$$

since both inventory and cost of goods sold are measured in terms of the cost to the firm, whereas sales includes a profit. If the information is available, average inventory should be used in the denominator of the ratio since the cost of goods sold is taken from the income statement, which covers a period of time while the inventory is a balance sheet item and is measured at a specific point in time. Therefore, if we had the 1994 balance sheet information for IMC, we could calculate the average inventory by summing the 1994 balance and the 1995 balance and dividing by two. For a firm with seasonal sales, a 12-month average would be appropriate if the analyst had monthly inventory balances available.

While we can interpret the inventory turnover ratio as we did the previous two ratios, i.e., for every dollar of inventory, how much the firm has spent for cost of goods sold, it is easier to think of the inventory turnover as the number of times inventory turns over in 1 year. As was discussed in an earlier frame, obsolete inventory or damaged goods will be reflected in this ratio. The inventory turnover ratio for IMC in 1995 is $52,000/$6,200 = 8.39.

? Calculate the inventory turnover ratio for IMC in 1996. Has it improved or deteriorated?

Answers: 9.24, improved.
The inventory turnover for 1996 is calculated by dividing the cost of goods sold by the inventory balance, so $61,000/$6,600 = 9.24. Since inventory is turning over more frequently, the ratio has improved.

8.   A second asset management ratio is the **average collection period**, which measures how well a firm manages its credit policy. The average collection period (ACP) is the average number of days in which credit sales are converted to cash—i.e., the average number of days that it takes a firm's customers to pay their bills to the firm.

$$\text{Average collection period} = \frac{\text{accounts receivable}}{\text{average daily sales}}$$

The average daily sales is found by taking the sales (only the sales made on credit should be used if this number is available; many times it is not, and the analyst typically assumes that all sales were made on credit in that case) and dividing by either 360 or 365, depending on whether the firm uses a banker's year or a calendar year in its calculations. The longer the average collection period, the longer the firm is waiting for its cash and the greater the opportunity loss. However, if a firm's average collection period is too low relative to the industry average, it may be losing sales due to a stricter credit policy. The average collection period for IMC in 1995 is 17 days. [$2,800/($60,000/365) = 17.0].

? Calculate the average collection period for IMC for 1996. Has it improved or deteriorated since 1995?

Answers: 33.6 days, deteriorated.
ACP = $6,900/($75,000/365) = 33.6 days. Since it is taking IMC longer in 1996 to convert its credit sales to cash, the ratio has deteriorated.

9.   Since IMC's liquidity ratios have improved while its average collection period has deteriorated, one can conclude that the improved inventory turnover contributed a large part to the improved liquidity. A firm can also measure how well its fixed assets are being utilized although these will not directly affect the firm's liquidity. The fixed asset turnover ratio is measured by dividing sales by net fixed assets.

$$\text{Fixed asset turnover} = \frac{\text{sales}}{\text{net fixed assets}}$$

Net fixed assets are a firm's plant, property and equipment less the accumulated depreciation. This ratio indicates how many dollars of sales are generated for each dollar invested in fixed assets. This ratio will be lower if a firm has excess capacity or if it has poorly maintained equipment that results in lower production efficiency. In the case of excess capacity, the firm may decide to sell off some of its fixed assets unless the excess capacity is viewed as a temporary situation. Since net fixed assets are used in the denominator, when a firm purchases new plant, property, or equipment that has not been in place long enough to generate sales (i.e., a slight time lag exists), its fixed asset turnover may fall slightly. Similarly, if a new firm is comparing itself to the industry average, this ratio may be lower since its net fixed assets will probably be higher than that of a more established firm that has some older assets that have been depreciated for several years. The use of straight-line depreciation rather than accelerated depreciation causes the net fixed asset account to be higher and results in a lower fixed asset turnover.

The fixed asset turnover ratio for IMC is 2.60 ($60,000/$23,087) in 1995. For every dollar invested in net fixed assets, IMC is generating $2.60 in sales.

? Calculate the fixed asset turnover for IMC in 1996. Has it improved or deteriorated?

Answers: 3.91, improved.
The 1996 fixed asset turnover ratio is $75,000/$19,200 = 3.91, indicating that in 1996 IMC generated $3.91 in sales for every dollar of net fixed assets. This is greater than the $2.60 in sales generated in 1995.

10.   The asset management ratio that gives a general picture of how well a firm is managing its assets is the **total asset turnover ratio**, which is calculated by dividing the sales by the total assets of the firm.

$$\text{Total asset turnover} = \frac{\text{sales}}{\text{total assets}}$$

(Again, whenever we use a number from the income statement in the same ratio as a balance sheet number, an *average* balance sheet number should be used if possible, so the average total assets should be used in the denominator.) If a firm is having problems with the management of any of its assets, this number should indicate it when it is compared with the industry average. However, if the firm is doing extremely well in one area, but poorly in another, the good performance may outweigh the bad, and the total asset turnover ratio will not reveal that a problem exists. The total asset turnover ratio indicates how many dollars in sales are generated for each dollar invested in total assets. The total asset turnover ratio for IMC in 1995 is $60,000/$35,167 = 1.71. For every dollar that IMC has invested in assets, it is generating $1.71 in sales.

? Calculate the total asset turnover ratio for IMC in 1996. Has it improved or deteriorated? Based on the previous analysis done, to what do you attribute the improvement or deterioration?

Answers: 1.93, improved, improved inventory turnover and more efficient use of fixed assets.
The total asset turnover ratio for 1996 is $75,000/$38,800 = 1.93, which means that in 1996 IMC generated $1.93 in sales for every dollar it had invested in assets. This is an improvement over 1995. Since we discovered in earlier frames that the inventory turnover and fixed asset turnover had improved while the average collection period had deteriorated, the improvement in the total asset turnover ratio must be attributed to the improvement in inventory turnover and a more efficient use of fixed assets.

11. While the liquidity ratios measure a firm's ability to handle its short-term debt obligations, the **leverage ratios** are designed to measure a firm's ability to handle its total debt obligations. The first of these is the **debt ratio**, which indicates how much of the firm is "owned" by its creditors—i.e., financed with borrowed funds.

% OF FIRM ASSETS FINANCED BY DEBT

$$\text{Debt ratio} = \frac{\text{total debt}}{\text{total assets}}$$

It measures how much debt a firm has for every dollar of assets it owns. The debt ratio of IMC in 1995 is $16,880/$35,167 = 0.48. So for every dollar of total assets that IMC has, it owes $0.48 to creditors, or stated in another fashion, the firm is financed with 48% debt.

? Calculate the debt ratio for IMC in 1996. Has it improved or deteriorated?

Answers: 0.49, deteriorated very slightly.
The 1996 debt ratio is $19,061/$38,800 = 0.49, so in 1996, 49% of the firm is financed with debt compared to 48% in 1995. This is a very slight deterioration.

12. A ratio that may be calculated in lieu of the debt ratio is the **debt/equity ratio**. This ratio also measures the amount of financial leverage that a firm is using. It indicates how much debt a firm has for every dollar of total equity.

$$\text{Debt/equity ratio} = \frac{\text{total debt}}{\text{total equity}}$$

Some firms use only long-term debt when calculating this ratio.

$$\text{Alternative debt/equity ratio} = \frac{\text{long-term debt}}{\text{total equity}}$$

The debt/equity ratio for IMC for 1995 is, therefore, $16,880/$18,287 = 0.92 if total debt is used in the calculation, indicating that for every dollar of equity financing, the firm uses $0.92 in debt financing. If only long-term debt is used in the calculation, the ratio becomes 0.36 ($6,500/$18,287). For every dollar of equity financing, IMC uses $0.36 in long-term debt.

? Calculate the debt/equity ratio for IMC in 1996 using both ratio definitions. How can you explain the fact that the ratio calculated using the first definition is higher than the 1995 figure while the ratio calculated using the alternative definition is lower than the 1995 figure?

Answers: 0.97, 0.35.
When total debt is used in the numerator, the debt/equity ratio becomes $19,061/$19,739 = 0.97. When long-term debt only is used, the debt/equity ratio is $7,000/$19,739 = 0.35. The difference in the trends depicted using the two definitions of the debt/equity ratio can be explained by the fact that although total debt increased relative to equity, IMC used less long-term debt as a percent of equity to finance the firm.

13. Yet a third ratio that measures the relative debt that a firm uses is called the **equity multiplier** or the **leverage ratio**. It measures the use of debt indirectly in that it indicates how many dollars of total assets a firm has for every dollar of equity. Since total assets must equal total liabilities plus equity, the higher the equity multiplier, the higher is the use of debt by the firm.

$$\text{Equity multiplier} = \frac{\text{total assets}}{\text{total equity}}$$

This ratio is 1.92 in 1995 for IMC, indicating that for every dollar of equity the firm has $1.92 in assets, which means that it must have $0.92 in debt. Note that this is the same result that we got when we calculated the debt/equity ratio in the previous frame using total debt in the numerator.

? Calculate the equity multiplier for IMC in 1996.

Answer: 1.97.
The 1996 equity multiplier is $38,800/$19,739 = 1.97.

14.   An increase in debt is not necessarily bad. If the firm can earn more on the money it borrows than it must pay for the debt service, the firm will be profitable. One ratio that can be used to measure this is the **times interest earned ratio (TIE)**, which is also called the **coverage ratio**. It measures how much operating profit a firm has to cover its interest expense.

$$\text{TIE} = \frac{\text{operating profit}}{\text{interest expense}} \qquad \frac{EBIT}{I}$$

In 1995, IMC's times interest earned ratio was 1.43, indicating that for every dollar of interest expense, IMC had $1.43 in operating profit to cover that expense.

? What is the times interest earned ratio for IMC in 1996? Based on the trend in the TIE and the debt ratios calculated previously, how would you evaluate IMC's debt management?

Answers: 4.61, very good debt management.
The 1996 times interest earned ratio for IMC is $6,000/$1,300 = 4.61. Therefore, IMC is much better able to pay its interest expense in 1996 than it was in 1995 even though it has taken on a little more debt in 1996. Its use of financial leverage appears to be good.

15.   If a firm has other fixed payments, such as lease payments, sinking fund payments, and/or preferred dividends, a **fixed charges coverage ratio (FCCR)** will indicate the firm's ability to handle all of those payments. We determine the profit earned by the firm before the payments and divide by the total of the payments. When sinking fund payments or preferred dividends are included, we must divide those payments by one minus the marginal tax rate of the firm to determine how many pretax dollars the firm needs to make those required payments since neither sinking fund payments nor preferred dividends are tax deductible; both are paid out of after-tax dollars.

$$\text{FCCR} = \frac{\text{EBIT} + \text{lease payments}}{\text{interest expense} + \text{lease payments} + \dfrac{\text{sinking fund payment} + \text{preferred dividends}}{1 - \text{tax rate}}}$$

There are no lease payments or sinking fund payments for IMC, but the firm does have preferred stock. The fixed charges coverage ratio for 1995 is therefore calculated as follows:

$$\text{FCCR} = \frac{\$2,000}{\$1,400 + \dfrac{\$13}{1 - 0.5}} = 1.40.$$

Since the preferred dividends are relatively small, the difference between this coverage ratio and the times interest earned ratio is negligible.

? Calculate the fixed charges coverage ratio for IMC for 1996.

Answer: 4.52.

$$FCCR = \frac{\$6,000}{\$1,300 + \dfrac{\$13}{1-0.5}} = 4.52$$

16. Another set of ratios are designed to measure the profitability of the firm and are referred to, therefore, as the **profitability ratios.** The profit margin ratios are a subset of these. The **gross profit margin** indicates how much a firm has left after it has paid for the direct cost of the goods it sells. It is calculated by dividing the gross profit by the sales.

$$\text{Gross profit margin} = \frac{\text{gross profit}}{\text{sales}}$$

IMC's 1995 gross profit margin is $8,000/$60,000 = 0.133 or 13.3%. For every dollar of sales that IMC generated in 1995, it had $0.133 left after paying for the cost of the goods it sold. The gross profit margin is most often expressed as a percentage, as are the other profit margin numbers we will calculate.

? Calculate the gross profit margin in 1996 for IMC.

Answer: 18.7%.
The gross profit margin is $14,000/$75,000 = 18.7%.

17. The **operating profit margin** indicates how much a firm has left after it has paid all of the expenses associated with general business operations, but before financing costs are considered. It is calculated by dividing the operating margin by sales.

$$\text{Operating profit margin} = \frac{\text{EBIT}}{\text{sales}}$$

The operating profit margin for IMC in 1995 is $2,000/$60,000 = 0.033 or 3.3%, indicating that IMC got to keep slightly more than 3 cents out of every dollar of sales after its operating expenses were paid.

? Calculate the operating profit margin for IMC in 1996. Has it improved or deteriorated from 1995?

Answers: 8.0%, improved.
The 1996 operating profit margin is $6,000/$75,000 = 0.08 or 8%. IMC got to keep 8 cents out of every dollar of sales after operating expenses were paid in 1996, so this is an improvement over 1995.

18. The **net profit margin** indicates how much a firm gets to keep once it has paid all of its expenses, including interest expenses. It is calculated by dividing the net income by sales.

$$\text{Net profit margin} = \frac{\text{net income}}{\text{sales}}$$

In 1995, IMC's net profit margin was $300/$60,000 = 0.005 or 0.5%, which means that for every dollar of sales, IMC kept one-half a cent as profit after paying all its expenses.

? Calculate the net profit margin for IMC in 1996.

Answer: 3.1%.
Net profit margin = $2,350/$75,000 = 0.031 or 3.1%

19. The **return on assets (ROA)** ratio is a profitability ratio by which management performance is often judged. It is calculated by dividing net income by total assets.

$$\text{ROA} = \frac{\text{net income}}{\text{total assets}}$$

IMC's return on assets in 1995 was $300/$35,167 = 0.009 or 0.9%. This means that in 1995, for every dollar invested in assets, IMC generated less than 1 cent in profits. The return on assets is the product of the net profit margin, which measures how well expenses were controlled, and total asset turnover, which measures how well the firm managed its assets.

$$\text{ROA} = \frac{\text{net income}}{\text{total assets}} = \frac{\text{net income}}{\text{sales}} \times \frac{\text{sales}}{\text{total assets}}$$

In 1995, IMC managed most of its assets fairly well, but its net profit margin was extremely low, making the return on assets very low.

? Calculate the return on assets for IMC for 1996. Has it improved or deteriorated since 1995? What was the bigger factor that was responsible for the improvement or deterioration?

Answers: 6.1%, improved, increased profitability.
The return on assets for 1996 is $2,350/$38,800 = 6.1%. This is a marked improvement over the ROA for 1995 of 0.9%. While the asset turnover ratio improved slightly from 1995 to 1996, the bigger factor affecting the improvement in the return on assets in 1996 was the profitability since the net profit margin increased from 0.5% to 3.1%.

20. Shareholders may be most interested in a firm's **return on equity (ROE)**, which measures the profit that the firm is earning for each dollar that shareholders' have invested in the firm.

$$\text{ROE} = \frac{\text{net income available for common shareholders}}{\text{common shareholders' equity}} = \frac{\text{net income} - \text{preferred dividends}}{\text{common shareholders' equity}}$$

When a firm has preferred stock outstanding, as IMC does, a return on total equity (ROTE) is sometimes also calculated.

$$\text{ROTE} = \frac{\text{net income}}{\text{preferred} + \text{common equity}}$$

The return on equity for IMC in 1995 is $287/$18,003 = 1.59%; the return on total equity is $300/$18,287 = 1.64%. For every dollar of common stockholders' investment, the shareholders' have earned $0.0159; for every dollar of total equity invested, the preferred and the common shareholders have earned $0.0164.

The return on total equity is comprised of three factors: the net profit margin of the firm, the total asset turnover, and the leverage ratio.

$$ROTE = \frac{\text{net income}}{\text{total equity}} = \frac{\text{net income}}{\text{sales}} \times \frac{\text{sales}}{\text{total assets}} \times \frac{\text{total assets}}{\text{equity}}$$

The return on total equity, therefore, is dependent upon the cost control of the firm, its asset management, and its use of debt. All else being equal, the greater the use of debt, the greater is the return on total equity; however, the greater the use of debt, the more risk that the equity holders bear, so they should expect a higher return.

? Calculate the return on total equity for IMC for 1996. Has it improved or deteriorated since 1995? Which factor contributed the most to the improvement or deterioration?

Answers: 11.9%, improved, the profitability of the firm.
The return on total equity for 1996 is equal to $2,350/$19,739 = 11.9%, so for every dollar that shareholders had invested, they earned slightly under 12 cents. This is an improvement over 1995 when they were earning only slightly more than 1½ cents on every dollar they had invested. While a better asset turnover ratio contributed partially to this improvement, the largest factor was a greatly increased net profit margin. The use of debt was only slightly higher in 1996 than in 1995 and thus played a negligible role in the improved return on equity.

21. In addition to a firm's profitability ratios, potential shareholders are also interested in **shareholder value ratios**, which are measures of the disposition of a firm's earnings and are used as indicators of the market value of the stock. The **earnings per share (EPS)** refers to the earnings available to common shareholders on a proportionate basis.

$$EPS = \frac{\text{net income} - \text{preferred dividends}}{\text{common shares outstanding}}$$

Much of the time, some of these earnings are retained by the firm for reinvestment purposes. The earnings that are paid out to the shareholders are the dividends, and shareholders are also interested in the **dividends per share (DPS)** since this indicates how much current cash flow they will receive for each share owned.

$$DPS = \frac{\text{total dividends declared}}{\text{common shares outstanding}}$$

IMC had 316 million shares outstanding in both 1995 and 1996. It retained $100 million of its earnings in 1995 and $1,452 million of its earnings in 1996. Its earnings per share in 1995 was, therefore, $287/316 = $0.91. Dividends paid in 1995 equal the 1995 distributable earnings minus the retained earnings, so dividends per share were ($287 − $100)/316 = $0.59 in 1995.

? Calculate the 1996 earnings per share and dividends per share for IMC.

Answers: $7.40, $2.80.
The earnings per share is $2,337/316 = $7.40, and the dividends per share is ($2,337 − $1,452)/316 = $2.80.

22. The **dividend payout ratio** indicates the percentage of a firm's earnings that the firm pays out in common stock dividends.

$$\text{Dividend payout ratio} = \frac{\text{dividends}}{\text{distributable earnings}}$$

The distributable earnings refers to the earnings available to common shareholders after preferred shareholders have been paid. Most firms follow a stable dividend policy, which means that the dividend payment is kept constant or is allowed to grow (or decline) at a steady rate. This can lead to a dividend payout ratio that is very volatile unless the firm has fairly stable earnings. Nevertheless, shareholders are interested in knowing whether the firm follows a policy of a high dividend payout ratio or a low dividend payout ratio. Investors who wish to augment current income from other sources with investment income will prefer a firm that has a high dividend payout ratio, while investors who wish to keep their money invested would prefer to invest in a firm that has a low, or even a zero, dividend payout ratio to avoid paying taxes on the dividends and brokerage fees to reinvest the money. This is referred to as the **clientele effect**.

The dividend payout ratio for IMC in 1995 was \$187/\$287 = 0.65. IMC paid out 65% of its 1995 distributable earnings in common dividends.

? Calculate the 1996 dividend payout ratio for IMC.

Answer: 38%.
Dividend payout ratio = \$885/\$2,337 = 38%

23. Financial analysts are interested in a firm's **price/earnings (P/E) ratio** when evaluating the stock as an investment. This number indicates how much investors are paying for the firm for each dollar of earnings that the firm produces.

$$\text{P/E ratio} = \frac{\text{market price per share}}{\text{earnings per share}}$$

If IMC was selling for \$35 in 1995, its P/E ratio was \$35/\$0.91 = 38.5. Investors were paying \$38.50 in price for each dollar of earnings per share. Why? Remember that the value of a stock is not based on its *current* earnings, but rather on expected *future* earnings. Investors must believe that IMC is going to perform well in the future.

? How much are investors paying for each dollar of earnings that IMC produced in 1996 if its market price is \$75 at that time?

Answer: \$10.10.
The price/earnings ratio is \$75/\$7.40 = 10.1, so for every dollar of earnings, investors are paying \$10.10 in price.

24. In addition to the ratios discussed in the previous frames, a common-size analysis can be very informative, especially when looking at a firm's financial statements over time. This analysis simply consists of restating all of the income statement accounts as a percent of sales and all of the balance sheet accounts as a percent of total assets. The income statements of IMC are restated on page 160.

Having expressed all the income statement accounts as a percent of sales, we can see in which categories IMC did better or worse at cost containment. Note that the firm reduced its cost of goods sold substantially, but selling and general administrative

---

International Motor Corporation

Common-Size Income Statement

for the years ending December 31,

	1995	% of sales	1996	% of sales
Sales	$60,000	100.0%	$75,000	100.0%
Cost of goods sold	52,000	86.7%	61,000	81.3%
Gross profit	$ 8,000	13.3%	$14,000	18.7%
Selling and general administrative expenses	6,000	10.0%	8,000	10.7%
Operating profit	$ 2,000	3.3%	$ 6,000	8.0%
Interest expense	1,400	2.3%	1,300	1.7%
Earnings before tax	$ 600	1.0%	$ 4,700	6.3%
Taxes	300	0.5%	2,350	3.1%
Earnings after tax	$ 300	0.5%	$ 2,350	3.1%

---

expenses rose slightly. Even though IMC increased its debt slightly, as we discovered when evaluating the leverage ratios of IMC, its interest expense actually decreased, both in dollars and as a percent of sales. (This may be possible if a firm refinances current debt at lower rates.) Thus, the improved profit margin that we observed is due largely to a decrease in the cost of goods sold and interest expense.

? Restate IMC's 1995 and 1996 balance sheets as a percent of total assets. Are there any evident changes in the asset mix of the firm? Has IMC made any significant changes in the method by which it chooses to finance its assets?

Answers:

International Motor Corporation

Common-Size Balance Sheet

as of December 31,

	1995	% of total assets	1996	% of total assets
Cash and marketable securities	$ 3,080	8.8%	$ 6,100	15.7%
Accounts receivable	2,800	8.0%	6,900	17.8%
Inventory	6,200	17.6%	6,600	17.0%
Total current assets	$ 12,080	34.3%	$19,600	50.5%
Net plant, property, and equipment	23,087	65.6%	19,200	49.5%
Total assets	$ 35,167	100.0%	$38,800	100.0%
Accounts payable	3,600	10.2%	4,600	11.9%
Notes payable	1,180	3.4%	1,250	3.2%
Accruals	5,600	15.9%	6,211	16.0%
Total current liabilities	$ 10,380	29.5%	$12,061	31.1%
Long-term debt	6,500	18.5%	7,000	18.0%
Total liabilities	$ 16,880	48.0%	$19,061	49.1%
Preferred stock	$ 284	0.8%	$ 284	0.7%
Common stock (at par)	521	1.5%	521	1.3%
Paid in surplus	1,930	5.5%	1,930	5.0%
Retained earnings	15,552	44.2%	17,004	43.8%
Total equity	$ 18,287	52.0%	$19,739	50.9%
Total liabilities and equity	$ 35,167	100.0%	$38,800	100.0%

Looking at the percentages calculated above, the asset mix of IMC has changed substantially between 1995 and 1996. In 1996, IMC has far more invested in current assets than it had in 1995. Accounts receivable have more than doubled as a percent of sales, supporting our previous analysis which indicated a lengthened average collection period. The firm is also holding a lot more cash as a percent of sales than it did in 1995. The firm is using slightly less long-term debt to finance the firm. Instead, it is using more trade credit (accounts payable), which is typically a more expensive method of financing, albeit more convenient.

 Apply It

1. Wagnall, Incorporated had $50,000 in revenues in 1995 while its cost of goods sold was $20,000. In addition, the firm had general selling and administrative expenses amounting to $12,000 and interest expense of $8,000. Wagnall has no preferred stock, but it paid its common shareholders a $0.25 per share dividend in 1995. There are 10,000 shares outstanding, and Wagnall is in the 35% marginal tax bracket.

   a. Prepare an income statement for Wagnall based on the information given. (Frame 1)

   b. What will be Wagnall's 1995 addition to its retained earnings account? (Frame 2)

   c. What is Wagnall's 1995 dividend payout ratio? (Frame 22)

2. You also have the following 1995 year-end information on Wagnall, Incorporated:

Cash	$ 5,000
Inventory	$ 8,000
Accounts payable	$ 3,500
Accrued wages	$ 1,200
Accounts receivable	$ 12,000
Notes payable	$ 10,000
Mortgages	$ 45,000
Common stock	$ 80,000
Retained earnings	$ 20,000
Marketable securities	$ 10,000
Net plant, property, and equipment	$124,700

   a. Prepare a balance sheet for Wagnall as of December 31, 1995. (Frame 2)

   b. Calculate Wagnall's liquidity ratios. (Frames 5 and 6)

   c. Calculate Wagnall's asset management ratios. (Frames 7, 8, 9, and 10)

   d. Calculate Wagnall's leverage ratios. (Frames 11, 12, 13, 14, and 15)

   e. Calculate Wagnall's profitability ratios. (Frames 16, 17, 18, 19, and 20)

   f. What is Wagnall's earnings per share in 1995? (Frame 21)

3. The following financial statements are available for Elves' Toy Shops, a toy manufacturing firm:

Elves' Toy Shops
Income Statement
for the years ending December 31,

	1996	1995
Sales	$2,700,000	$2,500,000
Cost of goods sold	1,250,000	1,100,000
Gross profit	$1,450,000	$1,400,000
Fixed operating expenses	1,280,000	1,200,000
Operating profit	$ 170,000	$ 200,000
Interest expense	48,000	35,000
Earnings before tax	$ 122,000	$ 165,000
Taxes (@ 40%)	48,800	66,000
Net income	$ 73,200	$ 99,000

Elves' Toy Shops
Balance Sheet

	1996	1995
Assets		
Cash	$ 111,000	$ 126,000
Accounts receivable	488,000	420,000
Inventory	360,000	219,000
Total current assets	$ 959,000	$ 765,000
Net plant, property, and equipment	280,000	250,000
Total assets	$1,239,000	$1,015,000
Liabilities		
Accounts payable	$ 135,000	$ 125,000
Accrued expenses	75,000	80,000
Notes payable	165,800	50,000
Total current liabilities	$ 375,800	$ 255,000
Long-term debt	240,000	210,000
Total liabilities	$ 615,800	$ 465,000
Equity		
Common stock ($0.50 par value, 100,000 shares outstanding)	$ 50,000	$ 50,000
Additional paid-in capital	150,000	150,000
Retained earnings	423,200	350,000
Total equity	$ 623,200	$ 550,000
Total liabilities and equity	$1,239,000	$1,015,000

Elves' common stock sold for $15 a share at the end of 1995 and for $11.125 a share at the end of 1996.

a. Calculate the ratios necessary to evaluate Elves' liquidity position. Has there been an improvement or deterioration? (Frames 5 and 6)

b. Calculate Elves' asset management ratios. Are there any strengths or weaknesses revealed? (Frames 7, 8, 9, and 10)

c. Calculate Elves' leverage ratios. Have they improved or deteriorated since 1995? (Frames 11, 12, 13, 14, and 15)

d. Calculate Elves' profitability ratios. Have they improved or deteriorated since 1995? (Frames 16, 17, 18, 19, and 20)

e. Break Elves' ROA and ROE ratios down into their component factors. What does this suggest about the major reason(s) for the improvement or deterioration revealed in part (d)? (Frames 19 and 20)

f. Calculate Elves' earnings per share and its price/earnings ratio for each year. (Frames 21 and 23)

4. Financial data for Dwarfs' Jewelry Stores is as follows:

Dwarfs' Jewelry Stores

Income Statement

for the year ending December 31, 1996

Sales	$3,000,000
Cost of goods sold	1,500,000
Gross profit	$1,500,000
General selling and administrative expenses	$1,000,000
Operating profit	$ 500,000
Interest expense	10,000
Earnings before tax	$ 470,000
Taxes (@ 34%)	166,600
Net income	$ 323,400

Dwarfs' Jewelry Stores

Balance Sheet

as of December 31, 1996

Assets		**Liabilities and Equity**	
Cash	$ 42,000	Accounts payable	$ 86,000
Accounts receivable	300,000	Accrued expenses	50,000
Inventory	863,000	Notes payable	36,000
Total current assets	$1,205,000	Total current liabilities	$ 172,000
Net plant, property, and equipment	$ 331,000	Long-term debt	$ 156,000
Total assets	$1,536,000	Common equity	$1,208,000
		Total liabilities and equity	$1,536,000

Dwarfs' has 1 million shares outstanding. The following ratios are available for a peer firm in the industry:

Peer Firm Ratios

Net profit margin	4%
Return on assets	12%
Return on equity	14%
Total asset turnover	1.94x
Average collection period	61 days
Inventory turnover	2.4x
Debt ratio	36%
Current ratio	4.02
Quick ratio	0.93
Price/earnings ratio	16

Evaluate how Dwarfs' is doing relative to its peer. In what areas are they doing better? In what areas do they appear to be doing worse? (Frames 6 through 21 and Frame 23)

Apply It Answers

1. a.

Wagnall, Incorporated

Income Statement

for the year ending December 31, 1995

Revenues	$50,000
Cost of goods sold	20,000
Gross profit	$30,000
General selling and administrative expenses	12,000
Operating profit	$18,000
Interest expense	8,000
Earnings before tax	$10,000
Taxes (@ 35%)	3,500
Net income	$ 6,500

b. Total dividends = $0.25 \times 10,000$ shares = $2,500
   1995 addition to retained earnings = net income − 1995 dividends paid
   = $6,500 − $2,500 = $4,000

c. Dividend payout ratio = $2,500/$6,500 = 38.5%

2. a.

Wagnall, Incorporated

Balance Sheet

as of December 31, 1995

Assets		Liabilities and Equity	
Cash	$ 5,000	Accounts payable	$ 3,500
Marketable securities	10,000	Accrued wages	1,200
Accounts receivable	12,000	Notes payable	10,000
Inventory	8,000	Total current liabilities	$ 14,700
Total current assets	$ 35,000	Mortgages	45,000
Net plant, property, and equipment	$124,700	Total liabilities	$ 59,700
Total assets	$159,700	Common stock	$ 80,000
		Retained earnings	20,000
		Total equity	$100,000
		Total liabilities and equity	$159,700

b. Current ratio = $35,000/$14,700 = 2.38
   Quick ratio = ($35,000 − $8,000)/$14,700 = 1.84

c. Inventory turnover = $20,000/$8,000 = 2.5
   Average collection period = $12,000/($50,000/365) = 87.6 days
   Fixed asset turnover = $50,000/$124,700 = 0.40
   Total asset turnover = $50,000/$159,700 = 0.31

d. Debt ratio = $59,700/$159,700 = 0.37
   Debt/equity ratio = $59,700/$100,000 = 0.597
   Alternative debt/equity ratio = $45,000/$100,000 = 0.45
   Equity multiplier = $159,700/$100,000 = 1.597
   Times interest earned = $18,000/$8,000 = 2.25
   Fixed charges coverage = $18,000/$8,000 = 2.25

e. Gross profit margin = $30,000/$50,000 = 0.60 = 60%

Operating profit margin = $18,000/$50,000 = 0.36 = 36%
Net profit margin = $6,500/$50,000 = 0.13 = 13%
Return on assets = $6,500/$159,700 = 0.04 = 4%
Return on equity = $6,500/$100,000 = 0.065 = 6.5%

f. Earnings per share = $6,500/$10,000 = $0.65

3. a. 1996 current ratio: $959,000/$375,800 = 2.55
1995 current ratio: $765,000/$255,000 = 3.00

1996 quick ratio: ($959,000 − $360,000)/$375,800 = 1.59
1995 quick ratio: ($765,000 − $219,000)/$255,000 = 2.14

Both the current ratio and the quick ratio indicate that Elves' liquidity position has deteriorated between 1995 and 1996.

b. 1996 inventory turnover ratio: $1,250,000/$360,000 = 3.47
1995 inventory turnover ratio: $1,100,000/$219,000 = 5.02

1996 average collection period: $488,000/($2,700,000/365) = 66 days
1995 average collection period: $420,000/($2,500,000/365) = 61.3 days

1996 fixed asset turnover ratio: $2,700,000/$280,000 = 9.6
1995 fixed asset turnover ratio: $2,500,000/$250,000 = 10.0

1996 total asset turnover ratio: $2,700,000/$1,239,000 = 2.18
1995 total asset turnover ratio: $2,500,000/$1,015,000 = 2.46

The biggest weakness is in the inventory turnover ratio. Elves' experienced a substantial drop in this ratio between 1995 and 1996. The average collection period lengthened slightly, and the fixed asset turnover ratio declined a bit. All of these elements contributed to a decline in the total asset turnover ratio.

c. 1996 debt ratio: $615,800/$1,239,000 = 0.50
1995 debt ratio: $465,000/$1,015,000 = 0.46

1996 debt/equity ratio: $615,800/$623,200 = 0.99
1995 debt/equity ratio: $465,000/550,000 = 0.85

1996 equity multiplier: $1,239,000/$623,200 = 1.99
1995 equity multiplier: $1,015,000/$550,000 = 1.84

1996 times interest earned: $170,000/$48,000 = 3.54
1995 times interest earned: $200,000/$35,000 = 5.71

Elves' has increased its debt from 1995 to 1996, as evidenced by both the debt ratio and the debt/equity ratio. The equity multiplier has also been calculated, but it is really redundant since it offers the same information as the debt ratio. The debt/equity ratio indicates that for every dollar of equity in 1996, Elves' owed $0.99 to its creditors. Increased use of debt is not necessarily a bad thing, so long as the firm is earning more on the funds than it is paying. The times interest earned ratio indicates that such is not the case. Elves' ability to cover its interest expense has also deteriorated sharply between the 2 years.

d. 1996 gross profit margin: $1,450,000/$2,700,000 = 54%
1995 gross profit margin: $1,400,000/$2,500,000 = 56%

1996 operating profit margin: $170,000/$2,700,000 = 6.3%
1995 operating profit margin: $200,000/$2,500,000 = 8.0%

1996 net profit margin: $73,200/$2,700,000 = $73,200/$2,700,000 = 2.7%
1995 net profit margin: $99,000/$2,500,000 = $99,000/$2,500,000 = 4.0%

1996 return on assets: $73,200/$1,239,000 = 5.9%
1995 return on assets: $99,000/$1,015,000 = 9.8%

1996 return on equity: $73,200/$623,200 = 11.7%
1995 return on equity: $99,000/$550,000 = 18%

All of the profitability ratios have deteriorated from 1995 to 1996.

e. ROA = net profit margin × total asset turnover
1996 ROA = 2.7% × 2.18 = 5.9%
1995 ROA = 4% × 2.46 = 9.8%

The deterioration in the return on assets is due to both a decrease in the firm's profitability and a less efficient use of assets. The biggest deterioration resulted from the reduced profitability.

ROE = net profit margin × total asset turnover × equity multiplier
1996 ROE = 2.7% × 2.18 × 1.99 = 11.7%
1995 ROE = 4% × 2.46 × 1.84 = 18%

The return on equity is also the result of a decrease in the firm's profitability and a less efficient use of assets. Even though the firm's leverage increased and, therefore, the risk to which its shareholders were exposed, the return on equity was pulled down.

f. 1996 earnings per share = $73,200/100,000 = $0.732
1995 earnings per share = $99,000/100,000 = $0.99

1996 price/earnings ratio = $11.125/$0.732 = 15.2
1995 price/earnings ratio = $15.00/$0.99 = 15.2

4. Dwarfs' ratios:
Current ratio: $1,205,000/$172,000 = 7.01
Quick ratio: ($1,205,000 − $863,000)/$172,000 = 1.99
Dwarfs' liquidity is much higher than that of its peer firm. In fact, the current ratio may actually be too high.

Inventory turnover: $1,500,000/$863,000 = 1.74
Average collection period: $300,000/($3,000,000/365) = 36.5 days
Total asset turnover: $3,000,000/$1,536,000 = 1.95

While Dwarfs' total asset turnover is the same of that of its peer firm for all intents and purposes, Dwarfs' inventory turnover is lower than that of its peer firm, indicating a possible problem. Its average collection period is very good relative to the peer firm, which helps to ameliorate the total asset turnover ratio.
Debt ratio: $328,000/$1,536,000 = 0.21 = 21%
Dwarfs' is using less leverage than the peer firm, so it probably has more financing flexibility and will be better able to take advantage of any unexpected opportunities that arise.

Net profit margin: $323,400/$3,000,000 = 10.8%
Return on assets: $323,400/$1,536,000 = 21.1%
Return on equity: $323,400/$1,208,000 = 26.8%

Dwarfs' profitability is much greater than that of the peer firm, which is reflected in both a higher return on assets and a higher return on equity. Since the return on assets is a function of the firm's profitability and its total asset turnover and the total asset turnover ratio for Dwarfs' was nearly identical to that of its peer firm, we can conclude that the higher ROA is due solely to the higher net profit margin. The return on equity is a function of the firm's profit margin, total asset turnover, and leverage ratios. Dwarfs' asset turnover ratio is identical to that of the peer firm, while its leverage ratio is actually lower than that of the peer firm (this was not calculated, but since Dwarfs' uses less debt, as indicated by the debt ratio, the leverage ratio will also be lower). We can conclude, therefore, that the higher ROE is solely attributable to the higher profitability of Dwarfs'.

FINANCIAL FORECASTING

In this module you will learn some basic techniques that are employed to produce forecasted income statements and balance sheets. Trend analysis and the percent-of-sales methods are the primary focus. You will also learn how constraints can be built into the forecasts. This module assumes a fundamental knowledge of accounting statements, a topic which was addressed more thoroughly in Module 8.

Equations introduced in this module

$$\text{Accounts receivable} = \text{average collection period} \times \frac{\text{sales}}{365}$$

$$\text{Accounts payable} = \text{average payment period} \times \frac{\text{cost of goods sold}}{365}$$

1. Financial decisions are based on future expectations regarding the revenues and expenses of a firm, which in turn determine the cash flows that a firm will have. Therefore, it is critical that a firm have a good set of forecasts on which to base its decision making. Forecasting involves considering the past, present, and future conditions that the firm faces. Since no firm operates in isolation, the analyst must examine global factors as well as industry-specific and company-specific factors.

The first step in creating forecasted, or **pro forma**, financial statements is to forecast sales. Sales is the most important account to forecast as well, since all of the firm's other income statement and balance sheet accounts are related to the firm's sales, either directly or indirectly. It is typical to forecast sales by first looking at the history of the sales growth over the last several years. This is what is known as a **trend analysis**. If an analyst were to observe that sales grew at an average rate of 18% a year over the past decade, he might forecast next year's sales to increase by 18% over this year's sales. A significant assumption that is made in this case is that past conditions will continue. This may not always be true. For example, assume that during the past decade the firm enjoyed patent protection that has now expired and that several competitors are waiting in line to begin production on the no-longer-protected product. To blindly forecast an 18% increase in sales would be a big mistake. As another example assume that the 18% growth rate was during a decade of strong economic conditions, but that economic forecasts look gloomy and it appears that the country may be entering a deep recession. Once again, to forecast an 18% growth rate would not be taking into consideration all of the relevant factors. A good sales forecast generally begins with a trend analysis, but the analyst adjusts for changing conditions.

? The Elizabethean Company (EC) has the following history of sales:

Year	Sales
1	$500,000
2	$550,000
3	$607,750
4	$669,741
5	$736,715
6	$810,386

If the past conditions are expected to continue into the next year, what would you forecast EC's sales to be in year 7?

Answer: $891,425.

The historical annual growth rate has been about 10 percent. (The growth rate can be calculated as [(ending value − beginning value)/beginning value] × 100%, so the growth in sales from the first year to the second year was [($550,000 − $500,000)/$500,000] × 100% = 10%.) The annual sales growth rates for each year were:

Year 1 to 2:	10%
Year 2 to 3:	10.5%
Year 3 to 4:	10.2%
Year 4 to 5:	10%
Year 5 to 6:	10%

Therefore, if past conditions are expected to continue, sales in year 7 should be $810,386(1.10) = $891,425. (Note that this *is* a conservative estimate since the average growth rate for the period is slightly *higher* than 10%.)

2. Once sales has been forecast, we can forecast other items on the income statement. Variable expenses are those that vary directly with sales and are usually forecast using the

percent of sales method. This method involves calculating the historical percentage of sales that the specific account represents and then using that same percentage of the forecasted sales to forecast the account. For example, suppose the Villella Corporation expects next year's sales to be $1 million, and its cost of goods sold has historically averaged 72% of sales. Then the Villella Corporation would forecast next year's cost of goods sold to be 0.72($1,000,000) = $720,000. Again, remember that a good analyst will always consider whether or not the historical average can be expected to continue in the future. For example, a war in the country of a major supplier of raw materials may decrease the availability of the raw materials, thereby increasing the price. Cost of goods sold can then be expected to be a higher percentage of sales than what the historical average would predict.

❓ The Elizabethean Corporation's cost of goods sold for the most recent 6 years has been as follows:

Year	Sales	Cost of Goods Sold
1	$500,000	$300,000
2	$550,000	$330,000
3	$607,750	$370,728
4	$669,741	$405,193
5	$736,715	$438,345
6	$810,386	$486,232

Use the percent of sales method to predict the cost of goods sold for year 7.

Answer: $534,855.

Cost of goods sold has averaged about 60% of sales for the past 6 years.

Year	Sales	Cost of Goods Sold	Percent of Sales
1	$500,000	$300,000	60%
2	$550,000	$330,000	60%
3	$607,750	$370,728	61%
4	$669,741	$405,193	60.5%
5	$736,715	$438,345	59.5%
6	$810,386	$486,232	60%

Assuming the past average is a reasonable predictor of what the future holds, the cost of goods sold for year 7 will be 60% of the sales forecast for year 7, or 0.60($891,425) = $532,855. (Note that we have rounded off the percent of sales to the nearest whole percentage. This is somewhat arbitrary although rounding errors should be less than the expected forecasting errors.)

3.   It is important to remember that not *all* income statement items will reasonably vary as a percent of sales. The general selling and administrative expenses may or may not. One way to tell is to calculate this account as a percent of sales and determine how constant the percentages are over time. If they are erratic, then the percent of sales is probably not the best predictor. A trend analysis might be done and the historical growth rate of this account used to forecast next year's general selling and administrative expenses. If it is listed as a separate account, the depreciation expense is best calculated by adjusting the past depreciation expense account for depreciation on any planned capital expenditures as well as for any changes in the depreciation rate that applies to existing assets. Interest expense is sometimes forecast as a percent of sales but, if the information is available, the forecast of this account might better be based on the long-term debt account. Unfortunately, this can sometimes lead the analyst into a vicious cycle since long-term debt requirements depend on other available financing sources that include retained earnings which, in turn, is determined by the amount of the current year's profits that are reinvested in the firm. Typically, the interest expense is forecast based on expected interest rates during the forecast period and any expected changes in the levels of short-term and long-term debt financing. This is added to any existing interest expense. Computer technology has been extremely helpful under these circumstances.

Taxes should be forecast using expected tax rates and the earnings before tax figure that results from the forecasted accounts.

? Which of the following income statement accounts is most likely to vary as a percent of sales?
   a. losses from extraordinary items
   b. interest expense
   c. labor expenses
   d. gain on the sale of an asset

Answer: labor expenses.
Since labor expenses are generally directly related to the service or product being sold, they are most likely to vary as a percent of sales. Interest expense is more dependent on the debt of the firm; gains or losses due to extraordinary items or the sale of assets are not accounts that can be expected to be directly related to sales. In fact, these accounts may not appear every year.

4. Likewise, there are balance sheet accounts that are often forecast as a percent of sales. On the asset side of the balance sheet accounts receivable are often forecast as a percent of sales since they result spontaneously with sales. Cash and inventory are also sometimes forecast as a percent of sales although a firm may choose to hold a minimum cash balance and/or may hold safety stock in inventory, in which case neither account should be forecast to drop below that. Similarly, if the analyst observes that the cash account has been, say, $2,000 every year for the past 5 years, it is reasonable to assume "no change." The marketable securities account is often used as a "plug." If excess funds are available when the forecast is completed, they are assumed to be invested in marketable securities. The plant, property, and equipment account generally does not vary directly as a percent of sales since a firm typically has some expansion potential before new capital expenditures must be made. However, if information regarding planned capital expenditures and/or current capacity requirements is not available (which may be the case when an external analysis is being done), this account is sometimes forecast as a percent of sales as well. It may also be forecast using a trend analysis.

On the right hand side of the balance sheet, accounts payable and accrued items are often considered to grow spontaneously with sales; however, long-term debt items and the common and preferred equity accounts should never be forecast as a percent of sales. These items change only if new bonds or stock are sold or old issues are retired or repurchased. Additionally, retained earnings, a common equity account, will be increased or decreased based on the current year's income statement. You might recall that this account is a cumulative account, so this year's retained earnings balance is equal to last year's balance plus any additions or reductions to retained earnings. If the firm has earned a profit in the current year, the addition to retained-earnings is the amount of profit that remains after dividends, if any, are paid. Notes payable, often a short-term liability account, can be used as the "plug" account on this side of the balance sheet. If additional funds are needed, this account is increased. (Note that there is always only *one* account that is plugged. If additional funds are needed, the notes payable account is plugged; if there are excess funds available, the marketable securities account is plugged.)

? Assume that the Elizabethean Corporation has $381,000 in its retained earnings this year. Next year's profits are forecasted to be $107,000. The firm has historically paid out 40% of its earnings in dividends (i.e., the dividend payout ratio is 40%). What would you forecast next year's retained earnings to be?

Answer: $445,200.

Since the dividend payout ratio is 40%, the firm has a history of reinvesting 60% of its profits in the firm. Next year's profits are forecasted to be $107,000, so 60% of this is $64,200. Adding that to the current year's retained earnings we get a forecasted balance of $445,200 ($64,200 + $381,000).

5. While forecasting many accounts as a percent of sales is the easiest method to use, an analyst sometimes has more information available and can do a more sophisticated and, therefore, a more accurate (hopefully) forecast. For example, suppose that a firm has had accounts receivable that have averaged 25% of sales in the recent several years. The firm, however, has decided to change its credit policy and hopes to reduce its average collection period from 91 days to 60 days by doing so. If the firm is expected to have $1 million in sales, and accounts receivable normally average 25% of sales, this would mean that accounts receivable would be forecast to be $250,000 if past conditions were to continue. This is an average collection period of 91.25 days ($250,000/[$1,000,000/365]). If the average collection period is expected to be reduced to 60 days, however, this information should be used to make the forecast. Since the average collection period is equal to the accounts receivable divided by average daily sales, the accounts receivable must be equal to the average collection period times average daily sales.

$$ACP = \frac{\text{Accounts receivable}}{\dfrac{\text{sales}}{365}}$$

$$\text{Accounts receivable} = ACP \times \frac{\text{sales}}{365}$$

Based on the assumption that the average collection period will be reduced to 60 days, the forecasted accounts receivable should be $60 \times (\$1,000,000/365) = \$164,384$.

The average payment period of a firm measures the average number of days that it takes the firm to pay its suppliers. This number is calculated by dividing the accounts payable by the average daily cost of goods sold.

$$\text{Average payment period} = \frac{\text{accounts payable}}{\dfrac{\text{cost of goods}}{365}}$$

Therefore,

$$\text{Accounts payable} = \text{average payment period} \times \frac{\text{cost of goods sold}}{365}.$$

? Currently, the Elizabethean Corporation is taking 73 days to pay its suppliers. The suppliers are threatening to make EC pay before goods are delivered. Furthermore, EC could be getting a 2.5% discount on the price of the goods if it pays within 15 days. If EC were to reduce its payment period to 15 days, what would its accounts payable be in year 7, based on the previous forecasts (sales = $891,425 and cost of goods sold = $534,855)?

Answer: $21,980.

If the average payment period is reduced to 15 days, then 15 = A/P/($534,855/365), so A/P = $534,855/365 × 15 = $21,980.

6. As the situation warrants, any and all of the above forecasting techniques may be used to forecast a complete set of financial statements. For example, assume that this year's income statement for Model Corporation is as follows:

Sales	$1,500,000
Cost of goods sold	870,000
Gross profit	$ 630,000
General selling and	
administrative expenses	180,000
EBIT	$ 450,000
Interest expense	35,000
Earnings before tax	$ 415,000
Tax (@ 40%)	166,000
Net income	$ 249,000

After reviewing the general economic and industry conditions and interviewing the vice-president of marketing to get his input, a financial analyst for Model estimates that the firm can expect an increase of 12% in sales revenues. He also expects general selling and administrative expenses to decrease by $1/2$% due to economies of scale. After talking to the director of capital budgeting, the analyst estimates that interest expense will increase by $5,000 due to an increase of $50,000 in capital expenditures that will be financed with a 10% 5-year note. Cost of goods sold is expected to remain at its current relationship to sales, and the tax rate is also expected to be the same next year. Based on these assessments, the pro forma income statement for Model Corporation will appear as follows:

Sales	$1,680,000	($1,500,000 × 1.12)
Cost of goods sold	974,400	(COGS was 58% of sales last year)
Gross profit	$ 705,600	
General selling and		
administrative expenses	179,100	($180,000 × [1 − 0.005] = $180,000 × 0.995)
EBIT	$ 526,500	
Interest expense	40,000	($35,000 + $5,000)
Earnings before tax	$ 486,500	
Tax	194,600	($486,500 × 0.40)
Net income	$ 291,900	

? This year's income statement for the Mimic Corporation is as follows:

Sales	$3,000,000
Cost of goods sold	1,860,000
Gross profit	$1,140,000
General selling and	
administrative expenses	400,000
EBIT	$ 740,000
Interest expense	50,000
Earnings before tax	$ 690,000
Tax (@ 40%)	276,000
Net income	$ 414,000

Next year's sales are expected to increase by 15%. Cost of goods sold is expected to remain the same in its historical relationship to sales. The general selling and administrative expenses have been increasing by 1.5% on average over the last decade, and this trend is expected to continue. The firm is not expecting to issue any new long-term debt, so the interest expense should remain the same. The tax rate is also not expected to change. Develop a pro forma income statement for the Mimic Corporation based on these facts.

Answer:

Sales	$3,450,000 ($3,000,000 × 1.15)
Cost of goods sold	2,139,000 (last year's COGS was 62% of sales)
Gross profit	$1,311,000
General selling and administrative expenses	406,000 ($400,000 × 1.015)
EBIT	$ 905,000
Interest expense	50,000 (expected to be the same as last year's)
Earnings before tax	$ 855,000
Tax (@ 40%)	342,000
Net income	$ 513,000

7.   The pro forma balance sheet is also largely based on the sales forecast. Assume that Model Corporation's balance sheet as of the end of the current year is as follows:

Assets		**Liabilities**	
Cash	$ 22,500	Accounts payable	$ 225,000
Accounts receivable	150,000	Accruals	30,000
Inventory	300,000	Notes payable	67,500
Total current assets	$ 472,500	Total current liabilities	$ 322,500
Plant, property, and		Long-term debt	250,000
equipment	550,000	Total liabilities	$ 572,500
Total assets	$1,022,500		
		Equity	
		Common stock	$ 100,000
		Retained earnings	350,000
		Total equity	$ 450,000
		Total liabilities and equity	$1,022,500

Assume that all the current asset accounts will remain at their current relationship to sales and that fixed assets will be increased by $50,000. In an effort to maintain an amicable relationship with suppliers, Model intends to decrease its current accounts payable balance by paying within 30 days. (Model currently has an average payment period of over 94 days. The average payment period is calculated as accounts payable divided by average daily cost of goods sold.) The capital expenditures are being financed by long-term debt, so that account will be increased by $50,000. Model will continue its historical dividend payout ratio of 40%. Any excess funds will be invested in marketable securities whereas any additional funds needed will be procured using the short-term liability account, notes payable. Based on the above data, a pro forma balance sheet for Model Corporation will appear as follows:

Cash	$ 25,200	(0.015 × $1,680,000; last year's cash/sales = 1.5%)
Accounts receivable	168,000	(0.10 × $1,680,000; last year's A/R/sales = 10%)
Inventory	336,000	(0.20 × $1,680,000; last year's inventory/sales = 20%)
Total current assets	$ 529,200	
Plant, property, and equipment	600,000	
Total assets	$1,129,200	
Accounts payable	$ 80,088	(30/365 × $974,400; a 365-day year is assumed)
Accruals	33,600	(0.02 × $1,680,000; last year's accruals/sales = 2%)
Notes payable	$ 90,372	(this figure is a plug after all other liability and equity accounts have been calculated)
Total current liabilites	$ 204,060	
Long-term debt	300,000	(increased $50,000 as per assumption)
Total liabilities	$ 504,060	
Common stock	100,000	(same as previous year; no new stock was sold)
Retained earnings	$ 525,140	($291,900 × 0.6 = $175,140 = addition to retained earnings)
Total equity	625,140	
Total liabilities and equity	$1,129,200	

? Mimic Corporation's balance sheet as of the end of the current year is as follows:

Cash	$ 1,500,000	Accounts payable	$ 240,000
Accounts receivable	360,000	Accruals	90,000
Inventory	750,000	Notes payable	224,000
Total current assets	$ 2,610,000	Total current liabilities	$ 554,000
		Long-term debt	800,000
Plant, property, and		Total liabilities	$1,354,000
equipment	1,000,000	Common stock	1,000,000
Total assets	$ 3,610,000	Retained earnings	1,256,000
		Total equity	2,256,000
		Total liabilities and equity	$3,610,000

Mimic is expected to maintain its current minimum cash balance. Furthermore, it hopes to reduce its average collection period to 30 days. (A 365-day calendar is used by Mimic.) Inventory will remain at its historical average percent of sales. Fixed assets are expected to increase by $200,000. On the liability side of the equation, both accounts payable and the accruals are expected to maintain their historical relationship to sales. The long-term debt account is expected to remain unchanged. Any excess funds will first be used to pay off notes payable. If there are additional excess funds, these will be invested in marketable securities, while any additional funds needed will be assumed to be procured by using notes payable, a short-term liability account. Mimic does not pay dividends, but instead reinvests 100% of its profits into the firm. Based on the above data, develop a pro forma balance sheet for Mimic Corporation.

Answer:

Cash	$1,500,000	(same as previous year)
Accounts receivable	284,000	(30/365 × $3,450,000)
Inventory	862,500	(0.25 × $3,450,000; last year's Inventory/sales = 25%)
Marketable securities	102,000	(plugged figure)
Total current assets	$2,748,500	
Plant, property, and		
equipment	1,200,000	(fixed assets are expected to increase by $200,000)
Total assets	$3,948,500	
Accounts payable	$ 276,000	(0.08 × $3,450,000; last year's A/P/sales = 8%)
Accruals	103,500	(0.03 × $3,450,000; last year's Accruals/sales = 3%)
Notes payable	0	(last year's balance paid off with excess funds)
Total current liabilities	379,500	
Long-term debt	800,000	(same as previous year)
Total liabilities	$1,179,500	
Common stock	$1,000,000	(same as previous year; no new stock sold)
Retained earnings	1,769,000	($1,256,000 + $513,000)
Total equity	$2,769,000	
Total liabilities and equity	$3,948,500	

8. There are oftentimes restrictions on how a firm may choose to finance its growth. Covenants on existing debt obligations may require that the debt ratio (total debt/total assets) not exceed a certain number, that the current ratio (current assets/current liabilities) be at least a certain number, or that net working capital (current assets − current liabilities) be at least a certain amount. Using our previous example of the Model Corporation as an illustration, let us assume that an existing bond covenant specifies that the debt ratio may not exceed 40%. This means that the maximum amount of total debt that the firm can have is 40% of the forecasted total assets, so 0.40 × $1,129,200 = $451,680. In the previous frame, the pro forma balance sheet for Model Corporation shows total debt to be $504,060, and this cannot occur given the new restriction we have just introduced. The difference, $504,060 − $451,680 = $52,380, must be raised by selling new stock or by using more retained earnings—i.e., reducing the amount of dividends that the firm is paying. If we assume that the adjustment is made to the notes payable account, the liability and equity accounts on the revised pro forma balance sheet would appear as follows:

Accounts payable	$ 80,088
Accruals	33,600
Notes payable	37,992 ($451,680 − $300,000 − $80,088 − $33,600)
Total current liabilities	$ 151,680
Long-term debt	300,000
Total liabilities	$ 451,680
Common stock	152,380 (assuming new stock is sold)
Retained earnings	525,140 (assumes the current dividend policy is maintained)
Total liabilities and equity	$1,129,200

? If another bond covenant specifies that the current ratio must be greater than or equal to 2.75, what is the maximum amount of short-term debt that the Model Corporation can use?

Answer: $192,436.

Since the current ratio is calculated as current assets/current liabilities and Model's forecasted current assets are $529,200, $529,200/x ≥ 2.75. Thus "x" can be no greater than $529,200/2.75 = $192,436.

Apply It

1. The Tinker Corporation is expecting sales of $2,800,000 next year. The firm's cost of goods sold has historically been 58% of its sales, and this relationship is expected to continue. Tinker hopes to be able to reduce its inventory balance so that its inventory turnover ratio (COGS/inventory) is equal to that of the industry average, 4.0. Based on this, what should the inventory account balance be on its pro forma balance sheet? (Frame 5)

2. The Valdez Company wants to reduce its average collection period to 40 days next year. It is expecting its sales to be $3,650,000, and all of its sales are on credit. If Valdez uses a 365-day year in its calculations, what should its accounts receivable balance be on its pro forma balance sheet? (Frame 5)

3. The Steady Corporation has the following sales history:

Year	Sales
1	$660,000
2	$706,200
3	$754,928
4	$809,283
5	$865,528

Assuming past conditions are expected to continue in the next year, what would you predict sales to be in year 6? (Frame 1)

4. The following historical information is available for the Carnac Corporation:

Year	Sales	Cost of Goods Sold
1	$500,000	$220,000
2	$550,000	$247,500
3	$616,000	$277,200

Sales in year 4 are expected to be $689,920. What would you forecast the firm's cost of goods sold to be in year 4? (Frame 2)

5. The following historical information is available for the Trial Corporation:

Year	Sales	Inventory	Accounts Payable
1	$1,000,000	$123,288	$30,825
2	$1,100,000	$114,521	$28,630
3	$1,215,500	$166,507	$43,292
4	$1,337,050	$146,526	$36,632

To predict the accounts payable balance for year 5, would it be better to use the ratio of accounts payable to sales or accounts payable to inventory? (Frame 3)

6. The Moore Company had $5,600,000 in sales this year. Net profits were $728,000, and the firm paid $254,800 in dividends. The retained-earnings account on the end-of-year balance sheet was $800,000. An analyst for Moore has forecast next year's sales to be $6,000,000. If you assume that Moore's net profit margin (net income/sales) and dividend payout ratio (dividends/net income) remain unchanged, what should the retained earnings account on the pro forma balance sheet be? (Frame 4)

7. The most recent 3-year financial statements for the Hypothetical Corporation are shown below:

Hypothetical Corporation

Income Statement (in thousands)

for the years ending

	1993	1994	1995
Sales	$1,620.0	$1,800.0	$2,000.0
Cost of goods sold	1,134.0	1,260.0	1,400.0
Gross profit	$ 486.0	$ 540.0	$ 600.0
General selling and administrative expenses	193.0	199.0	200.0
Operating profit	$ 293.0	$ 341.0	$ 400.0
Interest expense	35.0	42.0	38.0
Earnings before tax	$ 258.0	$ 299.0	$ 362.0
Tax (@ 40%)	103.2	119.6	114.8
Net income	$ 154.8	$ 179.4	$ 247.2

Hypothetical Corporation

Balance Sheet (in thousands)

as of December 31,

Assets	1993	1994	1995
Cash and marketable securities	$ 100.0	$ 118.5	$ 336.7
Accounts receivable	162.0	180.0	200.0
Inventory	324.0	360.0	400.0
Total current assets	$ 586.0	$ 658.5	$ 936.7
Plant, property, and equipment	648.0	700.0	700.0
Total assets	$1,234.0	$1,358.5	$1,636.7
Liabilities and Equity			
Accounts payable	$ 243.0	$ 270.0	$ 300.0
Accrued expenses	8.1	9.0	10.0
Notes payable	132.8	0	0
Total current liabilities	$ 383.9	$ 279.0	$ 310.0
Long-term debt	500.0	550.0	550.0
Total liabilities	$ 883.9	$ 829.0	$ 860.0
Common stock	100.0	100.0	100.0
Retained earnings	250.1	429.5	676.7
Total liabilities and equity	$1,234.0	$1,358.5	$1,636.7

Hypothetical is expecting sales to increase by 12% in 1996. The cost of goods sold will remain at its historical percentage of sales. General selling and administrative expenses are expected to increase by 3%, but the interest expense is expected to decrease by $4,000 due to the retirement of $10,000 in long-term debt. The tax rate is expected to remain at 40%. All earnings are reinvested in the firm. The accounts receivable, inventory, accounts payable, and accrued expenses are all expected to maintain their historical relationship to sales. Plant, property, and equipment will be increased only to the extent of the depreciation on these fixed assets. The cash and marketable securities will always have a minimum balance of $100,000, but if excess funds are available, they will be used to purchase marketable securities (which is what the firm did in 1995). If additional funds are needed, the notes payable account will be used as a plug. Based on this information, develop pro forma financial statements for the Hypothetical Corporation for 1996. (Frames 6 and 7)

8. The P & R Reicken Company has $8 million in assets. The assets are financed with $3.5 million debt and $4.5 million common equity. It has forecasted next year's assets to be $10 million. An existing debt covenant states that the debt ratio can be no greater than 45%.

   a. What is the maximum amount of debt the firm can use without violating the covenant? (Frame 8)

   b. How much new debt will the firm be allowed to raise to support the additional assets without violating the covenant? (Frame 8)

   c. If the firm expects to be able to add $400,000 next year to retained earnings, how much new stock must be sold to support the expected growth in assets? (Frame 8)

Apply It Answers

1. The expected level of the cost of goods sold account is 0.58($2,800,000) = $1,624,000. If Tinker wants its inventory turnover to be equal to the industry average, then $1,624,000/inventory = 4.0. Solving this equation for inventory, inventory = $1,624,000/4 = $406,000.

2. Since Valdez wants its average collection period to be 40 days, then its accounts receivable divided by the expected average daily sales must equal 40.

$$\frac{\text{accounts receivable}}{\dfrac{\$3,650,000}{365}} = 40$$

$$\text{accounts receivable} = 40(\frac{\$3,650,000}{365}) = 40(\$10,000) = \$400,000$$

3. The growth rates for years 1 through 5 have been approximately 7%.
   Years 1–2: ($706,200 – $660,000)/$660,000 = 7.0%
   Years 2–3: ($754,928 – $706,200)/$706,200 = 6.9%
   Years 3–4: ($809,283 – $754,928)/$754,928 = 7.2%
   Years 4–5: ($865,528 – $809,283)/$809,283 = 6.95%
   Assuming a 7% growth rate between years 5 and 6, sales in year 6 can be forecast to be $865,528(1.07) = $926,115.

4. Carnac's cost of goods sold has been about 45% of sales in the past.
   Year 1: $220,000/$500,000 = 44%
   Year 2: $247,500/$550,000 = 45%
   Year 3: $277,200/$616,000 = 45%
   If sales in year 4 are expected to be $689,920, then cost of goods sold can be expected to be 0.45($689,920) = $310,464.

5. The ratios of accounts payable to sales and accounts payable to inventory for the 4 years are shown below:

Year	Accounts Payable/Sales	Accounts Payable/Inventory
1	3.1%	25%
2	2.6%	25%
3	3.6%	26%
4	2.7%	25%

Since the ratio of accounts payable to inventory is much more constant than that of accounts payable to sales, the former will be a better predictor of next year's accounts payable than will the latter.

6. Moore's profit margin this year was $728,000/$5,600,000 = 13%. If this is expected to be stable, then next year's profits can be forecast to be 0.13($6,000,000) = $780,000. This year's dividend payout ratio was $254,800/$728,000 = 35%, which means Moore retained 65% of its earnings. Therefore, it can be expected to retain 0.65($780,000) = $507,000 of next year's profits. Since the retained earnings account this year has a balance of $800,000, next year's retained earnings account will have a balance of $800,000 + $507,000 = $1,307,000.

7. _____

Hypothetical Corporation

Pro Forma Income Statement (in thousands)

for the year ending December 31, 1996

Sales	$2,240.0	(12% increase over previous year)
Cost of goods sold	1,568.0	(historically, COGS has been 70% of sales)
Gross profit	$ 672.0	
General selling and administrative expenses	206.0	(a 3% increase over the previous year)
Operating profit	$ 466.0	
Interest expense	34.0	(a decrease of $4,000 from the previous year)
Earnings before tax	$ 432.0	
Tax (@ 40%)	172.8	
Net income	$ 259.2	

Hypothetical Corporation

Pro Forma Balance Sheet (in thousands)

as of December 31, 1996

Cash and marketable securities	$ 551.1	($100 minimum + $451.1 investment of excess funds)
Accounts receivable	224.0	(historically, A/R has been 10% of sales)
Inventory	448.0	(historically, inventory has been 20% of sales)
Total current assets	$1,223.1	
Plant, property, and equipment	700.0	(equipment replacement offset by depreciation)
Total assets	$1,923.1	
Accounts payable	$ 336.0	(historically, A/P has been 15% of sales)
Accrued expenses	11.2	(historically, accrued expenses have been 0.5% of sales)
Notes payable	0	(there are excess funds in 1996, so no borrowing is necessary)
Total current liabilities	$ 347.2	
Long-term debt	540.0	(decrease of $10,000)
Total liabilities	$ 887.2	
Common stock	$ 100.0	(no additional stock was sold)
Retained earnings	$ 935.9	(1995 balance of $676.7 + 1996 addition of $259.2)
Total liabilities and equity	$1,923.1	

8. a. Since forecasted assets are $10 million, and total debt/total assets cannot exceed 45%, total debt/$10,000,000 " 0.45. Solving the equation, total debt " 0.45($10,000,000) or $4,500,000.

   b. Since Reicken already has $3.5 million in debt on the books, it can only raise another million in new debt.

   c. Since assets = liabilities + equity, if Reicken has $10,000,000 in assets and can have only $4,500,000 in debt, it must finance the remaining $5,500,000 with equity. The firm currently has $4,500,000 in equity, so it must raise $1,000,000 more. However, $400,000 in new equity will come from retained earnings, so the firm will have to sell $600,000 in new stock.

SHORT-TERM ASSET MANAGEMENT

In this module, you will learn the various techniques that are employed in the management of the current assets of a firm—namely the cash, marketable securities, accounts receivable, and inventory. The benefits and the costs associated with these decisions are discussed. The Baumol Model and the Miller-Orr Model are presented as part of the cash management section. The types and characteristics of marketable securities in which a firm can invest its short-term funds as an alternative to holding cash are delineated. The requisite steps in establishing a credit policy are introduced, as well as tools used to track the accounts receivable management, such as the average collection period and aging schedules. Both the Economic Order Quantity and the Just-In-Time models are addressed in the inventory management section.

Equations introduced in this module

$$\text{Baumol Model: } Q = \sqrt{\frac{2TD}{k}}$$

Miller-Orr Model:

$$\text{Return point} = \text{lower limit} + \sqrt[3]{\frac{(0.75)TV}{k^*}}$$

$$\text{Upper limit} = \text{lower limit} + 3\sqrt[3]{\frac{(0.75)TV}{k^*}}$$

$$\text{Average collection period} = \frac{\text{accounts receivable}}{\dfrac{\text{credit sales}}{365}}$$

Cost of discounts = percentage discount × sales × percentage of customers taking discounts

Investment in accounts receivable = accounts receivable × variable cost ratio

Carrying cost of accounts receivable = investment in accounts receivable × r

Total inventory cost = acquisition costs + carrying costs + order costs

$$= (P \times D) + (C \times Q/2) + (O \times D/Q)$$

$$EOQ = \sqrt{\frac{2DO}{C}}$$

1. The current asset accounts on a firm's balance sheet are the firm's short-term assets. These are assets that are considered to be able to be converted to cash within one year or one operating cycle. They include cash, marketable securities, inventory, and accounts receivable. Management of these short-term assets involves a cost/benefit analysis. Once all of the benefits and all of the costs associated with a particular policy have been identified and quantified, if the benefits exceed the costs, the specific policy should be undertaken. If, however, the costs exceed the benefits, the policy should not be undertaken.

First, consider the cash account. Cash, which includes funds that a firm has in its checking account, is held for a number of reasons. A firm must have enough cash to pay its bills. This is sometimes referred to as a **transaction balance**. Like individuals, a firm may also wish to hold extra cash to meet unexpected needs. This is known as a **precautionary balance**. In addition, a firm may hold even a little more cash in order that it may be able to take advantage of a unique opportunity that arises and requires an immediate response. This is called a **speculative balance**. Sometimes a bank will require that a firm hold a minimum amount in an account at its institution in return for services that the bank agrees to provide to the firm. This is referred to as a **compensating balance** since it compensates the bank for its services. There is a cost associated with holding cash, however; it is an opportunity cost. If a firm has extra funds, it may choose to invest those funds in earning assets, such as short-term securities, instead of holding the funds as cash. The **opportunity cost** is what the firm *could have earned* on the funds had it invested them. There may also be a **transaction cost** associated with holding cash; this is the cost that the firm must incur to convert its short-term investments to cash if cash is needed to meet unexpected needs or opportunities. A brokerage fee is an example of a transaction cost. The more cash a firm holds, the fewer cash infusions it will need and, thus, the lower its transaction costs will be. However, the more cash a firm holds, the greater its opportunity cost will be.

? Cash balances that are held by the firm to enable the firm to react quickly to unexpected opportunities are called
   a. compensating balances.
   b. transaction balances.
   c. precautionary balances.
   d. speculative balances.

Answer: d.
This is the definition of a speculative balance.

2. The **Baumol Model** is a model that can be used to determine the amount of cash that a firm should hold to minimize the total costs, i.e., transaction costs and opportunity costs, associated with cash. This model assumes that cash is used uniformly throughout the period and, therefore, is not useful if a firm has seasonal needs for cash. Using "T" to represent the transaction cost associated with each cash infusion, "D" to represent the annual demand for cash, and "k" to represent the opportunity cost associated with holding cash, the amount of cash that a firm should obtain each time it gets a cash infusion, "Q", can be calculated using the following formula, known as the Baumol Model:

$$Q = \sqrt{\frac{2TD}{k}}.$$

As an example, assume that the Maximum Corporation has cash needs of $4 million per year. It can earn 5% on short-term investments, but it costs the firm $150 each time it needs a cash infusion. The amount of cash it should obtain with each cash infusion can be calculated as follows:

$$Q = \sqrt{\frac{2(\$150)(\$4,000,000)}{0.05}} = \$154,919.33 \approx \$154,920.$$

(Note that we always round *up* to the next dollar.) If Maximum obtains $154,920 each time it gets a cash infusion, the total of its opportunity cost and its transaction costs will be less than if it chooses any other amount as a cash infusion.

? The Predictable Company has cash needs of $2 million per year. These needs occur uniformly throughout the year. Each cash infusion costs the firm $100 in transaction costs. Predictable can earn 4% on short-term investments. What amount of cash should Predictable obtain with each cash infusion if it wishes to minimize its total costs associated with cash?

Answer: $100,000.

$$Q = \sqrt{\frac{2(\$100)(\$2,000,000)}{0.04}} = \$100,000$$

3.   Many firms do not have cash flows that occur evenly throughout the year, in which case the Baumol Model cannot be used. A second model, the **Miller-Orr Model**, assumes that cash flows vary unpredictably throughout the period. This model allows the cash balances to vary between the lower limit, which is the minimum cash balance that the firm should hold, and the upper limit, which is the maximum cash balance that the firm should hold. Whenever the cash balance drops below the lower limit, the firm must get a cash infusion to bring the cash balance to a level referred to in the model as the return point. Likewise, whenever the cash balance exceeds the upper limit, the firm should invest any cash that exceeds the return point amount in marketable securities. The lower limit can be thought of as the safety stock level of cash that management believes it should hold. The return point and the upper limit can be calculated using the following formulae:

$$\text{return point} = \text{lower limit} + \sqrt[3]{\frac{(0.75)TV}{k^\circ}}$$

$$\text{upper limit} = \text{lower limit} + 3\sqrt[3]{\frac{(0.75)TV}{k^\circ}},$$

where "T" is again the cost per transaction, "k°" is the opportunity cost per day, and "V" is the variance of daily cash flows.

To illustrate the application of this model, consider a firm that has cash flows that occur unevenly throughout the year. The variance of its daily cash flows has been calculated to be 10,000. Management wants to maintain a minimum cash balance of $2,000. It can invest any excess funds to earn 0.02% per day, and it costs the firm $100 for each cash infusion. In this example, the lower limit is $2,000, the minimum cash balance. The upper limit is calculated as

$$\text{upper limit} = \$2,000 + 3\sqrt[3]{\frac{0.75(\$100)(10,000)}{0.0002}} = \$6,660.85 \approx \$6,661.$$

So long as the firm has a cash balance between $2,000 and $6,661, nothing need be done. However, if the balance drops below $2,000 or exceeds $6,661, then action must be taken to bring the cash balance back to the return point, which is calculated below:

$$\text{return point} = \$2,000 + \sqrt[3]{\frac{0.75(\$100)(10,000)}{0.0002}} = \$3,553.615 \approx \$3,554.$$

? The Unpredictable Corporation has cash flow needs that occur sporadically throughout the year. The variance of the daily cash flows is 25,000. The firm's management has decided that its minimum cash balance must be $12,000. The firm has a daily opportunity cost of 0.005%, and it costs the firm $250 for each cash infusion. What action, if any, should the firm take if its cash balance is $15,000?

Answer: The firm need take no action if its cash balance is $15,000.

$$\text{upper limit} = \$12,000 + 3\sqrt[3]{\frac{0.75(\$100)(25,000)}{0.00005}} = \$25,628.40 \approx \$25,629$$

Since $15,000 lies between the lower limit of $12,000 and the upper limit of $25,629, the firm need take no action.

4. Besides determining the level of the cash balance that will minimize the total costs associated with cash, a firm will want to ensure that it has its cash working for it for the longest period possible. In order to do so, a firm will seek to reduce its **collection float** and to increase its **disbursement float**. Collection float is the amount of time it takes for a firm to have use of funds after a customer has paid for its goods. Collection float is determined by how long it takes the firm to receive the check after the customer has mailed it, how long it takes the firm to process the check and deposit it in the bank, and how long it takes before the bank gives the firm credit for the funds. Disbursement float is the amount of time it takes before payments to suppliers actually result in a cash outflow for the firm. While it, too, is a function of mail time, processing time, and check-clearing time, the firm is able to control only the mail time in the case of disbursement float. It may do so by mailing its checks from an office located in a remote area or by having its checking account at a bank that is located in a remote area, or at least at some distance from its suppliers. Since 1980 this practice has become less useful because the Federal Reserve now charges banks for float at the federal funds rate, and the banks pass these charges on to their customers. A firm may also have an arrangement with a bank to transfer only those funds needed to cover any checks that it wrote and which have now come back for payment to its checking account from an interest-bearing account. These are known as **zero balance accounts**, and they allow the firm to keep its funds working for it for the maximum amount of time.

There are several ways that a firm may elect to reduce its collection float. An obvious way is for the firm to streamline its in-house check-processing procedures as much as possible so that a minimum amount of time is spent on it. A second way is to use electronic collection. Under this method the funds are automatically transferred from the customer's bank account to the firm's bank account on the payment date, reducing the collection float to zero. Yet another method is to subscribe to a **lockbox system**. Under this setup, the customer is directed to mail its check to a post office box that is closest to the customer's business. This reduces mail float. A local bank picks up the check and processes it for clearing. The firm itself no longer has to process the check, so the firm processing time is reduced to zero.

? Which of the following is a method used to reduce collection float?
a. electronic collection
b. zero balance accounts
c. using a bank located in a remote location
d. mailing checks from an office located in a remote location

Answer: a.
Electronic collection allows the customer's funds to be deposited immediately into the firm's account, thus reducing collection float to zero. Zero balance accounts and remote disbursements are methods that help a firm control its disbursement float.

5. The methods that a firm can employ to reduce its collection float or to increase its disbursement float are not without costs. Therefore, in order to decide which, if any, a firm should employ, a cost/benefit analysis must be done. Consider, for example, a firm that is considering a lockbox system. The system will cost the firm $400,000 annually, but it is expected to reduce the firm's collection float by 3 days. The firm has average daily collections of $500,000 and uses a 365-day year in its calculations. It can earn 10% per year on its short-term investments.

The cost is obvious in this case—$400,000. The benefit is what the firm *can earn* on the freed funds. It is not the freed funds themselves, since that money already belongs to the firm. The firm is just receiving the money quicker. The freed funds in this case is $1,500,000 since the firm's daily collections average $500,000, and float will be reduced by 3 days. The firm can earn 10% on these funds, so the benefit of the system is 0.10 × $1,500,000 or $150,000. This is less than the $400,000 cost, so the firm *should not* adopt the lockbox system.

? Mailorder International averages $1,800,000 in daily collections. The firm is considering adopting a lockbox system that will cost $350,000. The system is expected to reduce collection float by 2 days, and Mailorder can earn 12% annually on its money. Should the firm adopt the system?

Answer: yes.
The freed funds are $1,800,000 × 2 = $3,600,000. The firm can earn 12% on these funds, and 0.12 × $3,600,000 = $432,000. This exceeds the $350,000 cost of the system.

6. In the above frames, it is assumed that the firm will invest any excess cash in short-term securities. There are a variety from which a firm may choose. These differ somewhat with regard to default risk and liquidity risk, and the greater the risk the higher the expected return on the investment. The financial manager must decide how much risk he is willing to take in return for a higher yield. If his firm expects to need the funds within the next 30 days, the manager will probably avoid the less liquid options. A brief description of the most frequently used short-term investments follows.

Treasury bills   Short-term debt of the U.S. government. The bills have maturities of 91, 192, or 365 days when newly issued. They are considered to be free of default risk and are considered very liquid and marketable. The minimum denomination is $10,000.

Negotiable certificates of deposit	Short-term debt issued by banks. These CDs have varying maturities up to 1 year and have a minimum denomination of $100,000. If the issuing bank is insured by the FDIC, any amount up to $100,000 is free of default risk since it is covered by the insurance; however, any amount in excess of $100,000 is not insured and is subject to default risk. Unlike CDs purchased by individuals, these CDs sell on the secondary market.
Repurchase agreements	Short-term financing agreements in which the borrower sells a security, such as a Treasury bill, to the lender with an agreement to buy the security back at a higher price within a short period of time, oftentimes just a few days. The security serves as collateral for the loan and, therefore, the lender is exposed to very little risk.
Banker's acceptances	Drafts written by the borrower and guaranteed by the bank on which the draft is drawn. They are typically used in international trade transactions. The borrower is an importer who writes the draft in payment for goods. When the exporter receives the draft, he may hold it until maturity and receive its full value or he may sell the draft at a discount prior to maturity. Since both the borrower and a bank have guaranteed the draft, banker's acceptances have very little risk.
Eurodollar deposits	Dollar-denominated time deposits held by banks outside the United States. The default risk depends on the credit worthiness of the issuing foreign bank.
Commercial paper	Short-term unsecured debt issued by large corporations. Maturities range up to 9 months, with the average maturity being 5 months. The minimum denomination is $25,000, but most commercial paper has a face value of $100,000 or more. The default risk depends on the credit-worthiness of the issuing corporation.

? If the financial manager of a firm wishes to invest $500,000 in a security that would expose him to no default risk, which of the following instruments should he select?

    a. certificate of deposit
    b. banker's acceptance
    c. treasury bill
    d. commercial paper

Answer: c.

Treasury bills are considered default-free. All of the other instruments have some, albeit little, default risk.

7. The management of accounts receivable involves several steps. First, a firm must decide on a credit policy. Management must decide on its credit standards—i.e., will it extend credit to anyone who applies for it or will it be selective and extend credit only to those customers that have a very low credit risk? Next it must establish its credit terms. Most sales to other firms are made on an open account, i.e., the customer receives the goods before making payment. Payment may be due in 30 days, which is designated as net 30 or n. 30. Sometimes the selling firm will provide the buying firm a discount if payment is made early. The terms $2/10$, net 30 means that the buying firm will receive a 2% discount if it pays for the goods within 10 days; otherwise, the full amount is due in 30 days. If the selling firm is a relatively small one in an industry, it will probably have to offer the same terms as its competitors. The last step in establishing a credit policy is to decide on its collection policy. This can range from doing nothing if a customer is paying late (generally not a good choice), to sending a polite letter of inquiry, to charging interest on payments extending beyond a specified period, to threatening legal action at the first late payment.

? If a firm purchased $1,000 of goods from another firm on terms of $1/15$, net 45, what will the firm have to pay for the goods if it makes payment on the fifteenth day?

Answer: $990.

The terms of $1/15$, net 45 means that the buying firm can take a 1% discount if it pays by the fifteenth day. Since $1,000 \times 0.01 = 10, the firm must pay only $990 for the goods.

8. Once a credit policy has been established, a firm must monitor its accounts receivable in order to be certain that its customers are being motivated by the terms offered and that the benefits still outweigh the costs. Two tools that can be used to monitor the accounts receivable are the average collection period and the aging schedule. The average collection period is the average number of days that it takes a firm to collect on its credit sales. It is calculated using the formula below:

$$\text{Average collection period} = \frac{\text{accounts receivable}}{\dfrac{\text{credit sales}}{365}}.$$

If the average collection period of a firm has been, say, 35 days for the past few years, and it is calculated to be 43 days this year, the firm may want to reexamine its credit policy. Of course, if the economy is sluggish, it may be the case that the entire industry is affected, in which instance the firm may adopt a "wait and see" attitude.

The average collection period is just one number, however, and can look reasonable even when a substantial percentage of the firm's customers are paying late. An aging schedule provides the firm with more information. An aging schedule categorizes accounts by the number of days they have been on the firm's books. It can be prepared using either the number of accounts or the dollar amount of the accounts receivable outstanding. For example, assume that a firm selling on terms of $2/15$, net 30 has $350,000 in accounts receivable that has been on the books for 15 days or less and that this represents 220 accounts. Another $450,000 has been on the books for 16 to 30 days, made up of 80 accounts, and $530,000 has been on the books for 31 to 40 days, representing 190 accounts. The firm has $200,000 that has been on the books for 41 to 50 days, and this represents 60 accounts. Yet another $70,000 has been on the books for 51 to 60 days, made up of 30 accounts, and there is $40,000, representing 20 accounts, that has been outstanding for over 60 days. An aging schedule based on the number of accounts is shown below:

Days Outstanding	Number of Accounts	Percent of Accounts
1 – 15	220	36.7%
16 – 30	80	13.3%
31 – 40	190	31.7%
41 – 50	60	10.0%
51 – 60	30	5.0%
Over 60	20	0.3%
	600	

An aging schedule based on the dollar amounts outstanding is as follows:

Days Outstanding	Amount Outstanding	Percent Outstanding
1 – 15	$ 350,000	21.4%
16 – 30	450,000	27.4%
31 – 40	530,000	37.3%
41 – 50	200,000	12.2%
51 – 60	70,000	4.3%
Over 60	40,000	2.4%
	$1,640,000	

The average collection period for the firm can be calculated to be approximately 30 days but, on closer examination, using the above aging schedules, we can see that 47% of the firm's customers are paying late, and this represents 51.2% of the total dollar amount outstanding.

? Financial Training Systems (FTS) bills its accounts on terms of $^3/_{10}$, net 30. There is $100,000 that has been outstanding for 10 days or less, $300,000 outstanding for 11 to 30 days, $100,000 outstanding for 31 to 40 days, $20,000 outstanding for 41 to 50 days, $10,000 outstanding for 51 to 60 days, and $2,000 outstanding for over 60 days. Prepare an aging schedule for FTS.

Answer:

Days Outstanding	Amount Outstanding	Percent Outstanding
1 – 10	$100,000	18.7%
11 – 30	300,000	56.3%
31 – 40	100,000	19.0%
41 – 50	20,000	3.8%
51 – 60	10,000	1.9%
Over 60	2,000	0.3%
	$532,000	

9. Any proposed change in a firm's credit policy can and should be analyzed prior to its inception by doing a cost/benefit analysis. Credit is extended in hopes of increasing sales and, therefore, profits. Therefore, the benefit associated with liberalizing a firm's credit policy is equal to the expected increase in sales multiplied by 1 minus the variable cost ratio of the firm. This gives us the gross profit associated with the sales increase. So, for example, if a firm expects sales to increase by $500,000 and variable costs are 55% of sales, the firm will enjoy a gross profit of $500,000(1 − 0.55) = $225,000 due to the sales increase.

? The Tirpak Company is examining a change in credit policy that is expected to increase sales by $650,000. If the variable cost ratio for the firm is 55%, what is the expected benefit to the firm of the proposed change?

Answer: $292,500.

$$\text{Benefit} = \$650,000(1 - 0.55) = \$292,500$$

10. One of the costs associated with extending credit is the cost of discounts if these are used. For example, if the S & G Corporation is currently offering terms of $^1/_{10}$, net 30 and 50% of its customers are currently taking the discount, we can calculate the amount of the discounts if sales are $3 million by taking the percentage discount times the dollar amount of the sales times the percent of customers taking the discount.

$$\text{Discount} = (0.01) \times (\$3,000,000) \times (0.50) = \$15,000$$

? Calculate the cost of the discounts if S & G decides to change its credit terms to $^2/_{10}$, net 40 and anticipates that this will increase sales to $3,800,000 and that 70% of its customers will then take the discount.

Answer: $53,200.

$$\text{Discount} = (0.02) \times (\$3,800,000) \times (0.70) = \$53,200$$

11. Another cost associated with extending credit is the carrying cost. The carrying cost is an opportunity cost. Had the firm not extended credit to its customers, it could have instead invested the money in other assets. Note, however, that the accounts receivable can be broken down into two parts: the cost of the goods or services to the firm and a profit on the sale. The amount of money that the firm has tied up in the accounts receivable is only the cost of the good or service to them. We refer to this as the firm's investment in its accounts receivable.

Investment in accounts receivable = accounts receivable × variable cost ratio

The firm's carrying cost is what it could have earned instead on this investment. If we let "r" represent what the firm could earn on an alternative investment, we can calculate the carrying cost as follows:

Carrying cost of accounts receivable = investment in accounts receivable × r.

To illustrate, assume that S & G has an average accounts receivable balance of $200,000 as a result of a policy change. Its variable cost ratio is 55%, and the firm can earn 10% on an alternative investment. The cost of carrying the accounts receivable is calculated below.

$$\text{Carrying cost} = \$200,000(0.55)(0.10) = \$11,000$$

? If S & G anticipates that its average accounts receivable balance will increase to $500,000 as a result of a credit policy change, what will the carrying cost associated with the accounts receivable be, assuming that all else remains the same?

Answer: $27,500.

$$\text{Carrying cost} = \$500,000(0.55)(0.10) = \$27,500$$

12. The more liberal the credit policy, the more likely the firm is to experience bad-debt losses. If S & G currently expects 2% in bad-debt losses on its $3 million in sales, the cost of bad-debt losses for the firm is 0.02($3,000,000) = $60,000.

? S & G expects bad debt losses to increase to 2.5% of sales under the new policy. Assuming that S & G expects sales to increase to $3,800,000, what is the cost of the bad-debt losses under the proposed policy?

Answer: $95,000.

$$\text{Bad-debt losses} = 0.025(\$3,800,000) = \$95,000$$

13. Processing and collection costs will also usually change with a change in credit policy. For the sake of example, we will assume that S & G's processing and collection costs are expected to increase from $100,000 to $200,000 under the new policy. We now have accumulated enough information to determine whether or not S & G should adopt the new credit policy.

The benefit of the policy change is $360,000, calculated as follows:

Gross profit under new policy = $3,800,000(1 − 0.55) =	$1,710,000	
−Gross profit under old policy = $3,000,000(1 − 0.55) =	$1,350,000	
Net change		$360,000

The change in costs are calculated below and totaled:

Discounts under new policy:	$ 53,200		
Discounts under old policy:	$ 15,000		
Net change		$ 38,200	
Carrying cost under new policy:	$ 27,500		
Carrying cost under old policy:	$ 11,000		
Net change		$ 16,500	
Bad-debt losses under new policy:	$ 95,000		
Bad-debt losses under old policy:	$ 60,000		
Net change		$ 35,000	
Processing and collection costs under new policy:	$200,000		
Processing and collection costs under old policy:	$100,000		
Net change		$100,000	
Total change in costs			$189,700
Net benefit or (cost)			$170,300

Since the policy change results in a net benefit to the firm, it should be adopted.

? The Mitchell Design Group (MDG) wants to examine the probable effect of changing their credit terms from $2/10$, net 40 to $3/10$, net 45. The firm hopes that the bigger discount will increase its annual sales from $1,500,000 to $2,000,000. Forty percent of its customers currently take the discount, but the credit manager believes that this will increase to 60% with the larger discount. Processing and collection costs are expected to rise from $50,000 to $62,000 under the proposed new terms, and bad debt losses are expected to increase 1% from 1.5% to 2.5%. MDG's average accounts receivable is expected to rise from $180,000 to $200,000 if the new terms are offered. The firm's variable cost ratio is 70%, and it can earn 8% on alternative investments. Should MDG change its credit terms as proposed?

Answer: Yes, the net benefit is $85,380.

Benefit:

Gross profit under new policy = $2,000,000(1 − 0.7)	= $600,000	
Gross profit under old policy = $1,500,000(1 − 0.7)	= $450,000	
Net change		$150,000

Costs:

Discounts under new policy = 0.03($2,000,000)(0.60)	= $ 36,000		
Discounts under old policy = 0.02($1,500,000)(0.40)	= $ 12,000		
Net change		$ 24,000	
Bad-debt losses under new policy = 0.025($2,000,000)	= $ 50,000		
Bad-debt losses under old policy = 0.015($1,500,000)	= $ 22,500		
Net change		$ 27,500	
Carrying costs under new policy = $200,000(0.7)(0.08)	= $ 11,200		
Carrying costs under old policy = $180,000(0.7)(0.08)	= $ 10,080		
Net change		$ 1,120	
Processing and collection costs under new policy	= $ 62,000		
Processing and collection costs under old policy	= $ 50,000		
Net change		$ 12,000	
Total change in costs			$ 64,620
Net benefit			$ 85,380

14.   A firm's inventory is considered to be a cost item. That is, the firm needs its inventory to be in business. Therefore, the object of inventory management is to minimize total costs. These costs can be divided into three categories: Acquisition costs, which are the costs of the inventory itself over the period being analyzed (usually 1 year); order costs, which are the total costs of placing orders over the period being analyzed (for a manufacturing firm these would include downtime and setup costs associated with switching from the manufacturing of one product to another); and carrying costs, which include storage costs, insurance, taxes, spoilage, obsolescence, and the opportunity cost of the funds tied up in the inventory. The total cost of inventory can be stated as shown below:

$$\text{Total cost} = \text{acquisition costs} + \text{carrying costs} + \text{order costs}$$

$$\text{Total annual cost} = (\text{annual demand} \times \text{cost to firm}) + (\text{unit carrying cost} \times \text{average inventory}) + (\text{cost per order} \times \text{number of orders in 1 year})$$

If we assign "Q" to be the quantity ordered each time an order is placed, "C" to designate the carrying cost per unit of inventory, "O" to be the cost per order, "P" to represent the cost of the inventory to the firm, and "D" to represent the annual demand for the firm's product, we can represent the total inventory cost symbolically as:

$$\text{Total cost} = P \times D + C \times Q/2 + O \times D/Q.$$

Note that Q/2 is the average inventory that the firm carries, assuming that there is no safety stock, and D/Q represents the number of orders placed per year (annual demand divided by the quantity ordered with each order).

Suppose the NMH company sells 1,000,000 marionettes a year. Each hand-painted marionette costs the firm $1. Since the marionettes are imported from Mexico, it costs NMH $20 for each order. Carrying costs are $0.20 per marionette, and NMH orders 20,000 of the puppets each time it orders. The total costs associated with NMH's inventory can be calculated as follows:

$$\text{Total costs} = \$1.00(1{,}000{,}000) + 0.2(20{,}000/2) + \$20(1{,}000{,}000/20{,}000) = \$1{,}003{,}000.$$

? Utensils Unlimited sells 500,000 spatulas a year. Each spatula costs the firm 10 cents. Carrying costs are 0.5 cents per unit. Utensils Unlimited orders 50,000 spatulas each time it places an order, and it costs the firm $2 per order. Calculate the total costs associated with the inventory for the firm.

Answer: $50,145.

$$\text{Total cost} = 0.10(500{,}000) + \$0.005(50{,}000/2) + \$2(500{,}000/50{,}000) = \$50{,}145$$

15.   Firms in some industries seek to reduce their carrying costs as much as possible. They may, in fact, use **"just-in-time" (JIT)** inventory management. Under this system the inventory is acquired precisely when needed so that the firm's inventory balance is always zero or very close to it. This technique requires exceptional coordination with suppliers as well as a predictable demand for the firm's products.

Other firms seek to minimize the total of their carrying costs and order costs, assuming that there are no quantity discounts and that, therefore, acquisition costs will be the same regardless. If the demand for the firm's product is even throughout the year, i.e., sales are not seasonal, the **economic order quantity (EOQ) model** will calculate the amount of inventory that the firm can order which will minimize the total of the order and carrying costs.

$$EOQ = \sqrt{\frac{2DO}{C}}$$

where "D" is the annual demand, "O" is the cost per order, and "C" is the carrying cost per unit. (Note that the greater the quantity ordered, the larger the carrying cost will be since the average inventory will be higher. At the same time, total order costs will be lower since the firm will need to order fewer times. There is an inverse relationship between carrying costs and order costs.)

In the example in the previous frame, NMH's annual demand was 1,000,000, and the cost per order was $20. The carrying cost per unit was $0.20. (Note that we round up regardless of the decimal value in order to avoid a stockout.) Thus,

$$EOQ = \sqrt{\frac{2(1,000,000)(\$20)}{0.20}} = 14,142.1 \approx 14,143 \text{ units}$$

if NMH were to order 14,143 units each time it ordered rather than its current policy of ordering 20,000 units, it would reduce its costs. As verification, the total costs of the inventory if 14,143 units are ordered each time is calculated below:

Total cost = $1(1,000,000) + $0.20(14,143/2) + $20(1,000,000/14,143) = $1,002,828.43.

This is less than the total cost of $1,003,000 that was calculated when 20,000 units were ordered each time.

? Use the EOQ model to determine if Utensils Unlimited is ordering the number of units that will minimize the total of its order and carrying costs. If not, determine the total cost associated with the economic order quantity.

Answers: No, $50,100.
Utensils Unlimited's annual demand was 500,000, the cost per order was $2, and the carrying cost per unit was 0.5 cents.

$$EOQ = \sqrt{\frac{2(500,000)(\$2)}{0.005}} = 20,000 \text{ units}$$

Since Utensils Unlimited had been ordering 50,000 spatulas with each order, the firm was not ordering the most cost effective amount. If 20,000 units are ordered each time, total costs will be reduced from $50,145 to $50,100 as calculated below:

Total costs = $0.10(500,000) + $0.005(20,000/2) + $2(500,000/20,000) = $50,100.

 Apply It

1. The Heiniger Company has cash needs of $60 million a year. It costs the firm $250 in transaction costs any time it sells marketable securities to obtain additional cash. It can earn 6% annually on these marketable securities. Heiniger's cash needs are fairly uniform throughout the year. How much cash should Heiniger obtain each time it needs a cash infusion? (Frame 2)

2. The Cougar Corporation has unpredictable cash flow needs and wishes to apply the Miller-Orr model in its cash management. Cougar's working capital manager,

Mr. Carter, has determined that the transaction costs associated with each cash infusion is $120. The variance of its daily cash flows has been calculated to be 5,000, and the opportunity cost of cash per day is 0.02%. Mr. Carter wants to maintain a minimum cash balance of $9,000. (Frame 3)

a. What is Cougar's lower limit?

b. What is Cougar's return point?

c. What is Cougar's upper limit?

d. If Cougar has a cash balance of $12,000, does the firm need to take any action? If so, what?

e. If Cougar has a cash balance of $14,000, does the firm need to take any action? If so, what?

f. If Cougar has a cash balance of $7,000, does the firm need to take any action? If so, what?

3. The Easy Reader Company supplies bulletin board services to numerous hotel chains nationwide. The owner of the company is investigating the desirability of employing another firm to do her billing and collections. Since the other firm specializes in these services, collection float will be reduced by 20 days. Average daily collections are $250, and the owner can earn 10% annually on her investments. The second firm charges $300 a month for this service. Should the owner employ the other firm? (Frame 5)

4. The Conservative Company is considering changing from its current policy of "cash only" to offering terms of $1/15$, net 30. The firm feels that by doing so it will increase its annual sales from $2,250,000 to $3,000,000. The firm estimates that 50% of its customers will take the discount and that its accounts receivable balance will average $320,000. It expects to experience bad-debt losses of 1.5% of sales if it decides to extend the credit. Variable costs are 65% of sales, and Conservative can earn 8% on short-term investments. The firm estimates that processing and collection costs will be $30,000 a year. Should Conservative adopt this credit policy or stay with its current "cash only" policy? (Frame 13)

5. The Mighty Power Corporation has the following accounts on its books:

Customer	Amount Owed	Age (In Days)
ABC	$50,000	35
DEF	$35,000	5
GHI	$15,000	10
KLM	$75,000	22
NOP	$42,000	40
QRS	$18,000	12
TUV	$82,000	53
WXY	$36,000	90

The firm extends credit on terms of $1/15$, net 30. Develop an aging schedule using 15-day increments through 60 days, and then indicate any accounts that have been outstanding for more than 60 days. (Frame 8)

6. The Hartlieb Beer Stein Company orders 400 steins each time it orders. The cost of each stein is $3. The cost of placing an order is $0.75, and carrying costs amount to $0.10 per stein. The company sells 100,000 steins a year, and the demand is fairly uniform throughout the year.

a. What is the total cost associated with its current inventory policy? (Frame 14)

b. Is Hartlieb ordering the most cost effective quantity? (Frame 15)

Apply It Answers

1. Since Heiniger's needs are uniform throughout the year, the Baumol model can be employed.

$$Q = \sqrt{\frac{2(\$250)(\$60,000,000)}{0.06}} = \$707,106.78 \approx \$707,107$$

2. a. The lower limit is Mr. Carter's minimum cash balance requirement of $9,000.

   b.

$$\text{return point} = \$9,000 + \sqrt[3]{\frac{0.75(\$120)(5,000)}{0.0002}} = \$10,310.37$$

   c.

$$\text{upper limit} = \$9,000 + 3\sqrt[3]{\frac{0.75(\$120)(5,000)}{0.0002}} = \$12,031.11$$

   d. Since $12,000 lies between the lower and upper limits designated by the Miller-Orr model, the firm need take no action.

   e. Since $14,000 exceeds the upper limit, the firm should invest any funds that exceed the return point in marketable securities. Thus, $14,000 − $10,310.37 = $3,689.63 should be invested in marketable securities.

   f. Since $7,000 is less than the lower limit, the firm should sell marketable securities to obtain a cash balance that is equal to the return point. Thus, the firm needs a cash infusion of $10,310.37 − $7,000 = $3,310.37.

3. No. The benefit of utilizing the services of the billing and collection firm is equal to what the firm can earn on the funds that are freed up. Since average daily collections are $250, and float will be reduced by 20 days, the amount that Easy Reader will have available to invest is $5,000 ($250 × 20). If the firm can earn 10% on this money, the annual benefit is $500 ($5,000 × 0.10). It will cost $300 a month for the services. This is an annual cost of $3,600, so the costs outweigh the benefits.

4. Conservative should adopt the credit policy. The benefits are $262,500 while the costs are only $106,640, as calculated below.

Benefits:		
Gross profit under credit policy	$3,000,000(1 − 0.65) =	$1,050,000
Gross profit under "cash only" policy	$2,250,000(1 − 0.65) =	$ 787,500
Net change		$ 262,500
−Cost of discounts = 0.01($3,000,000)(0.5) =		$ 15,000
−Cost of bad-debt losses = 0.015($3,000,000) =		$ 45,000
−Carrying cost of accounts receivable = ($320,000)(0.65)(0.08) =		$ 16,640
−Processing and collection costs		$ 30,000
Net benefit		$ 155,860

5.

Days Outstanding	Amount Owed	Percent of Accounts Receivable
0 – 15	$68,000	19.3%
16 – 30	$75,000	21.2%
31 – 45	$92,000	26.1%
46 – 60	$82,000	23.2%
Over 60	$36,000	10.2%

6. a. Total cost = $3.00(100,000) + $0.10(400/2) + $0.75(100,000/400) = $300,207.50

    b. No. Using the EOQ model, we determine that Hartlieb should be ordering 1,225 units each time in order to minimize total costs, as shown below.

$$EOQ = \sqrt{\frac{2(100,000)(\$0.75)}{0.10}} = 1,224.74 \approx 1,225 \text{ units}$$

SHORT-TERM LIABILITY MANAGEMENT

This module is designed to introduce you to various methods of short-term financing that are used by businesses. Bank loans, trade credit, commercial paper, and secured loans are discussed. You will learn how to calculate the explicit costs associated with each of these arrangements, and you will be introduced to some implicit costs that should also be considered when choosing a short-term financing source.

Equations introduced in this module

$$\text{Annual percentage rate (APR)} = \text{interest rate per period} \times \text{number of periods in 1 year}$$

$$\text{Effective annual rate (EAR)} = (1 + \text{interest rate per period})^{\text{number of periods per year}} - 1$$

$$\text{Interest rate per period} = \frac{\text{dollar amount of interest paid}}{\text{usable proceeds of loan}}$$

$$\text{Trade credit APR} = \frac{\text{percentage discount}}{100\% - \text{percentage discount}} \times \frac{365}{\text{payment period} - \text{discount period}}$$

$$\text{Average payment period} = \frac{\text{accounts payable}}{\text{average daily credit purchases}}$$

1. The matching principle of accounting stipulates that short-term assets should usually be financed with short-term debt while long-term assets should be financed with long-term debt. In choosing a source for its short-term financing needs, there are several factors that a firm takes into consideration. A firm may want a flexible source of funds that allows it to borrow as much or as little as necessary given the specific circumstances that the firm faces at a given point in time. A firm may also seek to avoid a source that will limit the firm's freedom in its operations. Some loans have restrictive covenants that require that the firm maintain a certain level of working capital or a minimum current ratio and/or that limit the amount of dividends that can be paid to the firm's shareholders. Of primary consideration, of course, is the cost of the financing.

The annual rate of interest that a firm is paying is typically quoted as an **annual percentage rate (APR)**. The annual percentage rate is also referred to as the **stated rate** or the **nominal rate** of interest. It is calculated by taking the interest rate per period and multiplying it by the number of periods in a year.

$$\text{APR} = \text{interest rate per period} \times \text{number of periods in 1 year}$$

This annual percentage rate does *not* take the effects of compounding into account. In order to compare the various sources of financing on the basis of their costs, the **effective annual rate (EAR)** must be calculated. The calculation of the effective annual rate incorporates the effects of compounding.

$$\text{EAR} = (1 + \text{interest rate per period})^{\text{number of periods per year}} - 1$$

Therefore, if a finance company stipulates that interest will be charged at the rate of 1.5% per month, the annual percentage rate is simply $0.015 \times 12 = 18.0\%$. The true interest rate that the borrower is paying is higher, however, as shown below:

$$\text{EAR} = (1.015)^{12} - 1 = 19.6\%.$$

? Timmons Towel and Diaper Service has received a quote for a loan from a commercial finance corporation. The loan stipulates that interest will be paid at the rate of 4% per quarter. Calculate the annual percentage rate and the effective annual rate of this loan.

Answers: 16%, 17%.
The annual percentage rate is $0.04 \times 4 = 16\%$ since there are 4 quarters in a year. The effective annual rate is $(1.04)^4 - 1 \approx 17\%$.

2. If we are quoted an annual percentage rate, rather than an interest rate per period, we can easily calculate the effective annual rate. If the stated rate is 12%, with interest paid semiannually, we know that the interest rate per period is 12%/2 = 6%. The effective annual rate is then $(1.06)^2 - 1 = 12.36\%$.

? If the stated annual rate is 12%, compounded quarterly, what is the effective annual rate?

Answer: 12.55%.
The interest rate per period is 12%/4 = 3%. The effective annual rate is then $(1.03)^4 - 1 = 12.55\%$.

3. One of the primary sources of short-term financing, especially for small businesses, is the commercial bank. Bank loans may be structured in several different fashions, so it is imperative to calculate the effective annual rate of each available loan in order to decide which is the best deal from the standpoint of cost.

The most straightforward type of bank loan is a single, end-of-period payment loan. This type of loan agreement requires that the firm pay the interest on the loan and pay back the principal in one lump sum at the end of the loan. We can calculate the interest rate per period by using the following formula:

$$\text{interest rate per period} = \frac{\text{dollar amount of interest paid}}{\text{usable proceeds of loan}}.$$

Thus, if the Timmons Towel and Diaper Service were offered a $500 loan for 3 months under the stipulation that it pay back the $500 and $26.25 in interest at the end of the period, the interest rate per period would be 5.25%.

$$\text{interest rate per period} = \$26.25/\$500 = 5.25\%$$

Since there are four 3-month periods in a year, this translates to an annual percentage rate of 21%.

$$\text{APR} = 4 \times 5.25\% = 21.0\%$$

The effective annual rate is 22.7%.

$$\text{EAR} = (1.0525)^4 - 1 = 22.7\%$$

? The Laughing Sun Sign Company needs to borrow $1,000 for 6 months. A bank has agreed to lend the firm the money provided that it repay the borrowed amount and $50 interest at the end of the 6-month period. Calculate the annual percentage rate and the effective annual rate of this loan.

Answers: 10%, 10.25%.

There are two 6-month periods in a year. The interest rate per period is $50/$1,000 = 5%, so the annual percentage rate is $2 \times 5\% = 10\%$. The effective annual rate is $(1.05)^2 - 1 = 10.25\%$.

4. Sometimes interest is paid on a **discount basis**, which means that the firm must pay the interest at the *beginning* of the loan period. The principal is repaid at the end of the period. This increases the effective cost of the loan to the firm over what it would be if the loan were an end-of-period payment loan as described in the previous frames. If we use our original example of the 3-month, $500 loan on which the interest charged was $26.25, but change the loan to a discount loan, the interest rate per period increases to 5.54% since the usable proceeds of the loan are now only $473.75. (This is the loan amount of $500 less the interest charge of $26.25 that the firm must pay up front.)

$$\text{interest rate per period} = \$26.25/\$473.75 = 5.54\%$$

The effective annual rate is now $(1.0554)^4 - 1 = 24.1\%$, significantly higher than the 22.7% effective annual rate that was calculated when the loan was structured as a single, end-of-period payment loan.

? If the $1,000, 6-month loan on which the interest charged was $50 is stipulated to be a discount loan, what is the effective annual rate on the loan?

Answer: 10.8%.

Since the $50 interest payment must be made at the outset of the loan, the usable proceeds are $950, and the interest rate per period is $50/$950 = 5.26\%$. The effective annual rate is, therefore, $(1.0526)^2 - 1 = 10.8\%$.

5. Regardless of whether the loan is structured as a discount loan or a single, end-of-period payment loan, the bank may have a **compensating balance requirement**. This means that the firm must hold a certain percent of the principal of the loan in an account at the bank. This serves to reduce the usable proceeds that the firm receives since the compensating balance is "held captive." Returning to our example of the $500, 3-month loan, with an interest charge of $26.25, we will assume that it is structured as a single, end-of-period payment loan, but that the bank has a compensating balance requirement of 10%. This means that the firm must hold $0.10 \times \$500 = \$50$ in an account at the bank. Therefore, the firm has only $450 of the loan proceeds available for its use. The interest rate per period is $26.25/$450 = 5.25\%. This translates to an effective annual rate of $(1.0525)^4 - 1 = 22.7\%$.

? Assume once again that the 6-month, $1,000 loan that requires a $50 interest payment is a single, end-of-period loan. Also assume, however, that the bank has a 10% compensating balance requirement. What is the effective annual cost of this loan?

Answer: 11.4%.
The compensating balance requirement is $0.10 \times \$1,000 = \$100$, so the usable proceeds of the loan is $900. The interest rate per period is $50/$900 = 5.56\%. The effective annual rate is $(1.056)^2 - 1 = 11.4\%$.

6. Other "fees" may be attached to a loan that can actually be thought of as interest charges under another name since these fees serve to increase the effective annual rate of the loan. One such fee is a **loan origination fee**, presumably charged to cover credit checks and legal fees and paid at the outset of the loan. Another type of fee is a **commitment fee**. This is a fee paid to a bank that legally binds the bank to stand ready to grant a firm a loan should the firm so require. Typically, the commitment fee is charged at the end of the loan period on any unborrowed balances as will be explained in more detail in a later frame.
  Suppose we have a single, end-of-period payment, 3-month, $500 loan. The interest is $26.25 for the 3-month period, but the loan also has a 1% loan origination fee. This fee increases the interest expense *and* reduces the usable proceeds since it must be paid at the beginning of the loan. The loan origination fee is charged on the principal of the loan, so in this case it amounts to $0.01 \times \$500 = \$5.00$. The total interest payment is $26.25 + $5.00 = $31.25, and the usable proceeds are $500 - $5 = $495. This makes the interest rate per period $31.25/$495.00 = 6.3\%. The effective annual cost of this loan is $(1.063)^4 - 1 = 27.7\%$.

? Assume that a 6-month $1,000 loan is a single, end-of-period payment loan with an interest charge of $50. There is also a 1% loan origination fee. What is the effective annual cost of this loan?

Answer: 12.5%.
The loan origination fee is $0.01 \times \$1,000 = \$10$. This makes the total interest payment $50 + $10 = $60. The usable proceeds of the loan are $1,000 - $10 = $990. The interest rate per period is, therefore, $60/$990 = 6.06\%. This translates to an effective annual cost of $(1.0606)^2 - 1 = 12.5\%$.

7. Oftentimes a bank loan is based on a **line of credit agreement**. Under this type of arrangement, a bank agrees to lend a firm any amount up to a stated maximum. This provides a firm with flexibility since the firm can draw upon the line of credit whenever it so chooses. The line of credit may be uncommitted, in which case it is a simple verbal agreement that does not legally bind the bank to provided the funds, or committed. If the line of credit is committed, the firm pays a commitment fee of $\frac{1}{4}$ to $\frac{1}{2}$% of the unused portion of the line of credit in addition to interest on the amount that the firm borrowed. A committed line of credit consists of a written, legally binding agreement. These arrangements will typically be accompanied by a compensating balance requirement and restrictions regarding the level of the firm's current ratio or net working capital. Lines of credit are renegotiated, usually on an annual basis, and a clean-up period of 1 to 2 months is generally required. During this period, the firm may have no outstanding balance drawn against its line of credit. This is to ensure that the firm is not using what is supposed to be short-term financing to finance long-term obligations. A **revolving credit agreement** is similar to a committed line of credit except that the agreement is extended for a longer period of time, often 2 to 3 years, and unlike a line of credit, the interest rate is variable.

The commitment fee associated with a committed line of credit or a revolving credit agreement increases the effective cost of the loan to the firm. To illustrate, we will assume that a firm has negotiated a committed line of credit with a stated maximum of $1 million and an interest rate of 10% with a bank. The commitment fee is 0.5%. During the year, the firm borrows $800,000, leaving $200,000 unused. The total cost of the loan is calculated below:

Interest on borrowed funds = 0.10($800,000) =	$80,000
Commitment fee paid on unused portion = 0.005($200,000) =	$ 1,000
Total cost	$81,000

? The Average Company has a committed line of credit with a stated maximum of $5 million with the Everyman's National Bank. The interest rate on borrowed funds is 12%, and the commitment fee is 0.3% on any unused portion of the line of credit. If Average borrows $3 million during the year, what is the total cost of the loan?

Answer: $366,000.

Interest on borrowed funds = 0.12($3,000,000) =	$360,000
Commitment fee on unused portion = 0.003($2,000,000) =	$ 6,000
Total cost	$366,000

8. Another source of short-term financing is **trade credit**. A firm's suppliers will generally sell their goods and services on open accounts, meaning that payment for the goods and services will be made at some designated time after delivery. Terms of "net 30" mean that payment is due 30 days from the date of the invoice. In this instance the cost of the trade credit is zero since it does not matter if the firm pays the bill immediately or at the end of 30 days, the cost of the goods and services is the same. However, many times suppliers will offer a discount to give their customers an incentive to pay early. Terms of "2/10, net 30" mean that the firm will get a 2% discount if it pays its bill within 10 days; otherwise, the full amount of the invoice is due in 30 days. If the firm chooses to forgo the discount, it is in effect paying a fee to delay payment beyond the discount period, which in this example is 10 days. The fee is the amount of the discount that the firm gives up, and the difference between the net payment period, 30 days, and the discount period of 10 days can be considered the term of a loan. For example, if a firm had purchased $100 worth of goods on these terms, it would only have to pay $98 for the goods if it paid within 10 days. It will have to pay the full $100 if it pays after the 10-day discount period. The interest it is paying to use its trade credit is $2, in return for which the firm has use of $98 for an additional 20 days (30 − 10). The interest rate per period is $2/$98 = 2.04%. If we assume a 365-day year, the number of 20-day periods in a year is 365/20 = 18.25. This makes the effective annual rate on this loan $(1.0204)^{18.25} − 1 = 44.6\%$. Trade credit tends to be an expensive source of short-term financing. However, it is easy to use because there is no paperwork involved; the firm simply does not pay the invoice amount within the discount period. It may also be the case that the firm's owner is unaware of the actual cost of the trade credit since it is an implicit cost rather than an explicit cost. It is a flexible source of funds that increases with the firm's needs since it is a direct result of a firm's purchases.

? Your firm purchases goods from its supplier on terms of $^1/_{15}$ net 40. What is the effective annual cost to your firm if it chooses not to take advantage of the trade discount offered?

Answer: 15.8%.

Since the discount is 1%, your firm must pay $1 to have the use of $99 for 25 (40 − 15) days. The interest rate per period is $1/$99 = 1.01%. There are 365/25 = 14.6 25-day periods in a year, so the effective annual rate is $(1.0101)^{14.6} - 1 = 15.8\%$.

9.   There is a formula that is sometimes used to calculate the approximate annual cost of using trade credit. It is actually a calculation of the annual percentage rate and, therefore, it ignores the effect of compounding.

$$APR = \frac{\text{percentage discount}}{100\% - \text{percentage discount}} \times \frac{365}{\text{payment period} - \text{discount period}}$$

Using the example in frame 8, we can approximate the annual cost of trade credit as follows:

$$APR = \frac{0.02}{0.98} \times \frac{365}{30 - 10} = 37.2\%.$$

? Calculate the approximate annual cost of trade credit for the credit terms $^1/_{15}$, net 40.

Answer: 14.7%.

$$APR = \frac{0.01}{0.99} \times \frac{365}{40 - 15} = 14.7\%.$$

10.   Given terms of $^2/_{10}$, net 30, some firms may ignore the payment due date and not pay until 45 days have passed. This practice is referred to as *stretching the accounts payable*. Doing so reduces the direct cost of trade credit. While the interest rate per period remains the same (it is still $2/$98 = 2.04%), the firm is now using the $98 for 35 days beyond the discount period. There are 10.43 35-day periods in a year. (365/35 = 10.43.) Thus, the effective annual rate is $(1.0204)^{10.43} - 1 = 23.4\%$.

? What is the effective annual rate of the credit terms of $^1/_{15}$, net 40 if the accounts payable are stretched to 60 days?

Answer: 8.49%.

The interest rate per period is $1/$99 = 1.01%. If payment is delayed until the sixtieth day, the firm has use of the funds for 45 days beyond the discount period. There are 365/45 = 8.11 45-day periods in 1 year. Thus, the effective annual rate is $(1.0101)^{8.11} - 1 = 8.49\%$.

11.   While the direct costs associated with stretching accounts payable may be lower, there are indirect costs that can be incurred. Suppliers may not be willing to accept the fact that a firm's payments are always late and may impose terms of cash on delivery (COD) or cash before delivery (CBD) on the delinquent firm. The delinquent firm then bears the additional cost associated with these terms and may have to negotiate a bank loan in order to have the cash available to pay under these new conditions. The supplier may also refuse to continue to do any business with the delinquent customer, leaving the customer to find another, perhaps more expensive, source. A poor credit rating may also result, making it difficult for the firm to obtain good terms with any other supplier. These indirect costs must be considered when deciding whether to stretch the accounts payable.

If accounts payable are not stretched, the firm should always pay on the latest day allowed. For example, if the discount period is 10 days and the firm is taking the discount, payment should be made on day 10, not on day 2. If the discount is not taken, and the terms are $^2/_{10}$, net 30, the full payment should be made on day 30, not on day 16. A firm should strive to keep its money working for it as long as possible. One way of tracking this is to calculate the average payment period and compare it to the credit terms.

$$\text{Average payment period} = \frac{\text{accounts payable}}{\text{average daily credit purchases}}$$

If the average payment period is calculated to be 40 days and the terms are $^2/_{10}$, net 30, the firm can conclude that it generally pays late and may be risking supplier difficulties. If the average payment period is 25 days, however, and the firm has not been taking the discount, it indicates that the firm is paying too early. It could be earning another 5 days' interest on its money.

? The Rowd Company has an average accounts payable balance of $250,000. Its average daily credit purchases are $14,000, and it receives terms of $^2/_{15}$, net 40. Rowd chooses to forgo the discount. Does the firm appear to be managing its accounts payable well?

Answer: No.

The average payment period is $250,000/$14,000 = 17.9 days. If Rowd made payment 3 days earlier, it could take advantage of the 2% discount. If, for some reason, it chooses to forgo the discount, it should not be paying the full amount until the fortieth day.

12.   Larger firms can sell commercial paper to obtain short-term funds. **Commercial paper** is short-term, unsecured debt. Only large corporations have the ability to raise funds in this fashion since the minimum face value is $25,000, and most commercial paper has a face value of at least $100,000. Investors are not willing to lend large amounts of money to smaller firms if there is no collateral involved.

The average maturity of commercial paper is 5 months, and the maximum maturity is usually 270 days due to the fact that extending the maturity beyond 270 days triggers a registration requirement with the SEC, which increases issue costs and creates a time delay in the sale of the issue. Commercial paper is referred to as either **direct paper**, meaning that the firm sells the security directly to the investors, or **dealer paper**. Dealers are utilized to sell the latter type to the investors, and they receive a spread for their services. The spread is normally 0.05% to 0.15% of the face value of the issue. This decreases the proceeds that the issuing firm receives, thus increasing the effective cost of the paper.

Commercial paper is sold at a discount, which means that it is sold for less than its face value. (In recent years, some interest-paying commercial paper has been issued as well.) The firm makes no interim interest payments, but pays the investor the face value at maturity. Let us suppose that a firm issues 6-month commercial paper with a face value of $100,000. The net proceeds received by the firm is $97,000. The interest that the firm is paying for the 6-month loan is $3,000, the difference between the face value and what the firm receives today. The interest rate per period is $3,000/$97,000 = 3.09%. Since there are two 6-month periods in 1 year, the effective annual rate is $(1.0309)^2 - 1 = 6.3\%$.

A firm issues 3-month commercial paper with a $100,000 face value and receives $98,000. What effective annual rate is the firm paying for its funds?

Answer: 8.4%.

The firm is paying $2,000 in interest for the 3-month loan. The interest rate per period is $2,000/$98,000 = 2.04%. Since there are four 3-month periods in a year, the effective annual rate is $(1.0204)^4 - 1 = 8.4\%$.

13.   Short-term financing can also be obtained using **secured loans**. These loans are collateralized with short-term assets. One such type loan is a **repurchase agreement**. Repurchase agreements use high quality, short-term, marketable securities, such as Treasury bills, as collateral. The borrower sells the securities to the lender with an agreement to buy them back in the near future for a higher specified price. The price for which the borrower sells the securities is less than their current market value, the difference being known as the **haircut**. Therefore, the lender has a security with a market value greater than the loan balance as collateral should the borrower default on the loan. Repurchase agreements have typical maturities ranging from 1 day to several weeks.

To illustrate how a repurchase agreement, or repo, works, let us assume that the People's Bank needs some quick short-term funds. People's has a portfolio of $2 million in Treasury bills, and it sells these securities to Best Bet Insurance for $1,960,000. The Treasury bills have a current market value of $1,970,000. People's agrees to buy the securities back in ten days for $1,965,000. The haircut is $10,000 ($1,970,000 − $1,960,000) in this transaction. People's is paying $5,000 ($1,965,000 − $1,960,000) in interest to borrow $1,960,000 for 10 days. The interest rate per period is $5,000/$1,960,000 = 0.255%. There are 36.5 10-day periods in a year (365/10 = 36.5), so the effective annual rate is $(1.00255)^{36.5} - 1 = 9.7\%$. (In this illustration, Best Bet, the lender, has purchased the repurchase agreement. It is referred to as a reverse repurchase agreement for People's Bank, the borrower.)

[?] In order to finance some construction, the National Power Company (NPC) has decided to sell $1 million of Treasury bills with a current market value of $930,000 for $915,000 with an agreement to buy the bills back for $920,000 in 30 days. What is the haircut associated with this transaction, and what is the effective annual cost of the loan for NPC?

Answers: $15,000, 6.9%.

The haircut is the difference between the current market value of the securities and the price at which NPC sold the securities, so $930,000 − $915,000 = $15,000. NPC is paying $5,000, the difference between the repurchase price of $920,000 and the selling price of $915,000, for the use of $915,000 for thirty days. The interest rate per period is $10,000/$915,000 = 0.546%. There are 12.17 30-day periods in a year (365/30 = 12.17), so the effective annual rate is $(1.00546)^{12.17} - 1 = 6.9\%$.

14.   A firm's accounts receivable can be used as security for a loan in a couple of ways: they may be pledged or factored. In a **pledging of accounts receivable** agreement, the lender reviews the invoices of the borrowing firm and decides which it is willing to accept as collateral for the loan, based on the credit standards of the lender. The lender then typically lends the borrower only 75% of the value of the accepted invoices. If the borrowing firm's customers default on their bills, the firm is still responsible to the lender for the money.

In a **factoring of accounts receivable** arrangement, the receivables are actually sold to the lender, (i.e., the factor), and the lender agrees to pay the firm the amount due from its customers at the end of the firm's payment period. For example, if a firm sells its goods on terms of net 30, then the factor will pay the firm the face value of its receivables, less a factor's fee, at the end of 30 days. The customers are usually instructed to make payments directly to the lender. In many cases the firm can borrow up to 80% of the face value of its receivables from the factor, thereby receiving its funds in advance. If such is the case, the firm will be charged interest on the loan in addition to the factor's fee. However, the factor's fee, which is typically ¾% to 1½% of the face value of the accounts receivable, is charged whether or not the firm borrows any of the available funds.

A factoring arrangement may be **with recourse**, meaning that the lender can seek payment from the borrower should the borrower's customers default on their bills, or **without recourse**, in which case the lender bears the risk of bad-debt losses. In this latter case, the factor will pay the firm the amount due regardless of whether or not the factor has received payment from the firm's customers. If the arrangement is with recourse, the lender may not require that it approve the customers' accounts before the sale is made, but if the factoring agreement is without recourse, the borrowing firm receives credit approval for a customer from the factor prior to shipping the goods. If approval is given, the goods are shipped and the customer is directed to make payment directly to the lender.

Suppose the National Brand Company (NBC) sells on terms of net 30 and wants to factor its accounts receivable, which total $6,250,000. The factor requires a 1.5% fee, payable at the beginning of the arrangement. The factor has agreed to lend NBC up to 80% of its receivables, and the stated annual rate on the loan is 12%. This makes the monthly interest rate 1%, but the factor's fee must also be considered as part of the cost of the loan. If NBC borrows the full 80% allowed, it must pay $50,000 ($0.01 \times \$5,000,000$) in interest plus $93,750 in commissions ($0.015 \times \$6,250,000$). Since the $93,750 must be paid at the beginning of the month, NBC has use of only $4,906,250. The interest rate per period is $143,750/\$4,906,250 = 2.93\%$. Since there are 12 periods in a year, the effective annual rate is $(1.0293)^{12} - 1 = 41.4\%$. When NBC is making its decision, it must weigh this cost against the benefits associated with a factoring arrangement, such as the reduced or eliminated need for in-house credit personnel, the elimination of other collection costs, and the elimination of risk if the agreement is without recourse.

? Universal Suppliers, Incorporated sells on terms of net 30 and wishes to factor its accounts receivable, which total $25 million. The factor charges a commission equal to ½% of the face value of the receivables, and this fee is payable at the beginning of the month. The stated annual rate on the loan is 12%, and Universal plans to borrow the maximum amount allowed by the factor, which is 80% of its receivables. What is the effective annual cost of this arrangement?

Answer: 21.6%.

The commission charged is $25,000,000 \times 0.005 = \$125,000$. Since it is payable at the beginning of the period, the firm's usable proceeds are only $19,875,000. The maximum amount that can be borrowed is $20 million (80% of $25 million). The interest is $0.01 \times \$20,000,000 = \$200,000$. Thus, the interest rate per period is $325,000/\$19,875,000 = 1.64\%$. Since there are 12 periods in a year, the effective annual cost is $(1.0164)^{12} - 1 = 21.6\%$.

15. Inventory can be used as collateral for a loan in one of three ways. In a **floating lien** or **general lien** arrangement, all of the inventory is used to secure the loan. This is the riskiest setup from the standpoint of the lender since the value of the collateral securing the loan is reduced as inventory is sold; therefore, this type of loan bears a higher interest rate than the next two arrangements that we discuss.

Lenders have less risk under what is referred to as a **trust receipts loan** or **floor planning**. This arrangement requires that inventory items be distinguishable from one another. For instance, the items may have different serial numbers. Specific items are held in a trust as security for the loan. As these items are sold, the proceeds from the sale are remitted to the lender in repayment of the loan. The lender will periodically send someone to ensure that the borrower has not sold some of the specified inventory while at the same time failing to make a repayment on the loan.

A **warehouse arrangement** is the least risky from the standpoint of the lender. This type of arrangement can be set up in one of two ways. The first method is to use a **public warehouse**, which is a business that exists for the sole purpose of storing and tracking the outflow of the inventory. The borrowing firm takes the inventory to the warehouse, and when it needs the inventory to sell, it returns to the warehouse and retrieves it. This works well for some types of inventory, such as wine, tobacco products, and salad oil, but it is not practical for items that are subject to spoilage and/or are bulky and therefore, difficult to transport to and from the warehouse. The second alternative is to use a **field warehouse**. A field warehouse is operated by a third party, but it is set up on the borrower's premises. The inventory is kept in a separate area and public notification is required. For example, bulky items may be contained within a fenced area with a sign on the fence proclaiming, "This is a field warehouse operated by the XYZ Company." This type of arrangement is more convenient for the borrower but it still gives the lender the added security of having the inventory that serves as collateral controlled by a third party. Warehouse arrangements are expensive in that the business operating the warehouse charges a fee on top of the interest that the borrower must pay the lender for the loan. However, the borrower may also save on inventory carrying costs. Since the warehouser is a professional at inventory control, there may be less damage and/or theft. Insurance costs are also sometimes lower.

? The Row Cannery wants to borrow $2 million for 1 month. Using its inventory as collateral, it can obtain a nominal annual rate of 12% on the loan. The lender requires that a warehouse arrangement be used, and the warehouse fee is $10,000, payable at the end of the month. Calculate the effective annual cost of this loan for Row Cannery.

Answer: 19.6%.
Since the nominal annual rate is 12%, the rate per month is 12%/12 = 1%. One month's interest on $2,000,000 is 0.01 × $2,000,000 = $20,000. The cannery will have the use of the full $2 million since the warehousing fee is paid at the end of the month. The interest rate per period is $30,000/$2,000,000 = 1.5%. The effective annual rate is $(1.015)^{12} - 1 = 19.6\%$.

Apply It

1. Which of the following 1-year $1,000 bank loans offers the lowest effective annual cost?
   a. a loan with a stated annual rate of 6%, compounded monthly (Frame 2)
   b. a discount loan with a stated annual rate of 6%, compounded annually (Frames 3 and 4)
   c. a loan with a stated annual rate of 6%, compounded annually, that also has a compensating balance requirement of 10% (Frames 3 and 5)
   d. a loan with a stated annual rate of 6%, compounded annually, that has a 1% loan origination fee (Frames 3 and 6)

2. A loan is quoted as having an annual percentage rate of 8%. If interest is compounded quarterly, what is the effective annual rate on this loan? (Frame 2)

3. What is the annual percentage rate and the effective annual rate on a loan that charges 1.9% a month in interest? (Frame 1)

4. A revolving credit agreement has a stated maximum of $10 million. The interest rate on the borrowed funds is 8%, and the commitment fee is 0.25%. If a firm were to borrow $6,000,000 under this agreement, what would its total cost be? (Frame 7)

5. Your firm purchases goods from its supplier on terms of $3/15$, net 40.
   a. What is the effective annual cost to your firm if it chooses not to take the discount and makes its payment on day 40? (Frame 8)
   b. What is the effective annual cost to your firm if it chooses not to take the discount and makes its payment on day 50? (Frame 10)

6. McClelland Kilts has an average accounts payable balance of $20,000. Its average daily credit purchases are $670, and the firm receives terms of $1/10$, net 30 from its suppliers. Based on this information, does McClelland Kilts appear to be managing its accounts payable well? (Frame 11)

7. The Treadwater Bank wants to raise $1 million using 3-month commercial paper. The net proceeds to the bank will be $980,000. What is the effective annual cost of this financing for Treadwater? (Frame 12)

8. In order to raise short-term funds, the First Bank of Chimera has sold the Second Bank of Chimera $3 million in Treasury securities for $2,550,000 with an agreement to repurchase the securities in 5 days for $2,552,000. The securities have a current market value of $2,600,000.
   a. What is the haircut on this repurchase agreement? (Frame 13)
   b. What is the effective annual cost of the financing? (Frame 13)

9. Uptown Clothiers sells on terms of net 30 and has factored $625,000 in accounts receivable. The factor has agreed to lend up to 80% of the receivables. The annual percentage rate on the loan is 6%, and the factor requires a 0.5% fee, payable at the end of the month. If Uptown borrows the maximum allowed, what is the effective annual cost of the arrangement? (Frame 14)

10. The Ohio Valley Steel Corporation has borrowed $5 million for 1 month at a stated annual rate of 9%, using inventory stored in a field warehouse as collateral. The warehouser charges a $5,000 fee, payable at the end of the month. What is the effective annual cost of this loan? (Frame 15)

11. Simple Simon's Bakery purchases supplies on terms of $1/10$, net 20. If Simple Simon's chooses to take the discount offered, it must obtain a bank loan to meet its short-term financing needs. The bank loan has an annual percentage rate of 18%, compounded quarterly. Which is the better deal for the bakery? (Frames 2, 8)

Apply It Answers

1. The effective annual rates of each of the alternatives are calculated as follows:
   a. Since the annual rate is 6%, the monthly rate is 6%/12 = 0.5%. This makes the effective annual rate $(1.005)^{12} - 1 = 6.2\%$.

b. The interest on this loan is $1,000 × 0.06 = $60. Since the interest is paid at the beginning of the loan period, this leaves only $940 of the $1,000 loan for the borrower to use. The interest rate per period is $60/$940 = 6.4%. Interest is compounded annually; therefore, one period is equal to 1 year, making 6.4% the effective annual rate.

c. The compensating balance is $1,000 × 0.10 = $100; therefore, the borrower will have the use of only $900 of the $1,000. The interest is 0.06 × $1,000 = $60. The interest rate per period is $60/$900 = 6.7%, and since this alternative uses annual compounding as well, the effective annual rate is 6.7%.

d. The interest expense is 0.06 × $1,000, and the loan origination fee is 0.01 × $1,000 = $10. The loan origination fee must be paid at the beginning of the loan, so the firm has use of only $990 for the loan period. The interest rate per period is $70/$990 = 7.1%, and since one period equals 1 year, this is the effective annual rate.

Alternative "a" offers the lowest effective annual cost.

2. The interest rate per period is 8%/4 = 2% since interest is compounded quarterly. The effective annual rate is $(1.02)^4 - 1 = 8.2\%$.

3. The annual percentage rate is simply the interest rate per period times the number of periods in a year. APR = 1.9% × 12 = 22.8%. The effective annual rate is $(1.019)^{12} - 1 = 25.3\%$.

4. The interest paid on the borrowed funds is $6,000,000 × 0.08 = $480,000. The commitment fee is levied on the $4,000,000 that was unused and is equal to $10,000 ($4,000,000 × 0.0025 = $10,000). The total cost is $490,000.

5. a. Your firm is paying $3 to borrow $97 for 25 days (40 − 15 = 25). The interest rate per period is $3/$97 = 3.09%. There are 365/25 = 14.6 25-day periods in a year. The effective annual rate is $(1.0309)^{14.6} - 1 = 55.9\%$.

b. Your firm is still paying $3 to borrow $97, so the interest rate per period is 3.09%. In this case the loan period is 35 days (50 − 15 = 35), and there are 365/35 = 10.43 35-day periods in a year. The effective annual rate is $(1.0309)^{10.43} - 1 = 37.4\%$.

6. McClelland's average payment period is $20,000/$670 = 29.9 days. Since this is just meeting the payment date stipulated in the credit terms, McClelland is managing its accounts payable well, given that it is not taking the discount. (There is not enough information supplied to determine if forgoing the discount is the best choice for short-term financing.)

7. The interest paid is the difference between the face value of the commercial paper, $1,000,000, and the proceeds to Treadwater, $980,000. The interest is, therefore, $20,000. Treadwater's usable proceeds is $980,000, so the interest rate per period is $20,000/$980,000 = 2.04%. Since there are four 3-month periods in a year, the effective annual cost is $(1.0204)^4 - 1 = 8.4\%$.

8. a. The haircut refers to the difference between the current market price of the securities and the selling price stated in the repurchase agreement. The haircut in this case is $2,600,000 − $2,550,000 = $50,000.

b. Since the First Bank of Chimera has agreed to buy the securities back for $2,552,000 and has sold them to the Second Bank for $2,550,000, the First Bank is paying interest of $2,000. It has use of the full $2,550,000 for the duration of the loan, which is 5 days. The interest rate per period is $2,000/$2,550,000 = 0.078%.

There are 73 5-day periods in 1 year (365/5 = 73). The effective annual rate is $(1.00078)^{73} - 1 = 5.9\%$.

9. Since the annual percentage rate on the loan is 6%, the monthly interest rate is 6%/12 = 0.5%, so Uptown Clothiers must pay $0.005 \times \$500,000 = \$2,500$ in interest. The factor's fee is $0.005 \times \$625,000 = \$3,125$. Since it is paid at the end of the month, Uptown Clothiers has use of the full $500,000 for the month. The interest rate per period is $5,625/$500,000 = 1.13%. Since there are 12 periods in 1 year, the effective annual rate is $(1.0113)^{12} - 1 = 14.4\%$.

10. The monthly interest rate is 9%/12 = 0.75%, so Ohio Valley Steel must pay $0.0075 \times \$5,000,000 = \$37,500$ in interest on the loan. Combining this with the $5,000 warehouser fee makes the monthly cost of the loan $42,500. Since the fee is paid at the end of the month, Ohio Valley Steel has use of the full $5,000,000 of borrowed funds. The interest rate per period is $42,500/$5,000,000 = 0.85%. Since there are 12 months in a year, the effective annual rate is $(1.0085)^{12} - 1 = 10.7\%$.

11. If Simple Simon's uses its trade credit, it will pay $1 to borrow $99 for 10 days since the full amount of the invoice is due 10 days after the discount period. The interest rate per period is $1/$99 = 1.01%. There are 36.5 10-day periods in a year, so the effective annual rate is $(1.0101)^{36.5} - 1 = 44.3\%$. The interest rate per period on the bank loan is 18%/4 = 4.5%. Since there are 4 quarters in a year, the effective annual rate is $(1.045)^4 - 1 = 19.3\%$. The bank loan is the better deal.

THE COST OF CAPITAL

In this module you will learn how to calculate the cost of capital—i.e., the cost of raising funds—for a firm. The cost of capital calculation may or may not include issue costs. While some firms integrate the costs associated with issuing securities into their costs of capital, other firms simply treat issue costs as an initial cash outflow when evaluating a project's feasibility. This module will address both methods, beginning with the second method first. You will first learn the correct methodology to use to determine the costs and proportions of debt, preferred stock, and common equity financing that a firm employs. Then, you will learn to adjust these components for issue costs if they are to be incorporated into the cost of capital. Part of this adjustment will require separating the common equity component into two separate components—retained earnings and new common stock sales.

Equations introduced in this module

$$WACC = p_d k_d + p_p k_p + p_c k_c$$

$$Price = coupon(PVIFA_{ytm,n}) + maturity\ value(PVIF_{ytm,n})$$

$$Alternatively,\ Net\ proceeds = coupon(PVIFA_{kd°,n}) + maturity\ value(PVIF_{kd°,n})$$

$$k_p = \frac{dividend}{price}$$

$$(Alternatively),\ k_p = \frac{dividend}{net\ proceeds}$$

$$k_c = \frac{dividend_1}{price} + g$$

211

or,

$$k_c = \frac{dividend_1}{net\ proceeds} + g$$

$$while\ k_{re} = \frac{dividend_1}{price} + g$$

$$k_c = rfr + \beta(\bar{r}_m - rfr)$$

---

1. A firm's **cost of capital** is the average cost of the securities that a firm uses to finance its operations. This cost is determined by the rate of return that investors require on the firm's securities. A weighted average is calculated by multiplying the cost of each type of financing that the firm uses by the proportion of that financing component that the firm uses. We can represent this in formula form as follows:

$$WACC = p_d k_d + p_p k_p + p_c k_c$$

where WACC is the "weighted average cost of capital," p_d is the proportion of debt financing used, p_p is the proportion of preferred stock financing used, p_c is the proportion of common equity financing used, k_d is the effective cost of debt for the firm, k_p is the effective cost of preferred stock for the firm, and k_c is the effective cost of common equity for the firm. Therefore, if the Krehlik Corporation uses 40% debt, 10% preferred stock, and 50% common stock to finance its operations and the effective cost of each is 5.4%, 8%, and 12%, respectively, then the firm's weighted average cost of capital is calculated as follows:

$$WACC = 0.4(5.4\%) + 0.1(8\%) + 0.5(12\%) = 8.96\%.$$

? Calculate the weighted average cost of capital for the Krehlik Corporation if the firm uses 30% debt, 15% preferred stock, and 55% common equity to finance its operations and the effective cost of each is 6%, 9%, and 12.5% respectively.

Answer: 10.02%.

$$WACC = 0.3(6\%) + 0.15(9\%) + 0.55(12.5\%) = 10.02\%$$

2. The weighted average cost of capital is the minimum acceptable rate of return for a firm's projects if and only if two conditions hold true:
(1) the project is of average risk for the firm; and
(2) the project will be financed using the same proportions of financing; i.e., the capital structure of the firm remains unchanged.
If a project is less risky than the average risk project of a firm, then its required rate of return will be less than the cost of capital for a firm, and if a project is more risky than the average risk project of a firm, it should be required to return more than the firm's cost of capital. Therefore, if a firm is in the retail ice cream business and has several establishments throughout the state of Ohio and is considering opening another store in Ohio in a location not unlike its current locations, the weighted average cost of capital can be used as a minimum acceptable rate of return for the new store, assuming that the new store will be financed in the same manner as the firm's other operations, since it is reasonable to assume that the new store is an average risk project for the firm. However, let us assume that another building has been purchased, but the firm's owner is bored with the retail ice cream business and instead has decided to open a pet funeral parlor in the newly purchased building. In this case, the weighted average cost of capital would not be a good

benchmark by which to judge the potential returns of the new project since a pet funeral parlor is probably a lot more risky for the firm than another ice cream store. The minimum rate of return that the firm should require from the pet funeral parlor should be greater than the minimum rate of return on an average risk project that the firm undertakes, reflecting the greater risk of the new project.

? Assume that the Krehlik Corporation has a weighted average cost of capital of 10%. It currently has some excess funds that it would like to invest for a short period of time. The firm is considering investing these funds in some Treasury bills that are currently offering a return of 5%. Given that these Treasury bills do not return at least the firm's cost of capital, should Krehlik Corporation invest in them?

Answer: Yes.

Since Treasury bills are risk-free instruments, they should not be required to return the firm's cost of capital. If a firm were to require all investments to return at least its cost of capital, the firm would become riskier in the long-run, since it would only be able to accept projects that are of the same or greater risk than the projects in which it currently invests.

3. Since the weighted average cost of capital is used as a benchmark by which to judge the acceptability of future projects that the firm is considering undertaking, we must use the most current data that we have when determining the proportions and the cost components of the weighted average cost of capital formula. Thus, when determining the proportions, we use the current market values of each type of security used to finance the firm, not the book values, which are historical numbers. For the same reason, when determining the effective cost of debt for the firm, we use the yield-to-maturity on the debt, not the coupon rate, since a firm would have to offer a coupon equal to the current yield-to-maturity on a new debt issue that it wanted to sell at par value since this is the investors' required rate of return on the firm's debt at the present time. If the debt is selling at its par value, the coupon rate *is* the yield-to-maturity on the debt. If it is selling for more or less than its par value, we need to determine its yield-to-maturity. The yield-to-maturity is the discount rate that makes the price of the debt equal to the present value of its expected future cash flows. Therefore, if we have a 9%, $1,000 bond that matures in 15 years and pays interest semiannually selling for $793.50, we can determine the yield-to-maturity on the bond by solving the following equation for i:

$$\$793.50 = \$45(\text{PVIFA}_{i,30}) + \$1,000(\text{PVIF}_{i,30}).$$

(Note that since the bond pays interest semiannually, an investor would receive $45 every 6 months, and there are 30 6-month periods in 15 years. The investor will also receive the face value of the bond, $1,000, at maturity, which is at the end of the thirtieth period.) Since the equation has two unknowns, we must use trial and error to solve it if a financial calculator is unavailable. The bond is selling at a discount, so the investor is receiving more than the coupon rate for a yield. The bond is paying a 4.5% coupon every 6 months, so we might try 5% for the 6-month rate as follows:

$$\$45(\text{PVIFA}_{5\%,30}) + \$1,000(\text{PVIF}_{5\%,30}) = \$45(15.3725) + \$1,000(0.2314) = \$923.16.$$

Since $923.16 is higher than the actual price of the bond, we know that the 5% rate is too low of a trial. We might, therefore, try 7%:

$$\$45(\text{PVIFA}_{7\%,30}) + \$1,000(\text{PVIF}_{7\%,30}) = \$45(12.4090) + \$1,000(0.1314) = \$689.81.$$

In this case our answer of $689.81 is less than the actual price of the bond, so we will try 6%:

$$\$45(\text{PVIFA}_{6\%,30}) + \$1,000(\text{PVIF}_{6\%,30}) = \$45(13.7648) + \$1,000(0.1741) = \$793.50.$$

Therefore, 6% is the 6-month yield. The yield-to-maturity is the average *annual* rate that an investor is promised if he holds the bond to maturity, so we will annualize the 6-month yield as follows:

$$\text{Effective annual rate} = (1 + \text{6-month rate})^2 - 1 = (1.06)^2 - 1 = 12.4\%.$$

? What is the yield-to-maturity on an 8%, $1,000 bond with 11 years left to maturity if interest is paid semiannually and the bond is currently selling for $1,159.40?

Answer: 6.1%.

To find the 6-month yield, we must solve the following equation for i:

$$\$1,159.40 = \$40(\text{PVIFA}_{i,\,22}) + \$1,000(\text{PVIF}_{i,\,22}).$$

Since we have an equation with two unknowns, we must use trial and error or a financial calculator to solve for the 6-month yield. The bond is selling for a premium, so we know that the yield-to-maturity must be less than the 8% coupon rate, and the 6-month yield is less than the semiannual coupon of 4%. We might try 2% as a first trial:

$$\$40(17.6580) + \$1,000(0.6468) = \$1,353.12.$$

Because $1,353.12 is greater than the actual price of the bond, we know that 2% was too low a discount rate. We will try 3%:

$$\$40(15.9369) + \$1,000(0.5219) = \$1,159.38.$$

The pennies difference is due to rounding, so the 6-month yield is 3%. The yield-to-maturity is the annualized rate, calculated as follows:

$$(1.03)^2 - 1 = 6.1\%.$$

4. The yield-to-maturity is the average annual return that investors are requiring on the firm's debt. However, since interest is tax deductible, the cost of debt (k_d) to the firm is actually less than the yield-to-maturity. We can determine the cost of debt by multiplying the yield-to-maturity by 1 minus the marginal tax rate of the firm. Thus, in our first example, while the yield-to-maturity was determined to be 12.4% if the firm is in the 30% marginal tax bracket, the cost of debt for the firm is actually only 12.4%(1 − 0.30) = 8.68%.

? If the yield-to-maturity is 6.1% and the firm is in the 40% marginal tax bracket, what is the cost of debt for the firm?

Answer: 3.66%.

$$k_d = 6.1\%(1 - 0.40) = 3.66\%$$

5. The required rate of return on preferred stock can be backed out of the equation for the price of preferred stock.

$$\text{Price} = \text{Dividend/Required rate of return} = \text{D/R}$$

So R = Dividend/Price. If an issue of preferred pays a $4.00 a share dividend and sells for $50 a share, then the required rate of return is calculated as R = $4.00/$50.00 = 8%. Since dividends on preferred stock are paid out of after-tax income, there is no tax savings for the firm, and the cost of the preferred stock is equivalent to the investors' required rate of return. Therefore, k_p = R = 8%.

? An issue of preferred stock pays a $3.50 dividend and sells for $40. What is the cost of preferred stock financing for the firm?

Answer: 8.75%.

$$k_p = \$3.50/\$40.00 = 8.75\%$$

6. The cost of common stock is more difficult to nail down since common stock does not usually pay a fixed dividend and it has no maturity. There are three methods that can be used to determine the cost of common stock: using a dividend discount model, applying the capital asset pricing model, and using current debt rates. Sometimes a firm uses more than one method and averages the results.

If a firm has been growing at a constant rate and that rate of growth is expected to continue indefinitely, the constant growth model, which is a dividend discount model, can be used. The constant growth model, when solved for R, indicates that the required rate of return on common stock is the sum of the dividend yield on the stock and the growth rate. This is demonstrated below:

$$P = \frac{D_1}{R - g}$$

so,

$$R = D_1/P + g$$

where D_1 is the expected future dividend, P is the current price of the stock, and g is the constant growth rate. The expected future dividend can be estimated from the current dividend the firm is paying by multiplying the current dividend by 1 plus the growth rate, or $D_1 = D_0(1 + g)$.

Assume that the Krehlik Corporation currently pays a dividend of $1.10 and is selling for $32 a share. The firm and its dividends are expected to grow at a constant rate of 6% indefinitely. The investors' required rate of return is calculated as follows:

$$D_1 = \$1.10(1.06) = \$1.166$$

$$R = \$1.166/\$32 + 0.06 = 9.6\%.$$

Since dividends on common stock are paid out of after-tax income, the investors' required rate of return *is* the firm's cost of common stock, so k_c = 9.6%.

? Assume that the Krehlik Corporation is currently selling at $20 a share and is expected to pay a dividend next year of $1.20 per share. The firm's earnings and dividends are expected to grow at a constant rate of 5% indefinitely. What is the firm's cost of common stock?

Answer: 11%.
Since $1.20 is the expected dividend, this is D_1. The cost of common stock is equivalent to the investors' required rate of return, so k_c = R = $1.20/$20 + 0.05 = 11%.

7. When a firm reaches maturity, its dividend is sometimes expected to remain the same indefinitely since no growth is anticipated. In this instance, the price of common stock can be determined in the same manner as the price of preferred stock, or Price = Dividend/R, where R is the required rate of return. Therefore, R = Dividend/Price. Again, the required rate of return, R, is also the firm's cost of common stock. So if the Krehlik Corporation currently sells for $13 a share and pays a dividend of $1.50 and that dividend is expected to remain constant indefinitely, the cost of common stock is calculated as follows:

$$k_c = \$1.50/\$13 = 11.5\%.$$

? If instead, the Krehlik Corporation pays a dividend of $2.50 and the dividend is expected to remain at this level indefinitely, and the stock sells for $15 a share, what is Krehlik's cost of common stock?

Answer: 16.7%.

$$k_c = \$2.50/\$15 = 16.7\%$$

8. A second method used to determine the cost of common stock is the capital asset pricing model, a model that asserts that the required rate of return on a stock is equal to the risk-free rate plus a risk premium. The risk premium for the stock is based on its systematic risk, which is measured by its beta (β) and indicates the degree to which the stock's returns move with the market in general. The capital asset pricing model (CAPM) is shown in formula form below:

$$R_j = rfr + \beta(\bar{r}_m - rfr)$$

where R_j is the required rate of return, rfr is the risk-free rate, and $\bar{r}_m$ is the expected return on the market in general. It is common practice to use the return on Treasury securities as a proxy for the risk-free rate, and the expected return on the S&P 500 as a proxy for the expected return on the market. So if the Krehlik Corporation has a beta of 0.9 and the relevant risk-free rate is 6% while the expected return on the market is 14%, the required rate of return on the firm's common stock is $R_j = 6\% + 0.9(14\% - 6\%) = 13.2\%$. This is also the firm's cost of common stock, k_c.

? Calculate the cost of common stock for Krehlik Corporation if its beta is 1.3, the expected return on the S&P 500 is 12%, and the relevant Treasury security rate is 4%.

Answer: 14.4%.

$$k_c = 4\% + 1.3(12\% - 4\%) = 14.4\%$$

9. The third method that is sometimes used to calculate the cost of common stock is to estimate the cost using current debt rates. It has been estimated that investors require 4% to 6% more on a firm's common stock than they do on the firm's debt. Therefore, if the yield-to-maturity on the debt of the Krehlik Corporation is 8%, we can estimate the cost of common equity by adding a premium of 4% to 6% to the 8% debt rate. We might choose 5%, in which case the cost of common stock for Krehlik will be 8% + 5% = 13%. Note that it is the yield-to-maturity on the debt and not the cost of debt to the firm that is used when estimating the cost of common equity. This is because the investors are requiring a return equal to the yield-to-maturity on the firm's debt. The cost of debt to the firm is lower than the required rate of return given the tax savings on the interest expense. It is the investors' required rate of return to which the premium is added.

? If the bonds of the Krehlik Corporation pay a 10% coupon and are priced to yield 9%, in what range is the cost of common stock for the firm if Krehlik is in the 34% marginal tax bracket?

Answer: 13% to 15%.

The yield-to-maturity on the debt, not its coupon rate, is the rate of return that investors are requiring on the firm's debt. Since they require a 4% to 6% premium on the common stock of the firm, k_c will have a range from 13% (9% + 4%) to 15% (9% + 6%).

10. The final step in determining the weighted average cost of capital is determining the proportions of each type of financing used. The following data has been collected for Krehlik Corporation:

	Book Value	Market Value
Debt	$10,000,000	$12,125,000
Preferred Stock	$ 6,000,000	$ 6,000,000
Common Stock	$20,000,000	$32,000,000

Since it is the market values rather than the book values that should be used in determining the proportions, we will total these and calculate the percentage of the total that each type of financing uses.

	Market Value	Proportion
Debt	$12,125,000	0.24
Preferred Stock	$ 6,000,000	0.12
Common Stock	$32,000,000	0.64
Total	$50,125,000	

? If the data collected for the Krehlik Corporation had instead been as follows, what would the appropriate proportions be?

	Book Value	Market Value
Debt	$ 14,000,000	$13,620,000
Preferred Stock	$ 1,500,000	$ 1,200,000
Common Stock	$ 12,000,000	$15,000,000

Answers: $p_d = 0.18$, $p_p = 0.06$, $p_c = 0.76$.

Since market values are the relevant numbers to use in calculating the proportions, we total them and determine what percentage each type of financing represents of the total.

	Market Value	Proportion
Debt	$13,620,000	0.18
Preferred Stock	$ 1,200,000	0.06
Common Stock	$15,000,000	0.76
Total	$19,820,000	

11. In order to put it all together, let us consider the Salt-of-the-Earth Corporation, which has the following balance sheet data:

Bonds (7% coupon, $1,000 face, 10 years to maturity)	$ 5,000,000
Preferred Stock ($2.60 dividend, 100,000 shares outstanding)	$ 2,500,000
Common Stock (1,000,000 shares outstanding)	$12,000,000

The bonds pay interest annually and are currently selling at $871.65 to yield 9%. Preferred stock is selling at par, and common stock is selling for $22 a share. The common stock is expected to pay a dividend of $0.75 a share next year. This dividend is expected to grow at 8% for the foreseeable future. The firm's marginal tax rate is 45%.

To calculate the weighted average cost of capital, we must first calculate the cost of each financing component. The cost of debt is the yield-to-maturity on the debt times 1 minus the firm's marginal tax rate, so

$$k_d = 9\%(1 - 0.45) = 4.95\%.$$

The cost of preferred is equal to the dividend divided by the price.

$$k_p = \$2.60/\$25.00 = 10.4\%$$

Lastly, information supplied in the problem allows us to use the constant growth model to estimate the cost of common stock.

$$k_c = \$0.75/\$22.00 + 0.08 = 11.4\%$$

Next, market values must be determined in order to calculate the relevant proportions. The number of bonds outstanding can be found by dividing the book value of the bonds by $1,000 since each bond has a $1,000 face value. The number of bonds is $5,000,000/$1,000 = 5,000. Since each bond is selling for $871.65, the total market value of the debt is 5,000 × $871.65 = $4,358,250. The preferred stock is selling at par, so its market value is equal to its book value of $2,500,000. And the market value of the common stock is equal to the price per share times the number of shares outstanding, so $22 × 1,000,000 = $22,000,000. We find the total market value and calculate the proportions as follows:

	Market Value	Proportion
Debt	$ 4,358,250	0.15
Preferred Stock	$ 2,500,000	0.09
Common Stock	$22,000,000	0.76
Total	$28,858,250	

The weighted average cost of capital is then calculated as follows:

$$WACC = p_d k_d + p_p k_p + p_c k_c$$
$$= 0.15(4.95\%) + 0.09(10.4\%) + 0.76(11.4\%) = 10.3\%.$$

The M & G Corporation's balance sheet contains the following information:

Bonds (12% coupon, $1,000 face value, 5 years to maturity)	$ 60 million
Preferred Stock ($5 dividend, 1 million shares outstanding)	$ 10 million
Common stock (10 million shares outstanding)	$100 million

The bonds pay interest annually and are selling at $1075.82 to yield 10%. Preferred stock is selling for $38.50 a share and the common stock is selling for $12.00 a share. The beta of the stock is 1.15. The relevant Treasury security rate is 5%, and the S&P 500 is expected to return 14% next year. M & G pays taxes at a rate of 39%.

? Calculate M&G's weighted average cost of capital.

Answer: 12.27%.
The first step requires finding the cost elements. The cost of debt is the bonds' yield-to-maturity of 10% adjusted for tax savings.

$$k_d = 10\%(1 - 0.39) = 6.1\%$$

The cost of preferred is found by dividing the dividend by the price of preferred.

$$k_p = \$5/\$38.50 = 12.99\%$$

The cost of common can be found by applying the capital asset pricing model. The risk-free rate is the Treasury security rate of 5%, and the expected return on the market is proxied by the expected return on the S&P 500.

$$k_c = 5\% + 1.15(14\% - 5\%) = 15.35\%$$

Next, the market value of each type of financing must be determined in order to find the relevant proportions. The market value of the debt can be found by multiplying the number of bonds outstanding by the current selling price per bond.

$$\text{Number of bonds} = \text{book value/face value per bond}$$

$$= \$60,000,000/\$1,000 = 60,000$$

$$\text{Market value of debt} = 60,000 \times \$1075.82 = \$64,549,200$$

The market value of both the preferred and the common is equal to the number of shares of each outstanding multiplied by the current price per share of that stock.

$$\text{Market value of preferred} = 1,000,000 \text{ shares} \times \$38.50 = \$38,500,000$$

$$\text{Market value of common} = 10,000,000 \text{ shares} \times \$12.00 = \$120,000,000$$

The total market value is $223,049,200, making the proportion of debt financing equal to $64,549,200/$223,049,200 = 0.29; the proportion of preferred stock financing equal to $38,500,000/$223,049,200 = 0.17; and the proportion of common stock financing equal to $120,000,000/$223,049,200 = 0.54. The weighted average cost of capital is, therefore,

$$\text{WACC} = (0.29)(6.1\%) + 0.17(12.99\%) + 0.54(15.35\%) = 12.27\%.$$

12.   Some firms also include the issue costs of each type of financing in their cost of capital calculation. To do this, the cost element of each type of financing is calculated based on the net proceeds that the firm receives rather than on the current price of the issue. For example, suppose a firm has a bond that pays a 7.5% coupon, has a $1,000 face value, and will mature in 20 years. Interest is paid annually. The firm will net $951 after flotation costs, and its marginal tax rate is 40%. Setting the discounted cash flows equal to the net proceeds received by the firm renders the following equation:

$$\$951 = \$75(\text{PVIFA}_{kd^\circ,20}) + \$1,000(\text{PVIF}_{kd^\circ,20}).$$

Using trial and error to solve for kd°, which is the cost of debt to the firm *after* flotation costs, but before the adjustment for taxes. We first try 9%. (Since the bond is selling at a discount, we know it is offering investors a greater return than the coupon rate.)

$$\$75(9.1285) + \$1,000(0.1784) = \$863.04$$

The price of $863.04 is less than the net proceeds received by the firm, so 9% is too high a discount rate. Next we try 8%.

$$\$75(9.8181) + \$1,000(0.2145) = \$950.85$$

The few cents difference is due to rounding, so 8% is the pre-tax cost of debt if issue costs are included. The cost of debt is therefore $8\%(1 - 0.40) = 4.8\%$.

? The Krehlik Corporation has a $1,000 face value, 15-year bond issue that pays a 5% coupon, with interest paid annually. The bond is selling at an original deep discount of $709.35 to net the firm $677.57. The firm's marginal tax rate is 50%. If Krehlik incorporates issue costs into its cost of debt, what is its after-tax cost of debt?

Answer: 4.5%.
If issue costs are incorporated into the cost of capital, the appropriate equation to solve for the pre-tax cost of debt is as follows:

$$\$677.57 = \$50(\text{PVIFA}_{kd°,15}) + \$1,000(\text{PVIF}_{kd°,15}).$$

Since the bond is selling at a discount, its pre-tax cost of debt is greater than the 5% coupon rate, so we might try 7%.

$$\$50(9.1079) + \$1,000(0.3624) = \$817.80$$

This answer is higher than $677.57, indicating that 7% is too low a discount rate. Next we will try 8%.

$$\$50(8.5595) + \$1,000(0.3152) = \$743.18$$

This answer is still too high, so we need to try a higher rate yet. Plugging 9% into the equation gives us the following result:

$$\$50(8.0607) + \$1,000(0.2745) = \$677.54.$$

The pre-tax cost of debt is 9%. The after-tax cost of debt is $9\%(1-0.5) = 4.5\%$. (Note: You may have chosen other interest rates before you arrived at 9% as the correct rate.)

13.   Similarly, the cost of preferred can be calculated by using net proceeds instead of price in the formula used to determine the cost of preferred. Suppose a firm has an issue of preferred stock that pays a dividend of $3.50 per share and sells for $48 a share. The flotation costs are $1.50 per share. If we wish to incorporate issue costs into the cost of capital, the cost of preferred is calculated as follows:

$$\text{net proceeds to the firm} = \$48.00 - \$1.50 = \$46.50$$

$$k_p = \$3.50/\$46.50 = 7.5\%.$$

? Suppose the Krehlik Corporation has an issue of preferred stock that pays a dividend of $3.75 a share and sells for $35 a share. Flotation costs are $2 a share, and the firm is in the 50% marginal tax bracket. What is the cost of preferred if issue costs are incorporated into the cost of capital?

Answer: 11.4%.
Since flotation costs are $2 a share, the net proceeds received by the firm is $33. Using this in the formula for the cost of preferred we get the following:

$$k_p = \$3.75/\$33.00 = 11.4\%.$$

14.   When issue costs are included in the cost of capital, there are two elements to the cost of common equity. One element is the cost of external common equity financing, i.e., the sale of new common stock, in which case the cost is adjusted for issue costs. The second element is the cost of internal financing, or the use of retained earnings. Since the use of retained earnings does not involve issue costs, the cost of retained earnings is not adjusted for those costs. Nevertheless, the use of retained earnings is not free. Retained earnings represents income that is reinvested in the firm rather than being distributed as dividends. Investors foregoing these dividend payments expect the reinvested earnings to earn their required rate of return, which they will realize as capital gains. Therefore, the cost of retained earnings is the same as the return that investors require on the firm's common equity, but it is not adjusted for issue costs. We can expand the weighted average cost of capital formula presented previously as follows:

$$\text{WACC} = p_d k_d + p_p k_p + p_c k_c + p_{re} k_{re}$$

where p_c and k_c represent the proportion of external common equity financing and the cost of external common equity financing, respectively, while p_{re} and k_{re} represent the proportion of internal common equity financing and the cost of internal equity financing, respectively.

As an illustration, suppose the common stock of a firm pays a dividend of $0.70 per share and sells for $52 a share. The dividends are expected to grow at an annual rate of 8% indefinitely. Issue costs are 3% of the selling price of the issue. The cost of external equity, k_c, will include these issue costs and can be calculated as follows:

$\text{Dividend}_1 = \$0.70(1.08) = \$0.756$
Issue cost per share $= 0.03(\$52) = \$1.56$
Net proceeds to the firm $= \$52.00 - \$1.56 = \$50.44$
$k_c = D_1/\text{net proceeds} + g = \$0.756/\$50.44 + 0.08 = 9.50\%.$

On the other hand, issue costs are not relevant when calculating the cost of internal financing, so $k_{re} = \$0.756/\$52.00 + 0.08 = 9.45\%$.

? The common stock of the Krehlik Corporation sells for $47 and is expected to pay a dividend of $1.20 a share. Dividends are expected to grow at a rate of 6% indefinitely, and issue costs are 5% of the selling price of the stock. Calculate the cost of external equity financing as well as the cost of retained earnings.

Answer: $k_c = 8.7\%$; $k_{re} = 8.6\%$.
The cost of external financing uses the net proceeds to the firm in its calculation. Issue costs are $0.05(\$47) = \$2.35$, so the firm nets $\$47.00 - \$2.35 = \$44.65$ per share. The expected dividend, D_1, is given as $1.20, so $k_c = \$1.20/\$44.65 + 0.06 = 8.7\%$. The cost of retained earnings, on the other hand, is $k_{re} = \$1.20/\$47 + 0.06 = 8.6\%$.

15. The **marginal cost of capital** is the cost of raising one additional dollar of capital. Suppose, for example, a firm uses 40% debt financing, 10% preferred stock financing, and 50% retained earnings. The costs of each are 5%, 7.1%, and 12%, respectively. Then its marginal cost of capital is calculated below:

$$\text{MCC} = 0.40(5\%) + 0.10(7.1\%) + 0.50(12\%) = 8.71\%.$$

On the other hand, suppose that the firm will exhaust its retained earnings and will have to sell new common stock in order to use 50% common equity financing. New common stock will cost the firm 12.4% due to flotation costs. Then the marginal cost of capital becomes

$$\text{MCC} = 0.40(5\%) + 0.10(7.1\%) + 0.25(12\%) + 0.25(12.4\%) = 8.81\%$$

since it will cost 8.81% to raise each new dollar of capital.

Calculate the marginal cost of capital for the firm above if it can finance its equity investment with 40% retained earnings and 10% new common stock.

Answer: 8.75%.

$$\text{MCC} = 0.40(5\%) + 0.10(7.1\%) + 0.40(12\%) + 0.10(12.4\%) = 8.75\%$$

Apply It

1. Why is the cost of debt adjusted for taxes while the cost of preferred stock and common equity are not? (Frame 4)

2. All else equal, if Congress increases tax rates, what happens to the relative cost of debt for a firm? (Frame 4)

3. The Marner Company pays a dividend on its common stock of $1 a share. This dividend is expected to grow indefinitely at a rate of 10%. The stock is currently selling for $50 a share, and its beta is 0.90. The relevant risk-free rate is 5%, and the S&P 500 is expected to return 14% in the next year. Marner recently sold a new debt issue that offered bondholders a yield of 7%. Marner is in the 34% tax bracket. Calculate the cost of common equity for Marner using

   a. a dividend discount model (Frame 6)

   b. the capital asset pricing model (Frame 8)

   c. current debt rates, assuming that investors require a 5% premium over their required rate of return on the firm's debt when investing in the firm's common stock (Frame 9)

4. Specialty Building Products' balance sheet contains the following information:

Bonds ($1,000 face value, 8% coupon, 6 years to maturity)	$30 million
Preferred Stock (6% dividend, 1,500,000 shares outstanding)	$15 million
Common Stock (5 million shares outstanding)	$60 million

   Both the bonds and the preferred stock are selling at par value. Common stock sells for $40 a share and pays a dividend of $0.90 a share. The dividend is expected to grow at 9% indefinitely. The firm is in the 40% marginal tax bracket.

   a. Calculate the after-tax cost of debt. (Frame 4)

   b. Calculate the after-tax cost of preferred stock. (Frame 5)

   c. Calculate the after-tax cost of common stock. (Frame 6)

   d. Calculate the firm's weighted average cost of capital. (Frame 11)

5. Pampered Pets, Incorporated is a nationwide pet grooming franchise. Its balance sheet contains the following information:

Bonds ($1,000 face value, 10% coupon, 10 years to maturity)	$ 80 million
Preferred Stock ($5.00 dividend, 1 million shares outstanding)	$ 10 million
Common Stock (6 million shares outstanding)	$100 million

   The bonds are selling at a price to yield 11% and pay interest annually. The preferred stock is selling for $40 a share while the common stock is selling for $22 a share. The beta of the equity is 1.4. The relevant Treasury security rate is 5.5%, and the S&P 500 is expected to return 14.8%. The firm is in the 34% marginal tax bracket.

   a. Calculate the after-tax cost of debt. (Frame 4)

   b. Calculate the after-tax cost of preferred stock. (Frame 5)

   c. Calculate the after-tax cost of common stock. (Frame 8)

   d. Calculate the firm's weighted average cost of capital. (Frame 11)

   e. If Pampered Pets is considering offering acting classes for animals, would the number calculated in part (d) be the appropriate minimum rate of return for this new venture? Why or why not? (Frame 3)

6. The Melmiss Corporation's balance sheet contains the following data:

Bonds ($1,000 face value, 9% coupon, 6 years to maturity)	$40 million
Preferred Stock (500,000 shares outstanding, $4.50 dividend)	$ 2 million
Common Stock (2 million shares outstanding)	$50 million

   The bonds are selling for $1,047 and pay interest semiannually. The preferred stock is selling for $45 a share. The common stock is expected to pay a dividend of $1.50 next year and currently sells for $32 a share. The dividends are expected to grow at a rate of 8% indefinitely. Melmiss is in the 30% marginal tax bracket.

   a. Calculate the after-tax cost of debt. (Frame 4)

   b. Calculate the after-tax cost of preferred stock. (Frame 5)

   c. Calculate the after-tax cost of common stock. (Frame 6)

   d. Calculate the weighted average cost of capital for the firm. (Frame 11)

7. Agnes Rochelle is planning to open an antique shop. The venture will cost her $30,000. She can borrow $7,500 from the bank at 11% and must put up $22,500 of her own money. Ms. Rochelle is in the 28% marginal tax bracket. If she wants a 15% return on her money, what minimum rate of return must she earn on this investment? (Frame 2)

8. An issue of preferred stock pays a $6.25 dividend and sells for $82 a share. Issue costs are $2 a share. The issuing firm pays taxes at a marginal rate of 39%. If the firm wants to include issue costs in its cost of capital calculation, what is the cost of the preferred stock? (Frame 13)

9. The Means Corporation needs $8 million. It plans to use 60% retained earnings and to finance the rest with debt. The company can raise the first $2 million of debt at 10.5%. Anything in excess of that will cost the firm 12%. The cost of internal equity is 16%, and the firm is in the 40% marginal tax bracket. What is the marginal cost of capital for Means? (Frame 15)

Apply It Answers

1. The interest that a firm pays on its debt is tax deductible, thereby creating a tax savings, so the cost of debt is actually less than what investors are requiring on the firm's debt. The dividends paid on preferred and common stock are paid out of after-tax income. The return that investors require *is* the cost to the firm.

2. If Congress were to raise tax rates, then the benefit of the tax deductibility of the interest expense also increases, reducing the after-tax cost of debt.

3. a. The expected future dividend is $1.00(1.10) = 1.10, so $k_c = $1.10/$50 + 0.10 = 12.2\%$.

 b. Using CAPM, $k_c = 5\% + 0.9(14\% - 5\%) = 13.1\%$.

 c. If investors require a 5% premium for holding common stock rather than debt of the firm, $k_c = 7\% + 5\% = 12\%$.

4. a. Since the bonds are selling at par, the yield-to-maturity is equal to the coupon rate on the bonds, so $k_d = 8\%(1 - 0.4) = 4.8\%$.

 b. Since the preferred stock is selling at par, its return is equal to its dividend rate; therefore $k_p = 6\%$.

 c. The expected dividend is $0.90(1.09) = 0.981. So $k_c = $0.981/$40 + 0.09 = 11.5\%$.

 d. In order to determine the proportions, we need to know the market value of each financing component. Since the bonds and the preferred stock are selling at par, their market values are the same as their book values of $30 million and $15 million, respectively. The market value of the common stock is equal to the price per share times the number of shares outstanding, so $5,000,000 \times $40 = $200,000,000$. The proportions are as follows:

	Market Value	Proportion
Debt	$ 30 million	0.12
Preferred Stock	$ 15 million	0.06
Common Stock	$200 million	0.82
Total	$245 million	

$$\text{WACC} = 0.12(4.8\%) + 0.06(6\%) + 0.82(11.5\%) = 10.37\%$$

5. a. Since the bonds are selling to yield 11%, $k_d = 11\%(1 - 0.34) = 7.26\%$.

 b. $k_p = \text{Dividend/Price} = $5/$40 = 12.5\%$

 c. We can find the cost of common by applying CAPM as follows:

$$k_c = 5.5\% + 1.4(14.8\% - 5.5\%) = 18.52\%.$$

 d. We need to first find the market value of each financing component in order to determine the correct proportions. The market value of the debt can be found by discounting back the total coupon payments and the maturity value at the yield-to-maturity as follows:

Total annual coupon payments $= 0.10($80,000,000) = $8,000,000$

Bond market value $= $8,000,000(\text{PVIFA}_{11\%,10}) + $80,000,000(\text{PVIF}_{11\%,10})$

$= $8,000,000(5.8892) + $80,000,000(0.3522)$

$= $75,289,600.$

The market value of the preferred stock is simply the price per share times the number of shares outstanding, or $40 \times 1,000,000 = 40 million.

The market value of the common stock is calculated in the same manner as that of the preferred stock, so $22 \times 6,000,000 = 132 million.

The proportions can now be calculated.

	Market Value	Proportion
Bonds	$ 75,289,600	0.30
Preferred Stock	$ 40,000,000	0.16
Common Stock	$132,000,000	0.53

The weighted average cost of capital is 0.30(7.26%) + 0.16(12.50%) + 0.53(18.52%) = 13.99%.

e. No. The weighted average cost of capital is the minimum acceptable rate of return only if the firm's capital structure remains unchanged *and* if the project is of average risk for the firm. It is unlikely that pet acting classes are in the same risk class as a pet grooming business. The acting classes are probably a more risky endeavor and should offer a higher minimum rate of return.

6. a. In order to calculate the after-tax cost of debt, we must first find the yield-to-maturity on the debt. We can determine the 6-month return by solving the equation below for i using trial and error:

$$\$1047 = \$45(PVIFA_{i,12}) + \$1,000(PVIF_{i,12}).$$

We will try a 6-month rate of 3% first since we know the 6-month yield is less than the 6-month coupon rate if the bond is selling at a premium.

$$\$45(9.9540) + \$1,000(0.7014) = \$1,149.33$$

The answer we get is greater than the current price of the bond, so we know that we have chosen a rate that is too low. We will now try 4%.

$$\$45(9.3859) + \$1,000(0.6246) = \$1,046.97$$

Therefore, 4% is the 6-month return. To find the yield-to-maturity, we need to annualize this rate. The effective annual rate is $(1.04)^2 - 1 = 8.16\%$. Therefore, $k_d = 8.16\%(1 - 0.3) = 5.7\%$.

b. The cost of preferred, $k_p = \$4.50/\$45 = 10\%$.

c. Since $1.50 is the *expected* dividend, $k_c = \$1.50/\$32 + 0.08 = 12.7\%$.

d. The number of bonds outstanding is equal to the book value divided by the face value per bond, so $40,000,000/$1,000 = 40,000 bonds. Since each bond sells for $1,047, the market value of the debt is $1,047 × 40,000 = $41,880,000. The market value of the preferred is 500,000 shares × $45 per share = $22,500,000. The market value of the common stock is 2,000,000 shares × $32 = $64,000,000. The proportions are shown below:

	Market Value	**Proportion**
Debt	$41,880,000	0.33
Preferred Stock	$22,500,000	0.17
Common Stock	$64,000,000	0.50

The weighted average cost of capital is then 0.33(5.7%) + 0.17(10%) + 0.50(12.7%) = 9.9%.

7. The minimum rate of return that she should require if she desires a 15% return on her money is her weighted average cost of capital. She is borrowing $7,500 of the $30,000, or 25% of her investment. She is financing the remaining 75% with her own money. The weighted average cost of capital is, therefore,

$$WACC = 0.25[11\%(1 - 0.28)] + 0.75(15\%) = 13.23\%.$$

8. The net proceeds to the firm are $82 - $2 = $80. Since preferred stock dividends are paid out of after-tax income, the tax rate is irrelevant, and $k_p = \$6.25/\$80 = 7.8\%$.

9. The Means Corporation will be using 0.4($8 million) = $3.2 million in debt for its financing. Two million of the total $8 million, or 25%, can be financed at 10.5%. The remaining $1.2 million of debt financing, which is 15% of the total funds needed, can be raised at 12%. The marginal cost of capital is calculated below:

$$MCC = 0.25(10.5\%)(1 - 0.4) + 0.15(12\%)(1 - 0.4) + 0.6(16\%) = 12.26\%.$$

CAPITAL BUDGETING

This module will introduce you to some techniques that firms use to select their long-term investments. The first step involves determining the cash flows associated with the investment, and the second step requires applying an evaluation technique. Four of the most commonly used evaluation techniques are presented in this module: payback period, net present value, internal rate of return, and profitability index. In addition, the problem of how to deal with projects that have unequal lives is addressed.

Equations introduced in this module

$$\text{Net present value} = \text{present value of cash inflows} - \text{present value of cash outflows}$$

$$\frac{\text{cash flow}_1}{(1+\text{irr})^1} + \frac{\text{cash flow}_2}{(1+\text{irr})^2} \ldots + \frac{\text{cash flow}_n}{(1+\text{irr})^n} - \text{initial investment} = 0$$

$$\text{Profitability index} = \frac{\text{present value of cash inflows}}{\text{present value of cash outflows}}$$

1.   Short-term assets are called **current assets**, while long-term assets are called **capital assets**. The process of selecting which long-term investments a firm should make is referred to as **capital budgeting**. There are two steps required in evaluating a long-term investment. The first involves forecasting the *cash flows* associated with the investment, and the second involves evaluating those cash flows using an appropriate evaluation method.

In forecasting the cash flows, determination of the timing of the cash flows is critical. Typically, a long-term investment will have initial cash flows, or cash flows that occur at the beginning of the project. These might include the cost of the asset, any investment tax credit that may be allowed, any increase in working capital that the project would require, and the sale of any existing asset if it is being replaced, net of taxes. To illustrate, consider the Talbot Corporation, which is considering replacing an existing machine. The new machine will cost the firm $60,000. An increase in spare parts inventory of $5,000 is also anticipated to prevent downtime. The existing machine is fully depreciated and can be sold today for $6,000. The new machine is more efficient and will save the firm $15,000 a year in operating expenses although it will have no effect on revenues. The new machine is 5-year property and will be depreciated using straight-line depreciation. (The half-year convention will be ignored.) It is expected that at the end of 5 years, the machine will have a salvage value of $10,000. It is felt that the spare parts inventory can be sold at cost at that time as well. Talbot pays taxes at a marginal rate of 39%. At the beginning of the project, the firm will have to pay for the machine and also buy the spare parts, so the initial cash flow is calculated as follows:

Cost of new machine	−$60,000
Cost of spare parts	−$ 5,000
Net cash flow	−$65,000

? The Burson Construction Company is considering the purchase of an additional concrete mixer. The mixer will cost the firm $105,000 and is expected to increase the firm's revenues by $35,000 a year. It qualifies for an investment tax credit equal to 8% of its cost. The new mixer will be depreciated over 7 years. It is expected that it will be sold at the end of this time for $32,000. An increase in inventory of $11,000 will be required with the purchase of the additional machine. This investment will be recouped when the new machine is sold. Burson is in the 45% marginal tax bracket. Determine the initial cash flows associated with this purchase.

Answer: Net initial cash flow = −$107,600.

Cost of new mixer	−$105,000
Investment tax credit	$ 8,400
Investment in inventory	−$ 11,000
Net cash flow	−$107,600

2.   The investment will also usually change annual cash flows from operations. It may increase revenues or expenses or decrease expenses. While depreciation of an asset is not a cash flow, it does affect the tax liability of the firm, so the change in the depreciation expense of the firm resulting from the purchase of an asset must be considered in calculating the after-tax cash flow from operations. Except in the evaluation of some mergers, interest expense on debt is not included in the calculation since the tax deductibility of the interest expense is included in the discount rate that is used to evaluate the project.

The operating cash flows for the Talbot Corporation, described in Frame 1, can be calculated as follows:

Change in revenues	$ 0
−Change in cash expenses	−$15,000
Change in before-tax cash flow	$15,000
−Change in depreciation	$12,000 ($60,000/5 = $12,000)
Change in taxable income	$ 3,000
−Change in taxes (@ 39%)	$ 1,170
Change in net income	$ 1,830
+Change in depreciation	$12,000
Change in after-tax cash flow	$13,830

? Calculate the annual operating cash flows for the Burson Company, described in the question for Frame 1, ignoring the half-year convention in the depreciation calculation.

Answer: $26,000 a year.

Change in revenues	$35,000
−Change in cash expenses	$ 0
Change in before-tax cash flow	$35,000
−Change in depreciation	$15,000 ($105,000/7 = $15,000)
Change in taxable income	$20,000
−Change in taxes (@ 45%)	$ 9,000
Change in net income	$11,000
+Change in depreciation	$15,000
Change in after-tax cash flow	$26,000

3. At the end of the project, there may be terminal cash flows involved, such as the sale of the asset, net of taxes, and the recoup of any initial investment that was made in working capital. For the Talbot Corporation described in Frame 1, this consists of the sale of the machine, taxes resulting from the sale, and the recoup of the investment in spare parts inventory. (The assumption is made in this module that the investment in spare parts is maintained at the initial level throughout the life of the equipment; i.e., if some are used, they are replaced. In practice, the actual value of the remaining spare parts would be used.) The net cash flow for the year will also include the cash flow from operations that were earned during that year. These were calculated in Frame 2.

Cash flow from operations	$13,830
Sale of machine at end of year 5	$10,000
Tax on gain realized by the sale	−$ 3,900 (the book value was zero)
Recoup of working capital investment	$ 5,000
Net cash flow for terminal year	$24,930

? Determine the terminal year net cash flow for the Burson Construction Company.

Answer: $54,600.

Cash flow from operations	$26,000 (calculated in answer to Frame 2)
Sale of mixer	$32,000
Tax on gain realized by the sale	−$14,400 (the book value was zero)
Recoup of working capital investment	$11,000
Net cash flow for terminal year	$54,600

4. Once the expected cash flows have been calculated, one of several evaluation techniques can be used to determine whether or not the project should be accepted. One such technique that is often used by firms is the payback period. The **payback period** calculates the number of years it takes to recoup the original investment. Consider the following project:

Project Venus

Year	Cash Flow
0	−$10,000
1	$ 4,000
2	$ 4,000
3	$ 4,000
4	$ 4,000
5	$ 4,000

The project will recoup $8,000 of the $10,000 investment by the end of the second year. If we can assume that the cash flows occur evenly throughout the year, the remaining $2,000 will be recouped halfway through year 3. Therefore, the payback period is 2½ years.

? Calculate the payback period for the following project:

Project Mercury

Year	Cash Flow
0	−$20,000
1	$ 6,000
2	$ 6,000
3	$ 6,000
4	$10,000
5	$15,000

Answer: 3⅕ years.

By the end of year 3, $18,000 of the $20,000 investment is recouped. If we assume that the cash flows occur evenly throughout the year, the remaining $2,000 will be recouped ⅕ ($2,000/$10,000) of the way into the fourth year.

5. While the payback period can be used as a quick and dirty technique, a final business decision should not be based on it. This technique ignores both the time value of money and cash flows that occur after the payback period. Note that for Projects Venus and Mercury, no difference is made between a dollar received 2 years from now and a dollar spent today. Also, the fact that the bulk of Project Mercury's cash flows occur in years 4 and 5 is totally ignored. Using the payback period technique, a decision maker would select Project Venus over Project Mercury since Venus has the shorter payback period, but it is intuitively obvious that Project Mercury will add more value to the firm.

A technique that takes both time value of money and *all* of a project's cash flows into account is the net present value evaluation technique. The **net present value (NPV)** is calculated by taking the present value of the project's cash inflows and subtracting the present value of the firm's cash outflows. The discount rate used should reflect the relative risk of the project. For an average risk project, the firm's cost of capital would be an appropriate discount rate. Project Venus' only cash outflow is the initial investment of $10,000. The cash inflows are $4,000 a year for 5 years. If we assume a 12% discount rate, the net present value of Project Venus is calculated as follows:

$$\text{NPV} = \$4,000(\text{PVIFA}_{12\%,5}) - \$10,000$$

$$= \$4,000(3.6048) - \$10,000 = \$4,419.20.$$

If the net present value is positive, the project should be accepted since a positive net present value indicates that when all the cash flows are translated to time zero dollars, the inflows exceed the outflows. Therefore, if the net present value is negative, the project should be rejected since the present value of the cash outflows exceeds the present value of the cash inflows. If the net present value is exactly zero, the firm might be indifferent about the project since the present value of the cash inflows exactly equals the present value of the cash outflows.

? Calculate the net present value for Project Mercury, assuming a 12% discount rate.

Answer: $9,276.80.

$$NPV = \$6,000(PVIFA_{12\%,3}) + \$10,000(PVIF_{12\%,4}) + \$15,000(PVIF_{12\%,5}) - \$20,000$$
$$= \$6,000(2.4018) + \$10,000(0.6355) + \$15,000(0.5674) - \$20,000 = \$9,276.80$$

6.   Note that while the payback period for Project Venus was lower than that of Project Mercury, the net present value of Project Mercury is higher than that calculated for Project Venus. The net present value represents the amount by which the project is expected to increase the firm's value, so if the firm has to choose between the two projects, in which case the projects are said to be **mutually exclusive projects**, Project Mercury should be the project that is selected. The payback period technique would have led to a non-wealth-maximizing decision. If the two projects are **independent projects**, i.e., if the decision to accept one does not affect the decision on the other, both Projects Venus and Mercury should be accepted, since they both have positive net present values and therefore increase the value of the firm.

? If the following two projects are mutually exclusive, which one should be undertaken, given a 10% discount rate for both?

	Cash Flows					
	Year 0	**Year 1**	**Year 2**	**Year 3**	**Year 4**	**Year 5**
Project Sun	−$20,000	$ 3,250	$ 3,250	$ 3,250	$ 3,250	$ 4,375
Project Moon	−$49,000	$14,260	$14,260	$14,260	$14,260	$17,560

Answer: Project Moon should be undertaken.

$$NPV_{SUN} = \$3,250(PVIFA_{10\%,4}) + \$4,375(PVIF_{10\%,5}) - \$20,000$$
$$= \$3,250(3.1699) + \$4,375(0.6209) - \$20,000 = -\$6,981.39$$
$$NPV_{MOON} = \$14,260(PVIFA_{10\%,4}) + \$17,560(PVIF_{10\%,5}) - \$49,000$$
$$= \$14,260(3.1699) + \$17,560(0.6209) - \$49,000 = \$7,105.78$$

Since Project Sun has a negative net present value, it should be rejected even if the projects had been independent, since it will erode close to $7,000 (NPV = −$6,981.39) of the firm's value. Project Moon, on the other hand, increases the firm's value by a little over $7,000 (NPV = $7,105.78).

7.   A second evaluation technique is the internal rate of return. The **internal rate of return (IRR)** of a project is the interest rate that makes the net present value of the project zero. We can determine the internal rate of return for Project Venus by solving the following equation for irr:

$$\$4,000(PVIFA_{irr,5}) - \$10,000 = 0.$$

Since this is an equation with one unknown, we will solve for the unknown quantity, $PVIFA_{irr,5}$.

$$PVIFA_{irr,5} = \$10,000/\$4,000 = 2.5000$$

We can now look in the tables for the present value of an annuity. Looking across the row for 5 periods, we see that 2.5000 lies between the interest factors for 28% and 30%. Therefore, the IRR is between 28% and 30%. If a financial calculator is available, the IRR can be calculated to be 28.6%.

With a few exceptions, if the internal rate of return is greater than the required rate of return on the project, the project should be accepted. It will have a positive net present value. If the internal rate of return is less than the required rate of return on the project, the project will have a negative net present value and should be rejected. If the internal rate of return is exactly equal to the required rate of return, the net present value is zero, and the firm may be indifferent about accepting the project. Since the required rate of return on Project Venus was 12% and its IRR has been calculated to be between 28% and 30%, the internal rate of return evaluation technique indicates that the firm should undertake the project.

The exceptions to these decision rules may occur when (1) mutually exclusive projects are being evaluated, as discussed in later frames, or (2) there is more than one sign change in the cash flows of a project. The latter case may result in multiple IRRs or in no IRR; in both instances, the net present value should be used to evaluate the project.

? Project Jupiter has the following expected cash flows:

Year	Cash Flow
0	−$12,000
1	$ 8,000
2	$ 8,000
3	$ 5,000

The project has a required rate of return of 18%. Use the internal rate of return evaluation technique to determine whether or not the project should be undertaken.

Answer: Yes.

The IRR of Project Jupiter is 37.3%, which is greater than the 18% required return. The equation to solve for the internal rate of return is as follows:

$$\$8,000(\text{PVIFA}_{irr,2}) + \$5,000(\text{PVIF}_{irr,3}) - \$12,000 = 0.$$

In this case, there are two unknown quantities, so trial and error must be used by substituting various interest rates in for IRR and determining if the resulting value is equal to zero. (It should be noted that it is more mathematically accurate to explain that the above equation is a third-degree polynomial with the IRR as the only unknown. Regardless, trial and error is used to produce the answer.) While you may have selected different rates for some of your trials, sample trials are shown below.

Using 20%: $8,000(1.5278) + $5,000(0.5787) − $12,000 = $3,115.90

Since we get a positive net present value using 20%, we know that the interest rate that will make the net present value equal to zero must be greater than 20%.

Using 30%: $8,000(1.3609) + $5,000(0.4552) − $12,000 = $1,163.20

Our answer is still a positive number, so we will try 40%.

Using 40%: $8,000(1.2245) + $5,000(0.3644) − $12,000 = −$382.00

Now the answer is negative, so we know that 40% is too high. The next lowest interest rate in the available tables is 35%.

Using 35%: $8,000(1.2894) + $5,000(0.4064) − $12,000 = $347.20

We now have isolated the IRR between 35% and 40%. Since this is greater than the 18% required rate of return, Project Jupiter should be undertaken. (If you have a financial calculator available, you should have calculated the IRR to be 37.3%.)

8. Like the net present value evaluation technique, the internal rate of return technique considers both the time value of money and *all* of a project's cash flows. It will result in the same wealth-maximizing decision as the net present value technique *except* when mutually exclusive projects are being evaluated (or when there is more than one sign change in the cash flow stream as mentioned in a previous frame). Consider again Projects Venus and Mercury. The cash flows are summarized again below.

Year	Project Venus	Project Mercury
0	−$10,000	−$20,000
1	$ 4,000	$ 6,000
2	$ 4,000	$ 6,000
3	$ 4,000	$ 6,000
4	$ 4,000	$10,000
5	$ 4,000	$15,000

The net present value of Venus was calculated to be $4,419.20 while the net present value of Mercury was $9,276.80. We determined the internal rate of return of Venus to be between 28% and 30% or, with the use of a financial calculator, 28.6%. The internal rate of return of Mercury is calculated to be 26.5%. Therefore, if we were to rank these two projects on the basis of their internal rates of return, Venus would be selected over Mercury. However, Mercury clearly has the higher net present value, thereby contributing more to the value of the firm. The conflict between the two evaluation techniques arises in this instance because the projects are of different sizes. Project Mercury, which requires a $20,000 investment compared to Project Venus' $10,000 investment, is twice as large as Venus. Thus, while the firm *is* earning a 28.6% return on Project Venus, that is a 28.6% return on a $10,000 investment. The firm is better off earning 26.5% on the larger $20,000 investment.

Even if the projects are the same size, it is incorrect to simply rank the projects based on their internal rates of return. Consider the information supplied for Projects Mars and Uranus, both of which have a required rate of return of 10%.

Year	Project Mars	Project Uranus
0	−$35,000	−$35,000
1	$10,000	$ 5,000
2	$10,000	$ 5,000
3	$10,000	$10,000
4	$10,000	$16,000
5	$10,000	$18,000
	NPV = $2,908	NPV = $3,296
	IRR = 13.2%	IRR = 12.9%

Project Uranus has a higher net present value than Project Mars, yet its internal rate of return is less. If a decision maker were to rank the projects on the basis of their internal rates of return, he would select Project Mars, which is not the wealth-maximizing decision. This conflict occurs because of the difference in the timing of the cash flows. As long as the required rate of return is relatively low, the firm is better off investing in Project Uranus, which has larger cash flows even though they occur later on down the road. At higher required rates of return, however, the larger, later cash flows would not be worth the wait since the opportunity cost of not having the funds to invest sooner is higher. In fact, if we had used 12% rather than 10% as a discount rate, Project Mars would have the higher net present value.

The internal rate of return technique can still be used in these cases and result in the correct decision, but it is the *incremental* internal rate of return that must be calculated. Returning to the examples of Projects Venus and Mercury, we will calculate the incremental cash flows, i.e., the difference in the cash flows that the firm experiences by investing in the larger project, Project Mercury.

Year	Project Venus	Project Mercury	Mercury – Venus
0	–$10,000	–$20,000	–$10,000
1	$ 4,000	$ 6,000	$ 2,000
2	$ 4,000	$ 6,000	$ 2,000
3	$ 4,000	$ 6,000	$ 2,000
4	$ 4,000	$10,000	$ 6,000
5	$ 4,000	$15,000	$11,000

? Calculate the incremental cash flows that a firm experiences by investing in Uranus, the project offering larger but later cash flows, instead of Mars.

Answer:

Year	Uranus – Mars
0	0
1	–$5,000
2	–$5,000
3	0
4	$6,000
5	$8,000

9.   Once the incremental cash flows involved with investing in the larger or the later paying project are determined, we can calculate the internal rate of return of these cash flows to determine if the larger or later paying project should be undertaken over the smaller or sooner paying project. If the incremental internal rate of return is greater than the required rate of return, the extra cost of the larger project or the extra wait on the later paying project is worth it. If the incremental internal rate of return is less than the required rate of return, the firm should invest in the smaller project or the project that offers the more immediate cash flows.

The incremental cash flows for "Mercury – Venus" were –$10,000, $2,000, $2,000, $2,000, $6,000, and $11,000, respectively, so the equation that must be solved for the incremental internal rate of return is as follows:

$$\$2,000(\text{PVIFA}_{irr,3}) + \$6,000(\text{PVIF}_{irr,4}) + \$11,000(\text{PVIF}_{irr,5}) - \$10,000 = 0.$$

If a financial calculator is unavailable, trial and error must be used.

  Using 15%: $2,000(2.2832) + $6,000(0.5718) + $11,000(0.4972) – $10,000 = $3,466.40

This indicates that 15% is too low a choice, so we now try 20%.

  Using 20%: $2,000(2.1065) + $6,000(0.4823) + $11,000(0.4019) – $10,000 = $1,527.70

Therefore, 20% is also too low a choice. Next we try 25%.

  Using 25%: $2,000(1.9520) + $6,000(0.4096) + $11,000(0.3277) – $10,000 = –$33.70

Since the net present value using a 25% discount rate is a very small negative number, we know that the incremental internal rate of return is approximately 25%. Since this exceeds the 12% required rate of return for Projects Venus and Mercury, it is worth the additional $10,000 to invest in Mercury over Venus. Note that this is the same conclusion that we came to when observing the net present values of the two projects.

? Calculate the incremental internal rate of return for the cash flows of "Uranus − Mars" and determine which project should be selected if the required rate of return is 10%.

Answers: Incremental IRR = 11.6%. Since this exceeds the required rate of return of 10%, it is worth it for the firm to wait for the larger but later cash flows associated with Project Uranus.

$$-\$5,000(PVIFA_{irr,\,2}) + 0(PVIF_{irr,\,3}) + \$6,000(PVIF_{irr,4}) + \$8,000(PVIF_{irr,5}) - 0 = 0$$

If a financial calculator is unavailable, you can use trial and error. Some sample trials are shown below.

Using 15%: −$5,000(1.6257) + 0 + $6,000(0.5718) + $8,000(0.4972) − 0 = −$720.10

Since the net present value using a 15% discount rate is negative, we know that the internal rate of return must be less than 15%.

Using 10%: −$5,000(1.7355) + 0 + $6,000(0.6830) + $8,000(0.6209) − 0 = $387.70

Now the net present value is positive. A larger discount rate is required for a zero net present value.

Using 11%: −$5,000(1.7125) + 0 + $6,000(0.6355) + $8,000(0.5935) − 0 = $137.70

The discount rate of 11% is still slightly too low.

Using 12%: −$5,000(1.6901) + 0 + $6,000(0.6355) + $8,000(0.5674) − 0 = −$98.30

We have determined that the internal rate of return lies between 11% and 12%. Using a financial calculator, we can obtain an answer of 11.6%. Regardless, we know that the incremental IRR is greater than the 10% required rate of return, indicating that it is worth the wait for the later but larger cash flows associated with Project Uranus.

10. A third evaluation technique that considers all of a project's cash flows as well as the time value of money is the profitability index. The **profitability index (PI)** is the ratio of the present value of the cash inflows of a project to the present value of the cash outflows of a project, or PI = PV of inflows/PV of outflows. To illustrate, consider the cash flows associated with Project Virgo, shown below:

Year	Cash Flow
0	−$5,000
1	$3,000
2	$3,000
3	$3,000
4	$2,000

Assuming a 12% discount rate, the present value of the cash inflows is calculated as follows:

$$PV = \$3,000(PVIFA_{12\%,3}) + \$2,000(PVIF_{12\%,3})$$
$$= \$3,000(2.4018) + \$2,000(0.6355) = \$8,476.40.$$

Since the only cash outflow is the initial investment of $5,000, the profitability index is equal to $8,476.40/$5,000 = 1.70. If the profitability index is greater than one, the present value of the cash inflows exceeds the present value of the cash outflows, and the project should be accepted. If the profitability index is less than one, the present value of the cash inflows is less than the present value of the cash outflows, indicating that the project should be rejected. A profitability index of 1.0 would occur if the net present value were zero. Therefore, the firm would be indifferent about the project. Project Virgo, with a profitability index of 1.70, should be undertaken. Mutually exclusive projects cannot be evaluated using the profitability index unless an incremental profitability index is calculated using the incremental cash flows of the two projects, just as was necessary with the internal rate of return evaluation technique.

? Use the profitability index technique to decide whether Project Leo, which has the following expected cash flows, should be accepted (assume a required rate of return of 12%).

Year	Cash Flow
0	−$15,500
1	$ 5,000
2	$ 5,000
3	$ 5,000
4	$ 5,000

Answer: No.
PI = 0.9797, which is less than 1.0, so Project Leo should be rejected.

$$PV \text{ of cash inflows} = \$5,000(PVIFA_{12\%,4})$$
$$= \$5,000(3.037) = \$15,185$$
$$PI = \$15,185/\$15,500 = 0.9797$$

11. One problem that arises when evaluating mutually exclusive projects, regardless of which evaluation technique is used, is evaluating projects with unequal lives. For example, assume a bakery is considering replacing an existing donut press with one of two new presses. One has an expected life of 4 years, will cost $18,000, and is expected to generate after-tax operating cash flows, which includes the maintenance expenses on the press, of $7,200 a year. The second press will cost $20,000, has an expected life of 6 years, and is expected to generate after-tax operating cash flows of $6,000 a year. The firm requires a 14% return on its investment regardless of which machine is purchased. If we were to calculate the net present value of the cash flows as stated, we would be ignoring the fact that the first press will have to be replaced more frequently than the second press. One versatile method of incorporating this fact into the analysis is called the **equivalent annual annuity approach**. There are three steps involved in using this approach:

Step 1: Find the net present value of each, given its expected life.

Step 2: Translate this value into an annual payment; i.e., determine what annual annuity is equivalent to the time zero value determined in Step 1.

Step 3: Determine the present value of the annuity payment calculated in Step 2, assuming that it will be received in perpetuity so long as the machine continues to be replaced.

Applying these steps to the problem stated above, we get:
Step 1: We find the net present value of each press, using four periods to evaluate press 1 and 6 periods to evaluate press 2.

$$NPV_1 = \$7,200(PVIFA_{14\%,4}) - \$18,000$$
$$= \$7,200(2.9137) - \$18,000 = \$2,978.64$$
$$NPV_2 = \$6,000(PVIFA_{14\%,6}) - \$20,000$$
$$= \$6,000(3.8887) - \$20,000 = \$3,332.20$$

Step 2: We translate each of the net present values into equal payments over the life of the press. Since PV = payment($PVIFA_{i\%,n}$), payment = $PV/PVIFA_{i\%,n}$.

$$payment_1 = \$2978.64/2.9137 = \$1,022.29$$
$$payment_2 = \$3332.20/3.8887 = \$856.89$$

Therefore, choosing press 1 will add value to the firm that is equivalent to receiving $1,022.29 a year for each of the 4 years of the press' life, while choosing press 2 will add value to the firm that is equivalent to receiving $856.89 a year for each of the 6 years of the press' life.

Step 3: If we assume that the firm will continue to replace whichever press it chooses, then the annual payment calculated in Step 2 will be a perpetuity. The present value of a perpetuity is found by dividing the payment by the required rate of return, so

$$PV_1 = \$1,022.29/0.14 = \$7,302.07$$
$$PV_2 = \$856.89/0.14 = \$6,120.64$$

Press 1 should be selected since it offers the highest present value. Note that this decision would not have been obvious by simply comparing the net present values of the two presses as calculated in Step 1.

? The Tom Tailor Company is expanding and needs to purchase more commercial sewing machines. It is considering two different models. The first model will cost $3,500, has an expected life of 3 years, and is expected to produce net cash flows of $2,300 a year. The second model will cost $5,000, has an expected life of 5 years, and is expected to produce net cash flows of $2,000 a year. The firm requires a 10% return on this investment. Which model should be purchased?

Answer: The first model should be purchased.
Since the two machines have different lives, it is necessary to use the equivalent annual annuity approach. The first step involves finding the net present value of each machine over its expected life.

$$NPV_1 = \$2,300(PVIFA_{10\%,3}) - \$3,500 = \$2,300(2.4869) - \$3,500 = \$2,219.87$$
$$NPV_2 = \$2,000(PVIFA_{10\%,5}) - \$5,000 = \$2,000(3.1699) - \$5,000 = \$1,339.80$$

We next find the annual annuity that is equivalent to the net present value for each machine.

$$pmt_1 = \$2,219.87/2.4869 = \$892.63$$
$$pmt_2 = \$1,339.80/3.1699 = \$422.66$$

Assuming that whichever machine is selected will be replaced in perpetuity, we calculate the present value of the payments calculated in Step 2, assuming they will be received so long as the machine continues to be replaced.

$$PV_1 = \$892.63/0.10 = \$8,926.30$$
$$PV_2 = \$422.66/0.10 = \$4,226.60$$

Since the present value of the stream of perpetual payments associated with machine 1 is greater than that of machine 2, machine 1 should be selected.

 Apply It

1. A machine will cost the Andrews Company $44,000. In addition, another $5,000 is needed to modify the machine for the specific needs of the Andrews Company. The machine will increase revenues by $8,000 a year. Labor costs will decrease by $10,000 a year. The machine will be depreciated over 7 years using straight-line depreciation. (Ignore the half-year convention.) The firm expects to be able to sell the machine at the end of the seventh year for $5,000. The Andrews Company pays taxes at a marginal rate of 34%.

   a. What are the initial cash flows associated with this project? (Frame 1)

   b. What are the annual operating cash flows associated with this project? (Frame 2)

   c. What are the terminal year cash flows associated with this project? (Frame 3)

   d. What is the payback period of this project? (Frame 4)

   e. Use the net present value evaluation technique to determine whether this machine should be purchased, assuming that Andrews requires a 15% return from it. (Frame 5)

2. Use the incremental internal rate of return methodology to determine which of the following two mutually exclusive projects should be undertaken. The required rate of return is 16%. (Frame 9)

Year	Project Saturn	Project Neptune
0	−$10,000	−$50,000
1	$ 5,000	$20,000
2	$ 5,000	$25,000
3	$ 8,000	$25,000
	IRR = 29.9%	IRR = 18.1%

3. A machine will cost a firm $40,000. The machine is not expected to affect revenues, but it is expected to decrease labor costs by $25,000 per year. The machine is 5-year property and will be depreciated using straight-line depreciation. (Ignore the half-year convention.) It is expected that the machine can be sold for $7,000 at the end of 5 years. The firm is in the 34% marginal tax bracket, and it requires a 14% return on this project.

   a. Calculate the initial, annual operating, and terminal year cash flows associated with the investment in this machine. (Frames 1, 2, and 3)

   b. Calculate the payback period for the machine. (Frame 4)

   c. Use the net present value evaluation technique to determine if the machine should be purchased. (Frame 5)

   d. Use the internal rate of return evaluation technique to determine if the machine should be purchased. (Frame 7)

   e. Use the profitability index evaluation technique to determine if the machine should be purchased. (Frame 10)

4. Davis Realty and Insurance Company is considering the purchase of a new computer system for its three offices. The system will cost $28,000. There will be an additional $7,000 needed for installation and set-up. The firm's current system can be sold for $5,000. The new system will allow the firm to access a broader information base and to provide more services for its clientelle. It is expected that revenues will be

increased by $10,000 a year due to this advantage. The system will be depreciated over 7 years using straight-line depreciation. (Ignore the half-year convention.) It is expected to have a salvage value of $6,000 at the end of this period. Davis pays taxes at a marginal rate of 28% and requires a 15% return on this investment.

  a. Calculate the initial, annual operating, and terminal cash flows associated with the system. (Frames 1, 2, and 3)

  b. Use the net present value evaluation technique to determine if the system should be purchased. (Frame 5)

  c. Use the internal rate of return evaluation technique to determine if the system should be purchased. (Frame 7)

  d. Use the profitability index evaluation technique to determine if the system should be purchased. (Frame 10)

5. Two machines have the following expected cash flows.

Year	Machine A	Machine B
0	−$100,000	−$25,000
1	$ 50,000	$15,000
2	$ 50,000	$15,000
3	$ 50,000	$15,000
	IRR = 23.4%	IRR = 36.3%

The machines are mutually exclusive, and the firm requires a 16% return on this investment.

  a. Use the net present value evaluation technique to determine which machine should be purchased. (Frame 6)

  b. Use the correct internal rate of return methodology to determine which machine should be purchased. (Frame 9)

6. The Easy Reader Company provides bulletin board services to hotels in three cities. The proprietor has decided to purchase a fax machine that will save her travel costs as well as employee salaries. She is trying to decide between two different models. The cheaper model will cost $3,000 and will probably last 3 years with heavy usage. The more expensive model will cost $5,500, but it is expected to last 6 years. In either case, the net annual cash flows from the investment will be $6,200 due to the cost savings. The proprietor requires a 12% return on any investment she makes in the business. Which model should she purchase? (Frame 11)

Apply It Answers

1. a.

Machine cost	−$44,000
Modifications	−$ 5,000
Total	−$49,000

  b.

Change in revenues	$ 8,000	
−Change in cash expenses	−$10,000	
Change in before-tax cash flow	$18,000	
−Change in depreciation	$ 7,000	($49,000/7)
Change in taxable income	$11,000	
−Change in taxes (@ 34%)	$ 3,740	
Change in net income	$ 7,260	
+Change in depreciation	$ 7,000	
Change in after-tax cash flow	$14,260	

c.

Change in cash flow from operations	$14,260
Sale of machine	$ 5,000
Tax on gain on sale of machine	−$ 1,700
Total	$17,560

d. $14,260 \times 3 = \$42,780$ is recouped after 3 years, leaving $6,220 to be recouped out of the cash flow for year 3. If the cash flows occur evenly throughout the year, $6,220/\$14,260 = 0.43 \approx 0.5$, so the payback period is $3\frac{1}{2}$ years.

e.

$$NPV = \$14,260(PVIFA_{15\%,6}) + \$17,560(PVIF_{15\%,7}) - \$49,000$$

$$= \$14,260(3.7845) + 17,560(0.3759) - \$49,000 = \$11,567.77$$

The project should be accepted since it has a positive net present value.

2.

	Cash Flows			
	Year 0	Year 1	Year 2	Year 3
Neptune − Saturn	−$40,000	$15,000	$20,000	$17,000

The IRR of the incremental project, "Neptune − Saturn" can be found by solving the following equation for IRR:

$$\$15,000(PVIF_{irr,1}) + \$20,000(PVIF_{irr,2}) + \$17,000(PVIF_{irr,3}) - \$40,000 = 0.$$

Using either trial and error or a financial calculator, the incremental IRR is approximately 14%. Since this is less than the 16% required rate of return, the additional investment in the larger project, Neptune, is not worth it, and the firm should invest in the smaller project, Saturn.

3. a. Initial cash flow = cost of the machine = −$40,000

Annual operating cash flows years 1–5:

Change in revenues	0
− Change in cash expenses	−$25,000
Change in before-tax cash flow	$25,000
− Change in depreciation	$ 8,000 ($40,000/5)
Change in taxable income	$17,000
− Change in taxes (@ 34%)	$ 5,780
Change in net income	$11,220
+ Change in depreciation	$ 8,000
Change in after-tax cash flow	$19,220

Terminal year cash flows:

Change in after-tax cash flow from operations	$19,220 (from above)
Sale of machine	$ 7,000
Tax on sale of machine	−$ 2,380
Total	$23,840

b. $38,440 ($19,220 \times 2) of the original investment is recovered in the first 2 years of the project. The remaining $1,560 will be recovered in the next $\frac{1}{10}$ of a year. ($1,560/\$19,220 = 0.08 \approx 0.10$). The payback period is, therefore, $2\frac{1}{10}$ years.

c.

$$NPV = \$19,220(PVIFA_{14\%,4}) + \$23,840(PVIF_{14\%,5}) - \$40,000$$

$$= \$19,220(2.9137) + \$23,840(0.5193) - \$40,000 = \$28,381$$

Since the net present value is positive, the machine should be purchased.

d. To find the internal rate of return, the following equation must be solved for IRR using trial and error:

$$\$19,220(\text{PVIFA}_{irr,4}) + \$23,840(\text{PVIF}_{irr,5}) - \$40,000 = 0$$

Using 15%: $19,220(2.7982) + $23,840(0.4972) − $40,000 = $25,634.65

Using 25%: $19,220(2.3616) + $23,840(0.3277) − $40,000 = $13,202.32

Using 36%: $19,220(1.9658) + $23,840(0.2149) − $40,000 = $3,004.18

Using 40%: $19,220(1.8492) + $23,840(0.1859) − $40,000 = −$26.52

The internal rate of return is between 36% and 40%, and is approximately 40% since the net present value is close to zero at that discount rate. A financial calculator indicates that the internal rate of return is 39.96%. Since this is greater than the required rate of return of 14%, the machine should be purchased.

e. The present value of the cash inflows at the required rate of return of 14% is equal to $19,220(2.9137) + $23,840(0.5921) = $70,117. The profitability index is then $70,117/$40,000 = 1.75. Since this is greater than zero, the project should be accepted.

4. a. Initial cash flow:

Cost of system	−$28,000
Installation	−$ 7,000
Sale of old computer	$ 5,000
Tax on sale	−$ 1,400
Net cash flow	−$31,400

Annual operating cash flows for years 1 – 7:

Change in revenues	$10,000
− Change in cash expenses	0
Change in before-tax cash flow	$10,000
− Change in depreciation	$ 5,000 ($35,000/7)
Change in taxable income	$ 5,000
− Change in taxes (@ 28%)	$ 1,400
Change in net income	$ 3,600
+ Change in depreciation	$ 5,000
Change in after-tax cash flow	$ 8,600

Terminal year cash flow:

Change in cash flow from operations	$ 8,600 (from previous step)
+ Sale of system	$ 6,000
− Tax on sale	$ 1,680
Net cash flow	$12,920

b.

$$\text{NPV} = \$8,600(\text{PVIFA}_{15\%,6}) + \$12,920(\text{PVIF}_{15\%,7}) - \$31,400$$

$$= \$8,600(3.7845) + \$12,920\,(0.3759) - \$31,400 = \$6,003.32$$

Since the system has a positive net present value, it should be purchased.

c. The internal rate of return can be found by solving the following equation for IRR:

$$\$8,600(\text{PVIFA}_{irr,6}) + \$12,920(\text{PVIF}_{irr,7}) - \$31,400 = 0$$

Using 20%: $8,600(3.3255) + $12,920(0.2791) − $31,400 = $805.71

Using 25%: $8,600(2.9514) + $12,920(0.2097) − $31,400 = −$3,309.64

Using 24%: $8,600(3.0205) + $12,920(0.2218) − $31,400 = − $2,558.04

From the tables, the internal rate of return can be established to be between 20 and 24% (a calculator will give an answer of 20.9%); therefore, the system should be undertaken, since the IRR is greater than the required rate of return of 15%.

d. The present value of the cash inflows at the required rate of return of 15% is $8,600(3.7845) + $12,920(0.3759) = $37,403.33. PI = $37,403.33/$31,400 = 1.19. Since the profitability index is greater than 1.0, the system should be purchased.

5. a.

$$NPV_A = \$50,000(PVIFA_{16\%,3}) - \$100,000 = \$50,000(2.2459) - \$100,000 = \$12,295$$

$$NPV_B = \$15,000(PVIFA_{16\%,3}) - \$25,000 = \$15,000(2.2459) - \$25,000 = \$8,689$$

Since machine A will increase the value of the firm the most, it should be the machine purchased.

b. Since the machines are mutually exclusive, we need to find the incremental IRR. First we determine the incremental cash flows; i.e., the cash flows associated with the additional investment in the more expensive machine, machine A.

	Cash Flows			
	Year 0	**Year 1**	**Year 2**	**Year 3**
A − B	−$75,000	$35,000	$35,000	$35,000

So for the additional $75,000 invested in machine A, the firm will realize additional net cash flows of $35,000 a year. The internal rate of return of the incremental investment is determined by solving the following equation for IRR:

$$\$35,000(PVIFA_{irr,3}) - \$75,000 = 0.$$

Since this is an equation with one unknown, we can solve for the present value interest factor of an annuity and estimate the interest rate from the tables.

$$PVIFA_{irr,3} = \$75,000/\$35,000 = 2.1429$$

Looking this factor up in the table, we determine the IRR to be between 18% and 19%. If a financial calculator is available, the IRR can be calculated to be 18.9%. Since this is greater than the 16% required rate of return, the additional investment in machine A is worth it, and machine A should be undertaken.

6. Since the two fax machines have unequal lives, the equivalent annual annuity method must be used. First we must determine the net present value of each machine based on its expected life.

$$NPV_1 = \$6,200(PVIFA_{12\%,3}) - \$3,000$$

$$= \$6,200(2.4018) - \$3,000 = \$11,891.16$$

$$NPV_2 = \$6,200(PVIFA_{12\%,6}) - \$5,500$$

$$= \$6,200(4.1114) - \$5,500 = \$19,990.68$$

Next we must translate these net present values into equivalent annual annuities.

$$\text{payment}_1 = \$11,891.16/2.4018 = \$4,950.94$$

$$\text{payment}_2 = \$19,990.68/4.1114 = \$4,862.26$$

If the machine selected is replaced each time it wears out, the machine will produce discounted cash flows that are equivalent to the payments calculated above for that machine indefinitely. We therefore find the present value of a perpetual stream of the payments associated with each machine.

$$PV_1 = \$4,950.94/0.12 = \$41,257.83$$

$$PV_2 = \$4,862.26/0.12 = \$40,518.83$$

Since the present value of the cash flows associated with the infinite replacement of the first fax machine is higher, the first fax machine, i.e., the less expensive model, should be purchased.

LEVERAGE AND CAPITAL STRUCTURE

This module provides an introduction to the concepts of leverage and capital structure. The amount of leverage that a firm has can result from both its fixed operating expenses and its fixed financing costs. Both the degree of operating leverage and the degree of financial leverage are discussed, and the methods used to calculate each are presented. The concept of capital structure, which refers to the amount of debt, preferred stock, and common equity financing that a firm uses, is introduced along with major conflicting viewpoints regarding its importance in business management. The EBIT/EPS analysis methodology is presented as one tool that can be used in the capital structure decision-making process.

Equations introduced in this module

$$DOL = \frac{\%\ change\ EBIT}{\%\ change\ sales} = \frac{sales - variable\ costs}{EBIT}$$

$$q = \frac{f}{p - c}$$

$$DFL = \frac{\%\ change\ EPS}{\%\ change\ EBIT} = \frac{EBIT}{EBIT - I - \dfrac{PfD}{1 - tax\ rate}}$$

$$DTL = \frac{\%\ change\ EPS}{\%\ change\ sales} = DOL \times DFL$$

$$\frac{(EBIT - I_{plan\,1})(1 - tax\ rate) - PfD_{plan\,1}}{common\ shares\ outstanding_{plan\,1}} = \frac{(EBIT - I_{plan\,2})(1 - tax\ rate) - PfD_{plan\,2}}{common\ shares\ outstanding_{plan\,2}}$$

1. The risk associated with a firm can be separated into two broad categories: **Business risk**, which is the uncertainty of the operating profits (EBIT) of a firm, and **financial risk**, to which the common stockholders of a firm are exposed when a firm uses debt or preferred stock to finance part of its operations. Business risk is higher the more uncertain the demand for a firm's product or services, the selling price per unit, and/or the cost of goods sold. The greater the amount of the fixed costs of operations, the greater the business risk will be as well. This is due to the fact that the firm must cover these fixed costs even if sales drop off due to a sluggish economy. For example, suppose that a shoemaker employs elves to help make the shoes that he sells. He pays the elves a fixed wage per shoe. If sales decline, he simply employs fewer elves or pays each elf less since the number of shoes he needs to manufacture is less. If the shoemaker decided to replace these elves with a machine, he would have to cover the cost of the machine regardless of how many shoes he could sell. He has increased the fixed costs of his operations. This is referred to as his **operating leverage**. As is the case with any type of leverage, when a firm's operating leverage increases so does the risk of the firm. Leverage has both its advantages and its disadvantages. In the example described previously, if the shoemaker is selling a lot of shoes and his operating leverage is high (i.e., he has replaced the elves with a machine), he can keep all the profits once he has covered the fixed expenses associated with the machine. If he had continued to use the elves, he would have to pay the elves for each shoe regardless of how many he sold, so he would never be able to be quite as profitable as he could once he has covered the fixed costs of the machine. On the other hand, as mentioned above, if his sales declined, he could simply lay off some of the elves, whereas if he had replaced the elves with a machine, the fixed costs associated with the machine would continue regardless of the sales level. The **degree of operating leverage (DOL)** measures the percentage change in operating profit that will be realized for each percentage change in sales, given a beginning level of sales.

$$DOL = \frac{\% \text{ change EBIT}}{\% \text{ change sales}}$$

Thus, if we calculate the degree of operating leverage at a sales level of $50,000 to be 2.0, and we expect sales to increase to $75,000 (a 50% increase), we can expect that the firm's operating profit will increase by 100% (2 × 50%).

? The Galpin Company currently has sales of $200,000 and operating profit of $70,000. The degree of operating leverage at the $200,000 sales leverage has been calculated to be 2.50. If Galpin expects its sales to increase to $275,000 next year, what can it expect its operating profit to be?

Answer: $135,625.
The expected change in sales is ($275,000 − $200,000)/$200,000 = 37.5%. Since the DOL is given as 2.50, the expected change in operating profit should be 2.5 times this or 93.75%. (2.5 × 37.5% = 93.75%). Therefore, the expected level of operating profit at the $275,000 sales level should be ($70,000)(1.9375) = $135,625.

2. An algebraic manipulation of the equation for the degree of operating leverage yields the following formula:

$$DOL = \frac{\text{sales} - \text{variable costs}}{\text{EBIT}}.$$

Thus, if we know that a firm has $50,000 in sales, $10,000 in fixed operating expenses, and that variable costs are 50% of sales, the degree of operating leverage of the firm at $50,000 in sales is calculated as follows:

$$DOL = \frac{\$50,000 - \$25,000}{\$50,000 - \$25,000 - \$10,000} = \frac{\$25,000}{\$15,000} = 1.67.$$

If we expect sales to increase to $60,000, which is a 20% increase ($60,000 − $50,000)/$50,000 = 0.20), then we can expect operating profit to increase by 20% × 1.67 or 33.4%. Therefore, the expected operating profit is $15,000 × 1.334 = $20,010.

Remember that the DOL calculated above is the degree of operating leverage *at a sales level of $50,000*. If sales increase, the DOL will decrease, all else equal. For example, if sales do increase to $60,000, the new DOL will be as follows:

$$DOL = \frac{\$60,000 - \$30,000}{\$60,000 - \$30,000 - \$10,000} = \frac{\$25,000}{\$15,000} = 1.50.$$

This means that an increase of 20% from the new $60,000 sales level will increase operating profit by only 30% (20% × 1.50 = 30%).

? The Belmont Corporation has $500,000 in sales and $300,000 in fixed operating expenses. Variable costs are 30% of sales. If sales were to increase to $800,000, what would Belmont's operating profit be?

Answer: $260,000.

$$DOL = \frac{\$500,000 - \$150,000}{\$500,000 - \$150,000 - \$300,000} = \frac{\$350,000}{\$50,000} = 7.0.$$

The expected percentage change in sales is ($800,000 − $500,000)/$500,000 = 60%, so the expected percentage change in operating profit is 7 × 60% = 420%. The expected level of operating profit is the current level of $50,000 times 1 plus the expected percentage increase, or $50,000(5.20) = $260,000.

3.   The greater the fixed operating costs of the firm, the higher the **breakeven point**, which is the volume of sales at which the total revenues equals the total costs. This is the point at which the operating profit will be equal to zero. Since this is the point at which sales − variable costs − fixed operating costs = zero, and sales = volume × unit price and variable costs = volume × unit costs, we can calculate the breakeven point as follows:

$$qp - qc - f = 0$$

$$q(p - c) = f,$$

$$so \ q = \frac{f}{p - c}$$

where q is the number of units sold, p is the selling price per unit, c is the variable cost per unit, and f is the fixed operating costs. As an example, suppose that you are deciding whether you should market hand-painted marionettes. Each marionette will cost you $2, and you believe you can sell the marionettes for $8 apiece. Your fixed operating costs will be $2,000. Your break-even point is then $2,000/($8.00 − $2.00) = 500 marionettes. If you sell less than 500 of the puppets, you will lose money; if you sell more than 500, you will earn a profit.

? Josie has decided to try to market some beaded barrettes that she designs. Each barrette costs her $1.75 to make, with materials and labor included. Her fixed costs include her registration fees at the various craft shows at which she will sell her wares as well as her beading looms. She estimates these costs to be $1,000. How many barrettes must she sell to break even if she can sell each barrette for $6.50?

Answer: 211 barrettes.

$$q = \$1,000/(\$6.50 - \$1.75) = 210.5$$

Since Josie cannot sell one-half a barrette, she must sell 211 to break even.

4. A firm's financial risk increases with the increased use of securities that require fixed payments, i.e., debt and preferred stock, to fund the firm's activities. The greater the use of these types of securities, the greater the risk that the firm will be unable to make the required payments. (Even though nonpayment of preferred dividends cannot cause a firm to go bankrupt, certain benefits, such as limited voting rights, may accrue to the preferred stockholders if dividends are missed too many consecutive times.) Since interest and preferred dividend payments are not considered when calculating EBIT, financial leverage does not affect the operating profit of a firm. It does, however, affect the earnings available to common shareholders. The **degree of financial leverage (DFL)** is the percentage change in the earnings per share for each percentage change in operating profit, given a beginning level of sales.

$$DFL = \frac{\% \text{ change EPS}}{\% \text{ change EBIT}}$$

Therefore, if a firm has a degree of financial leverage of 1.55 and is expecting operating profits to increase by 100%, then it can expect earnings per share to increase by 155% ($1.55 \times 100\%$).

? The Galpin Company is expecting its operating profit to increase from $70,000 to $135,625. Its degree of financial leverage at its current sales level is 1.30, and its current earnings per share is $0.82. What is Galpin's expected earnings per share if its operating profit increases to the expected level?

Answer: $1.82.
The percentage change in operating profit is 93.75% [($135,625 − $70,000)/$70,000]. Since the degree of financial leverage is 1.30, earnings per share should increase by 1.3 times as much as the percentage change in operating profit. $1.3 \times 93.75\% = 121.875\%$. Therefore, the new earnings per share will be $0.82(2.21875) = $1.82.

5. Using algebraic manipulation, the formula for the degree of financial leverage can also be expressed as follows:

$$DFL = \frac{EBIT}{EBIT - I - \dfrac{PfD}{1 - \text{tax rate}}}$$

where I is the interest expense and PfD represents the preferred dividends. Since preferred dividends are not tax deductible, we divide the amount needed to pay them by "1 − tax rate" in order to determine how much is needed *before* taxes in order for the firm to have enough *after-tax* dollars to pay them.

Suppose a firm has sales of $1,000,000, fixed operating costs of $200,000, and a variable cost ratio of 40%. Additionally, the firm pays $50,000 in interest expenses and will pay $5,000 in preferred dividends. The firm is in the 40% marginal tax bracket. We can calculate its degree of financial leverage as follows:

$$DFL = \frac{\$1,000,000 - \$200,000 - \$400,000}{\$1,000,000 - \$200,000 - \$400,000 - \$50,000 - \dfrac{\$6,000}{1-0.4}}$$

$$= \frac{\$400,000}{\$400,000 - \$50,000 - \dfrac{\$6,000}{1-0.4}}$$

$$= \frac{\$400,000}{\$340,000} = 1.18.$$

If the firm's operating profit increases from $400,000 to $600,000, which is a 50% increase, then its earnings per share will increase by 1.18 × 50% = 59%.

? The Taggert Corporation has sales of $800,000, fixed operating costs of $100,000, and a variable cost ratio of 50%. Additionally, the firm pays $80,000 in interest expense and is in the 45% marginal tax bracket. At the current sales level, its earnings per share is $1.58. If its sales were to increase to $1,000,000, what would its earnings per share be?

Answer: $2.30.

The current level of operating profit is $800,000 − $100,000 − $400,000 = $300,000. The degree of financial leverage is $300,000/($300,000 − $80,000) = 1.36. If sales increase to $1,000,000, operating profit will increase to $1,000,000 − $100,000 − $500,000 = $400,000. (The fixed costs of $100,000 do not change with the level of sales.) This is an increase of 33⅓% ([$400,000 − $300,000]/$300,000 = 0.33333). The degree of financial leverage indicates that for each percentage increase in operating profit, earnings per share will increase by 1.36 times as much, which means that in this case earnings per share will increase by 1.36 × 0.33333 = 45.33%. The new earnings per share will be $1.58(1.4533) = $2.30.

6. The effects of financial leverage can be observed by doing an EBIT/EPS analysis. This analysis depicts the effect of changes in financial leverage on the earnings per share of the firm. For example, assume that a firm needs to raise $1 million, and it can do so either by selling 100,000 new shares of common stock for $10 a share or by issuing debt that has a 9% coupon. Further assume that the firm is currently financed with all equity and that there are 500,000 shares outstanding. To examine the effects of the two financing plans on the earnings per share of the firm, we first select two hypothetical levels of operating profit and calculate the earnings per share at each level under each of the two plans. For the purposes of this illustration, we will use EBIT = 0 and EBIT = $5 million. The interest expense under the new stock plan will be 0, and the interest expense under the debt plan will be 0.09($1,000,000) = $90,000. The number of shares outstanding under the new stock plan will be 600,000 while the number of shares outstanding under the debt plan will remain at 500,000. We will assume a 40% tax rate.

	New Common Stock		**Debt**	
EBIT	0	$5,000,000	0	$5,000,000
−Interest	0	0	$90,000	90,000
EBT	0	$5,000,000	−$90,000	$4,910,000
−Tax	0	$2,000,000	−$36,000°	$1,964,000
EAT	0	$3,000,000	−$54,000	$2,946,000
÷ shares outstanding	600,000	600,000	500,000	500,000
EPS	0	$ 5.00	−$ 0.108	$ 5.892

°The negative tax dollars represents a tax savings since before-tax income is negative. This loss can be carried back or forward to offset taxable income in other years.

It can be observed that at higher levels of operating profit, the use of debt results in a higher earnings per share than the use of equity financing. However, if operating profit is low, debt financing will yield a lower earnings per share than will equity financing. Since the relationship between EBIT and EPS is linear, we can depict this graphically. We have established the two points necessary to plot each financing plan above.

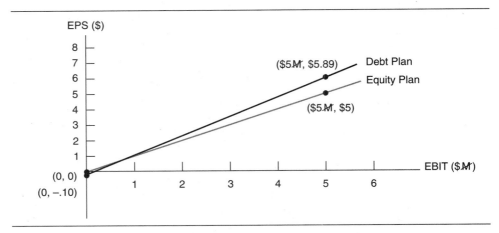

? The Teller Company needs to raise $500,000. It can sell 20,000 new shares at $25 per share, or it can raise the money by issuing bonds with a coupon rate of 10%. The firm is currently financed entirely with common equity, and there are 150,000 shares outstanding. Teller is in a 25% tax bracket. Use hypothetical EBIT levels of 0 and $1,000,000 and develop an EBIT/EPS graph depicting the two plans.

Answer:

	Equity Plan		Debt Plan	
EBIT	0	$1,000,000	0	$1,000,000
−Interest	0	0	$ 50,000	$ 50,000
EBT	0	$1,000,000	− $ 50,000	$ 950,000
−Tax	0	$ 250,000	− $ 12,500°	$ 237,500
EAT	0	$ 750,000	− $ 37,500	$ 712,500
÷ shares outstanding	170,000	170,000	150,000	150,000
EPS	0	$ 4.41	− $ 0.25	$ 4.75

°The negative tax dollars represents a tax savings since before-tax income is negative. This loss can be carried back or forward to offset taxable income in other years.

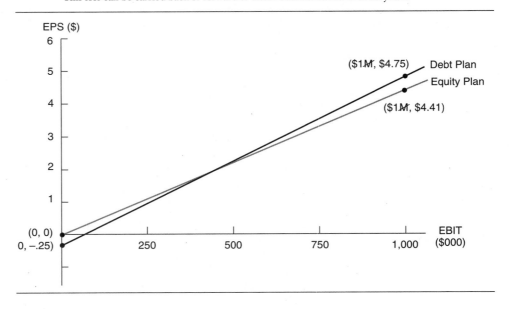

7. We can calculate the exact point at which the two lines representing the two plans cross algebraically. This point is sometimes referred to as the *indifference point*, but that is really a misnomer since a firm should *not* be indifferent between the two financing plans at this point. Note that in the example in the above frame, the equity plan provides the higher earnings per share at all levels of operating profit below the point of intersection, while the debt plan provides the higher level of earnings per share at all levels of operating profit above the point of intersection. If operating profit is exactly at the level indicated for the point of intersection, *equity* should be the choice based on this analysis since it is the less risky alternative for the shareholders and, for the same level of earnings, the less risky alternative should be selected.

Since the point of intersection is the point at which earnings per share for the two plans are equal, we express earnings per share in terms of operating profit and set the two plans equal to one another as follows:

$$\frac{(\text{EBIT})(1-0.40)}{600,000} = \frac{(\text{EBIT}-\$90,000)(1-0.40)}{500,000}.$$

The numerator of each side is a shorthand calculation of the after-tax income of the firm under each plan. The denominator of each side is the number of shares outstanding under each plan. Thus, each side of the equation represents the earnings per share under that plan. We cross multiply to begin to solve for EBIT.

$$300,000\text{EBIT} = 360,000\text{EBIT} - \$32,400,000,000$$

$$60,000\text{EBIT} = \$32,400,000,000$$

$$\text{EBIT} = \$540,000$$

Based on this analysis, if operating profit is expected to be less than or equal to $540,000, the equity plan should be undertaken. If operating profit is expected to be greater than $540,000, the debt plan should be chosen since it will provide the firm with the higher earnings per share.

? Calculate the point of intersection for the two plans that the Teller Company is considering. If the operating profit is expected to be $400,000, which plan should the Teller Company select?

Answer: The lines intersect at an EBIT of $425,000. Since the equity plan produces a higher level of EPS at all levels of operating profit below this, the equity plan should be selected.

$$\frac{\text{EBIT}(1-0.25)}{170,000} = \frac{(\text{EBIT}-\$50,000)(1-0.25)}{150,000}$$

$$112,500\text{EBIT} = 127,500\text{EBIT} - \$6,375,000,000$$

$$15,000\text{EBIT} = \$6,375,000,000$$

$$\text{EBIT} = \$425,000$$

8. The effects of both operating leverage and financial leverage is measured by the **degree of total leverage (DTL)**. The degree of total leverage indicates the percentage change in earnings per share that results from each percentage change in sales.

$$\text{DTL} = \frac{\%\text{ change EPS}}{\%\text{ change sales}}$$

Therefore, if a firm has a degree of total leverage of 3.12 and is expecting sales to increase by 8%, then the expected increase in earnings per share is 24.96% (3.12 × 8%).

? Arapaho Mining Company has a degree of total leverage of 2.90. Sales are currently $3,000,000 and earnings per share is $0.50. If sales were to decrease to $2,700,000, what is the expected level of earnings per share?

Answer: $0.355.

The change in sales is calculated below:

$$\% \text{ change sales} = \frac{\$2,700,000 - \$3,000,000}{\$3,000,000} = -10\%.$$

The change in earnings per share will be 2.90 times this, or 29%. Since this will be a *decrease* of 29%, $0.50(1 − 0.29) = $0.355.

9. The degree of total leverage is actually the product of the degree of operating leverage and the degree of financial leverage.

$$DTL = DOL \times DFL$$

If a firm is in a capital intensive industry and, therefore, has a high degree of operating leverage *and* uses a lot of debt to finance its operations, it will have a very high degree of total leverage. When sales are good, this will produce very attractive levels of earnings per share. However, when sales are poor, earnings per share can plummet. It is generally considered unwise for firms that have high fixed operating costs and, therefore, high degrees of operating leverage, to use high levels of debt to finance the firm since the degree of total leverage would then be excessively high.

? Which of the following firms could afford to have a higher debt ratio, given its degree of operating leverage?
  a. Delta Air Lines
  b. U.S. Steel
  c. McDonald's
  d. Anheuser-Busch

Answer: c.

Of the four choices, McDonald's would be expected to have the lowest level of fixed assets since its profits are derived from its inventory. The airlines industry has high fixed operating costs relative to its variable costs as do manufacturing firms such as U.S. Steel and Anheuser-Busch.

10. Capital structure refers to the manner in which a firm funds its operations, i.e., the proportions of debt, preferred stock, and common equity (retained earnings and new issues of common stock) financing that it uses. It has long been debated among academics whether or not an *optimal* capital structure exists for a firm. A study done by Franco Modigliani and Merton Miller in 1958 concluded that the only optimal capital structure was 100% debt financing since debt was tax deductible. The assumptions under which this conclusion was reached were extremely unrealistic (e.g., no brokerage costs or personal taxes exist), and since that time other researchers, as well as Modigliani and Miller themselves, relaxed some of the assumptions. Personal taxes, increased costs of both debt and equity with increased levels of debt, and bankruptcy costs were incorporated into empirical studies. To date, no formula for an optimal capital structure has been determined. There are indications that a firm may not be financing itself optimally, however. These include a lowering of debt ratings, an increase in the costs of debt and/or equity for the firm, and a decreasing stock price.

In making a capital structure decision, a firm should consider qualitative as well as quantitative factors. The EBIT/EPS analysis can be used to examine the differences in expected income levels under various plans. The riskiness involved must also be considered since use of debt or preferred stock financing exposes common shareholders to more risk. Their required rate of return will, therefore, increase. Control is another factor that may be important. Issuing new common stock will reduce the ownership interests of the existing shareholders, which may be a concern to them. A firm will also want to remain as flexible as possible so that it can take advantage of unexpected opportunities. It should make current financing decisions with regard to potential future financing needs and not close the door to any future financing options, if possible. Issue costs and the speed with which it can obtain the funds may also be factors in some instances.

? How would bankruptcy costs affect the attractiveness of debt financing to the firm?

Answer: The costs of bankruptcy will reduce the attractiveness of debt financing since it will somewhat offset the tax savings associated with the interest deductibility of the debt.

 ## Apply It

1. Why would a firm that has a lot of fixed operating costs relative to its variable costs choose to use less debt financing in its capital structure than a firm that was less capital-intensive? (Frame 1)

2. A firm has a degree of operating leverage of 1.50 and a degree of financial leverage of 2.66. If its sales increases by 15%, by how much should its earnings per share increase? (Frames 8 and 9)

3. A firm has a degree of operating leverage of 1.70 and a degree of financial leverage of 2.78. If sales were to decrease by 25%, what would the earnings per share decrease by? (Frames 8 and 9)

4. The Calico Company has sales of $6 million. Variable costs are 50% of sales, and fixed operating costs are $1 million. The firm also has $500,000 in annual interest expense. Its earnings per share is $1.75.
   a. What is the degree of operating leverage for Calico Company, and what does the number mean? (Frames 1 and 2)
   b. What is the degree of financial leverage for Calico Company, and what does the number mean? (Frames 4 and 5)
   c. What is the degree of total leverage for Calico Company? (Frame 9)
   d. If sales were to increase to $6,900,000, what is the expected level of earnings per share? (Frame 8)

5. The Kinsel Corporation has sales of $12 million. Variable costs are 65% of sales, and fixed operating costs are $2.2 million. The firm pays $500,000 a year in interest. Preferred dividends are $200,000. There are 2 million shares of common stock outstanding, and the firm pays taxes at the marginal rate of 50%.
   a. Calculate the firm's degree of operating leverage. (Frame 2)

b. Calculate the firm's degree of financial leverage. (Frame 5)

c. Calculate the firm's degree of total leverage. (Frame 9)

d. If sales were to decrease to $10.5 million, what would happen to Kinsel's earnings per share? (Frame 8)

6. The American Gothic Corporation needs to raise $5 million to build a new barn, silo, stables, and corral. The firm currently is financed entirely with equity. There are 3 million shares of common stock outstanding. The firm is trying to decide between the following two alternatives for raising the needed funds:

(1) sell 100,000 shares of new common stock at the current market price of $50 a share or

(2) issue bonds that pay a 10% coupon.

American Gothic pays taxes at a marginal rate of 45%.

a. Using hypothetical EBIT levels of 0 and $50 million, develop an EBIT/EPS analysis graph depicting the two alternatives. (Frame 6)

b. Calculate the point of intersection of the two lines in the EBIT/EPS analysis graph. (Frame 7)

c. If American Gothic expects an EBIT of $30 million, which financing plan should it choose based on this analysis? Why? (Frame 7)

d. What other factors should American Gothic consider in making this decision? (Frame 10)

Apply It Answers

1. A firm that has a lot of fixed operating costs relative to its variable costs has a high degree of operating leverage. If, on top of that, the firm uses a lot of debt financing, its degree of total leverage will expose the firm to an excessive level of risk.

2. The degree of total leverage gives us the percentage change in earnings per share for each percentage change in sales. DTL = DOL × DFL = 1.50 × 2.66 = 3.99. If sales increase by 15%, the earnings per share should increase by 3.99 × 15% = 59.85%.

3. The degree of total leverage gives us the percentage change in earnings per share for each percentage change in sales. DTL = DOL × DFL = 1.70 × 2.78 = 4.726. If sales fall by 25%, the earnings per share will fall by 4.726 × 25% = 118.15%.

4. a.

$$DOL = \frac{\text{sales} - \text{variable costs}}{\text{EBIT}} = \frac{\$6,000,000 - \$3,000,000}{\$6,000,000 - \$3,000,000 - \$1,000,000} = 1.50$$

This indicates that for every percentage change in sales, operating profit will change by 1.50% in the same direction.

b.

$$DFL = \frac{\text{EBIT}}{\text{EBIT} - I} = \frac{\$6,000,000 - \$3,000,000 - \$1,000,000}{\$6,000,000 - \$3,000,000 - \$1,000,000 - \$500,000} = 1.33$$

This indicates that for every percentage change in operating profit, earnings per share will change by 1.33% in the same direction.

c. DTL = DOL × DFL = 1.50 × 1.33 = 2.00

    d. The percentage change in sales is ($6,900,000 − $6,000,000)/$6,000,000 = 15%. The degree of total leverage indicates the percentage change in earnings per share for each percentage change in sales, so earnings per share should increase by 2 × 15% = 30%. The current earnings per share is $1.75, and $1.75(1.30) = $2.27.

5. a. Variable costs are 0.65 × $12,000,000 = $7,800,000. The degree of operating leverage is calculated below:

$$\text{DOL} = \frac{\text{sales} - \text{variable costs}}{\text{EBIT}}$$

$$= \frac{\$12,000 - \$7,800,000}{\$12,000 - \$7,800,000 - \$2,200,000} = 2.10.$$

    b.

$$\text{DFL} = \frac{\text{EBIT}}{\text{EBIT} - \text{I} - \dfrac{\text{PfD}}{1 - \text{tax rate}}}$$

$$= \frac{\$12,000,000 - \$7,800,000 - \$2,200,000}{\$12,000,000 - \$7,800,000 - \$2,200,000 - \$500,000 - \dfrac{\$200,000}{(1-0.5)}} = 1.82$$

    c. DTL = DOL × DFL = 2.10 × 1.82 = 3.822

    d. The percentage decrease in sales would be ($10,500,000 − $12,000,000)/$12,000,000 = 12.5%. The degree of total leverage indicates that for every percentage change in sales, earnings per share will change by 3.822 × 12.5% = 47.775%. The current earnings per share is $0.275, as calculated below:

$$\text{EPS} = \frac{\text{Earnings available for common shareholders}}{\text{shares of common stock outstanding}} = \frac{\text{Net income} - \text{preferred dividends}}{\text{shares of common stock outstanding}}$$

$$= \frac{(\$12,000,000 - \$7,800,000 - \$2,200,000 - \$500,000)(1 - 0.50) - \$200,000}{2,000,000} = \$0.275.$$

    If the sales decrease by 12.5%, earnings per share will decrease by 47.77% to $0.275(1 − 0.47775) = $0.144.

6. a.

	Equity Plan		**Debt Plan**	
EBIT	0	$50,000,000	0	$50,000,000
−Interest	0	0	$ 500,000	$ 500,000
EBT	0	$50,000,000	($ 500,000)	$49,500,000
−Taxes	0	$22,500,000	($ 225,000)°	$22,275,000
EAT	0	$27,500,000	($ 275,000)	$27,225,000
÷ shares outstanding	3,100,000	3,100,000	3,000,000	3,000,000
EPS	$0	$ 8.87	$ 0.46	$ 9.08

°This number represents a tax savings.

b.

$$\frac{\text{EBIT}(1-0.45)}{3,100,000} = \frac{(\text{EBIT}-\$500,000)(1-0.45)}{3,000,000}$$

$$1,650,000\,\text{EBIT} = 1,705,000\,\text{EBIT} - 852,500,000,000$$

$$55,000\,\text{EBIT} = 852,500,000,000$$

$$\text{EBIT} = \$15,500,000$$

c. Since the debt plan provides the higher earnings per share at an operating profit of $30 million, it should be chosen.

d. One factor to consider is flexibility, but since the firm is currently financed entirely with equity, it is unlikely that the firm will be so highly leveraged that it has closed a door on any future financing options. If the debt option is selected, existing shareholders will not have to worry about losing their proportionate share of ownership, i.e., their control. The riskiness of the earnings needs to be taken into account as well. Unless earnings are extremely volatile, it is unlikely that they will drop from the expected level of $30 million to the indifference point of $15,500,000. This is further support for the debt option. In addition, issue costs on debt are lower than those on equity, so this factor favors the debt option as well.

INTERNATIONAL FINANCE

In this module you will become familiar with the basic terminology and concepts underlying international finance. Exchange rates are introduced, and their quotations in *The Wall Sreet Journal* are explained. Both spot rates and forward rates are discussed. The Balance of Payments is presented and explained as well as the effects of devaluation and revaluation of a country's currency on that country. Theories used to predict exchange rates, such as purchasing power parity and the International Fisher Effect, are explained. Issues faced by multinational corporations are discussed, along with methods that can be used to reduce their risk exposure.

Equations introduced in this module

$$\text{Amount of foreign currency received per dollar} = \frac{\$1.00}{\text{price of foreign currency in dollars}}$$

1.   An understanding of exchange rates is fundamental to understanding international finance. An **exchange rate** is simply the price of one currency in terms of another. Like all prices, exchange rates are set by supply and demand. If the demand for a certain currency exceeds its supply, the price (exchange rate) of that currency will go up relative to other currencies. Similarly, if the supply of a currency exceeds the demand for it, that currency's exchange rate will fall relative to other currencies. The supply and demand for a country's currency depends on the supply and demand for goods and services produced by that country. If the American demand for Japanese goods and services exceeds the Japanese demand for American goods and services, the Japanese yen will increase in value relative to the American dollar, assuming that exchange rates are allowed to float freely without intervention. (In reality, the central banks of various countries often intervene in order to stabilize their country's currency, as is discussed in a later frame.) Another way of stating this is that the American dollar will fall in value relative to the Japanese yen. The supply and demand for a country's currency and, therefore, the price of that currency, can be affected by many different factors, such as war, weather conditions, natural disasters, and even fads.

?   The primary export of the country of Imogene is a medicine made from a native plant, the miraculeum. Imogene experienced an unusual drought this year that all but destroyed the plant. Assuming that there is no offsetting demand for any of Imogene's other products, what would you expect to happen to the value of Imogene's currency, the rainbo, relative to other currencies?

Answer: The value of the rainbo should fall relative to other currencies since the demand for the currency will decrease with the demand for Imogene's exports.

2.   We can calculate the amount of a specific foreign currency that we will receive for each dollar by dividing $1 by the price of that currency in dollars. For example, if one Belgium franc is currently equal to $0.03175, then we can expect to get $1/$0.03175 = 31.50 Belgium francs for each dollar that we exchange.

?   A British pound is currently equal to $1.5745. How many pounds will you receive if you exchange $100?

Answer: £63.51.
One dollar is equivalent to 0.6351 pounds ($1/$1.5745 = £0.6351), so $100 can be exchanged for 100 × 0.6351 = £63.51.

3.   When we refer to the current price of one currency relative to another currency we are talking about the spot rate. The formal definition of a **spot rate** is the exchange rate quoted when delivery and payment is to be made within two business days. Exhibit 1 below shows spot rates in existence on January 23, 1995. (In the case of currencies for which more than one quotation appears, the first quote is the spot rate.) These quotes, taken from *The Wall Street Journal*, are for interbank transactions of $1 million and more, so an individual seeking to exchange a mere thousand dollars would receive fewer units of any given foreign currency per dollar than the quote would indicate. The quotes in *The Wall Street Journal* are **ask prices**, or the prices for which dealers are willing to sell the currency. Dealers also have a **bid price**, which does not appear in *The Wall Street Journal*. This is the price for which dealers are willing to buy the currency.
　　　The first two columns of quotes (labelled "U.S. $ equiv.") give us the amount of U.S. dollars that would be received for one unit of the foreign currency for the current day and one day prior. One Danish krone could be exhanged for 16 3/4 cents on January 23, 1995, (one krone is equal to $0.1675); it has dropped slightly in value from the previous day

Exhibit 1

CURRENCY TRADING

EXCHANGE RATES
Monday, January 23, 1995

The New York foreign exchange selling rates below apply to trading among banks in amounts of $1 million and more, as quoted at 3 p.m. Eastern time by Bankers Trust Co., Dow Jones Telerate Inc. and other sources. Retail transactions provide fewer units of foreign currency per dollar.

Country	U.S. $ equiv. Mon.	U.S. $ equiv. Fri.	Currency per U.S. $ Mon.	Currency per U.S. $ Fri.
Argentina (Peso)	1.00	1.00	1.00	1.00
Australia (Dollar)	.7680	.7693	1.3022	1.3000
Austria (Schilling)	.09422	.09390	10.61	10.65
Bahrain (Dinar)	2.6524	2.6526	.3770	.3770
Belgium (Franc)	.03209	.03209	31.16	31.17
Brazil (Real)	1.1757790	1.1785504	.85	.85
Britain (Pound)	1.5960	1.5895	.6266	.6291
30-Day Forward	1.5955	1.5892	.6268	.6292
90-Day Forward	1.5949	1.5887	.6270	.6295
180-Day Forward	1.5938	1.5878	.6274	.6298
Canada (Dollar)	.7051	.7029	1.4183	1.4228
30-Day Forward	.7044	.7015	14.2065	1.4255
90-Day Forward	.7016	.6989	1.4253	1.4308
180-Day Forward	.6987	.6959	1.4313	1.4371
Czech. Rep. (Koruna)				
Commercial rate	.0363332	.0363332	27.5230	27.5230
Chile (Peso)	.002452	.002449	407.75	408.35
China (Renminbi)	.118488	.118481	8.4397	8.4402
Colombia (Peso)	.001169	.001171	855.75	854.30
Denmark (Krone)	.1675	.1676	5.9686	5.9650
Ecuador (Sucre)				
Floating rate	.000421	.000421	2374.00	2372.50
Finland (Markka)	.21338	.21372	4.6865	4.6790
France (Franc)	.19114	.19102	5.2317	5.2350
30-Day Forward	.19122	.19109	5.2295	5.2331
90-Day Forward	.19138	.19125	5.2252	5.2289
180-Day Forward	.19168	.19153	5.2171	5.2211
Germany (Mark)	.6612	.6614	1.5123	1.5120
30-Day Forward	.6619	.6620	1.5108	1.5106
90-Day Forward	.6633	.6634	1.5076	1.5073
180-Day Forward	.6660	.6662	1.5015	1.5011
Greece (Drachma)	.004246	.004246	235.50	235.50
Hong Kong (Dollar)	.12926	.12928	7.7363	7.7350
Hungary (Forint)	.0090277	.0090163	110.7702	110.9101
India (Rupee)	.03188	.03188	31.37	31.37
Indonesia (Rupiah)	.0004509	.0004511	2217.62	2216.75
Ireland (Punt)	1.5806	1.5745	.6327	.6351
Israel (Shekel)	.3336	.3335	2.9978	2.9982
Italy (Lira)	.0006304	.0006274	1586.22	1594.00
Japan (Yen)	.010038	.010055	99.63	99.45
30-Day Forward	.010072	.010087	99.28	99.13
90-Day Forward	.010139	.010156	98.63	98.46
180-Day Forward	.010261	.010280	97.46	97.27
Jordan (Dinar)	1.4347	1.4306	.6970	.6990
Kuwait (Dinar)	3.3462	3.3495	.2989	.2986
Lebanon (Pound)	.000608	.000608	1644.00	1644.00
Malaysia (Ringgit)	.3911	.3917	2.5568	2.5528
Malta (Lira)	2.7585	2.7561	.3625	.3628
Mexico (Peso)				
Floating rate	.1748251	.1763668	5.7200	5.6700
Netherland (Guilder)	.5898	.5900	1.6955	1.6948
New Zealand (Dollar)	.6441	.6424	1.5527	1.5568
Norway (Krone)	.1511	.1511	6.6185	6.6195
Pakistan (Rupee)	.0324	.0324	30.83	30.83
Peru (New Sol)	.4596	.4591	2.18	2.18
Philippines (Peso)	.04049	.04057	24.70	24.65
Poland (Zloty)	.41211000	.41350000	2.43	2.42
Portugal (Escudo)	.006398	.006408	156.30	156.05
Saudi Arabia (Riyal)	.26663	.26664	3.7505	3.7504
Singapore (Dollar)	.6900	.6908	1.4493	1.4475
Slovak Rep. (Koruna)	.0325520	.0322789	30.7201	30.9800
South Africa (Rand)				
Commercial rate	.2831	.2829	3.5322	3.5348
Financial rate	.2395	.2421	4.1750	4.1300
South Korea (Won)	.0012621	.0012616	792.35	792.65
Spain (Peseta)	.007599	.007609	131.60	131.43
Sweden (Krona)	.1344	.1347	7.4420	7.4230
Switzerland (Franc)	.7886	.7865	1.2680	1.2715
30-Day Forward	.7902	.7879	1.2656	1.2692
90-Day Forward	.7930	.7909	1.2610	1.2644
180-Day Forward	.7980	.7959	1.2531	1.2564
Taiwan (Dollar)	.038020	.038057	26.30	26.28
Thailand (Baht)	.03987	.03988	25.08	25.08
Turkey (Lira)	.0000245	.0000246	40887.00	40633.89
United Arab (Dirham)	.2723	.2723	3.6728	3.6728
Uruguay (New Peso)				
Financial	.172414	.172414	5.80	5.80
Venezuela (Bolivar)	.00589	.00589	169.87	169.87
— — —				
SDR	1.47008	1.47272	.68024	.67902
ECU	1.25100	1.25010		

Special Drawing Rights (SDR) are based on exchange rates for the U.S., German, British, French and Japanese currencies. Source: International Monetary Fund.

European Currency Unit (ECU) is based on a basket of community currencies.

z-Not quoted.

Source: *The Wall Street Journal*, Volume CXXXII No. 16, January 24, 1995, p. C17.

when a krone was worth $0.1676. These two columns are referred to as direct quotes in the United States. A **direct quote** is the price in the domestic (home) currency equal to one unit of the foreign currency.

The last two columns of quotes (labelled "Currency per U.S. $") give us the amount of foreign currency that we will receive for each U.S. dollar that we wish to exchange. Again, these quotes are given for the current day and 1 day prior. One U.S. dollar could be exchanged for 5.9686 Danish krone on January 23, 1995, and only 5.9650 Danish krone on January 22, 1995. This is because the krone dropped in value relative to the U.S. dollar between the 2 days as we noted above. These quotes, expressed as the amount of foreign currency to be received for one unit of the home currency, are **indirect quotes** in the United States. They would be considered *direct quotes* in Denmark, however, since in Denmark the home currency is the krone and the foreign currency is the dollar. Currency dealers use **European terms** for most of their negotiations, meaning that they use quotes that would be considered indirect quotes in the United States. An exception to this occurs when the exchange rate between the U.S. dollar and the British pound is quoted. In that case, dealers use the direct quote from the United States point of view; the worldwide quotation would be expressed as $1.5960 per pound.

❓ According to Exhibit 1, how many U.S. dollars were received for each Bahrain dinar on January 23, 1995?

Answer: $2.6524.

The U.S. dollar price of one dinar is a direct quote in the United States. The direct quote for January 23, 1995, appears in the first column of the quotations.

4. Some of the currencies in Exhibit 1 have more than one line of quotes associated with them. The quotations following the first line of quotes for each currency are forward rates. **Forward rates** are exchange rates that are agreed upon today while the actual delivery and purchase of the currency will not occur until some future date. Forward rates are often quoted for delivery and purchase dates that are 1, 2, 3, 6, and/or 12 months into the future. As in the case of spot transactions, settlement (i.e., the actual purchase and delivery) may take place 2 days after the maturity date on the forward contract. Settlement of a 30-day forward contract would take place 32 days in the future. (If the thirty-second day is a holiday, settlement will occur on the next business day.) The currency is said to be at a **forward premium** from the spot rate if the direct price in the forward market is greater than the direct spot rate. The currency is at a **forward discount** from the spot rate if the direct price in the forward market is lower than the direct spot rate.

❓ Is the 90-day forward rate for the French franc at a premium or a discount from the spot rate?

Answer: Premium.
The direct quote for the spot rate is F.F. = $0.19114. The 90-day forward rate direct quote is F.F. = $0.19138. Since the forward rate is greater than the spot rate, it is selling at a premium.

5. The quotes shown in Exhibit 1 are called **outright quotations**, which means that the full price is given. Dealers in forward contracts speak in terms of **points** or **swap rates**. A point is the difference between the spot rate and the forward rate, carried out to the number of decimal points traditionally used in the trading of the two currencies involved. In most cases this is four decimal points. Translating the data for January 23, 1995, from Exhibit 1 to point quotations, in American terms (i.e., using the direct quote in the U.S.) the 90-day forward rate for the German deutschemark is +21 points, or 21 points above the spot rate (6633 − 6612 = 21). Using European terms, the 90-day forward rate would be quoted as − 47 points, or 47 points below the spot rate (15076 − 15123 = − 47).

❓ Express the 180-day forward rate for the Swiss franc, using American terms, in points.

Answer: +94.
In American terms the outright quotation for the 180-day forward rate for the Swiss franc is 0.7980 and the outright quotation for the spot rate is 0.7886. Dropping the decimal point and subtracting, we get 7980 − 7886 = +94 points.

6. Foreign exchange rate policy is influenced by a set of international rules that have been agreed upon by the central banks of various nations. After World War II, an agreement was made by the Allied Powers in Bretton Woods, New Hampshire. This 1944 accord established a fixed exchange-rate policy in hopes of aiding international trade. The **International Monetary Fund (IMF)** was created to help countries maintain their exchange rates by lending funds to any member country whose currency might be in danger of weakening relative to other currencies unless that weakening was due to a long-term problem, in which case that country's currency was allowed to fall in value relative to other currencies. Only the U.S. dollar was convertible to gold, and foreign entities could demand gold in exchange for dollars.

By the 1960s the fixed exchange rate system was becoming harder to maintain. The demand for American exports had lessened since European factories were now rebuilt after having been damaged and destroyed by the war. This resulted in a surplus of dollars held by foreign governments. These were exchanged for gold, and by 1971 the U.S. gold supply was being severely depleted. At this point President Richard Nixon suspended the convertibility of the dollar into gold, and exchange rates were allowed to freely float, which meant that the rates would be determined by supply and demand. In March 1973, the gold exchange standard was ended.

At the present time, the exchange rate system in existence is somewhere between fixed and floating. In 1972, the European Economic Community (EEC) members decided to maintain their currencies within established limits of each other, an arrangement that became known as the **snake**. This system failed for much the same reason as the post World War II fixed exchange-rate system failed—market pressures caused some of the currencies to fluctuate outside their established limits. Due to these problems, the European Monetary System (EMS) was established in 1979. Under this new arrangement, the exchange rates of member countries are held to specified limits and are also pegged to the **European Currency Unit (ECU)**. The ECU is not a currency; it is a unit of account that is a weighted average of the exchange rates of the member countries. Each weight is determined by the member country's gross national product and its activity in intra-European trade.

While the members of the EEC have pegged their currencies to the ECU, a number of countries have tied their currencies to another currency. Some Latin American and Asian countries, for example, have tied their currencies to the U.S. dollar. Central banks will sometimes intervene to prevent their country's currency from rising or falling too much relative to other currencies. This is referred to as **managed float** or **dirty float**.

? True or False: An American tourist in Europe would be wise to exchange his dollars for ECUs, which can be spent in any of the member countries, in order to minimize currency exchange transaction costs.

Answer: False.
The ECU is not a currency.

7. When a foreign currency that is pegged to gold or another currency decreases in value relative to other currencies, it is said to have been **devalued**; when it increases in value relative to other currencies, it is said to have been **revalued**. The terms "revalued" and "devalued" are often applied to all currencies. Technically, if a *floating* currency drops in value relative to other currencies, the appropriate terminology is that the currency has **weakened**, **deteriorated**, or **depreciated**. If a floating currency increases in value relative to other currencies, the appropriate terminology is that the currency has **strengthened** or **appreciated**. When a currency is expected to drop relative to major currencies or when the currency is being artificially supported through central bank intervention, it is said to be **soft**. A currency is said to be **hard** if it is expected to increase in value relative to other currencies.

When a currency has depreciated or been devalued, foreign goods are more expensive for domestic consumers while domestic goods are cheaper for foreign consumers. When a currency has appreciated or been revalued, foreign goods become cheaper to domestic consumers, but domestic goods are more expensive for foreign consumers. Consider, for example, a meat pie that sells in London for £2.00. If the current exchange rate is $1.5960 per pound, the meat pie will cost the American consumer $3.19 ($1.5960 × 2.00 = $3.192). If the pound subsequently depreciates to $1.5500, the meat pie will now cost the American consumer only $3.10 ($1.5500 x 2.00 = $3.10). Note that the meat pie will still cost the British consumer £2.00. If exchange rates are left to float freely, the reduced price may eventually increase the demand for the product, which will increase the demand for British pounds and thereby cause the pound to appreciate in value.

? If the pound had, instead, appreciated to $1.6000, what would the cost of the meat pie be to the American consumer? What would it be to the British consumer?

Answers: $3.20, £2.00.

The meat pie will now cost the American consumer $1.6000 × 2.00 = $3.20. The price remains the same for the British consumer since the price of the meat pie did not change; only the price of the British currency changed.

8. As described in a previous frame, the central bank of a country will sometimes intervene to keep its country's currency from rising or falling too much in value relative to other currencies. If the currency increases too much in value relative to other currencies, as did the Japanese yen in the early 1990s, the country's products become too expensive for foreign consumers and the demand for those products decreases. If, on the other hand, the currency decreases too much in value relative to other currencies, foreign goods become very expensive.

In order to prevent its country's currency from being revalued or appreciating relative to other currencies, the central bank of a country will flood the market with its currency by exchanging it for other currencies. For example, if the Federal Reserve, the central bank of the United States, wanted to prevent the dollar from appreciating in value, it would use dollars to buy foreign currencies. This will increase the supply of dollars in foreign markets. If the supply of dollars exceeds the demand for dollars, the value of the dollar will fall. To prevent its currency from being devalued or depreciating relative to other currencies, the central bank of the country will use foreign currencies in its possession to buy back its own currency. The Federal Reserve would use foreign currencies to buy back dollars.

While the central bank of a country can directly intervene to adjust the exchange rate for its currency, the government of that country can also use indirect means that will affect its exchange rate. Import taxes make foreign products more expensive for domestic consumers, reducing the demand for the imported goods and, by extension, the demand for foreign currencies, thereby strengthening the home currency. Import quotas achieve the same results. A reduction in or elimination of taxes on investment income earned by foreign investors on domestic securities increases the demand for that country's securities and will increase the demand for the home currency, exerting upward pressure on its value.

? If the United States government were to levy a heavy tax on interest income earned on U.S. securities by foreign investors, what effect would you expect this to have on the value of the dollar?

Answer: The dollar could be expected to weaken since the demand for U.S. securities and, therefore, the demand for U.S. dollars would be reduced.

9. The ability to accurately predict changes in exchange rates would give any business an edge over its competitors. There are several economic theories that are utilized to this end. The theory of **purchasing power parity** states that, over time, the differential rate of inflation between two countries will be offset by an equal but opposite change in their exchange rates. Therefore, if the rate of inflation in the United States is expected to be 2% higher than the rate of inflation in Britain, the U.S. dollar should devalue by 2% during the coming year relative to the pound. If the dollar did not drop in value, American goods would be more expensive than comparable British goods. At some point, consumers in the U.S., Britain, and in other countries will decrease their demand for the more expensive American product and increase their demand for the British substitute. This should cause the value of the American currency to decrease and the value of the British currency to increase if rates are allowed to float freely. Empirical tests of purchasing power parity have demonstrated that this theory holds true in the long run for most currencies. There are a few currencies, however, (like the U.S. dollar) that do not respond in the manner described above in the short to medium term, due partly to lags in adjustments and central bank intervention.

? If you expect the rate of inflation in Germany to be 6% higher than the rate of inflation in the United States, what would you expect to happen to the exchange rates of the deutschemark and the dollar?

Answer: The deutschemark should fall in value by 6% against the dollar if the theory of purchasing power parity holds true.

10. **Interest rate parity** is a theory that states that a difference in interest rates in the foreign and domestic currency markets for securities of similar risk and maturity should be approximately equal but opposite in sign to the forward exchange rate discount or premium on the foreign currency. In other words, if a 6-month Treasury bill is yielding 6% and a 6-month Swedish government security is yielding 10%, then the 180-day forward discount for the Swedish krona is 4%. If interest rate parity did not exist and the actual forward discount were less than 4%, there would be an opportunity for investors to make unlimited profits by borrowing in dollars, converting the dollars to krona and purchasing the Swedish securities, and selling forward contracts for krona (i.e., entering an agreement to exchange the krona for dollars 6 months from now at the 6-month forward rate). This would increase the demand for the Swedish securities, driving down their yield. At the same time, the demand to sell krona 6 months from now should drive down the 6-month forward rate as well, making the discount larger. (Note that if the actual forward discount were *greater than* 4%, it would pay to borrow Swedish krona and invest in dollar-denominated securities.)

? If a 1-year U.S. Treasury bill is currently yielding 8%, and a 1-year German government security is yielding 15%, what should happen to the 1-year forward rate on the deutschemark if interest rate parity exists?

Answer: Interest rate parity states that there should be a forward discount of 7% on the deutschemark.

11. The **International Fisher Effect** states that the expected change in the spot exchange rate between two countries should be equal but opposite in direction to the difference in interest rates between the countries. If American investors expect to lose 5% when converting money earned on German investments back to dollars, then they must be compensated for this by earning 5% more on the German securities than on similar U.S. securities or they will not purchase the securities. If the investors only expect to lose 3% in exchanging the currency, the demand for the German securities would increase, driving their prices up and their yields down.

? If U.S. government securities are yielding 6% and Japanese government securities are yielding 12%, what can you predict about the spot exchange rate between the two countries?

Answer: The yen should drop in value by 6% against the dollar according to the International Fisher Effect. American investors would earn 6% more on Japanese securities, but they would lose this amount when converting yen to dollars, so the effective yields on the two investments will be the same.

12. Some empirical studies have indicated that the forward rate is the best predictor of the future spot rate. That is, if the 90-day forward rate quote for Japanese yen is

¥98.63 per dollar, then the expected spot exchange rate between the dollar and the yen 90 days from now is ¥98.63 per dollar. When these studies compare the use of the forward rate as a predictor of the future spot rate to methods used by forecasting firms, the forecasting firms' methodology has not tended to be any more accurate on average.

? Refer to Exhibit 1 and use the forward rate to predict the exchange rate that will exist between the U.S. dollar and the Swiss franc 6 months from now. Express your quote in European terms.

Answer:

S.F. 1.2531/U.S.$.

European terms refer to quoting the amount of foreign currency that will be received for each dollar. The 180-day forward rate is used to predict what the spot exchange rate will be 6 months from now.

13. The **balance of payments** is a record of all the monetary transactions that have occurred between one country and all the other countries in the world. A simplified balance of payments statement for the United States appears below:

Balance of Payments

(in billions of U.S. dollars)

A. Current Account	
Merchandise exports	$360
Merchandise imports	−475
Trade balance	−115
Other exports	143
Income from investment abroad	100
Other imports	−93
Income paid to foreign investors in American securities	−130
Government spending abroad	−13
Current balance	−108
B. Direct Investment and Other Long-Term Capital	
Direct investment in United States	72
Direct investment abroad	−32
Foreign investment in American securities	24
American investment in foreign securities	−20
Basic balance	−64
C. Short-term Capital	
Net investment in short-term capital	16
D. Errors and Omissions	23
Official settlements balance	−25
E. Total Change in Reserves	
Monetary gold	2.05
SDRs	3.20
Reserve position in IMF	8.75
Foreign exchange assets	11.00

This statement contains five major sections. The first section is the **current account** and lists the value of goods and services that have been imported and exported, government spending abroad, and foreign investment income for the specified time period. An often quoted figure, the **trade balance**, is contained in the current account section of the balance of payments. The trade balance is the net balance on *merchandise trade*, which refers to imports and exports such as wheat, machinery, oil, aircraft, and automobiles. The trade balance does not include income and expenditures for services that are imported or exported or receipts and payments resulting from tourism although these items are still part of the current account.

A second section is the **direct investment and capital account**, which tracks long-term capital flows. These include the country's investment abroad in plant, property, and equipment (listed as "direct investment abroad"), foreign investment in plant, property, and equipment in the country (listed as "direct investment in the country by foreign investors"), investment in foreign securities, and foreign investment in domestic securities. (Income *earned* on the investments is included in the current account.) The sum of these first two sections is referred to as the **basic balance**. Analysts study this balance to evaluate long-term trends in a country's balance of payments since these accounts do not include the more volatile short-term capital investments.

The third section of the balance of payments is the **short-term capital account** which tracks bank deposits and investment in money market instruments. The entries under this heading are often affected by the monetary policies of various countries, and for this reason they are considered to be more volatile and reversible than the entries in the previous two sections.

The fourth section, **Errors and omissions**, adjusts for statistical discrepancies that exist for a number of reasons, including illegal activities. The **official settlements balance** is the sum of these first four sections. It is used to judge a country's competitive position relative to the rest of the world. A positive balance generally means that the country has had more currency inflow than outflow, which would indicate a strengthening position for the home currency. A negative balance indicates that the country has had more currency outflow than inflow. This would have a negative effect on the exchange rate of the home currency.

The last section on the balance of payments, the **total change in reserves**, is simply a balancing account. If the official settlements balance is +$2 billion, then the total change in reserves section must equal − $2 billion. The reserves include monetary gold, SDRs, reserves held by the country with the IMF, and foreign exchange assets. (**SDR** stands for "special drawing rights." An SDR is actually the value of a basket of five major currencies—the U.S. dollar, the French franc, the German mark, the British pound, and the Japanese yen.)

? A negative trade balance means that
  a. the country has imported more goods than it has exported.
  b. the country has exported more goods than it has imported.
  c. foreign firms have invested in more plant, property, and equipment in the country than domestic firms have invested in foreign countries.
  d. more currency has flowed into the country than has flowed out.

Answer: a.
The trade balance is calculated by netting merchandise exports, which create a currency inflow, with merchandise imports, which create a currency outflow. When a country imports more goods than it exports, it has a net currency outflow, making the trade balance negative.

14. As the balance of payments indicates, a country's currency inflows and outflows are in part affected by the activity of domestic firms in foreign countries and of foreign firms in the home country. **Multinational corporations** are firms that have operations in several different countries. These firms may enjoy special benefits, but they also face unique risks. Multinational firms have a greater opportunity for growth since they have expanded the market for their goods and services. It may be less costly for a firm to grow by investing in plant, property, and equipment in another country than for the firm simply to export its goods and/or services. Transportation costs are reduced, and land and/or labor may be less expensive in another country. A firm with international operations also enjoys diversification benefits. While the home country's economy is sluggish, another country may be experiencing an economic boom. Also, the firm may enjoy a greater access to raw materials than it otherwise would.

On the other hand, the foreign country may be facing economic difficulties instead; it may be entering a period of recession or high inflation, an increased risk that is faced by the multinational firm. The firm also faces political risk—a risk that results from the local politics of the countries in which the firm has operations. Although the political environment may have been friendly for the firm when it initiated operations in the foreign country, that environment may change, leaving the firm to face threats such as the expropriation (i.e., seizure) of its assets. The more unstable the politics of a country, the greater the political risk faced by a firm.

Fluctuations in exchange rates are yet another added risk for the multinational corporation since exchange rates can move in a way that will adversely affect the firm's profits. There are three measures of exchange rate risk:

1. **Operating** or **economic exposure** refers to the change in a firm's value that results from an *unexpected* change in exchange rates.
2. **Accounting** or **translation exposure** refers to the change in equity that occurs due to accounting requirements when financial statements denominated in a foreign currency are converted to the domestic currency.
3. **Transaction exposure** refers to changes in the value of outstanding payments (incoming or outgoing) that were agreed upon prior to a change in exchange rates, but that will not be settled until some future date.

? Which of the following is *not* a benefit that may be enjoyed by a multinational corporation?
   a. an expanded market for the firm's goods and services
   b. lower labor costs
   c. expropriation
   d. diversification

Answer: c.
Expropriation refers to the seizure of a firm's assets by the foreign government, typically without compensation. This is a risk faced by a multinational firm, not a benefit.

15. While the additional risk involved in international operations cannot be eliminated, it can be minimized. Engaging in a joint venture with the government of the foreign country can minimize political risk and may reduce some legal constraints regarding the use of domestic labor, exportation of the currency of the host country, and taxation. Since the government also stands to profit from the firm's operations in its country, it is more likely to act in a manner that will be profitable for the firm. The political risk is not eliminated, however, since the existing government may be overthrown and existing agreements rendered null and void.

Multinational firms seek to reduce their economic exposure through diversification—i.e., expanding operations into more than one other country. In doing so, a firm is in a position to better react to unexpected changes in exchange rates. Beyond diversification, since the changes are *unexpected* and, therefore, cannot be predicted, the firm can do nothing.

? True or False: Economic exposure includes the risk that a firm's assets will be seized by the host government with no compensation given to the firm.

Answer: False.
The risk that a firm's assets will be expropriated is classified as political risk. Economic exposure relates to an unexpected change in exchange rates that affects a firm's profits.

16. Translation exposure occurs because of accounting requirements. Different countries use different methods of accounting for international activities. The official method used in the United States since December 1981 is the **current-rate method**. Under this method assets and liabilities are translated into the home currency at the current rate of exchange. The existing equity accounts are translated at the rate of exchange that existed when the transaction took place—i.e., the historical exchange rate. The change in the retained earnings account does not reflect the transaction gains and losses due to the change in the exchange rates. These are reported in a separate equity account, "cumulative translation adjustment." Income statement accounts are converted to the home currency at the exchange rate that actually existed on the date that the transaction took place or at a weighted average rate. Dividends paid are converted at the exchange rate that existed on the date that the dividends were paid. An advantage of this method of accounting is that the relative proportions of the individual balance sheet accounts remains the same, making ratio analysis easier.

Another method that is used by some other countries is the monetary/nonmonetary method. Under this method, the monetary assets—cash, marketable securities, accounts receivables and long-term receivables—and the monetary liabilities—current liabilities and long-term debt—are converted to the home currency at the current exchange rates. All other assets and liabilities are converted at historical rates. Income statement entries are translated at the average rate for the period with the exception of the cost of goods sold and depreciation accounts. Those are translated at the historical rate. This method has the advantage of allowing the foreign nonmonetary assets to be carried at their original cost on the parent company's consolidated balance sheet, just as domestic nonmonetary assets are.

Regardless of which method is used, the translation of accounts into the currency of the home country of the parent corporation can result in a loss. This loss can be minimized by matching exposed foreign currency assets and liabilities, which is referred to as a balance sheet hedge. If exposed assets are equal to exposed liabilities, any change in exchange rates that changes the value of the exposed assets will also change the value of the exposed liabilities in an equal but opposite direction so that the net accounting exposure is equal to zero. The transactions required to ensure that exposed assets are equal to exposed liabilities are not free, however, and since the loss is only a paper loss (i.e., the firm is in no better or worse financial condition in actuality), it is recommended that a firm do nothing to reduce translation exposure. The costs of a balance sheet hedge outweigh the benefits. Furthermore, it is almost impossible to offset both translation *and* transaction exposure. Transaction exposure involves *real* losses, as is discussed in the next section, and the firm should concentrate its efforts on minimizing it.

? Under the current rate method of translating foreign currency transactions into the home currency, all income statement accounts are converted into the home currency
  a. at the exchange rate in existence on the day that the conversion takes place.
  b. at the exchange rate in existence on the day that the actual transaction took place.
  c. at the average rate for the period with the exception of the cost of goods sold and the depreciation accounts.
  d. Any of the above are acceptable choices under the current rate method.

Answer: b.
Under the current rate method all income statement accounts may be converted at the exchange rate that existed on the day the transaction took place or at a weighted average rate for the period.

17. Transaction exposure results when a firm purchases or sells goods and services on credit and the prices are in a foreign currency or when it borrows or lends funds with repayment to be made in a foreign currency. For example, if an American firm has sold goods to a Mexican firm on credit with payment due in 30 days and the peso drops in value relative to the dollar before payment is made, the American firm will receive pesos that are worth less when converted to dollars than they were when the sale took place. This affects the *real* profits of the firm. The American firm has five options available to it:

1. It can do nothing.
2. It can demand payment to be made in dollars, thereby transferring the exchange rate risk onto the Mexican firm.
3. It can do a money market hedge.
4. It can hedge using the forward market or the futures market.
5. It can hedge using the options market.

If the American firm believes that the probability of the peso's depreciating relative to the dollar is low, it may choose the first alternative and do nothing since most of the remaining alternatives have an explicit cost associated with them. The second alternative, demanding payment in dollars, may also be used. (Note that the payment terms must be specified at the point of sale and cannot be changed later.) While this alternative does not have an explicit cost, it may have an implicit cost that needs to be considered. If the American firm has competitors that bear the exchange rate risk themselves while charging a similar price for their products, the firm might lose its customers to its competition.

A money market hedge involves borrowing an amount of money in the foreign currency such that the principal and interest on the loan is exactly equal to the payment that is due the firm. The maturity of the loan should match the payment due date. The borrowed funds can then be converted immediately to the home currency at the current exchange rates. The customer's payment is then used to repay the loan. The firm no longer faces exchange rate risk, but even if the customer fails to make payment in a timely fashion, the firm is still responsible for the loan repayment.

? An American firm sold $100,000 worth of goods to a Finnish firm. Payment is due from the Finnish firm in 60 days, but the American firm is concerned that the Finnish markka will depreciate in value relative to the dollar prior to the receipt of its payment. The American firm wants to do a money market hedge. To do so it will borrow an amount in _____ such that the _____ and _____ payments on the loan are exactly equal to the $_____. It will then exchange that currency immediately for _____ and use the Finnish firm's future payment to pay off the loan.

Answers: markkas, principal, interest, 100,000, dollars.
To conduct a money market hedge, the hedger borrows an amount in the foreign currency such that the principal and interest payments on the loan are equal in size and maturity to the payment owed the hedger by the customer. The hedger immediately converts the currency received to its home currency and pays off the loan at some time in the future with the payment(s) received from its customer.

18. The firm can also purchase an options contract to hedge its position in the foreign currency market. If the firm is expecting to receive payment in a foreign currency, it can buy an option that allows it to exchange the foreign currency for dollars at some future date for an exchange rate that is agreed upon today. This prespecified exchange rate is called the **strike price** or **exercise price**. The option described in this scenario is an option to *sell* the foreign currency and is called a **put option**. The firm pays a price for this option, which can be considered to be the cost of insurance. If the foreign currency depreciates in value relative to the home currency, the firm will exercise its option and exchange the foreign currency at the strike price on the option if it is better than the existing exchange rate. On the other hand, if the foreign currency appreciates in value relative to the home currency, the firm can simply let its option expire, losing only the cost of the option.

If the firm needs to make a payment at some point in the future in a foreign currency, it can hedge its position by buying an option to *purchase* the foreign currency at some future date for an exchange rate agreed upon today. This option is called a **call option**. As in the case of the put option, the firm pays a price for this option. If the foreign currency appreciates in value relative to the home currency, the firm will exercise its call option and exchange the home currency for the foreign currency at the strike price on the option if it is less than the existing exchange rate. If, however, the foreign currency depreciates in value relative to the home currency, such that the strike price is higher than the existing exchange rate, the firm will simply let its option expire and lose the price that it paid for the option.

? An American firm is planning to invest in a plant in Geneva, Switzerland. It will need to make a payment of one million Swiss francs 3 months from today. If the firm wants to use an options contract to hedge against an increase in the value of the franc relative to the dollar, it should purchase a _____ option.

Answer: call.

A call option gives the American firm the right to buy Swiss francs at the exercise price stipulated on the option. A put option would give the firm the right to sell Swiss francs at the exercise price. Since the firm will need to make payment in Swiss francs, it will need to purchase the call option.

19. A forward market transaction and a futures market transaction are similar in design. Both give the investor the right to buy or sell the underlying currency at some point in the future for a price specified today. These contracts differ from options contracts in that the investor cannot simply let the contract expire. In order to get out of the contract, an investor must take the opposite position in the contract.

If a firm buys a forward contract or a futures contract (takes a **long position**), it is agreeing to take delivery of the specified number of units of the foreign currency on the specified future date for the price stipulated today. If a firm sells a forward contract or a futures contract (takes a **short position**), it is agreeing to deliver the specified number of units of the foreign currency on the specified future date for the price stipulated today. Therefore, if an American firm is expecting to receive a payment denominated in Canadian dollars, it can hedge against a possible decline in the value of the Canadian dollar relative to the American dollar by *selling* Canadian dollars forward or by taking a short position in a futures contract on Canadian dollars. In doing so, the firm has *locked in* the exchange rate that it will get when it exchanges the Canadian dollars for American dollars. On the other hand, if the American firm is expecting to *make* a payment that is denominated in Canadian dollars, it can lock in the exchange rate that it will get when it converts its American dollars to the Canadian currency by *buying* Canadian dollars forward or by taking a long position in a futures contract on Canadian dollars.

Refer back to Exhibit 1 in this module. The exchange rates for forward contracts on Canadian dollars 30, 90, and 180 days into the future are listed. Note that if the American firm expects to receive payment in Canadian dollars 90 days from now, it can lock in an exchange rate for the Canadian dollars of U.S.$0.7016 for each Canadian dollar it receives by selling the Canadian dollars forward—i.e., by agreeing to deliver Canadian dollars 90 days from now in exchange for U.S.$0.7016/C$. If the American firm is fearful that the spot exchange rate 90 days from now will be less than this rate, it will use the hedge. On the other hand, if the American firm needs to make a payment denominated in Canadian dollars in 90 days and expects the Canadian dollar to *increase* in value relative to the American dollar, it will buy Canadian dollars forward—i.e., it will agree to buy Canadian dollars in 90 days and pay U.S.$0.7016 for each Canadian dollar it receives, thereby locking in what it hopes will be a lower exchange rate than the actual spot rate 90 days from now.

A German firm is expecting to receive payment denominated in Australian dollars 60 days from now. The firm is concerned about the value of the Australian dollar and wants to hedge against the possibility that the Australian dollar will depreciate relative to the German deutschemark prior to its receiving payment. How can the firm use the forward market to hedge its position?

Answer: It should sell Australian dollars forward.

Since the German firm is expecting payment in Australian dollars in 60 days and will want to exchange the dollars for deutschemarks, it will sell Australian dollars forward. In doing so, the German firm locks in the exchange rate that it will get for the Australian dollar 60 days from now.

20.   Multinational corporations also enjoy the added availability of additional financing sources. In addition to selling debt and equity in their home countries, the multinational corporation can more readily sell debt and equity to investors in other countries due to their international visibility. The debt can be denominated in the home currency of the investors or in the home currency of the corporation. It could even be denominated in some third currency.

Eurocurrencies refer to currencies deposited in banks in countries other than the home country of the currency. The first Eurocurrency to exist was the **Eurodollar**. Eurodollars are dollar deposits held by foreign banks or by International Banking Facilities (IBF) in the U.S. A foreign bank can make a loan that is denominated in dollars. The loan is called a **Eurodollar loan**. These loans tend to be short to intermediate term loans, with a typical maturity of less than or equal to 6 months. The maturity date is fixed, but the interest rate is typically variable and fluctuates with **LIBOR**, which is the short-term rate at which British banks borrow from each other. The Eurodollar loan is a specific type of **Eurocurrency loan**, which simply refers to a loan denominated in a currency other than the home currency of the lender.

Commercial paper is an unsecured debt obligation of the borrower. **Euro-commercial paper** is an unsecured debt obligation that is denominated in a eurocurrency. Like commercial paper, it is sold at a discount. Euro-commercial paper has typical maturities of 1, 2, or 6 months. Over 90% of the Euro-commercial paper issued is denominated in dollars.

A **Eurobond** is a long-term debt instrument that is denominated in a currency other than the home currency of the country in which the bond is sold. Eurobonds are underwritten by international syndicates of banks and other security firms. They are bearer bonds, and interest is fixed and paid annually. Eurobonds were initially bonds that were denominated in dollars and sold in a country other than the United States. There are also bonds issued by foreign borrowers but denominated in the home currency of the lender. **Yankee bonds** refers to foreign bonds sold in the United States that are denominated in dollars. **Samurai bonds** are foreign bonds sold in Japan denominated in yen. **Bulldogs** are bonds issued in the United Kingdom by a foreign borrower and denominated in pounds. **Dual currency bonds** are bonds which have the purchase price of the bond and the coupon payment of the bond denominated in one currency and the principal redemption price denominated in a second currency. These bonds are attractive to firms which wish to borrow and pay debt service in one currency, but want to repay the principal in a second currency to which it expects to have access when this payment is due.

Bonds such as Eurobonds are, for the most part, free of regulation. If an American firm sells a bond denominated in dollars overseas, that bond does not have to be registered with the Securities and Exchange Commission, which saves the firm time and money. The American firm also avoids the disclosure requirements associated with registering an issue, which prevents competition from having access from information that the firm wishes to keep private. Eurobonds also tend to have favorable tax treatment, making them even more attractive to the issuer.

? A dual currency bond is a bond for which
a. the principal and interest payments are denominated in a currency other than the home currency of the issuer.
b. the price of the bond and the principal repayment are denominated in a currency other than the currency in which the interest payments are denominated.
c. the issuer is a foreign entity, but the bond is denominated in the home currency of the country in which the bond is issued for sale.
d. the purchase price of the bond and the coupon payments are denominated in the same currency while the principal redemption price is denominated in a second currency.

Answer: d.

A dual currency bond is denominated in two currencies. The coupon payments are denominated in the same currency as the price of the bond. The principal repayment is denominated in a second currency to which the issuing firm expects to have access at the time the bond matures.

21.   In addition to the International Monetary Fund mentioned in a previous frame that serves as the central bank for the central banks of all nations, there are a number of other agencies that oversee the international flow of funds. The **World Bank**, the formal name of which is **The International Bank for Reconstruction and Development**, was also established in 1944. Its primary objective is to grant loans to countries to enhance their economic development. It sells bonds to both private investors and governments to finance its operations.

The **International Financial Corporation (IFC)** has as its main purpose the promotion of private enterprise within countries. It utilizes the private rather than the government sector to achieve its objectives. It provides loans to corporations and also purchases stock of corporations. Historically it has received funding from the World Bank, but it also borrows on its own cognizance.

The **International Development Association (IDA)** was created in 1960 and concentrates on lending to the less prosperous nations. It extends loans to nations that are not able to qualify for loans from the World Bank at low interest rates.

The **Bank of International Settlements (BIS)** is sometimes referred to as "the lender of the last resort" because it provides assistance to countries that are experiencing a financial crisis.

? The institution that was created to make loans to countries in order to enhance economic development was the
a. International Development Association.
b. World Bank.
c. International Monetary Fund.
d. International Financial Corporation.

Answer: b.
The primary objective of the World Bank is to make loans to countries to stimulate their economic development.

 Apply It

1. A current fad in Hungary involves American-made blue jeans. If the American demand for a Hungarian export does not increase, what would you expect to happen to the value of the Hungarian forint relative to the U.S. dollar? (Frame 1)

2. If one Belgian franc is equal to $0.03170, how many Belgian francs will be received in exchange for $50? (Frame 2)

3. Refer to the following *Wall Street Journal* clipping to answer the following questions:

Exhibit 2

CURRENCY TRADING

EXCHANGE RATES

Tuesday, May 30, 1995

The New York foreign exchange selling rates below apply to trading among banks in amounts of $1 million and more, as quoted at 3 p.m. Eastern time by Bankers Trust Co., Dow Jones Telerate Inc. and other sources. Retail transactions provide fewer units of foreign currency per dollar.

Country	U.S. $ equiv. Tue	U.S. $ equiv. Fri	Currency per U.S. $ Tue	Currency per U.S. $ Fri
Argentina (Peso)	1.00	1.00	1.00	1.00
Australia (Dollar)	.7212	.7195	1.3866	1.3899
Austria (Schilling)	.1023	.1031	9.7705	9.6965
Bahrain (Dinar)	2.6525	2.6525	.3770	.3770
Belgium (Franc)	.03501	.03531	28.563	28.317
Brazil (Real)	1.1031	1.1154	.9065	.8965
Britain (Pound)	1.6025	1.6065	.6240	.6225
30-Day Forward	1.6019	1.6056	.6243	.6228
90-Day Forward	1.6002	1.6037	.6249	.6236
180-Day Forward	1.5961	1.5999	.6265	.6251
Canada (Dollar)	.7286	.7290	1.3725	1.3718
30-Day Forward	.7277	.7275	1.3742	1.3745
90-Day Forward	.7261	.7260	1.3772	1.3775
180-Day Forward	.7239	.7238	1.3815	1.3817
Chile (Peso)	.002655	.002662	376.65	375.65
China (Renminbi)	.1204	.1204	8.3077	8.3063
Colombia (Peso)	.001140	.001144	877.50	874.50
Czech. Rep. (Koruna)	....	....		
Commercial rate	.03852	.03854	25.958	25.944
Denmark (Krone)	.1842	.1856	5.4295	5.3872
Ecuador (Sucre)	....	....		
Floating rate	.0004047	.0004068	2471.00	2458.00
Finland (Markka)	.2336	.2362	4.2800	4.2335
France (Franc)	.2042	.2064	4.8980	4.8455
30-Day Forward	.2038	.2057	4.9065	4.8605
90-Day Forward	.2033	.2053	4.9185	4.8716
180-Day Forward	.2028	.2049	4.9302	4.8801
Germany (Mark)	.7202	.7265	1.3885	1.3765
30-Day Forward	.7209	1.3745	1.3872	.7275
90-Day Forward	.7228	1.3709	1.3835	.7294
180-Day Forward	.7255	1.3657	1.3784	.7322
Greece (Drachma)	.004437	.004471	225.36	223.65
Hong Kong (Dollar)	.1293	.1293	7.7355	7.7348
Hungary (Forint)	.008085	.008109	123.69	123.32
India (Rupee)	.03188	.03186	31.370	31.392
Indonesia (Rupiah)	.0004490	.0004486	2227.00	2229.00
Ireland (Punt)	1.6485	1.6450	.6066	.6079
Israel (Shekel)	.3339	.3339	2.9946	2.9948
Italy (Lira)	.0006144	.0006098	1627.50	1639.99
Japan (Yen)	.01207	.01210	82.818	82.660
30-Day Forward	.01213	.01217	82.447	82.189
90-Day Forward	.01223	.01227	81.776	81.517
180-Day Forward	.01238	.01242	80.795	80.530
Jordan (Dinar)	1.4327	1.4286	.6980	.7000
Kuwait (Dinar)	3.3744	3.3647	.2964	.2972
Lebanon (Pound)	.0006154	.0006154	1625.00	1625.00
Malaysia (Ringgit)	.4055	.4067	2.4658	2.4590
Malta (Lira)	2.8729	2.8729	.3481	.3481
Mexico (Peso)	....	....		
Floating rate	.1612	.1622	6.2050	6.1650
Netherland (Guilder)	.6434	.6486	1.5543	1.5417
New Zealand (Dollar)	.6674	.6690	1.4985	1.4948
Norway (Krone)	.1615	.1629	6.1935	6.1405
Pakistan (Rupee)	.03232	.03232	30.939	30.939
Peru (new Sol)	.4451	.4454	2.2465	2.2450
Philippines (Peso)	.03872	.03861	25.825	25.900
Poland (Zloty)	.4132	.4132	2.4200	2.4200
Portugal (Escudo)	.006823	.006902	146.57	144.90
Saudi Arabia (Riyal)	.2666	.2666	3.7508	3.7506
Singapore (Dollar)	.7190	.7194	1.3908	1.3900
Slovak Rep. (Koruna)	.03421	.03431	29.230	29.150
South Africa (Rand)	.2731	.2727	3.6612	3.6675
South Korea (Won)	.001316	.001315	759.95	760.55
Spain (Peseta)	.008258	.008337	121.10	119.95
Sweden (Krona)	.1377	.1376	7.2640	7.2680
Switzerland (Franc)	.8734	.8822	1.1450	1.1335
30-Day Forward	.8751	.8847	1.1427	1.1303
90-Day Forward	.8790	.8891	1.1376	1.1247
180-Day Forward	.8845	.8949	1.1306	1.1175
Taiwan (Dollar)	.03910	.03953	25.572	25.300
Thailand (Baht)	.04066	.04067	24.595	24.590
Turkey (Lira)	.0000235	.0000234	42625.75	42716.79
United Arab (Dirham)	.2723	.2723	3.6727	3.6727
Uruguay (New Peso)	....	....		
Financial	.1618	.1618	6.1800	6.1800
Venezuela (Bolivar)	.005890	.005890	169.78	169.78
SDR	1.5756	1.5763	.6347	.6344
ECU	1.3264	1.3343		

Special Drawing Rights (SDR) are based on exchange rates for the U.S., German, British, French, and Japanese currencies. Source: International Monetary Fund.

European Currency Unit (ECU) is based on a basket of community currencies.

z-not quoted.

Source: *The Wall Street Journal,* Volume CXXXII No. 105, May 31, 1995, p. C21.

a. In European terms, what was the spot exchange rate between the U.S. dollar and the Brazilian real on May 30, 1995? (Frame 3)

b. Is the direct quote for the 180-day forward rate on the Canadian dollar at a premium or a discount from the spot rate? (Frame 4)

c. Express the 180-day forward rate for the Canadian dollar, using European terms, in points. (Frame 5)

d. Using the theory that the forward rate is the best predictor of the expected future spot rate, what would you predict that the direct quote spot rate between the U.S. dollar and the Japanese yen will be 6 months from the date of the quotes? (Frame 12)

4. What is the ECU? (Frame 6)

5. If the American dollar depreciates against the Japanese yen, what will happen to the price of an automobile produced by the Ford Motor Company as far as the American consumer is concerned? (Frame 7)

6. If the Federal Reserve system is afraid that the American dollar is depreciating too rapidly relative to other currencies, what action will it take in the foreign exchange market? (Frame 8)

7. If inflation in Germany is 8% and inflation in Colombia is 25%, what would you predict will happen to the exchange rate between the deutschemark and the peso? (Frame 9)

8. If the 12-month Treasury bill is yielding 7% and a 12-month British government security is yielding 10%, what would you expect to happen to the 12-month forward rate between the U.S. dollar and the British pound? (Frame 10)

9. If the 12-month Treasury bill is yielding 7% and a 12-month British government security is yielding 10%, what would you predict about the spot exchange rate between the U.S. dollar and the British pound? (Frame 11)

10. Given the following data, calculate the trade balance for the United States: (Frame 13)

Merchandise imports	−$368 billion
Government spending abroad	−$ 15 billion
Basic balance	−$ 94 billion
Direct investment in U.S.	$ 6 billion
Merchandise exports	$223 billion
Exported services	$ 70 billion
Imported services	−$ 75 billion
Net investment in short-term capital	$ 30 billion

11. Which of the three types of exposure—translation, transaction, or economic—is it most important for a firm to hedge against? (Frames 14, 15, 16, and 17)

12. If a Canadian firm is expecting to receive payment in British pounds in 30 days, what procedure can the firm use to do a money market hedge? (Frame 17)

13. If a Canadian firm is expecting to receive payment in British pounds in 30 days, what procedure can the firm use to hedge using the options market? (Frame 18)

14. If a Canadian firm is expecting to receive payment in British pounds in 30 days, what procedure can it use to hedge using forward contracts? (Frame 19)

15. What are the advantages associated with a Eurobond from the standpoint of the issuer? (Frame 20)

16. What international institution serves as a central bank for the central banks of all nations? (Frame 21)

Apply It Answers

1. The increased demand for American dollars will cause the value of the dollar to rise relative to the forint.

2. The number of Belgian francs that can be received in exchange for $50 is equal to $50/$0.03170 = B.F.1,577.2871.

3. a. European terms for most currencies is expressed as the number of units of foreign currency to be received for each U.S. dollar. Referring to the clipping 0.9065 Brazilian reals are equal to one U.S. dollar.

   b. The direct quote is the quote in the first column, the U.S. dollar equivalent of one Canadian dollar. Since the 180-day forward rate of U.S.$0.7239/C$ is less than the spot exchange rate of U.S.$0.7286/C$, the forward rate is at a discount.

   c. A point is the difference between the spot rate and the forward rate, carried out to the number of decimal points traditionally used. European terms refer to the number of Canadian dollars per U.S. dollar. The swap rate is $13815 - 13725 = +90$ points.

   d. Using the forward rate as the best predictor, the expected 6-month spot rate is equivalent to the 6-month forward rate of $0.01238/¥. As an indirect quote, this is ¥80.795/U.S.$.

4. An ECU or European currency unit is a unit of account that is a weighted average of the currencies of the countries that are members of the European monetary system.

5. Nothing. The prices of domestic products do not change for the domestic consumer regardless of whether the home currency appreciates or depreciates.

6. If the American dollar is falling relative to other currencies, the supply of dollars exceeds the demand, so the Federal Reserve will buy up U.S. dollars in the foreign exchange market, using its holdings of foreign currencies to do so.

7. Purchasing power parity states that the differential rate of inflation between two countries will be offset by an equal but opposite change in their exchange rates. Therefore, if Colombia's inflation rate is 17% higher than Germany's, you should expect the Colombian peso to depreciate by 17% against the German deutschemark.

8. Interest rate parity states that a difference in the interest rates for securities of the same risk and maturity will be equal but opposite in sign to the forward exchange rate discount or premium on the foreign currency. Therefore, if the difference in interest rates between a British security and a U.S. security of similar risk and maturity is 3%, there should be a 3% discount on the forward rate for the British pound.

9. The International Fisher Effect states that the expected change in the spot rate between two countries should be equal but opposite in direction to the difference in the interest rates between the countries. Thus, if the Treasury bill is yielding 7% and a similar maturity British government security is yielding 10%, the British pound should be expected to drop in value by 3% against the U.S. dollar.

10. The trade balance is simply the difference between merchandise exports and merchandise imports. $223 billion - $368 billion = -$145 billion.

11. Transaction exposure is the most important to hedge against since it can be predicted, unlike economic exposure, and it creates a real loss rather than a paper loss like translation exposure.

12. If the Canadian firm is expecting to receive payment in British pounds, it can borrow an amount in pounds such that the principal and interest payments combined equal the amount of payment due it. It should then convert the proceeds of the loan to Canadian dollars at the current exchange rate. When payment is received (in pounds), it can be used to pay off the loan.

13. If the Canadian firm is expecting to receive payment in pounds, it will want to buy a put option on British pounds. This gives the firm the right to sell the pounds it receives at the specified exchange rate on the option contract.

14. If the Canadian firm is expecting to receive payment in pounds, it will want to sell British pounds forward. This locks in the exchange rate that it will receive for the pounds 30 days from now.

15. Eurobonds are subject to less regulation than domestic bonds. In the United States, domestic bonds must be registered with the SEC, which subjects them to disclosure requirements. Eurobonds, on the other hand, do not have to be registered with the SEC, which saves the firm both time and money. The firm also avoids having to disclose information that might be useful to its competitors.

16. The International Monetary Fund (IMF) serves as the central bank of the central banks of all nations. It lends member nations funds in order to stabilize exchange rates.

Future Value of $1

Interest Rate (percent)

Periods	0.50	0.75	1.00	1.50	2.00	3.00	4.00	5.00	6.00
1	1.0050	1.0075	1.0100	1.0150	1.0200	1.0300	1.0400	1.0500	1.0600
2	1.0100	1.0151	1.0201	1.0302	1.0404	1.0609	1.0816	1.1025	1.1236
3	1.0151	1.0227	1.0303	1.0457	1.0612	1.0927	1.1249	1.1576	1.1910
4	1.0202	1.0303	1.0406	1.0614	1.0824	1.1255	1.1699	1.2155	1.2625
5	1.0253	1.0381	1.0510	1.0773	1.1041	1.1593	1.2167	1.2763	1.3382
6	1.0304	1.0459	1.0615	1.0934	1.1262	1.1941	1.2653	1.3401	1.4185
7	1.0355	1.0537	1.0721	1.1098	1.1487	1.2299	1.3159	1.4071	1.5036
8	1.0407	1.0616	1.0829	1.1265	1.1717	1.2668	1.3686	1.4775	1.5938
9	1.0459	1.0696	1.0937	1.1434	1.1951	1.3048	1.4233	1.5513	1.6895
10	1.0511	1.0776	1.1046	1.1605	1.2190	1.3439	1.4802	1.6289	1.7908
11	1.0564	1.0857	1.1157	1.1779	1.2434	1.3842	1.5395	1.7103	1.8983
12	1.0617	1.0938	1.1268	1.1956	1.2682	1.4258	1.6010	1.7959	2.0122
13	1.0670	1.1020	1.1381	1.2136	1.2936	1.4685	1.6651	1.8856	2.1329
14	1.0723	1.1103	1.1495	1.2318	1.3195	1.5126	1.7317	1.9799	2.2609
15	1.0777	1.1186	1.1610	1.2502	1.3459	1.5580	1.8009	2.0789	2.3966
16	1.0831	1.1270	1.1726	1.2690	1.3728	1.6047	1.8730	2.1829	2.5404
17	1.0885	1.1354	1.1843	1.2880	1.4002	1.6528	1.9479	2.2920	2.6928
18	1.0939	1.1440	1.1961	1.3073	1.4282	1.7024	2.0258	2.4066	2.8543
19	1.0994	1.1525	1.2081	1.3270	1.4568	1.7535	2.1068	2.5270	3.0256
20	1.1049	1.1612	1.2202	1.3469	1.4859	1.8061	2.1911	2.6533	3.2071
21	1.1104	1.1699	1.2324	1.3671	1.5157	1.8603	2.2788	2.7860	3.3996
22	1.1160	1.1787	1.2447	1.3876	1.5460	1.9161	2.3699	2.9253	3.6035
23	1.1216	1.1875	1.2572	1.4084	1.5769	1.9736	2.4647	3.0715	3.8197
24	1.1272	1.1964	1.2697	1.4295	1.6084	2.0328	2.5633	3.2251	4.0489
25	1.1328	1.2054	1.2824	1.4509	1.6406	2.0938	2.6658	3.3864	4.2919
26	1.1385	1.2144	1.2953	1.4727	1.6734	2.1566	2.7725	3.5557	4.5494
27	1.1442	1.2235	1.3082	1.4948	1.7069	2.2213	2.8834	3.7335	4.8223
28	1.1499	1.2327	1.3213	1.5172	1.7410	2.2879	2.9987	3.9201	5.1117
29	1.1556	1.2420	1.3345	1.5400	1.7758	2.3566	3.1187	4.1161	5.4184
30	1.1614	1.2513	1.3478	1.5631	1.8114	2.4273	3.2434	4.3219	5.7435
36	1.1967	1.3086	1.4308	1.7091	2.0399	2.8983	4.1039	5.7918	8.1473
48	1.2705	1.4314	1.6122	2.0435	2.5871	4.1323	6.5705	10.4013	16.3939
60	1.3489	1.5657	1.8167	2.4432	3.2810	5.8916	10.5196	18.6792	32.9877
72	1.4320	1.7126	2.0471	2.9212	4.1611	8.4000	16.8423	33.5451	66.3777
84	1.5204	1.8732	2.3067	3.4926	5.2773	11.9764	26.9650	60.2422	133.5650
96	1.6141	2.0489	2.5993	4.1758	6.6929	17.0755	43.1718	108.1864	268.7590
100	1.6467	2.1111	2.7048	4.4320	7.2446	19.2186	50.5049	131.5013	339.3021
108	1.7137	2.2411	2.9289	4.9927	8.4883	24.3456	69.1195	194.2872	540.7960
120	1.8194	2.4514	3.3004	5.9693	10.7652	34.7110	110.6626	348.9120	1,088.188
180	2.4541	3.8380	5.9958	14.5844	35.3208	204.5034	1,164.129	6,517.392	35,896.80
360	6.0226	14.7306	35.9496	212.7038	1,247.561	41,821.62	1,355,196	42,476,396	

Interest Rate (percent)

7.00	8.00	9.00	10.00	11.00	12.00	13.00	14.00	15.00	20.00
1.0700	1.0800	1.0900	1.1000	1.1100	1.1200	1.1300	1.1400	1.1500	1.2000
1.1449	1.1664	1.1881	1.2100	1.2321	1.2544	1.2769	1.2996	1.3225	1.4400
1.2250	1.2597	1.2950	1.3310	1.3676	1.4049	1.4429	1.4815	1.5209	1.7280
1.3108	1.3605	1.4116	1.4641	1.5181	1.5735	1.6305	1.6890	1.7490	2.0736
1.4026	1.4693	1.5386	1.6105	1.6851	1.7623	1.8424	1.9254	2.0114	2.4883
1.5007	1.5869	1.6771	1.7716	1.8704	1.9738	2.0820	2.1950	2.3131	2.9860
1.6058	1.7138	1.8280	1.9487	2.0762	2.2107	2.3526	2.5023	2.6600	3.5832
1.7182	1.8509	1.9926	2.1436	2.3045	2.4760	2.6584	2.8526	3.0590	4.2998
1.8385	1.9990	2.1719	2.3579	2.5580	2.7731	3.0040	3.2519	3.5179	5.1598
1.9672	2.1589	2.3674	2.5937	2.8394	3.1058	3.3946	3.7072	4.0456	6.1917
2.1049	2.3316	2.5804	2.8531	3.1518	3.4785	3.8359	4.2262	4.6524	7.4301
2.2522	2.5182	2.8127	3.1384	3.4985	3.8960	4.3345	4.8179	5.3503	8.9161
2.4098	2.7196	3.0658	3.4523	3.8833	4.3635	4.8980	5.4924	6.1528	10.6993
2.5785	2.9372	3.3417	3.7975	4.3104	4.8871	5.5348	6.2613	7.0757	12.8392
2.7590	3.1722	3.6425	4.1772	4.7846	5.4736	6.2543	7.1379	8.1371	15.4070
2.9522	3.4259	3.9703	4.5950	5.3109	6.1304	7.0673	8.1372	9.3576	18.4884
3.1588	3.7000	4.3276	5.0545	5.8951	6.8660	7.9861	9.2765	10.7613	22.1861
3.3799	3.9960	4.7171	5.5599	6.5436	7.6900	9.0243	10.5752	12.3755	26.6233
3.6165	4.3157	5.1417	6.1159	7.2633	8.6128	10.1974	12.0557	14.2318	31.9480
3.8697	4.6610	5.6044	6.7275	8.0623	9.6463	11.5231	13.7435	16.3665	38.3376
4.1406	5.0338	6.1088	7.4002	8.9492	10.8038	13.0211	15.6676	18.8215	46.0051
4.4304	5.4365	6.6586	8.1403	9.9336	12.1003	14.7138	17.8610	21.6447	55.2061
4.7405	5.8715	7.2579	8.9543	11.0263	13.5523	16.6266	20.3616	24.8915	66.2474
5.0724	6.3412	7.9111	9.8497	12.2392	15.1786	18.7881	23.2122	28.6252	79.4968
5.4274	6.8485	8.6231	10.8347	13.5855	17.0001	21.2305	26.4619	32.9190	95.3962
5.8074	7.3964	9.3992	11.9182	15.0799	19.0401	23.9905	30.1666	37.8568	114.4755
6.2139	7.9881	10.2451	13.1100	16.7386	21.3249	27.1093	34.3899	43.5353	137.3706
6.6488	8.6271	11.1671	14.4210	18.5799	23.8839	30.6335	39.2045	50.0656	164.8447
7.1143	9.3173	12.1722	15.8631	20.6237	26.7499	34.6158	44.6931	57.5755	197.8136
7.6123	10.0627	13.2677	17.4494	22.8923	29.9599	39.1159	50.9502	66.2118	237.3763
11.4239	15.9682	22.2512	30.9127	42.8181	59.1356	81.4374	111.8342	153.1519	708.8019
25.7289	40.2106	62.5852	97.0172	149.7970	230.3908	352.9923	538.8065	819.4007	6,319.749
57.9464	101.2571	176.0313	304.4816	524.0572	897.5969	1,530.053	2,595.919	4,383.999	56,347.51
130.5065	254.9825	495.1170	955.5938	1,833.388	3,497.016	6,632.052	12,506.89	23,455.49	502,400.1
293.9255	642.0893	1,392.598	2,999.063	6,414.019	13,624.29	28,746.78	60,257.00	125,492.7	4,479,450
661.9766	1,616.890	3,916.912	9,412.344	22,439.13	53,079.91	124,603.6	290,312.5	671,417.5	39,939,224
867.7163	2,199.761	5,529.041	13,780.61	34,064.18	83,522.27	203,162.9	490,326.2	1,174,313	82,817,975
1,490.898	4,071.605	11,016.96	29,539.97	78,502.18	206,798.1	540,097.2	1,398,698	3,592,252	
3,357.788	10,252.99	30,987.02	92,709.07	274,636.0	805,680.3	2,341,064	6,738,794	19,219,445	
194,571.8	1,038,188	5,454,684	28,228,209						

APPENDIX A-2

Present Value of $1

Interest Rate (percent)

Periods	0.50	0.75	1.00	1.50	2.00	3.00	4.00	5.00	6.00
1	0.9950	0.9926	0.9901	0.9852	0.9804	0.9709	0.9615	0.9524	0.9434
2	0.9901	0.9852	0.9803	0.9707	0.9612	0.9426	0.9246	0.9070	0.8900
3	0.9851	0.9778	0.9706	0.9563	0.9423	0.9151	0.8890	0.8638	0.8396
4	0.9802	0.9706	0.9610	0.9422	0.9238	0.8885	0.8548	0.8227	0.7921
5	0.9754	0.9633	0.9515	0.9283	0.9057	0.8626	0.8219	0.7835	0.7473
6	0.9705	0.9562	0.9420	0.9145	0.8880	0.8375	0.7903	0.7462	0.7050
7	0.9657	0.9490	0.9327	0.9010	0.8706	0.8131	0.7599	0.7107	0.6651
8	0.9609	0.9420	0.9235	0.8877	0.8535	0.7894	0.7307	0.6768	0.6274
9	0.9561	0.9350	0.9143	0.8746	0.8368	0.7664	0.7026	0.6446	0.5919
10	0.9513	0.9280	0.9053	0.8617	0.8203	0.7441	0.6756	0.6139	0.5584
11	0.9466	0.9211	0.8963	0.8489	0.8043	0.7224	0.6496	0.5847	0.5268
12	0.9419	0.9142	0.8874	0.8364	0.7885	0.7014	0.6246	0.5568	0.4970
13	0.9372	0.9074	0.8787	0.8240	0.7730	0.6810	0.6006	0.5303	0.4688
14	0.9326	0.9007	0.8700	0.8118	0.7579	0.6611	0.5775	0.5051	0.4423
15	0.9279	0.8940	0.8613	0.7999	0.7430	0.6419	0.5553	0.4810	0.4173
16	0.9233	0.8873	0.8528	0.7880	0.7284	0.6232	0.5339	0.4581	0.3936
17	0.9187	0.8807	0.8444	0.7764	0.7142	0.6050	0.5134	0.4363	0.3714
18	0.9141	0.8742	0.8360	0.7649	0.7002	0.5874	0.4936	0.4155	0.3503
19	0.9096	0.8676	0.8277	0.7536	0.6864	0.5703	0.4746	0.3957	0.3305
20	0.9051	0.8612	0.8195	0.7425	0.6730	0.5537	0.4564	0.3769	0.3118
21	0.9006	0.8548	0.8114	0.7315	0.6598	0.5375	0.4388	0.3589	0.2942
22	0.8961	0.8484	0.8034	0.7207	0.6468	0.5219	0.4220	0.3418	0.2775
23	0.8916	0.8421	0.7954	0.7100	0.6342	0.5067	0.4057	0.3256	0.2618
24	0.8872	0.8358	0.7876	0.6995	0.6217	0.4919	0.3901	0.3101	0.2470
25	0.8828	0.8296	0.7798	0.6892	0.6095	0.4776	0.3751	0.2953	0.2330
26	0.8784	0.8234	0.7720	0.6790	0.5976	0.4637	0.3607	0.2812	0.2198
27	0.8740	0.8173	0.7644	0.6690	0.5859	0.4502	0.3468	0.2678	0.2074
28	0.8697	0.8112	0.7568	0.6591	0.5744	0.4371	0.3335	0.2551	0.1956
29	0.8653	0.8052	0.7493	0.6494	0.5631	0.4243	0.3207	0.2429	0.1846
30	0.8610	0.7992	0.7419	0.6398	0.5521	0.4120	0.3083	0.2314	0.1741
36	0.8356	0.7641	0.6989	0.5851	0.4902	0.3450	0.2437	0.1727	0.1227
48	0.7871	0.6986	0.6203	0.4894	0.3865	0.2420	0.1522	0.0961	0.0610
60	0.7414	0.6387	0.5504	0.4093	0.3048	0.1697	0.0951	0.0535	0.0303
72	0.6983	0.5839	0.4885	0.3423	0.2403	0.1190	0.0594	0.0298	0.0151
84	0.6577	0.5338	0.4335	0.2863	0.1895	0.0835	0.0371	0.0166	0.0075
96	0.6195	0.4881	0.3847	0.2395	0.1494	0.0586	0.0232	0.0092	0.0037
100	0.6073	0.4737	0.3697	0.2256	0.1380	0.0520	0.0198	0.0076	0.0029
108	0.5835	0.4462	0.3414	0.2003	0.1178	0.0411	0.0145	0.0051	0.0018
120	0.5496	0.4079	0.3030	0.1675	0.0929	0.0288	0.0090	0.0029	0.0009
180	0.4075	0.2605	0.1668	0.0686	0.0283	0.0049	0.0009	0.0002	0.0000
360	0.1660	0.0679	0.0278	0.0047	0.0008	0.0000	0.0000	0.0000	0.0000

Interest Rate (percent)

7.00	8.00	9.00	10.00	11.00	12.00	13.00	14.00	15.00	20.00
0.9346	0.9259	0.9174	0.9091	0.9009	0.8929	0.8850	0.8772	0.8696	0.8333
0.8734	0.8573	0.8417	0.8264	0.8116	0.7972	0.7831	0.7695	0.7561	0.6944
0.8163	0.7938	0.7722	0.7513	0.7312	0.7118	0.6931	0.6750	0.6575	0.5787
0.7629	0.7350	0.7084	0.6830	0.6587	0.6355	0.6133	0.5921	0.5718	0.4823
0.7130	0.6806	0.6499	0.6209	0.5935	0.5674	0.5428	0.5194	0.4972	0.4019
0.6663	0.6302	0.5963	0.5645	0.5346	0.5066	0.4803	0.4556	0.4323	0.3349
0.6227	0.5835	0.5470	0.5132	0.4817	0.4523	0.4251	0.3996	0.3759	0.2791
0.5820	0.5403	0.5019	0.4665	0.4339	0.4039	0.3762	0.3506	0.3269	0.2326
0.5439	0.5002	0.4604	0.4241	0.3909	0.3606	0.3329	0.3075	0.2843	0.1938
0.5083	0.4632	0.4224	0.3855	0.3522	0.3220	0.2946	0.2697	0.2472	0.1615
0.4751	0.4289	0.3875	0.3505	0.3173	0.2875	0.2607	0.2366	0.2149	0.1346
0.4440	0.3971	0.3555	0.3186	0.2858	0.2567	0.2307	0.2076	0.1869	0.1122
0.4150	0.3677	0.3262	0.2897	0.2575	0.2292	0.2042	0.1821	0.1625	0.0935
0.3878	0.3405	0.2992	0.2633	0.2320	0.2046	0.1807	0.1597	0.1413	0.0779
0.3624	0.3152	0.2745	0.2394	0.2090	0.1827	0.1599	0.1401	0.1229	0.0649
0.3387	0.2919	0.2519	0.2176	0.1883	0.1631	0.1415	0.1229	0.1069	0.0541
0.3166	0.2703	0.2311	0.1978	0.1696	0.1456	0.1252	0.1078	0.0929	0.0451
0.2959	0.2502	0.2120	0.1799	0.1528	0.1300	0.1108	0.0946	0.0808	0.0376
0.2765	0.2317	0.1945	0.1635	0.1377	0.1161	0.0981	0.0829	0.0703	0.0313
0.2584	0.2145	0.1784	0.1486	0.1240	0.1037	0.0868	0.0728	0.0611	0.0261
0.2415	0.1987	0.1637	0.1351	0.1117	0.0926	0.0768	0.0638	0.0531	0.0217
0.2257	0.1839	0.1502	0.1228	0.1007	0.0826	0.0680	0.0560	0.0462	0.0181
0.2109	0.1703	0.1378	0.1117	0.0907	0.0738	0.0601	0.0491	0.0402	0.0151
0.1971	0.1577	0.1264	0.1015	0.0817	0.0659	0.0532	0.0431	0.0349	0.0126
0.1842	0.1460	0.1160	0.0923	0.0736	0.0588	0.0471	0.0378	0.0304	0.0105
0.1722	0.1352	0.1064	0.0839	0.0663	0.0525	0.0417	0.0331	0.0264	0.0087
0.1609	0.1252	0.0976	0.0763	0.0597	0.0469	0.0369	0.0291	0.0230	0.0073
0.1504	0.1159	0.0895	0.0693	0.0538	0.0419	0.0326	0.0255	0.0200	0.0061
0.1406	0.1073	0.0822	0.0630	0.0485	0.0374	0.0289	0.0224	0.0174	0.0051
0.1314	0.0994	0.0754	0.0573	0.0437	0.0334	0.0256	0.0196	0.0151	0.0042
0.0875	0.0626	0.0449	0.0323	0.0234	0.0169	0.0123	0.0089	0.0065	0.0014
0.0389	0.0249	0.0160	0.0103	0.0067	0.0043	0.0028	0.0019	0.0012	0.0002
0.0173	0.0099	0.0057	0.0033	0.0019	0.0011	0.0007	0.0004	0.0002	0.0000
0.0077	0.0039	0.0020	0.0010	0.0005	0.0003	0.0002	0.0001	0.0000	0.0000
0.0034	0.0016	0.0007	0.0003	0.0002	0.0001	0.0000	0.0000	0.0000	0.0000
0.0015	0.0006	0.0003	0.0001	0.0000	0.0000	0.0000	0.0000	0.0000	0.0000
0.0012	0.0005	0.0002	0.0001	0.0000	0.0000	0.0000	0.0000	0.0000	0.0000
0.0007	0.0002	0.0001	0.0000	0.0000	0.0000	0.0000	0.0000	0.0000	0.0000
0.0003	0.0001	0.0000	0.0000	0.0000	0.0000	0.0000	0.0000	0.0000	0.0000
0.0000	0.0000	0.0000	0.0000	0.0000	0.0000	0.0000	0.0000	0.0000	0.0000
0.0000	0.0000	0.0000	0.0000	0.0000	0.0000	0.0000	0.0000	0.0000	0.0000

APPENDIX A-3

Future Value of an Ordinary Annuity of $1

Interest Rate (percent)

Periods	0.50	0.75	1.00	1.50	2.00	3.00	4.00	5.00	6.00
1	1.0000	1.0000	1.0000	1.0000	1.0000	1.0000	1.0000	1.0000	1.0000
2	2.0050	2.0075	2.0100	2.0150	2.0200	2.0300	2.0400	2.0500	2.0600
3	3.0150	3.0226	3.0301	3.0452	3.0604	3.0909	3.1216	3.1525	3.1836
4	4.0301	4.0452	4.0604	4.0909	4.1216	4.1836	4.2465	4.3101	4.3746
5	5.0503	5.0756	5.1010	5.1523	5.2040	5.3091	5.4163	5.5256	5.6371
6	6.0755	6.1136	6.1520	6.2296	6.3081	6.4684	6.6330	6.8019	6.9753
7	7.1059	7.1595	7.2135	7.3230	7.4343	7.6625	7.8983	8.1420	8.3938
8	8.1414	8.2132	8.2857	8.4328	8.5830	8.8923	9.2142	9.5491	9.8975
9	9.1821	9.2748	9.3685	9.5593	9.7546	10.1591	10.5828	11.0266	11.4913
10	10.2280	10.3443	10.4622	10.7027	10.9497	11.4639	12.0061	12.5779	13.1808
11	11.2792	11.4219	11.5668	11.8633	12.1687	12.8078	13.4864	14.2068	14.9716
12	12.3356	12.5076	12.6825	13.0412	13.4121	14.1920	15.0258	15.9171	16.8699
13	13.3972	13.6014	13.8093	14.2368	14.6803	15.6178	16.6268	17.7130	18.8821
14	14.4642	14.7034	14.9474	15.4504	15.9739	17.0863	18.2919	19.5986	21.0151
15	15.5365	15.8137	16.0969	16.6821	17.2934	18.5989	20.0236	21.5786	23.2760
16	16.6142	16.9323	17.2579	17.9324	18.6393	20.1569	21.8245	23.6575	25.6725
17	17.6973	18.0593	18.4304	19.2014	20.0121	21.7616	23.6975	25.8404	28.2129
18	18.7858	19.1947	19.6147	20.4894	21.4123	23.4144	25.6454	28.1324	30.9057
19	19.8797	20.3387	20.8109	21.7967	22.8406	25.1169	27.6712	30.5390	33.7600
20	20.9791	21.4912	22.0190	23.1237	24.2974	26.8704	29.7781	33.0660	36.7856
21	22.0840	22.6524	23.2392	24.4705	25.7833	28.6765	31.9692	35.7193	39.9927
22	23.1944	23.8223	24.4716	25.8376	27.2990	30.5368	34.2480	38.5052	43.3923
23	24.3104	25.0010	25.7163	27.2251	28.8450	32.4529	36.6179	41.4305	46.9958
24	25.4320	26.1885	26.9735	28.6335	30.4219	34.4265	39.0826	44.5020	50.8156
25	26.5591	27.3849	28.2432	30.0630	32.0303	36.4593	41.6459	47.7271	54.8645
26	27.6919	28.5903	29.5256	31.5140	33.6709	38.5530	44.3117	51.1135	59.1564
27	28.8304	29.8047	30.8209	32.9867	35.3443	40.7096	47.0842	54.6691	63.7058
28	29.9745	31.0282	32.1291	34.4815	37.0512	42.9309	49.9676	58.4026	68.5281
29	31.1244	32.2609	33.4504	35.9987	38.7922	45.2189	52.9663	62.3227	73.6398
30	32.2800	33.5029	34.7849	37.5387	40.5681	47.5754	56.0849	66.4388	79.0582
36	39.3361	41.1527	43.0769	47.2760	51.9944	63.2759	77.5983	95.8363	119.1209
48	54.0978	57.5207	61.2226	69.5652	79.3535	104.4084	139.2632	188.0254	256.5645
60	69.7700	75.4241	81.6697	96.2147	114.0515	163.0534	237.9907	353.5837	533.1282
72	86.4089	95.0070	104.7099	128.0772	158.0570	246.6672	396.0566	650.9027	1,089.629
84	104.0739	116.4269	130.6723	166.1726	213.8666	365.8805	649.1251	1,184.845	2,209.417
96	122.8285	139.8562	159.9273	211.7202	284.6467	535.8502	1,054.296	2,143.728	4,462.651
100	129.3337	148.1445	170.4814	228.8030	312.2323	607.2877	1,237.624	2,610.025	5,638.368
108	142.7399	165.4832	192.8926	266.1778	374.4129	778.1863	1,702.988	3,865.745	8,996.600
120	163.8793	193.5143	230.0387	331.2882	488.2582	1,123.700	2,741.564	6,958.240	18,119.80
180	290.8187	378.4058	499.5802	905.6245	1,716.042	6,783.445	29,078.22	130,327.8	598,263.4
360	1,004.515	1,830.743	3,494.964	14,113.59	62,328.06	1,394,021	33,879,878		

Interest Rate (percent)

7.00	8.00	9.00	10.00	11.00	12.00	13.00	14.00	15.00	20.00
1.0000	1.0000	1.0000	1.0000	1.0000	1.0000	1.0000	1.0000	1.0000	1.0000
2.0700	2.0800	2.0900	2.1000	2.1100	2.1200	2.1300	2.1400	2.1500	2.2000
3.2149	3.2464	3.2781	3.3100	3.3421	3.3744	3.4069	3.4396	3.4725	3.6400
4.4399	4.5061	4.5731	4.6410	4.7097	4.7793	4.8498	4.9211	4.9934	5.3680
5.7507	5.8666	5.9847	6.1051	6.2278	6.3528	6.4803	6.6101	6.7424	7.4416
7.1533	7.3359	7.5233	7.7156	7.9129	8.1152	8.3227	8.5355	8.7537	9.9299
8.6540	8.9228	9.2004	9.4872	9.7833	10.0890	10.4047	10.7305	11.0668	12.9159
10.2598	10.6366	11.0285	11.4359	11.8594	12.2997	12.7573	13.2328	13.7268	16.4991
11.9780	12.4876	13.0210	13.5795	14.1640	14.7757	15.4157	16.0853	16.7858	20.7989
13.8164	14.4866	15.1929	15.9374	16.7220	17.5487	18.4197	19.3373	20.3037	25.9587
15.7836	16.6455	17.5603	18.5312	19.5614	20.6546	21.8143	23.0445	24.3493	32.1504
17.8885	18.9771	20.1407	21.3843	22.7132	24.1331	25.6502	27.2707	29.0017	39.5805
20.1406	21.4953	22.9534	24.5227	26.2116	28.0291	29.9847	32.0887	34.3519	48.4966
22.5505	24.2149	26.0192	27.9750	30.0949	32.3926	34.8827	37.5811	40.5047	59.1959
25.1290	27.1521	29.3609	31.7725	34.4054	37.2797	40.4175	43.8424	47.5804	72.0351
27.8881	30.3243	33.0034	35.9497	39.1899	42.7533	46.6717	50.9804	55.7175	87.4421
30.8402	33.7502	36.9737	40.5447	44.5008	48.8837	53.7391	59.1176	65.0751	105.9306
33.9990	37.4502	41.3013	45.5992	50.3959	55.7497	61.7251	68.3941	75.8364	128.1167
37.3790	41.4463	46.0185	51.1591	56.9395	63.4397	70.7494	78.9692	88.2118	154.7400
40.9955	45.7620	51.1601	57.2750	64.2028	72.0524	80.9468	91.0249	102.4436	186.6880
44.8652	50.4229	56.7645	64.0025	72.2651	81.6987	92.4699	104.7684	118.8101	225.0256
49.0057	55.4568	62.8733	71.4027	81.2143	92.5026	105.4910	120.4360	137.6316	271.0307
53.4361	60.8933	69.5319	79.5430	91.1479	104.6029	120.2048	138.2970	159.2764	326.2369
58.1767	66.7648	76.7898	88.4973	102.1742	118.1552	136.8315	158.6586	184.1678	392.4842
63.2490	73.1059	84.7009	98.3471	114.4133	133.3339	155.6196	181.8708	212.7930	471.9811
68.6765	79.9544	93.3240	109.1818	127.9988	150.3339	176.8501	208.3327	245.7120	567.3773
74.4838	87.3508	102.7231	121.0999	143.0786	169.3740	200.8406	238.4993	283.5688	681.8528
80.6977	95.3388	112.9682	134.2099	159.8173	190.6989	227.9499	272.8892	327.1041	819.2233
87.3465	103.9659	124.1354	148.6309	178.3972	214.5828	258.5834	312.0937	377.1697	984.0680
94.4608	113.2832	136.3075	164.4940	199.0209	241.3327	293.1992	356.7868	434.7451	1,181.882
148.9135	187.1021	236.1247	299.1268	380.1644	484.4631	618.7493	791.6729	1,014.346	3,539.009
353.2701	490.1322	684.2804	960.1723	1,352.700	1,911.590	2,707.633	3,841.475	5,456.005	31,593.74
813.5204	1,253.213	1,944.792	3,034.816	4,755.066	7,471.641	11,761.95	18,535.13	29,219.99	281,732.6
1,850.092	3,174.781	5,490.189	9,545.938	16,658.08	29,133.47	51,008.09	89,327.78	156,363.3	2,511,995
4,184.651	8,013.617	15,462.20	29,980.63	58,300.17	113,527.4	221,121.4	430,400.0	836,611.6	22,397,244
9,442.523	20,198.63	43,510.13	94,113.44	203,983.0	442,324.2	958,481.5	2,073,654	4,476,110	
12,381.66	27,484.52	61,422.68	137,796.1	309,665.2	696,010.5	1,562,784	3,502,323	7,828,750	
21,284.26	50,882.56	122,399.6	295,389.7	713,647.1	1,723,309	4,154,586	9,990,693	23,948,338	
47,954.12	128,149.9	344,289.1	927,080.7	2,496,682	6,713,994	18,008,174	48,134,233		
2,779,583	12,977,337	60,607,594							

APPENDIX A-4

Present Value of an Ordinary Annuity of $1

Interest Rate (percent)

Periods	0.50	0.75	1.00	1.50	2.00	3.00	4.00	5.00	6.00
1	0.9950	0.9926	0.9901	0.9852	0.9804	0.9709	0.9615	0.9524	0.9434
2	1.9851	1.9777	1.9704	1.9559	1.9416	1.9135	1.8861	1.8594	1.8334
3	2.9702	2.9556	2.9410	2.9122	2.8839	2.8286	2.7751	2.7232	2.6730
4	3.9505	3.9261	3.9020	3.8544	3.8077	3.7171	3.6299	3.5460	3.4651
5	4.9259	4.8894	4.8534	4.7826	4.7135	4.5797	4.4518	4.3295	4.2124
6	5.8964	5.8456	5.7955	5.6972	5.6014	5.4172	5.2421	5.0757	4.9173
7	6.8621	6.7946	6.7282	6.5982	6.4720	6.2303	6.0021	5.7864	5.5824
8	7.8230	7.7366	7.6517	7.4859	7.3255	7.0197	6.7327	6.4632	6.2098
9	8.7791	8.6716	8.5660	8.3605	8.1622	7.7861	7.4353	7.1078	6.8017
10	9.7304	9.5996	9.4713	9.2222	8.9826	8.5302	8.1109	7.7217	7.3601
11	10.6770	10.5207	10.3676	10.0711	9.7868	9.2526	8.7605	8.3064	7.8869
12	11.6189	11.4349	11.2551	10.9075	10.5753	9.9540	9.3851	8.8633	8.3838
13	12.5562	12.3423	12.1337	11.7315	11.3484	10.6350	9.9856	9.3936	8.8527
14	13.4887	13.2430	13.0037	12.5434	12.1062	11.2961	10.5631	9.8986	9.2950
15	14.4166	14.1370	13.8651	13.3432	12.8493	11.9379	11.1184	10.3797	9.7122
16	15.3399	15.0243	14.7179	14.1313	13.5777	12.5611	11.6523	10.8378	10.1059
17	16.2586	15.9050	15.5623	14.9076	14.2919	13.1661	12.1657	11.2741	10.4773
18	17.1728	16.7792	16.3983	15.6726	14.9920	13.7535	12.6593	11.6896	10.8276
19	18.0824	17.6468	17.2260	16.4262	15.6785	14.3238	13.1339	12.0853	11.1581
20	18.9874	18.5080	18.0456	17.1686	16.3514	14.8775	13.5903	12.4622	11.4699
21	19.8880	19.3628	18.8570	17.9001	17.0112	15.4150	14.0292	12.8212	11.7641
22	20.7841	20.2112	19.6604	18.6208	17.6580	15.9369	14.4511	13.1630	12.0416
23	21.6757	21.0533	20.4558	19.3309	18.2922	16.4436	14.8568	13.4886	12.3034
24	22.5629	21.8891	21.2434	20.0304	18.9139	16.9355	15.2470	13.7986	12.5504
25	23.4456	22.7188	22.0232	20.7196	19.5235	17.4131	15.6221	14.0939	12.7834
26	24.3240	23.5422	22.7952	21.3986	20.1210	17.8768	15.9828	14.3752	13.0032
27	25.1980	24.3595	23.5596	22.0676	20.7069	18.3270	16.3296	14.6430	13.2105
28	26.0677	25.1707	24.3164	22.7267	21.2813	18.7641	16.6631	14.8981	13.4062
29	26.9330	25.9759	25.0658	23.3761	21.8444	19.1885	16.9837	15.1411	13.5907
30	27.7941	26.7751	25.8077	24.0158	22.3965	19.6004	17.2920	15.3725	13.7648
36	32.8710	31.4468	30.1075	27.6607	25.4888	21.8323	18.9083	16.5469	14.6210
48	42.5803	40.1848	37.9740	34.0426	30.6731	25.2667	21.1951	18.0772	15.6500
60	51.7256	48.1734	44.9550	39.3803	34.7609	27.6756	22.6235	18.9293	16.1614
72	60.3395	55.4768	51.1504	43.8447	37.9841	29.3651	23.5156	19.4038	16.4156
84	68.4530	62.1540	56.6485	47.5786	40.5255	30.5501	24.0729	19.6680	16.5419
96	76.0952	68.2584	61.5277	50.7017	42.5294	31.3812	24.4209	19.8151	16.6047
100	78.5426	70.1746	63.0289	51.6247	43.0984	31.5989	24.5050	19.8479	16.6175
108	83.2934	73.8394	65.8578	53.3137	44.1095	31.9642	24.6383	19.8971	16.6358
120	90.0735	78.9417	69.7005	55.4985	45.3554	32.3730	24.7741	19.9427	16.6514
180	118.5035	98.5934	83.3217	62.0956	48.5844	33.1703	24.9785	19.9969	16.6662
360	166.7916	124.2819	97.2183	66.3532	49.9599	33.3325	25.0000	20.0000	16.6667

282

Interest Rate (percent)

7.00	8.00	9.00	10.00	11.00	12.00	13.00	14.00	15.00	20.00
0.9346	0.9259	0.9174	0.9091	0.9009	0.8929	0.8850	0.8772	0.8696	0.8333
1.8080	1.7833	1.7591	1.7355	1.7125	1.6901	1.6681	1.6467	1.6257	1.5278
2.6243	2.5771	2.5313	2.4869	2.4437	2.4018	2.3612	2.3216	2.2832	2.1065
3.3872	3.3121	3.2397	3.1699	3.1024	3.0373	2.9745	2.9137	2.8550	2.5887
4.1002	3.9927	3.8897	3.7908	3.6959	3.6048	3.5172	3.4331	3.3522	2.9906
4.7665	4.6229	4.4859	4.3553	4.2305	4.1114	3.9975	3.8887	3.7845	3.3255
5.3893	5.2064	5.0330	4.8684	4.7122	4.5638	4.4226	4.2883	4.1604	3.6046
5.9713	5.7466	5.5348	5.3349	5.1461	4.9676	4.7988	4.6389	4.4873	3.8372
6.5152	6.2469	5.9952	5.7590	5.5370	5.3282	5.1317	4.9464	4.7716	4.0310
7.0236	6.7101	6.4177	6.1446	5.8892	5.6502	5.4262	5.2161	5.0188	4.1925
7.4987	7.1390	6.8052	6.4951	6.2065	5.9377	5.6869	5.4527	5.2337	4.3271
7.9427	7.5361	7.1607	6.8137	6.4924	6.1944	5.9176	5.6603	5.4206	4.4392
8.3577	7.9038	7.4869	7.1034	6.7499	6.4235	6.1218	5.8424	5.5831	4.5327
8.7455	8.2442	7.7862	7.3667	6.9819	6.6282	6.3025	6.0021	5.7245	4.6106
9.1079	8.5595	8.0607	7.6061	7.1909	6.8109	6.4624	6.1422	5.8474	4.6755
9.4466	8.8514	8.3126	7.8237	7.3792	6.9740	6.6039	6.2651	5.9542	4.7296
9.7632	9.1216	8.5436	8.0216	7.5488	7.1196	6.7291	6.3729	6.0472	4.7746
10.0591	9.3719	8.7556	8.2014	7.7016	7.2497	6.8399	6.4674	6.1280	4.8122
10.3356	9.6036	8.9501	8.3649	7.8393	7.3658	6.9380	6.5504	6.1982	4.8435
10.5940	9.8181	9.1285	8.5136	7.9633	7.4694	7.0248	6.6231	6.2593	4.8696
10.8355	10.0168	9.2922	8.6487	8.0751	7.5620	7.1016	6.6870	6.3125	4.8913
11.0612	10.2007	9.4424	8.7715	8.1757	7.6446	7.1695	6.7429	6.3587	4.9094
11.2722	10.3711	9.5802	8.8832	8.2664	7.7184	7.2297	6.7921	6.3988	4.9245
11.4693	10.5288	9.7066	8.9847	8.3481	7.7843	7.2829	6.8351	6.4338	4.9371
11.6536	10.6748	9.8226	9.0770	8.4217	7.8431	7.3300	6.8729	6.4641	4.9476
11.8258	10.8100	9.9290	9.1609	8.4881	7.8957	7.3717	6.9061	6.4906	4.9563
11.9867	10.9352	10.0266	9.2372	8.5478	7.9426	7.4086	6.9352	6.5135	4.9636
12.1371	11.0511	10.1161	9.3066	8.6016	7.9844	7.4412	6.9607	6.5335	4.9697
12.2777	11.1584	10.1983	9.3696	8.6501	8.0218	7.4701	6.9830	6.5509	4.9747
12.4090	11.2578	10.2737	9.4269	8.6938	8.0552	7.4957	7.0027	6.5660	4.9789
13.0352	11.7172	10.6118	9.6765	8.8786	8.1924	7.5979	7.0790	6.6231	4.9929
13.7305	12.1891	10.9336	9.8969	9.0302	8.2972	7.6705	7.1296	6.6585	4.9992
14.0392	12.3766	11.0480	9.9672	9.0736	8.3240	7.6873	7.1401	6.6651	4.9999
14.1763	12.4510	11.0887	9.9895	9.0860	8.3310	7.6911	7.1423	6.6664	5.0000
14.2371	12.4805	11.1031	9.9967	9.0895	8.3327	7.6920	7.1427	6.6666	5.0000
14.2641	12.4923	11.1083	9.9989	9.0905	8.3332	7.6922	7.1428	6.6667	5.0000
14.2693	12.4943	11.1091	9.9993	9.0906	8.3332	7.6923	7.1428	6.6667	5.0000
14.2761	12.4969	11.1101	9.9997	9.0908	8.3333	7.6923	7.1429	6.6667	5.0000
14.2815	12.4988	11.1108	9.9999	9.0909	8.3333	7.6923	7.1429	6.6667	5.0000
14.2856	12.5000	11.1111	10.0000	9.0909	8.3333	7.6923	7.1429	6.6667	5.0000
14.2857	12.5000	11.1111	10.0000	9.0909	8.3333	7.6923	7.1429	6.6667	5.0000

GLOSSARY

Accounting exposure The change in a firm's equity that occurs due to accounting requirements when financial statements denominated in a foreign currency are converted to the domestic currency.

Adjustable rate preferred stock (ARPS) An issue of preferred stock on which the dividends are not fixed, but instead change periodically with some benchmark rate, such as the long-term Treasury bond yield.

All-or-nothing commitment A best-efforts agreement wherein the investment banker and the issuing firm further agree that if the entire issue cannot be sold, none of the securities will be sold.

Annual percentage rate The nominal or stated rate of interest. This rate does not take the effects of compounding into account.

Annuity A series of equal deposits or withdrawals.

Annuity due A series of equal deposits or withdrawals that occur *at the beginning of each period.*

Articles of incorporation Documents filed with the secretary of state by a corporation that seeks to be incorporated in that state.

Ask price The price at which dealers are willing to sell a security.

Asset management ratios A set of ratios that measure how well a firm is utilizing its assets.

At the money option An option on which the strike price is approximately equal to the current market price of the stock. The option can be either a call option or a put option.

Authorized shares The maximum number of shares that a corporation can sell as indicated in the articles of incorporation.

Average collection period An asset management ratio that measures the average number of days that it takes a firm's credit customers to pay their bills.

Balance of payments A record of all the monetary transactions that have occurred between one country and all the other countries in the world.

Balance sheet A financial statement that presents a picture of the financial position of a firm at a specific point in time.

Bank holding companies A corporation that controls a large number of individual banks, each of which has its own board of directors and executive management team.

Bank Holding Company Act of 1956 A federal law that defined a bank as an institution that accepts deposits that can be withdrawn upon demand and that makes commerical loans.

Bank of International Settlements (BIS) An international organization that provides assistance to countries that are experiencing a financial crisis.

Bankers' acceptances Drafts that are dual obligations of the writer of the draft and the bank on which the draft is drawn. These are short-term debt obligations used primarily in international trade.

Barter system The direct transfer of goods and services without the use of money.

Basic balance On the balance of payments, the sum of the current account and the direct investment and capital account.

Baumol Model A cash management model that is used to determine the amount of cash that a firm should hold to minimize its total costs. This model assumes that cash is used uniformly throughout the period.

Bearer bonds Bonds which are owned by whoever has physical possession of them. The issuing firm has no record of the investor's name and address, and the investor must clip coupons and send them to the issuing firm's agent in order to receive the interest payments. The investor must also send the bond to the issuing firm's agent upon maturity in order to receive the maturity value.

Best-efforts agreement A situation wherein the investment banker agrees to do his best to sell an issue for the issuing firm. However, the investment banker does not buy the issue from the firm and receives only a commission for the securities that are sold. Any unsold securities are returned to the issuing firm.

Beta A measure of systematic risk.

Bid price The price at which dealers are willing to buy a security.

Block trade A trade consisting of 10,000 or more shares.

Blue sky laws State securities regulations.

Bond market The market on which debt issues are traded.

Bond rating A measure of the default risk of a debt issue of a firm.

Bond series Several bond issues that are issued under one blanket indenture provision.

Breakeven point   The volume of sales at which total revenues equal total costs.

Breakpoints   Sales volume levels at which investors in a load mutual fund can receive a reduced sales charge.

Broker   An individual who matches buyers and sellers of securities in return for a commission.

Bulldogs   Bonds issued in the United Kingdom by a foreign borrower and denominated in pounds.

Business risk   The uncertainty regarding the operating profits of a firm.

Bylaws   Rules of a corporation that are established by its founders and govern the internal affairs of the firm. They may be changed only with shareholder approval.

Call option   An instrument that gives the investor the right to purchase the underlying asset at a prespecified price for a price agreed upon today.

Callable bond   A bond that may be repurchased by the issuing firm from the investor at a prespecified price.

Callable preferred stock   An issue of preferred stock that allows the issuing firm to buy back the stock from the investors at a prespecified price.

CAMEL ratings   A common framework agreed upon by the Comptroller of the Currency, the Federal Reserve, and the FDIC that is used to assess a bank's soundness.

Capital Asset Pricing Model   The relationship between the systematic risk of a security and its expected equilibrium rate of return.

Capital assets   Long-term assets.

Capital budgeting The process of selecting which long-term investments a firm should make.

Capital gains   A gain on the sale of any capital asset. For a bond, the difference between the purchase price of the bond and the amount that the investor receives when the bond matures.

Capital market   The market on which long-term securities (i.e., securities with greater than 1 year to maturity) are traded.

Capital structure   The amount of debt, preferred stock, and common equity that a firm uses to finance its operations.

Certificates of deposit   Short-term debt issued by banks that have varying maturities up to 1 year and have minimum denominations of $100,000.

Chicago Board Options Exchange (CBOE)   Initially, the only trading floor on which existing options could be bought and sold.

Clientele effect   The phenomenon that refers to the fact that different investors have different preferences for the type of income they want—i.e., dividend income versus capital gains.

Closed-end investment company   A company that pools the money of its investors and invests in a set of securities according to a stated investment objective. A closed-end company has a fixed number of shares that are traded on exchange floors. The share prices are set by supply and demand.

Coefficient of variation   A relative measure of variability that is calculated by dividing the standard deviation by the expected value.

Collar   The maximum and minimum dividend rates specified on an issue of adjustable rate preferred stock.

Collateral trust receipts   Bonds that are backed by stocks and bonds owned by the borrowing firm.

Collection float   The amount of time it takes for a firm to have use of the funds after a customer has paid for its goods.

Commercial paper   Short-term, unsecured debt issued by large corporations.

Commission broker   An employer of a brokerage firm who occupies the firm's seat on the exchange floor.

Commitment fee   A fee that is paid to a bank that legally binds the bank to loan a firm up to a maximum amount upon request by the firm.

Commodity Futures Trading Commission (CFTC) The regulatory agency for the futures markets.

Compensating balance requirement   Proceeds that a firm must hold at a bank, often in a noninterest bearing account, in return for services that the bank has agreed to provide.

Competitive Banking Equality Act of 1987   A federal law that defined a bank as any institution that is insured by the FDIC. This law applies only to those institutions that were established after March 4, 1986.

Competitive underwriting   A situation wherein the issuing firm announces its plans to issue a security and requests bids from the investment banking industry.

Compound interest   Interest that is paid on both the principal and any accumulated interest.

Compounding The process of finding a future value when a present value is known.

Consumer Price Index (CPI) The cost of a market basket of goods that is perceived to reflect the purchases made by the average consumer. Changes in the CPI are used to measure inflation.

Contiguous county branching A state law under which banks may establish branches only in counties that are adjacent to those in which they already have operations.

Continuous probability distribution A probability distribution having an infinite number of possible outcomes.

Conversion price The amount of a bond's face value that is exchanged for each share of stock.

Conversion ratio The number of shares of common stock that will be received for each share of preferred stock or for each bond that is exchanged.

Conversion value The market price of the common stock times the conversion ratio. The value of the convertible security *if* it is converted to common stock.

Convertible bond A bond that can be exchanged for shares of the firm's common stock.

Convertible preferred stock An issue of preferred stock that allows its shareholders to redeem the preferred shares for shares of common stock of the firm.

Corporate charter A document granted by the state that binds the corporation to abide by the articles of incorporation and the laws of that state.

Corporation A legal entity that is empowered by the state in which it is incorporated to own assets in its own name.

Correlation coefficient A measure of the comovement of two variables. The correlation coefficient can have values between negative one and positive one, inclusive.

Correspondent bank A large metropolitan bank that serves as a depository for smaller banks in the area.

Cost of capital The average cost of the securities that a firm uses to finance its operations.

Coupon The dollar amount of interest that is paid annually on a note or bond.

Coupon rate The nominal annual interest rate that a note or bond is paying. The annual dollar amount can be determined by multiplying the coupon rate by the face value of the note or bond.

Coverage ratio (TIE ratio) A leverage ratio that indicates how much operating profit a firm has to cover its interest expense.

Covered option A call option written by an investor who owns the underlying stock.

Cumulative preferred stock An issue of preferred stock on which any missed dividend payments must be paid in arrears before common shareholders can receive any payments.

Cumulative voting A system of voting which allows each shareholder a number of votes equal to the number of seats on the board of directors that are up for election times the number of shares owned by the shareholder. This system is designed to allow shareholders who hold a minority of the shares to gain representation on the board.

Current account A section on the balance of payments that lists the value of goods and services that have been imported and exported, government spending abroad, and foreign investment income for the specified time period.

Current assets Assets that are considered to be quickly converted to cash, within 1 year or 1 operating cycle.

Current liabilities Debt obligations that are due within 1 year or 1 operating cycle.

Current-rate method The official method used in the United States to account for international activities.

Current ratio A liquidity ratio that measures how many dollars of current assets a firm has for each dollar of short-term debt.

Current yield The return that a bondholder is earning on the interest income only. Capital gains or losses are not included. The current yield is calculated by dividing the annual amount of interest by the price of the bond.

Day order A limit order that is cancelled at the end of the trading day. Unless a time limit is specified, a limit order is automatically considered to be a day order.

Dealer An individual who buys and sells securities from his or her own inventory.

Dealer paper Commercial paper that is sold to investors through dealers, who charge the issuing firms a spread for their services.

Dealer's spread The difference between the ask price and the bid price.

Debt/equity ratio A leverage ratio that measures how much debt a firm has for every dollar of shareholders' investment. Either total debt or long-term debt may be used in this calculation.

Debt ratio   A leverage ratio that indicates how much debt the firm has supporting every dollar in assets.

Declaration date   The day on which the board of directors announce that dividends will be paid.

Default risk   The risk that the bond issuer will be unable to meet the required payments.

Deferred call   A feature on a callable bond that stipulates that the issuing firm cannot buy the bond back from the investor until a certain amount of time has passed.

Deflation   A general decrease in price levels.

Degree of financial leverage   The percentage change in earnings per share that will result from each percentage change in operating profit.

Degree of operating leverage   The percentage change in operating profit that will result from each percentage change in sales.

Degree of total leverage   The percentage change in earnings per share that results from each percentage change in sales.

Demand deposits   Checking accounts.

Depository Institution Deregulation and Monetary Control (DIDMC) Act of 1980   A federal law that provided for the phase out of interest rate ceilings that depository institutions could pay its depositors, allowed thrift institutions to make commerical loans and to offer checking accounts. It also allowed interest to be paid on checkable deposits.

Depository institutions   Financial intermediaries that accept deposits from its customers—namely, commercial banks, savings and loan associations, mutual savings banks, and credit unions.

Detachable warrant   A warrant that is sold attached to a bond that allows the investor to keep the bond and sell the warrant or vice versa if he so chooses.

Devalued   A term that is used when a foreign currency that is pegged to gold or to another currency has decreased in value relative to other currencies. If a floating currency loses value, it is said to have **weakened, deteriorated,** or **depreciated.**

Direct investment and capital account   A section on the balance of payments that tracks long-term capital flows.

Direct paper   Commercial paper that is sold directly to investors by the firm.

Direct quote   The price in the home currency that is equal to one unit of a foreign currency.

Disbursement float   The amount of time it takes before payments to suppliers result in an actual cash outflow for the firm.

Discount basis loan   A loan for which the interest is paid at the beginning of the loan period.

Discount bond   A bond that is selling for less than its face value.

Discount forward rate   A forward rate for which the direct quote is less than the direct spot rate.

Discount rate   The interest rate that the Federal Reserve charges depository institutions for Federal advances.

Discounting   The process of finding a present value when a future value is known.

Disinflation   A decrease in the rate of inflation.

Disintermediation   A phenomenon that refers to investors' pulling money out of accounts with financial intermediaries and investing directly in stocks and bonds.

Dividend payout ratio   The percentage of a firm's earnings that is distributed to its common shareholders.

Dividend per share   The amount of a firm's profits that a shareholder will receive for each share that he or she owns.

Dividend yield   The return that an investor receives from the dividend income only. Capital gains and losses are not included. The dividend yield is calculated by dividing the dividend by the price of the stock.

Dividends per share   The current cash flow that shareholders' will receive for each share that they own.

Douglas Amendment   An amendment to the McFadden Act that prohibits bank holding companies from crossing state lines unless the authorities of the individual states are in agreement.

Dual banking system   The system that exists in the United States whereby banks may be chartered by either the federal government or a state government.

Dual currency bonds   Bonds for which the purchase price and the coupon payment are denominated in one currency and the principal redemption price is denominated in a second currency.

Dual listings   Stocks that are listed both on a major exchange and on a regional exchange.

Due diligence A specification requiring investment bankers to verify the information that the issuing firm provides in its registration statement, even to the extent of investigating the issuing firm's corporate charter, past financial statements, corporate minutes, patents, and customers.

Earnings per share The earnings available to a firm's common shareholders on a proportionate basis.

Economic exposure The change in a firm's value that results from an *unexpected* change in exchange rates.

Economic order quantity model An inventory management model that calculates the amount of inventory that a firm can order which will minimize the total of the order and carrying costs.

Edge Act of 1919 A federal law that allows bank holding companies to form interstate subsidiary corporations for the specific purpose of accepting deposits and making loans related to international business transactions. The subsidiary corporations are referred to as "Edge corporations."

Effective annual rate The actual annual interest rate that is being paid when the effects of compounding are considered.

Equipment trust receipts Bonds that are backed by specific equipment that is owned by the borrowing firm.

Equity multiplier A leverage ratio that indicates how many dollars of assets a firm has for each dollar of shareholders' investment.

Equivalent annual annuity approach A capital budgeting evaluation procedure that is used when evaluating mutually exclusive projects that have unequal lives.

Errors and omissions A section on the balance of payments that adjusts for statistical discrepancies that exist.

Euro-commercial paper An unsecured debt obligation that is denominated in a eurocurrency.

Eurobond Long-term debt that is denominated in a currency other than the home currency of the country in which the bond is sold.

Eurocurrencies Currencies deposited in banks in countries other than the home country of the currency.

Eurocurrency loan A loan that is denominated in a currency other than the home currency of the lender.

Eurodollar deposits CDs issued by banks outside the United States, but denominated in U.S. dollars. The maturities range up to 6 months.

Eurodollar loan A dollar-denominated loan made by a foreign bank.

Eurodollars Dollar deposits held by foreign banks.

European Currency Unit (ECU) A unit of account that is a weighted average of the exchange rates of the member countries. Each weight is determined by the member country's gross national product and its activity in intra-European trade.

European terms The quotes used by foreign currency dealers. The amount of foreign currency to be received for each U.S. dollar. An exception to this is the quote for the U.S. dollar and the British pound.

Ex-dividend date The day that is 4 business days before the record date. An investor purchasing the stock on or after this date will *not* receive the announced dividend payment.

Excess reserves Cash that a depository institution has that is more than the amount mandated by the Federal Reserve.

Exchange rate The price of one currency in terms of another.

Exercise period The time period during which an option has value. At the end of the exercise period, the option expires worthless.

Exercise price The price at which the holder of an option can buy or sell the underlying security.

Expectations Hypothesis A theory regarding the term structure of interest rates. It states that future interest rates are based on investor expectations about future inflation rates.

Expected value A measure of the central tendency of a probability distribution. It is calculated as a weighted average of the possible outcomes, using probabilities as weights.

Face value (or **maturity value** or **par value**) The amount that the investor in a debt instrument will receive when the instrument matures.

Factoring of accounts receivable agreement An agreement through which the accounts receivable of a firm are sold to a lender. The agreement may be made *with recourse*, in which case the lender can seek payment from the borrower should the borrower's customers default on their bills, or *without recourse*, in which case the lender bears the risk of any bad-debt losses.

Fed funds rate The interest rate that is paid on short-term interbank loans.

Federal advance   A loan from the Federal Reserve to a depository institution.

Federal Deposit Insurance Corporation (FDIC)   A federal government agency that insures bank deposits of its member banks for up to $100,000 per account.

Federal funds borrowings   Short-term (often overnight or weekend) interbank loans.

Federal Reserve System   A quasi-government agency that consists of a seven-member Board of Governors, 12 district banks, and 25 district branch banks. This agency controls the money supply of the nation through its use of monetary policy tools, and it has regulatory power over the depository type financial institutions. It was established for the purpose of creating conditions conducive to full employment and balanced economic growth with stable prices.

Field warehouse arrangement   A secured loan arrangement wherein the inventory items that serve as collateral for a loan are controlled by a third party who is affiliated with neither the borrower nor the lender. The inventory is stored on the borrower's premises, but is physically separated from the business operations. Public notification that the separated area is a field warehouse is required.

Financial risk   The uncertainty regarding the earnings available to common shareholders due to the manner in which the firm chooses to finance its operations.

First mortgage bonds   Bonds that are secured by real estate owned by the borrower that have the highest claim on that real estate in the event of default.

Fiscal policy   Policies adopted by Congress that affect the economy and the money supply—namely, taxation, government spending, and deficit management.

Fixed-asset turnover ratio   An asset management ratio that measures how many dollars of sales are generated for each dollar the firm has invested in fixed assets.

Fixed-charges coverage ratio (FCCR)   A leverage ratio that measures a firm's ability to handle all its fixed payments, including interest, leases, sinking funds, and preferred dividends.

Floating lien or **General lien**   A loan arrangement in which all of the inventory of a firm is used as collateral for a loan. The value of the collateral decreases as the inventory is sold.

Floor planning or **Trust receipts loan**   A loan arrangement in which specific inventory items are identified as collateral to secure a loan.

Forward rate   An exchange rate agreed upon today while actual delivery and purchase of the currency will not occur until some future date.

Future value   The value of $1 invested today at some later time.

Futures options   Option contracts for which the underlying asset is a futures contract.

General obligation (GO) bonds   A type of municipal bond that is backed by the full taxing power of the issuing government.

Glass-Steagall Act of 1933   A federal law that prohibits banks from underwriting securities.

Good until cancelled order   A limit order that is (theoretically) left on the books indefinitely.

Government deficit   The amount by which the expenses of the federal government exceed its revenues.

Government surplus   The amount by which revenues generated by the federal government exceed its expenses.

Gross profit margin   A profitability ratio that indicates how much a firm has left after it has paid for the direct cost of goods sold.

Haircut   In a repurchase agreement, the difference between the price for which the borrower sells the securities and the actual market price of the securities.

Hard currency   A currency that is expected to increase in value relative to other currencies.

Holding period return   The total return that an investor earned over a specified period of time.

In-the-money call option   A call option on which the strike price is less than the current market price of the stock.

In-the-money put option   A put option on which the strike price is greater than the market price of the stock.

Income statement   A financial statement that reports the revenues and expenses for a firm over a period of time.

Independent projects   Projects for which the acceptance of one has no effect on the acceptance of the others.

Indirect quote   The amount of foreign currency to be received for one unit of the home currency.

Industrial revenue bond A type of municipal bond for which the proceeds raised are used to benefit a business venture, such as an industrial park.

Inflation A general increase in price levels.

Initial public offering (IPO) The initial public sale of a firm's stock.

Interest rate The price of credit.

Interest rate parity A theory that states that a difference in interest rates for securities of similar risk and maturity should be equal but opposite in sign to the forward exchange rate discount or premium on the foreign currency.

Internal rate of return The interest rate that will make the net present value of a project equal to zero.

International Development Association (IDA) An international organization created in 1960 for the purpose of making loans to the less prosperous nations that cannot qualify for loans from the World Bank.

International Financial Corporation (IFC) An international organization that provides loans to corporations and purchases stock of corporations for the purpose of promoting private enterprise within countries. It obtains some of its funding from the World Bank.

International Fisher Effect A theory that states that the expected change in the spot exchange rate between two countries should be equal but opposite in direction to the difference in interest rates between the countries.

International Monetary Fund (IMF) An organization originally established in 1944 by the Bretton Woods agreement to help countries maintain their exchange rates by lending funds to any member country whose currency might be in danger of weakening.

Intrastate offerings Securities that are sold only to investors living in one state.

Intrinsic value (of a call option) The difference between the market price of the underlying asset and the strike price of the option. This is the minimum price at which the option should sell.

Inventory turnover ratio An asset management ratio that indicates how often inventory needs to be replaced each year.

Investment Company Act of 1940 A federal law that requires that investment companies be registered with the SEC and provides for the regulation of these companies.

Issued shares The number of shares (ownership interests) that have been sold.

Just in time (JIT) An inventory management technique under which inventory is acquired precisely when needed so that the firm's inventory balance is always zero or very close to it.

Killer Bs Shares of common stock that have more powerful voting privileges than other shares.

Lagged reserve requirement A term that refers to the fact that a depository institution has a certain amount of time (2 days as of April 1995) in which to come up with the cash necessary to meet the Federal Reserve mandated amount, based on its daily average deposit balance over a reserve period.

Lead underwriter (or **managing house**) The investment banking firm that negotiates the terms with the issuing firm.

Letter of intent A document signed by an investor indicating that he plans on purchasing enough shares within the next 13-month period to meet a breakpoint that entitles him to a reduced sales charge on a load fund.

Leverage ratios A set of ratios that measures a firm's ability to handle its debt obligations.

LIBOR The short-term rate at which British banks borrow from each other.

Limit order An order to buy or sell a security at a prespecified price or better.

Line of credit agreement An agreement between a bank and a firm under which the bank agrees to lend the firm any amount up to a stated maximum amount upon request by the firm. The agreement is generally renegotiated on an annual basis. The line of credit may be committed, which makes it a legal obligation of the bank, or uncommitted.

Liquidity ratios A set of ratios that measures a firm's ability to handle its short-term debt obligations.

Load fund A mutual fund that has a front-end sales charge. Its shares are purchased at net asset value plus the sales charge, or load.

Loan origination fee A fee that must be paid to the lender at the beginning of the loan period.

Lockbox system A cash management technique that is used to reduce collection float. A firm's customer is directed to mail its check to a post office box that is closest to its business. The checks are retrieved by a local bank and processed for clearing.

Long hedge A futures contract position that is used to guard against adverse price movements that are related to the future purchase of a financial instrument.

Long position A position taken in a futures contract wherein the investor agrees to buy the underlying asset.

Long-term assets The fixed assets of a firm—namely, the equipment, land, and buildings that a firm owns.

Long-term debt Debt obligations that are due in more than 1 year.

M-1 A measure of the money stock that includes coin, currency, and demand deposits.

M-2 A measure of the money stock that includes coin, currency, demand deposits, savings accounts, and certificates of deposit that have a face value of $100,000 or less.

M-3 A measure of the money stock that includes coin, currency, demand deposits, savings accounts, all certificates of deposit, and money market accounts.

Maintenance margin The minimum percentage of the total value of an investor's portfolio that must be on deposit with the broker as cash. If the cash falls below this amount, a margin call will be triggered.

Maloney Act of 1938 An amendment to the Securities Exchange Act of 1934 that provides for SEC registration of national securities associations and for the establishment of standards for such organizations. The NASD is registered under this Act.

Managed (or **dirty**) **float** A reference to the intervention of central banks to prevent their country's currency from rising or falling too much relative to other currencies.

Mandatory convertible preferred stock An issue of convertible preferred stock that requires the stockholders to convert their preferred shares into common shares within a specified amount of time.

Margin A good faith deposit. The investor's equity position.

Margin call A request for an additional deposit of cash into an investor's brokerage account. If the deposit is not made, the broker will sell the investor's portfolio in order to pay off the loan that was made to the investor to allow him to purchase the securities.

Margin transaction The purchase of securities using borrowed funds.

Market order An order to buy or sell a security at the prevailing price.

Market risk premium The difference between the expected return on the market and the risk-free rate. This is the amount that the market has to pay above the risk-free rate to get investors to invest in its risky assets.

Matched order A securities transaction that does not involve a true ownership change.

McFadden Act of 1927 A law that stipulated that branching within a state could be regulated by the individual state.

Mean A measure of the central tendency of a probability distribution, or the average of the set of numbers. (See expected value.)

Miller-Orr Model A cash management model that assumes that cash flows vary unpredictably throughout the period. The model allows cash balances to vary between a lower limit and an upper limit without requiring any adjustments.

Monetary policy tools These are tools that are controlled by the Federal Reserve and are used to manipulate the supply of money in the economy. The three tools are the reserve requirement, the discount rate, and open market operations.

Money market The market on which short-term securities (i.e., securities with less than 1 year to maturity) are traded.

Money market instrument A security that has a maturity of 1 year or less.

Mortgage bonds Bonds that are secured by real estate owned by the borrower.

Multinational corporations Firms that have operations in several different countries.

Municipal bonds Debt of state and local governments.

Mutual fund An open-end investment company that pools the money of its investors and invests in a set of securities according to a stated investment objective. A mutual fund does not have a fixed number of shares but, instead, will create new shares to meet demand. The shares are bought and sold through the company itself at a price that is based on the net asset value.

Mutually exclusive projects Projects for which the acceptance of one necessarily excludes the acceptance of the others.

Naked option An uncovered option. A call option written by an investor who does not own the underlying stock.

NASDAQ The National Association of Securities Dealers Automated Quotation System. One of the computerized quotation systems on which security dealers enter their bid and ask quotes.

National Association of Securities Dealers (NASD) The only national securities association that is registered with the SEC to date (April 1995).

National Market Issues The most actively traded over-the-counter stocks.

Negotiable order of withdrawal accounts Interest-bearing checking accounts.

Negotiated underwriting An agreement for which the terms are settled between a single investment banking firm and the issuing firm.

Net asset value The value of the assets owned by an investment company minus any liabilities of the company, divided by the number of shares outstanding.

Net present value The present value of a project's cash inflows minus the present value of a project's outflows.

Net profit margin A profitability ratio that indicates how much a firm gets to keep from each dollar of sales after all its expenses are paid.

No load fund A mutual fund that has no front-end sales charge. Its shares can be purchased at net asset value.

Nominal (or stated) interest rate The observed interest rate. This interest rate incorporates a premium for inflation.

Noncumulative (or straight) preferred stock An issue of preferred stock on which any missed dividend payments are lost to the preferred shareholder forever.

Nondetachable warrant A warrant that is attached to a bond and may not be sold separately.

Nonparticipating preferred stock An issue of preferred stock that pays only a predetermined dividend to its shareholders regardless of the level of earnings of the firm.

Nonrefunding provision A bond feature that prohibits the bond issuer from buying the bond back by using the proceeds from the sale of a new, lower coupon bond.

Normal distribution A continuous probability distribution that results in a bell-shaped curve.

Odd lot A unit of trading which, for most stocks, is an order for less than 100 shares.

Offering price The price for which load mutual fund shares can be purchased. The offering price is equal to the net asset value of the fund plus a sales charge.

Official settlements balance The sum of the first four sections on the balance of payments. It is used to judge a country's competitive position relative to the rest of the world.

Open-end investment company A mutual fund.

Open interest The number of futures contracts that remain active.

Open-market operations A monetary policy tool used by the Federal Reserve. They involve the purchase or sale of Treasury securities by the Federal Reserve from (or to) the public.

Open-market purchase The purchase of Treasury securities by the Federal Reserve from the public. This is a monetary policy tool used to expand money supply.

Open-market sale The sale of Treasury securities by the Federal Reserve to the public. This is a monetary policy tool used to contract money supply.

Operating exposure See economic exposure.

Operating leverage The amount of risk that a firm has as a result of the amount of fixed operating costs it incurs relative to its variable costs.

Operating profit margin A profitability ratio that indicates how much a firm has left after it has paid all of the expenses associated with general business operations.

Opportunity cost The return that an investor could have earned on an alternative investment of similar risk.

Option contract An agreement to buy or sell an underlying asset within a specified time period for a price specified today.

Option premium The price that an investor must pay for an option.

Option writer (or **seller**) The investor who agrees to abide by the terms of the option if the option holder chooses to exercise the option. The seller of the option receives the option premium.

Ordinary annuity A series of equal deposits or withdrawals that occur *at the end of each period.*

Out-of-the-money call option A call option on which the strike price is greater than the current market price of the stock.

Out-of-the-money put option A put option on which the strike price is less than the market price of the stock.

Outright quotations   A foreign currency quotation that indicates the full price.

Outstanding shares   Shares that remain in the hands of the investors.

Par value bond   A bond that is selling for its face value.

Participating preferred stock   An issue of preferred stock that entitles the preferred shareholders to receive a percentage of the firm's earnings in addition to the stated dividend, based on a prespecified formula.

Payback period   The number of years that it takes a firm to recoup its original investment in a project.

Payment date   The day on which the dividend checks are mailed.

Penny stocks   Stocks that trade for under $1 a share.

Percent of sales method   A forecasting technique that assumes that the future value of a financial statement account will be based on that account's historical relationship to sales.

Perfectly negatively correlated   Variables that have a correlation coefficient of −1. The variables *always* move in opposite directions.

Perfectly positively correlated   Variables that have a correlation coefficient of +1. The variables *always* move together.

Perpetuity   A series of equal payments that are to continue forever.

Pledging of accounts receivable agreement   A secured loan agreement that is collateralized by the accounts receivable of the borrower. The lender reviews the invoices of the borrowing firm, decides which are acceptable as collateral, and lends the borrower a certain percentage of the value of the accepted invoices.

Poison put   A put feature on a bond that stipulates that the put option can be exercised only in the event of a hostile takeover attempt on the firm. It is used to discourage such takeovers and, as such, is one of several *shark repellants*.

Portfolio   An investment consisting of more than one asset.

Precautionary balance   The amount of extra cash that a firm holds to meet unexpected needs.

Preemptive rights   The right of a shareholder to buy any new shares that are offered for sale in a firm in order to maintain his or her percentage ownership in the firm. Preemptive rights are authorized in the corporate charter.

Preferred stock   An equity issue that has a priority claim over common stock.

Premium bond   A bond that is selling for more than its face value.

Premium forward rate   A forward rate for which the direct quote is greater than the direct spot rate.

Present value   The value of an investment today.

Price-earnings (P/E) ratio   The amount that investors are paying for a share of a firm's stock relative to each dollar of earnings that the firm has. The P/E ratio is calculated by dividing the close price of the stock by the most recent 12 months' earnings per share figure.

Primary market   The market on which new issues are traded.

Principal   The amount that is invested today. The present value.

Pro forma   A projected financial statement.

Probability distribution   A set of possible outcomes and the likelihood of their occurrence.

Profitability index (PI)   The ratio of the present value of the cash inflows to the present value of the cash outflows of a project.

Profitability ratios   A set of ratios that is designed to measure the profitability of a firm.

Prospectus   An abbreviated registration statement containing the financial statements of a firm and other information that allows an investor to judge the quality of an issue. The prospectus must be given to an investor when the security is offered for sale.

Proxy card   A document that is included with the proxy statement on which the shareholder indicates his vote.

Proxy fight   A situation that occurs when one or more groups is trying to gain control of a firm and solicits the firm's shareholders for the right to vote their shares.

Proxy statement   A statement that must be sent to shareholders of publicly held corporations that explains all the issues on which the shareholders will vote.

Public warehouse arrangement   A secured loan arrangement wherein the inventory items that serve as collateral for a loan are stored in a warehouse that is off the premises of the borrowing firm and are controlled by a third party who is affiliated with neither the borrower nor the lender.

Purchasing power parity   The theory that states that, over time, the differential rate of inflation between two countries will be offset by an equal but opposite change in their exchange rates.

Put option   An instrument that gives the investor the right to sell the underlying asset at a prespecified price for a price agreed upon today.

Putable bond   A bond that allows the bondholder to sell the bond back to the issuing firm at a prespecified price.

Quick ratio   A liquidity ratio that measures how many dollars of current assets, excluding inventory, a firm has to cover its short-term debt obligations.

Range   A statistical measure that is calculated as the difference between the highest and lowest possible outcomes.

Real interest rate   The true price of credit. The interest rate that would exist if inflation were zero.

Rear-end load   A redemption fee on a mutual fund.

Recession   An extended period (usually 6 months or more) of increased unemployment and a reduction in the national output.

Record date   In theory, the day on which an investor must own stock in order to receive the announced dividend payment. In reality, the investor must have purchased the stock 5 business days before the record date in order to receive the dividend.

Red herring prospectus   An incomplete, preliminary prospectus that has not been approved by the SEC, a fact which must be prominently stated on the front cover of the prospectus in red ink.

Redemption fee   A rear-end load. A fee that is charged mutual fund investors when they sell their shares. The investors receive net asset value minus this fee for their shares.

Registered bonds   The name and address of the bondholder is registered with the issuing firm, which sends its required payments automatically to the investor.

Registration statement   A document that must be filed with the SEC prior to the sale of a new security. The document contains the financial statements of the firm and other information that allows an investor to judge the quality of an issue.

Regulation Q   A federal law passed in 1933 that set a ceiling on the interest rates that depository institutions could pay its depositors.

Repurchase agreements   A type of secured loan in which the borrower sells high quality, short-term, marketable securities to a lender with an agreement to buy the securities back in the near future for a higher specified price.

Reserve period   The time period during which a daily average deposit balance is calculated. This balance, in turn, determines how much cash a depository institution must have. As of April 1995, this period is 2 weeks.

Reserve requirements   One of the three monetary policy tools of the Federal Reserve. These requirements mandate the amount of cash that a depository institution must hold based on the dollar amount and type of deposits that the institution has.

Return on assets   A profitability ratio that is sometimes used to judge management performance. It indicates how much income is generated for every dollar invested in total assets.

Return on equity   A profitability ratio that measures the profit that a firm is generating for each dollar of shareholders' investment. This ratio can be calculated using both common and preferred equity or using common equity only.

Revalued   A term that is used when a foreign currency that is pegged to gold or to another currency has increased in value relative to other currencies. If a floating currency increases in value, it is said to have **strengthened** or **appreciated**.

Revenue bond   A type of municipal bond that is backed by the proceeds of a specific project.

Reverse split   An accounting technique that decreases the number of shares outstanding and increases the par value of the firm's stock. The total value of the equity remains unchanged.

Reversing trade   A position taken in a futures contract that is the opposite of the position that the investor currently holds. The reversing trade cancels the contract for the investor.

Revolving credit agreement   An agreement between a bank and a firm under which the bank agrees to lend the firm any amount up to a stated maximum amount upon request by the firm. The agreement is generally longer than a line of credit agreement and may extend for 2 or 3 years. A commitment fee is paid to the lender in return for this legally binding agreement.

Rights offering   A formal procedure through which a firm issues rights to its shareholders that the shareholders can use to purchase new shares that are being sold by the firm.

Risk   The uncertainty associated with expected values.

Risk-free rate The interest rate paid on a risk-free instrument. Since Treasury securities are considered to be free from default risk, the yield on a Treasury security is used as a proxy for the risk-free rate for that specific time period.

Round lot A unit of trading which, for most stocks, is 100 shares.

Rule 134 A regulation of the SEC that establishes the guidelines for tombstone advertisements.

Rule 135A A regulation of the SEC that establishes guidelines for advertisements made by investment companies that need not be accompanied by a prospectus.

Rule 156 A regualtion of the SEC that establishes guidelines for sales literature of investment companies.

Samurai bonds Foreign bonds sold in Japan and denominated in yen.

Second (or **junior**) **mortgage bonds** Bonds that are secured by real estate owned by the borrower but that have a secondary claim on that real estate.

Secondary market The market on which used issues are traded.

Secondary reserves High quality, short-term, liquid investments held by a depository institution. These can be sold to meet reserve requirements if necessary.

Secured loans Loans that are collateralized with assets owned by the borrower.

Securities Act of 1933 A federal law that requires full and fair disclosure of information regarding new securities issues in an attempt to prevent fraud. This law instituted registration requirements for new securities.

Securities Exchange Act of 1934 A federal law that established rules for the operation of the exchange floors and the over-the-counter markets. This act also established the Securities and Exchange Commission as the regulatory agency of the securities markets.

Securities and Exchange Commission (SEC) A group of five people who are appointed by the president of the United States with Senate approval and who have the responsibility of administering all of the federal securities laws.

Securities Investor Protection Act A federal law passed in 1970 that established the Securities Investor Protection Corporation (SIPC).

Securities Investor Protection Corporation (SIPC) A federally chartered, nonprofit membership corporation that guarantees clients of insolvent member securities firms that they will be paid up to $500,000 to cover unreturned cash and/or securities. All registered brokers and dealers and members of the national securities exchanges are automatically members of the SIPC unless they are exempt.

Security Market Line The graph of the Capital Asset Pricing Model.

Selling group A group of investment bankers, brokers, and dealers who agree to sell a security issue in return for a commission for those securities that they sell.

Serial debt Debt that is issued at the same point in time but that matures at different points in time.

Settlement price The average closing price on a futures contract for any given day. Contracts are then marked to market at this price.

Share One unit of ownership of a corporation.

Shareholder value ratios A set of ratios that measures the disposition of a firm's earnings. These ratios are used as indicators of the market value of a firm's stock.

Short hedge The sale of a financial futures contract to hedge (i.e., ensure against losses in) a position that the investor currently holds in a financial instrument.

Short position A position taken in a futures contract wherein the investor agrees to sell the underlying asset.

Short sale The sale of borrowed stock.

Short-term capital account A section on the balance of payments that tracks bank deposits and investment in money market instruments.

Simple interest Interest that is paid on the principal only.

Sinking fund A bond provision that mandates that the issuing firm put aside a specified amount of money each year that can be used to retire the bond.

Snake An agreement by the members of the European Economic Community to maintain their currencies within established limits of each other.

Soft currency A currency that is expected to drop in value relative to major currencies or when the currency is being artificially supported through central bank intervention.

Special drawing rights (SDRs)   The value of a basket of five major currencies—the U.S. dollar, the French franc, the German mark, the British pound, and the Japanese yen.

Specialist   A dealer in assigned stocks on an exchange floor.

Speculative balance   The amount of extra cash that a firm holds in order to be able to take advantage of unexpected opportunities that arise.

Spot rate   The exchange rate quoted when delivery and payment is to be made within 2 business days.

Stagflation   A term that refers to a period of high unemployment coexisting with a sluggish economy.

Standard deviation   A statistical measure of dispersion. The standard deviation is the square root of the variance.

Stock   A certificate that represents an owner's investment in a firm.

Stock dividend   A distribution of additional stock to a firm's existing shareholders based on their current ownership interest in the firm. The total value of the equity remains unchanged; only the value of the individual equity accounts are changed.

Stock market   The market on which equity issues are traded.

Stock split   An accounting technique that increases the number of shares outstanding and decreases the par value of the firm's stock. The total value of the equity remains unchanged.

Strike price   The exercise price on an option contract. The prespecified price at which the investor can buy or sell the underlying asset.

Subordinated debenture   Unsecured debt that has a secondary claim to other unsecured debt issues of a firm.

Subscription price   The price at which the owner of a right can purchase one new share of the firm.

Super Dot   An electronic order-routing system that allows a firm that is a member of the NYSE to transmit an order directly to the specialist unit at which the security is traded or to the member firm's booth.

Swap rates (or **points**)   The difference between the spot rate and the forward rate, carried out to the number of decimal points traditionally used in the trading of the two currencies involved. This method of quotation is the one most often used by dealers in forward contracts.

Systematic risk   Risk that is associated with the market in general.

Term structure of interest rates   The relationship between time to maturity and yields.

Third market   Over-the-counter trading of listed securities.

Thrift institutions   This refers specifically to savings and loan associations, mutual savings banks, and credit unions.

Time value (of an option)   The amount by which the option premium exceeds the intrinsic value of the option. This amount is due to the fact that the option has more time to expiration, and the stock price can move in a direction during that time to make the option more valuable.

Times interest earned (TIE) ratio   See coverage ratio.

Tombstone advertisements   An advertisement that can be placed prior to the approval of the registration statement by the SEC. This ad need not be accompanied by a prospectus, but is limited in the amount of information that it can convey.

Total asset turnover ratio   An asset management ratio that measures how many dollars of sales are generated for each dollar the firm has invested in assets.

Total change in reserves   The balancing account on the balance of payments.

Total reserves   The total cash that a depository institution has.

Trade balance   The net balance on merchandise trade, which refers to imports and exports such as wheat, machinery, oil, aircraft, and automobiles.

Trade credit   An informal loan arrangement in which a firm chooses to pay its supplier for goods and services received later rather than sooner, often forgoing a reduction in price to do so.

Transaction balance   The amount of cash that a firm holds to have the requisite amount necessary to pay its bills.

Transaction cost   The cost associated with selling assets in order to raise cash.

Transaction exposure   Changes in the value of outstanding payments (incoming or outgoing) that were agreed upon prior to a change in exchange rates, but that will not be settled until some future date.

Translation exposure   See accounting exposure.

Treasury bill   Short-term debt of the U.S. government. Treasury bills have maturities of 3, 6, and 12 months, and their minimum face value is $10,000.

Treasury bonds Long-term debt issued by the United States government. Treasury bonds usually have maturities of greater than 7 years and have a face value of $1,000.

Treasury notes Intermediate-term debt issued by the United States government. Treasury notes usually have maturities of 7 years or less and have a face value of $5,000.

Treasury stock Issued shares that have been repurchased by the firm.

Treasury strips Debt instruments sold by brokerage firms that are backed by the firms' investments in Treasury securities. Treasury strips pay no periodic interest payments.

Trend analysis A forecasting technique that uses historical growth rates to predict the future value of a financial statement account.

Uncovered option A naked option. A call option written by an investor who does not own the underlying stock.

Underwriting The purchase of securities for immediate resale to the public.

Underwriting spread The difference between what an investment banker receives for the securities it sells and what it paid the issuing firm for them.

Underwriting syndicate A group of investment bankers who agree to underwrite an issue together, each purchasing a portion of the issue.

Unit branching A state law under which banks may not establish any branches.

Unsecured debt Bonds that are backed only by the creditworthiness of the issuer.

Unsystematic risk Risk that is unassociated with the system. Company-specific risk.

Variance A statistical measure of dispersion.

Warrant A call option that gives the holder the right to buy a firm's stock from the firm at a prespecified price within a specified period of time.

Wash sale A transaction in which one individual purchases and sells the same stock at approximately the same time.

World Bank The International Bank for Reconstruction and Development. It was established in 1944 to grant loans to countries to enhance their economic development.

Yankee bonds Foreign bonds sold in the United States and denominated in dollars.

Yield curve A graph that is used to depict the term structure of interest rates. It plots the yields on similar risk securities that mature at different points in time.

Yield-to-maturity The promised average annual yield that an investor will receive if he purchases the bond for its current price and holds it until it matures.

Zero balance accounts A cash management technique that allows a firm to keep its funds working for it for the maximum amount of time. The firm's bank transfers only those funds needed to cover any checks that it wrote and are now being cleared from an interest-bearing account to its checking account.